Charles Williams
"The Place of the Lion"
"The Descent of the Dove"
(subtitled "A History of the Holy
Spirit in the Church"
poems by —
"Shadows of Ecstasy" (novel)
✱ "All Hallows Eve" ✱ p134

The Passionate God

The Passionate God

ROSEMARY HAUGHTON

PAULIST PRESS   *New York/Ramsey*

First published in 1981
Darton, Longman & Todd Ltd
89 Lillie Road
London SW6 1UD

ISBN: 0-8091-2383-5 (paper)
    0-8091-0324-9 (cloth)

Library of Congress
Catalog Card Number: 81-80049

Published in the U.S.A.
by Paulist Press,
545 Island Road,
Ramsey, N.J. 07446

Printed and bound in the
United States of America

This book is dedicated to The Company of the friends of Wisdom, for whom—

'The hint half-guessed, the gift half understood is Incarnation. Here the impossible union of the spheres of existence is actual.'

References

Biblical quotations are in general from the Jerusalem Bible, published and © 1966, 1967 and 1968 by Darton, Longman & Todd Ltd and Doubleday & Co. Inc., and from the Revised Standard Version of the Bible, copyrighted 1952 and 1971 by the Division of Christian Education of the National Council of the Churches of Christ in the USA.

References in the text have been kept to a minimum, but full publication details of works cited can be found in the bibliography at the back of the book.

Contents

Acknowledgements

The three extracts taken from *Selected Poems* and *Duino Elegies* by Rainer Maria Rilke are reproduced by permission of The Hogarth Press.

The extracts from *The Nuclear State* by Robert Jungk © Kindler Verlag 1978 are reproduced by permission of John Calder (Publishers) Ltd and Grosset & Dunlap, Inc., New York.

The excerpts from *Taliessin Through Logres* by Charles Williams (1938) are reprinted by permission of Oxford University Press.

Introduction
Wisdom, Poetry and Romance

As a confirmed introduction-skipper myself, I hesitate to ask, but finally do ask, the reader not to skip this one. The book is its own best explanation but it will make sense more rapidly if I begin by giving some account not of why—the book will show that—but of how it came to be written. Out of that arises a kind of 'scene-setting' exercise, to show the necessary locus of what is being done, including some explanation of apparent oddities which might cause a degree of culture shock in the reader if encountered unprepared.

The ground from which this book grew was an increasing preoccupation, over many years, with an apparently naive question: What difference did the resurrection of Jesus make? It seemed to me that Christians talked as if the answer to that question were obvious, but on examination there seemed to be much talk and little evidence. What *kind* of difference *should* it make? Does it make a difference to how we feel about life? Or does it affect our bodily being? If so, precisely how? What difference did Paul see? Have his views been proved right or do we just *assume* he was right? And anyway, what did he really *mean*?

This has to do first of all with the nature of material reality; resurrection is bodily or it is nothing. We are, after all, talking about the event Christians call 'incarnation', flesh-taking, before all else a bodily, material event. So what happened to material reality, what happened to *bodies*, when Jesus rose from the dead? And embedded in all this there was the other question: why did he die at all? Why death? Why *evil*? And what is it?

In Arthur Koestler's mammoth book *The Act of Creation* he shows how a sudden transformation such as conversion, a new scientific insight or (on a more everyday scale) the catharsis of laughter, or of tears, occurs when two irreconcilable 'matrices' of thought and experience coincide in the mind. What makes people laugh at the pompous gentleman slipping on the banana skin is the incompatibility of his dignity and his sudden predicament. What makes people

1

weep is the break in one order of comprehensible and imaginable living caused by a disaster which 'undoes' it. Discoveries, spiritual and intellectual, are the outcome not of a progression of reasoning along one line but of disparate experiences knocking up against each other. Without conscious thought or will, at a certain narrow point, they touch, explode, and something new is born. This process is the one which created this book, for my wrestling with the theological questions produced for a long time nothing but a quantity of waste paper. But at the same time I rediscovered Charles Williams, the strange poet-novelist-dramatist-theologian who was a friend of C.S. Lewis and J.R.R. Tolkien, and in the last years of his life (he died aged 46 in 1945) one of the group around Lewis called the 'Inklings' who met in an Oxford pub to read and discuss each other's work. Brilliant as the group was, and rightly revered as Lewis and Tolkien have become in different ways, Williams was in a class by himself. Where they saw things head on, with beautiful and uncompromising clarity, Williams saw them all round and with a stereoscopic vision of unparalleled intensity. But his thought is, therefore, ambivalent, obscure and richly allusive. He could not be popular, but those who catch fire from him are never the same again.

Williams had first come into my life when I was in my teens and a new Christian. I knew him only through a few of his poems, and for some time I was delightfully drunk on the stuff, but I have a poor head for strong poetry, and I forgot him. I rediscovered him through *The Descent of the Dove*, sub-titled 'A History of the Holy Spirit in the Church', his idiosyncratic book of historical theology or theological history. Thrilled, I went back to the poems, found and read all his six weird and unclassifiable novels (recently republished in paperback). I discovered the doctrine of Exchange which is the mainspring of this book. One day or other, this idea knocked up against the questions on my mind about resurrection, an explosion occurred and a breach was made into new regions. In exploring the territory to which this explosion gave me access I needed a language. I had it to hand in the study of Romance and Romantic love which I had pursued for some time.

Finally, there was a third thing which proved to be the context and in one sense the reason for the whole adventure. Over the last six years I had been part of a small, new, poor, insecure but

2

obstinately hopeful community of mixed Christians and not-particularly-Christians, trying to help each other to find ways and values to make sense of life now, and to help those damaged by the evils of life now (including their own). At the same time and for many years before that, my work as a lecturer had taken me all over North America, staying always where possible in homes, and in the very rapid intimacy of such visits getting to know lives, hopes, efforts, experiments. And everywhere I found evidence that people were being drawn together in just such little, unknown, yet obstinately hopeful groups as that from which I came. In country or city, permanently or briefly, people were gathering to live, study, work, pray together.

After a long time, through events in my own life, I became aware of all this in a new way. Finally this awareness touched that other awareness already at work as I explored the world in the light of the doctrine of Exchange. The explosion this time was much greater. In a sense this book is a photograph of that event. But my questions continued. Why am I seeing these things *now*? Why are the things that I am seeing going on *now*? And what is the reason for the intersection of the events, and my seeing them, and the kind of language available to me to express what I see?

My knowledge of my own past partially answered the first question for me. My knowledge of cultural history, interpreted by means of a peculiar language I had developed for this, partially answered the second. The answer to my third question can only emerge from the assertion that true answers to fundamental human questions must have the nature of poetry. Poetry brings to a point the experiences of the past and mediates them to the future through the narrows of the present. The present is now, this minute, with all the people in it. It is the menu at the restaurant this evening, the people in the local prison tonight, the lessons the kids are learning in class this afternoon, the debate going on in the chambers of government and business—the open one and the secret one. It is the conversation in the supermarket check-out line and by the tractor still hot from ploughing. It is the unquestioned basis of work in the laboratory, of the kinds of questions well-trained, well-paid people are feeding into computers and of the kinds of questions the dying are asking (or wanting to ask) in their hospital beds. Now is a cultural moment of the most bewildering concreteness and of a

3

totally inmeasurable precision. Therefore 'now' is our stifling limitation and our essential challenge, but our particular 'now' has deprived us of so many poetical tools that the challenge is more acute than perhaps it has ever been.

I was driven to pursue connections and enabled to perceive gaps and openings which well-trained and -equipped craftsmen did not notice, for they were busy with their craft. And at a cultural moment when history itself was revealing, through cracks, the light of new worlds, I groped for tools to deal verbally with the extraordinary nature of what I was perceiving and found them under my untutored hands. My use of them is clumsy, but I believe that in use they will be seen to be the right ones because they are not more complicated than they need be. They are not crude, nor are they sophisticated. They are simple, made of old materials but shaped for new needs and by new techniques. They are, in fact, common to all, like divine Wisdom.

'Wisdom' is a human gift and a name of God. It is both subject and context. In Scripture Wisdom is 'she', and she sets her table in public and summons one and all. What Wisdom offers, as I have attempted to follow her signs, is intended for the little ones, the people in the highways and hedges, and not only for those with gilt-edged invitations. In one sense this book's purpose is to extend that invitation. It is an invitation to experience Heaven and Hell, life and death, to know them in facts of nuclear power and food co-ops and police methods, of attitudes to babies and the poor and the handicapped and what we put in the soil. So it has to do with God, and with bread, and with sex, because there is a God-bread-sex continuum as there is a matter-energy continuum, and in exactly the same way. Wisdom is simply the apprehension of God in human experience through its whole extent.

That is Christian theology, for Christianity is the revelation of that Wisdom in one historical yet eternal point, physical and spiritual and personal and cosmic. People become Christians because they discover Wisdom in Christianity. They discover that it is true, in the clear and obvious sense of truth which is that it corresponds with their experience of reality. This is so in two distinct but related ways. People 'discover' that Christianity is true by a conversion experience, in which they perceive, very simply and directly and without argument, that the revelation of God in Christ is what life

4

is all about. And again they 'discover' its truth over a lifetime's experience, in which personal growth and reflection, and increased and increasingly sensitive knowledge of the environment—social, 'natural', biological and historical—in which one lives, come together to confirm, year by year, the fundamental and living truthfulness of what Christianity has to say about the nature of reality. Inward deepening and outward observation interact with revelation, and the result is the growth of Wisdom. But it can only be communicated in poetic terms.

A book such as this must therefore include, as poetic, description and allusion, direct address to the hearer and at the same time indirect evocation of matters which lie deep in the region where speaker and hearer meet. To do this is theology, which is a particularly exacting kind of poetry. This may appear to be one of those statements which are intended to provoke thought rather than to be taken seriously as a statement of fact, but it is a statement of a fact which is important not only for this book but for all thinking about religion, God, faith. There are 'areas of concern' which are so ultimate that they are literally out of sight and can easily be not only out of mind but dismissed as not worthy of being in mind because they cannot be thought of in the way we think about breakfast, or geography, or pneumonia. But this is the case not only about religious matters but about all those things in human life which are, in the end, of greatest importance—not only concepts like 'God' and 'faith' but 'compassion', 'loyalty' and 'truth'.

Kipling, in his short story 'Wireless', said that he thought the most powerful lines in all poetry were Keats':

Magic casements opening on the foam
Of perilous seas and faery-lands forlorn.
('Ode to a Nightingale')

Not all may agree, but the lines do have an extraordinary terror and beauty. For a moment, those windows are opened in the mind of the hearer, and he leans over the sill, afraid and breathless, aware of the unquestionable and untameable reality of an inner and common world, twilit and yet lucent, still and yet tingling with arrested movement, so new it has no language, yet dying. This is the land where Psyche searches for lost Eros, where the hermit ventures in

5

search of God, where the child lives familiarly in her moments of solitary fantasy, where the poet goes, in fear and trembling, to find the materials of his craft, and where he meets the prophet and visionary on the same errand.

The theologian also must open those windows onto the land whence culture draws its common life and whence it must continually revivify it, if it is not to stagnate in cliché and rhetoric. The languages of poetry and of theology, therefore, are always searching for words which will convey a truth whose essence is (so the poet and the theologian know) infinitely precise yet never capable of complete articulation. Poetry is not 'illustration' of prose by adding imagery; it is rather the most accurate way in which some inkling of an incommunicable experience can be communicated, and theology is exactly that also. It is in the struggle to articulate truthfully that the words become capable of actually communicating truth, for if they are the right words they take to themselves some of the power of the experience and break through into the mind that listens, creating a communion of experience.

This book has in its title not only the word 'God', but the word 'Passion', and the ordinary experience just mentioned is an example of the kind of experience from which the theology of this book takes its name and its symbols and its dynamics. For its thesis is that we can begin to make some sense of the way God loves people if we look very carefully at the way people love people, and in particular at the way of love we can refer to as 'passionate' because that kind of love tells us things about how love operates which we could not otherwise know. We can say 'love' and mean a restful, gentle and essentially kind experience. But if we say 'passion' we evoke something in motion—strong, wanting, needy, concentrated towards a very deep encounter. It is a violent word. Yet it has, in its roots, obviously a 'passive' sense. 'Passion' also implies a certain helplessness, a suffering and undergoing for the sake of what is desired and, implicitly, the possibility of a tragic outcome.

This is a book about the passion of God for human beings; it is a phenomenology of divine love for, in, through and between people, which means the entire, mysterious and infinitely complex system of inter-relationships which is creation, and the Creator in creation. But most of all it is about that point at which the passion of God drove him to become incarnate, and that is how 'Romance' language

6

is able to help me to answer the question which I asked at first, for it leads, quickly and surely, to ways of thinking about Incarnation.

'Incarnation' is a word to which most people find it hard to give a meaning. It violates, as a concept, our sense of divine and human decency, it crosses a barrier which we require, for our mental and psychological comfort, to be impermeable. A God who creates, who orders, a God whose bliss we can, maybe, come to share beyond death—this kind of God many can accept as *thinkable*, even if not believable. He is whole, glorious, benevolent and (if sometimes inexplicable) comforting. And an 'All' kind of God who has no distinctness but is a presence within, the Ultimate Ground, our final Good—such a God can command intellectual assent and even adoration. He is sufficiently numinous for worship, sufficiently pervasive to be attainable. But a God who is immediate, historical, demanding, personal, passionately human—that is altogether too much.

And Jesus, also, we can take. Jesus who was heroic, gentle, 'whole', healing, poor and persecuted—we have plenty of time for him. Everyone can love Jesus, as long as he is not God. But Jesus who is God is too difficult and demanding. Separately they will do, God and Jesus, in some kind of close but imaginable relationship. But a totally unimaginable oneness, a God so passionate he has to be Jesus, a Jesus so passionate he has to be God—he is so outrageous a demand on human intellect and human courage that there are only two possible responses: utter faith or utter rejection.

In practice, the inability to cope with the concept of Incarnation has always gone hand in hand with an inability to accept the miraculous element in the gospel accounts, and so with a desire to dispose of it either by making Jesus so much God and so little human that the 'miraculous' is merely his home territory, or by making him so much a man and so little God (no more than every human being) that miracles become an affront and must be disbelieved. This real and huge mental stumbling-block is important and has to be understood at the beginning of such a book as this. It is helpful to realize that what is acceptable as miraculous in this sense, and what is not, varies, and the reasons for this will illuminate our prejudices. At one time, *all* the 'miraculous' things in the Gospels were explained away as either suggestion, fabrication or hallucination. Nowadays, many people find 'miraculous' physical and mental healing acceptable, and the reason for this has to do with styles of thinking, those changes in a culture about what it is or is not possible for people to think at a given time. We do not often realize to what an extent our theology is also limited and directed by such cultural fashions.

In the emergence of scientific disciplines as a reliable guide to the nature and operation of the universe, during the eighteenth and nineteenth centuries, the climate of thought created was naturally inimical to anything that could not be fitted into available scientific categories. It was not any process of reasoning which excluded all non-scientifically-verifiable phenomena as 'unreal', but rather a profound human need for a manageable universe. The medieval universe had been manageable because of God, an intellectually manageable kind of God. The 'Enlightenment' exploded religion (though some 'enlightened' people kept God as a pet) but quickly and necessarily offered a substitute with which to prop up the universe. It is intolerable to human beings to live in a meaningless universe. Even those few who attempt this in the name of realism end up, like the Existentialists, making a kind of meaning out of the conscious assertion of meaninglessness. So, when scientific discovery seemed to be about to explain everything, it was natural that things which it manifestly could not explain should be dismissed not as unexplainable—this would have left a hole in science—but as simply non-existent. But time and experience have shown the limits to strictly 'scientific' exploration, and travel in the border areas of scientific discovery has led scientists to draw on imaginative rather than strictly 'scientific' concepts. In this changed climate of opinion Jesus the healer, for instance, is once more intellectually respectable, but only so long as he is not divine.

What has happened is not that people have learned to accept a different category of experience, one in which 'inexplicable' things happen, but that they have widened the original category within which they find it possible to think. This category can be called 'everydayness'. Things which at one time were dismissed as fables or frauds by all 'reasonable' people are now quite thinkable; in fact it is even fashionable to think about them and speculate on their relationship to other, more usual, phenomena. They are included, therefore, in the category of the 'everyday', or if they cannot quite be fitted in there they are on the borders of it, in the category we

8

can call 'strange'. These are not precise terms, but they evoke very precisely the state of mind with which we approach and judge the status of experiences, as 'everyday', or strange, or perhaps as so-strange-they-can't-have-happened, though we have now moved the borders of this category a long way outwards.

'Romantic' experience is one kind of verifiable human experience which is both 'strange' and 'everyday'. It opens on 'perilous seas and faery lands forlorn', but one stands at the window with one's feet firmly in the house of verifiable everydayness. That is why it will help us to ask and answer the question: What happens if we take Incarnation seriously?

There has been a move not only among non-Christians but among many Christians, since the last century, to answer this question by saying, '*Don't* take it seriously; in fact don't take it at all.' But the rejection of the idea of Incarnation is not primarily an intellectual decision but an emotional and spiritual revulsion against inadequate (un-poetic) theology and therefore inadequate (un-poetic) Christianity. Instead of refuting, therefore, I am trying to discover the radical implications of the poetic and scandalous statement that God became, and remains, human. This brings me finally to a brief discussion of Scripture as poetry. As soon as we move out of the areas of life in which things have names and uses and not much else, we find that the words we are using change. We flounder and gasp in the unfamiliar atmosphere, trying to find words to express what we experience. We cannot, for instance, convey the experience of a really good Christmas celebration by describing the food we ate, or the presents we received, or who was there. So we say it was 'wonderful', or some such word, and hope desperately that the person who was not there will, from his or her own experience, evoke the proper response. But we still feel there must *be* words to express 'what it was like', and if we find them they will be poetic words, evoking by imagery and association an experience impossible to describe in 'everyday' terms. This is why poetry is essential for *accurate description* of any sphere of experience beyond the 'everyday'. Wordsworth had no doubt seen thousands of daffodils in the course of his life before the day in which he suddenly 'saw' them differently and wrote the poem about them which, alas, is too often now used to insulate bored school-children against any such experience in their own lives. But for him, thenceforwards, daffodils must have carried the 'feel' of that other sphere of experience into which, seeing them, he had momentarily entered.

This perception is important in understanding the language used in Scripture. In this book I have drawn on the only direct sources of information we have on the subject, which are the four Gospels and other New Testament writings. And since I do not want to spend a great deal of space within the discussion itself over questions of exegesis and biblical criticism, it may help if I outline here the nature of my approach to the New Testament writings.

My approach to the Gospels in particular may strike some as naive, since it is based on the assumption that all four evangelists were writing about things actually seen and heard (not necessarily by themselves, of course, but by witnesses) and using whatever poetic categories of religious and historic imagery they needed to clarify the nature of what was seen and heard.

The assumption of many exegetes seems to be that one cannot do *both* these things. Either one reports something actually seen with the bodily eyes or heard with the ears, or one evokes an inner experience by means of relevant symbols and associations. This separation is, however, quite contrary to normal experience. If, for instance, I visit a house where I was once intensely happy, my memory of that happiness will transform my experience of the house in the present. The familiar covers on the chairs, the view from the window, cause me deep emotion which actually changes the way I *see* them and which I cannot possibly account for by acknowledging that the design of the furnishing fabric is beautiful, or the view dramatic, though both things may be true. I am not tempted to say, therefore, that I don't see the chairs or the view but am only 'really' experiencing a memory. I am doing both, authentically and simultaneously. The objects I see evoke the emotion, and the memory gives unique meaning to the objects.

It seems to me reasonable and realistic to assume that this is what the evangelists were doing, too. Of course, the reason why many people cannot accept this in the Gospel accounts, though they would have no difficulty with the example just given, is that the events reported by the evangelists are often of a kind we do not expect to see. Being unwilling to accept the breakdown of categories on which we rely to make sense of our physical and even spiritual surroundings, we want to enclose the report in one manageable

10

'sphere'. If the incident cannot be explained in terms that fit our normal expectations of the physical world, then we explain it in (equally expected) terms of symbolic evocation of inner experience. But my bold assumption in working with the Gospel account is that this is unreasonable. I think it is, in fact, an *a priori* assumption, not a conclusion based on evidence, and that it is only maintained by excluding without examination all evidence which seems to contradict it.

If we can say of a reported action or reaction, 'that rings true as a report of human behaviour', then we are saying something important, and it is the criterion by which we are accustomed to judge the 'truthfulness to life' of novels or biographies. It is difficult (though not impossible) to analyse just why we react to a description of a human incident by a definite, and usually immediate, acceptance or rejection of its 'truthfulness', but we do, and we recognize this as proper.

So, too, in the Gospels I find it helpful and reasonable to use this criterion. I can say, 'this rings true', this is how human beings might be expected to behave in the circumstances described. But someone may say: 'Such circumstances *couldn't* exist, therefore he/she/they must have been reacting to something else—or maybe the evangelist wrote this to evoke some deeper truth.' Then we reach the point at which I want to say that what 'rings true' might well *be* true, and that it is simplest to suppose so unless there is strong evidence that it did not happen.

I quote here a somewhat unkind but witty comment on what happens to the minds of those students of Scripture who are perhaps insufficiently aware of the cultural influences which shape their thinking. The quotation is from *John Who Saw* by A.H.N. Green-Armytage, itself quoted by J.A.T. Robinson in his book *Re-dating the New Testament*:

> There is a world—I do not say a world in which all scholars live but one at any rate into which all of them sometimes stray, and which some of them seem permanently to inhabit—which is not the world in which I live. In my world, if *The Times* and *The Telegraph* both tell one story in somewhat different terms, nobody concludes that one of them must have copied the other, nor that the variations in the story have some esoteric significance. But

in that world of which I am speaking this would be taken for granted. There, no story is ever derived from facts but always from somebody else's version of the same story . . . In my world, almost every book, except some of those produced by Government departments, is written by one author. In that world almost every book is produced by a committee, and some of them by a whole series of committees. In my world, if I read that Mr. Churchill, in 1935, said that Europe was heading for a disastrous war, I applaud his foresight. In that world, no prophecy, however vaguely worded, is ever made except after the event. In my world we say, 'The first world war took place in 1914–1918'. In that world they say, 'The world war narrative took shape in the third decade of the twentieth century.' In my world men and women live for a considerable time—seventy, eighty, even a hundred years—and they are equipped with a thing called memory. In that world (it would appear) they come into being, write a book, and forthwith perish, all in a flash, and it is noted of them with astonishment that they 'preserve traces of primitive tradition' about things which happened well within their own adult lifetime.

The fashion for detecting multiple authorship has faded somewhat since the above was written, and memory as a normal human attribute has been given more credit, but the outcry which arose when Dr Robinson suggested (only *suggested*) that the New Testament took its present form within about forty years of the events described in the Gospels was extraordinary, not because his impeccably presented evidence and arguments were inadequate (some of his critics did not wait to read the book) but because he was as disturbing as a circus clown in a clubroom in which decorum is maintained because members never ask each other real questions. Robinson asked real questions, and so revealed once more the more drastic question-asking tendencies of the New Testament writers themselves. This needed doing, for the 'fashionableness' of some exegetical schools is worrying. If an explanation is easily and smoothly acceptable in any particular culture the chances are great that its terms are culturally conditioned—that is, adapted to the expectations and subliminal exclusions of that society, and so designed to provide reassurance rather than the challenge of real exploratory thinking.

I shall, therefore, treat the writers of the four Gospels as reliable and competent authors who were trying to present to their various audiences the most astounding material in the history of mankind and in doing so perforce became poets (or rather, were able to do it only because they discovered they *were* poets). They drew on religious and historical allusions and symbols in order to convey, by the use of imaginatively familiar categories, the significance of the events they were describing, when the events themselves were so strange that it was going to be hard for the hearers to make any sense of them. They were recounting both what was seen by the bodily eyes, where this was possible and as far as possible, and also in the same words the intensely strange and revolutionary significance of what was seen, not only for those present but *chiefly* for the later hearers for whom they wrote.

There is a perfect contemporary example of this double vision in an Israeli government pamphlet by a Yemeni Jew who came to the new State of Israel. His story is a factual account of what happened, but its vivid reality is due to the fact that his mind is soaked in the images of his people's older history. For him, the Exodus from Egypt, the return from exile in Babylon, the call to travel to the State of Israel and the final coming of the Messiah are all simultaneous, in a sense, yet there is no confusion. We see these very poor people, leaving every possession and security to travel to the new land in utter ignorance and utter trust, and we realize the justification of that reckless hope in the language of the exiled people of God as they travel towards their God who calls them home:

We lived in exile and waited for the Redemption, not knowing whether it would come. One of our number went to the capital and came back announcing: 'There is a State of Israel'. We did not know if it was true. Many days passed without a word or sign. But rumours spread. People came from afar to tell us: 'There is a king in Israel'. Later they came and said: 'There is an army in Israel, an army of heroes.' Finally they came and said: 'These are the plagues which herald the Messiah, there is war in Israel.' And we remained in exile and did not know if it was true. We went on hoping for the Redemption, but the spirit

13

was weary. We rejected exile and it seemed to us that the spirit of God was in us and exhorted us: 'Come with Me, go into the land of Israel.' We did not stop asking ourselves, 'Is there news of the Redemption?' And we were told: 'Wait, the prediction will be fulfilled in due time.' And then one day a letter came from the *Shaliyah* (emissary): 'Arise my brothers! Get up, the hour has struck. Our country needs its sons and builders for its redemption and for our own, to raise up its arms and cultivate its desert lands . . . .' We sold our houses and our goods without money. We left our synagogues to the Gentiles . . . . And we took with us the scrolls of the Law and the sacred objects. And we made ready provisions for the journey, each family its own, griddle cake and melted butter, dried meat and spices and coffee. And we carried flour for the journey, and the women gathered twigs and made fire in empty tins in the middle of the fields and baked our bread, or wrapped stones in dough and set them on the fire . . . and groups came from all the corners of Yemen and we felt sick with longing to set eyes on the land of Israel. So we came to Aden, at our last breath, footsore and plundered, weak and bereft of everything. And we were gathered into a great camp near the town. It stretched into the sands of the desert and yet was too small to shelter us all. And we lay down in great numbers on the sand itself, with the sky for our roof, family by family, and great sandstorms raged and in our hearts we prayed for our aliyah: 'May we be borne by eagles' wings to our country!' And we were borne into the air.

They were, in fact, air-lifted into Israel and were not all all afraid, though most had never seen a plane before. If the Redemption was to be accomplished by means of peculiar and noisy machines, so be it. The poetic imagery *is* the description. This is theology—the poetic evocation of human events in such a way as to make clear their divine significance. So if I say that God is passionate, and that this gives us the key to the whole nature of reality, I am making a theological statement which is strictly poetic. The poetry of passionate love is the accurate language of theology.

It is not possible to write a book like this in a sequence which will be truthful. Whatever sequence I choose will be an imposed and therefore misleading order, simply because there is no 'order',

14

except, from one point of view, a chronological one. The construction of this book is, therefore, related more to a circle than to a line, and though it naturally has to consist of successive chapters it is a help to think of it as some enormous wall-chart, with chapters radiating out from the centre, which is the chapter called 'Resurrection'. The rest lead towards it and away from it, and the earlier ones in the book depend on it for their significance as much as do the later ones. The structure of the book therefore has something of the character of concentric spheres, as in the image I use in the book itself.

Like all books, this one has a date, and the date shapes and drives it. C.S. Lewis said of his Christ-symbol in the Narnia books, 'he is not a tame lion'. The lion is roaring now to some effect, and this book is a response to that sound, as the prophet Amos indicated. *Because* it is a whole theology of the passionate God it grows from and leads into the awareness growing in so many minds and hearts that divine love is breaking through in a new way. The response of humankind to this new approach of its lover is, at first, tentative, yet increasingly delighted, awed and joyful, even under the shadow of death.

A few years ago Donald Heinz, who was worried by the tendency to seek escape from real problems and challenges by concentrating on 'self-actualization' in various forms, wrote an article called 'The Consuming Self' (*America*, 4 June 1977). Heinz was prophetic in his 'program' for those seeking a real human future rather than an escape into either technology or 'fulfilment':

> I think we can protest every fore-shortening of the human story, every time a truth is told about humanity which is much less than the truth we have caught sight of. We can seek ways to blow spirit back into a flattened language. The deposit laid down in our language by centuries of religious symbols has been seriously eroded in our time. That erosion has not only separated us from our past but significantly limited the ability of language to open up our present and future for us.
>
> Further I think we can become listeners for 'rumours of angels'. We can entertain strangers. We can engage in non-violent acts of transcendental imagination. We can become story-tellers. We can stage events in which the human condition becomes

15

transparent to the sacred. We can tend symbols and lend our groanings to the birth-pangs of new ones. We can revisit old friends, like the Hebrew prophets, who knew something about alternatives to self-consumption. . . .

We cannot kid ourselves. The boundaries of the possible have been narrowed. Failure at political and symbolic tasks must not, however, reduce us to harmless isolation in the web of an alienating society. Perhaps we shall have to begin with handfuls of others to create (or let re-emerge) at first only a microcosm of meaning, small networks that allow a scaled-down joy in existence. Memory and hope will lay anchor there. The dreams will be dreams that can be shared around. Into our language will be deposited our commonality and our openness to what is beyond us. We will tell ancient stories and strain towards new ones, and we will keep lighting the sacred fires, even if, at first, in private for fear of the winds. They will be the flames from which the torch is carried to other small tents erected outside a now secularized canopy. Rebirth of the human potential waits to happen in such communities.

It is an enormous task which is laid on us, and we have little equipment for it. But it is the only task, the one God lays on us, and so it can be done because it is his work. The work is, as Charles Williams once put it,

> . . . the regeneration of mankind. The word has, too often, lost its force, it should be recovered. The apostles set out to generate mankind anew. They had not the language; they had not the ideas; they had to discover everything. They had only one fact, and that was that *it had happened*.

So with us. We have lost the language, and our ideas are tangled and dulled. We have to discover everything, but we have the same fact—it happened; the passion of God broke through in Christ, and in him it is breaking through once more. It is breaking through in a new way, but we are enabled to perceive its newness because what we are seeing causes constant little shocks of recognition. It has not 'happened before' yet it is piercingly familiar, as each spring is unique, yet recognized in its uniqueness as the breakthrough of

16

an eternal newness, deeply familiar yet never to be held, always to be freshly discovered.

Like spring, this breakthrough of newness is violent. We are sentimental about spring. We concentrate on fluffy birds, the chubby pinkness of apple-blossom, the reassuring soft green of new grass. But spring is not gentle or cosy. It is an eruption of life so strong it can push bricks apart and make houses fall down. It thrusts through, and because of, layers of rotted past. The diamond brilliance of the cuckoo's note is the result of many fledglings shouldered out of the nest to their deaths, as all new life thrusts aside whatever impedes it. Even in the sheer perfection of each growing thing there is an integrity which is painful in its accuracy. The scent of lilacs in the dawn cuts through fuzziness of disordered desire, the etched whiteness of lily of the valley against dark leaves sears the imagination. These are not soft things; they have a tenderness ascetically fined down to an essential longing. This is the violence of absolute love, which takes the Kingdom of Heaven by storm in a silence of total concentration on the one thing necessary.

1 Exchange of Life

The incarnation is a happening both unique and ordinary. It is so complete and absolute of its kind that it has no parallels, no precedents, no successors, but the flesh-taking of God as Jesus is a unique example of the kind of ordinary event I want to call 'breakthrough'. An impulse—of need, of love, of will-to-power—manages to overcome some obstacle and pass through to a new and desired sphere of experience. This can be a small personal event, such as the achievement of a shared understanding. It can be a physical event, such as the breaking of a dam, when the 'need' of the water to find a way forward breaks the barriers and crashes through to the valley below. It can be a mystical experience or a scientific discovery. It can be a chicken breaking its shell or the signing of a peace treaty.

Even this random collection of examples shows that 'breakthrough' is a category of events which makes nonsense of the division of reality into material and spiritual. It has to do with the nature of reality as such—physical, psychological and spiritual reality; and even to use those words introduces a misleading separation, yet a necessary one, since we cannot talk about the oneness of experience unless we can also talk about the fact that we experience reality in ways that can only be described by developing such distinctions. But it shows us that we also need a language about reality which will make it easier not to be handicapped by the separation of those categories. And in attempting to realize the meaning of the Flesh-taking it is essential to transcend those categories if we are to realize it as the manifestation not just of God but of the nature of reality, at its peak. Incarnation is breakthrough, and it involves every level of reality from the most basic particles to the ultimate Being of God.

In order to begin to understand this I want to propose a kind of language about reality which makes it possible to realize Incarnation as breakthrough, and as 'ordinary', and as unique, but which also enables us to realize how the concept of 'breakthrough' is linked intimately to the way reality 'works' altogether. This language is derived from a very simple model of reality which helps to make sense of apparent contradictions.

We use simple imaginative models of reality all the time, without realizing it, even if we give sophisticated and subtle explanations of ones we are conscious of using. These models are, for most people (including the highly educated), a fearful hotch-potch of successive philosophical fashions, each providing certain mental patterns to ease our struggle to make sense of the world around us. If my account of them is deliberately ludicrous, this helps to show up the unexamined nature of our use of them.

One of the most respectable and ancient teaches us to think of cause and effect as if it were a row of boulders, which might just as well keep still, bumping each other in succession, each impelled towards the next by the one before. (When we add to this excruciating mental picture a 'prime mover' who kicks the first boulder, but might equally well have refrained from doing so, the argument for the non-existence of God becomes persuasive.) But, side by side with this very dull model of reality, we have learned to think of the growth of plants and animals through evolution, each adding greater complexity and efficiency as generation upon generation adapts to a changing environment. This is comforting, like a warm bath after battling with the chill blast of scientific rationalism. It gives a feeling of being inside some vast and splendid Process, supportive, inexorable and ultimately Good. Although one version of this is, of course, associated with Teilhard de Chardin, this is certainly not what Teilhard was actually getting at, any more than the boulders are what the schoolmen were talking about. It is the residual model of reality which settles in the imaginations not only of the half-educated but of the sophisticated and erudite, in those parts of their minds which are off-duty professionally.

There is also a version of Plato's model. Like all these 'residual' models it does scant justice to Plato, but it helps people to live with certain otherwise unexplainable nostalgias and feelings of incompleteness. The notion that phenomenal experience is a fragmented and inadequate reflection of a perfect archetype has the effect of making experienced reality manageable, yet not too restrictive, since however inadequate and unsatisfying it seems it is not the whole story. But this model is also 'static'. The reflections do not grow *towards* the archetype; they can only, perhaps, fade away or be absorbed into it, as in Charles Williams's astonishing novel, *The Place of the Lion,* in which archetypal realities 'get loose' and all the butterflies in the world are drawn irresistibly towards a great and terrifyingly beautiful butterfly into which they disappear. It is a powerful book, but its model of reality is very 'impersonal' and ultimately (though I think Williams failed to see this) deterministic.

The jargon of depth psychology (valuable as it is in its proper context) also provides a way of dealing with reality which takes the form of a mythology, not replacing but coexisting with the other models. Jung's archetypes or (in the Freudian model) powerful gods like Id and Ego rule a world of human insides, for which exterior matter and events exist, it sometimes seems, only to provide images for the Interior Realities. The whole thing is like a kind of sacred drama, taking place on the little human stage which contains it. Again, this is not what Jung, at least, was saying—he said almost the opposite—but it is the model of reality which remains in the imagination.

Obvious examples of models which explain aspects of reality at the cost of excluding intractable experience as 'unreal' are Behaviourism and Communism, both based on a cause-and-effect model of personal or social behaviour. Even the 'process' models are caught in another kind of 'staticness'—that of the gradual building up in a body towards some kind of destined perfection, at which point it all stops.

I am definitely not talking about the really complex and agonizingly worked out conceptual languages with which philosophers and scientists of various schools and disciplines have attempted to make the vastness of reality manageable in some way by the staggering human mind. I am speaking of the rough but usable 'pictures' which are seized on by the dazed imagination, without our even being aware that such a thing is happening. Many, indeed, would hotly deny that they had internalized such naive models, but the presence of these models is betrayed by word and attitude, by unquestioned inclusions and exclusions and by those emotional reactions to intellectual challenges which betray the presence of hidden terms of reference. Among such indications of a concealed model of reality is the use of the words 'material' and 'spiritual' as

20

mutually exclusive categories. We can talk about their essential interdependence, or even oneness, but that is not how we 'feel' them.

The theology of this book is based on the use of a different kind of model, expressing itself in a different kind of language. The mental picture I am proposing is just as naive as all the others and manageable by anyone, but it does not exclude any kind of experience or known reality. It is simply a picture of life as given and received in exchange, without ceasing, forever.

'Life' in this context means all of reality, apprehensible and inapprehensible, all that is and all that could be, and it involves thinking of everything not just as part of an infinitely complex web of interdependence, but as a *moving* web, a pattern of flowing, a never-ceasing in-flow and out-flow of being. But to say that is not enough; the language is still wrong because the word 'being' has for us a 'stopped' quality. For that word, let us substitute another: love.

This is the best word, because it is impossible to conceive of love as simply 'there'. To be 'there' means to be, except accidentally, *alone*. But love cannot be alone or it is not love—it has to be *given* or it belies its name. And if it is given it must be received, even if the reception is chilly. But somewhere (if we are to call it love) it must have a return by another *given* love responding to it. Or is it 'another'? Is this not, also as given, just 'love', equally with the origin of it? And is this not, therefore, essentially an *exchange* of love? And is not the name of this exchange also simply love? And what is that but a description (as far as anything can be) of what Christians call the Blessed Trinity, the nature of God as love?

But that is going too fast, perhaps. We began with material reality and must remain with it, through literal thick and thin. And in fact we are doing so, even when we struggle to deal with what appear to be disembodied concepts. They never are really disembodied, and that brief description of the operation of love as exchange is a description of the basic nature of material reality, as it is a description of the most intense human experience and of the very life of God. This last we can only conceive because its operation is also the experienced operation of exchanged love in our own bodies and minds, and those same bodies and minds exist only in exchange

21

with other kinds of life and of un-living matter, from the basic rocks to the heart of divine love itself.

If it seems strange to talk of love in connection with rocks or the cellular structure of living beings, that is because we are accustomed to static models of reality. But we all learned even before we went to school that the earth was once a 'ball of fire', whirling out from the sun, as if the sun could not bear its own privacy but must share itself with space. And within the whirling, incandescent core 'chemicals' constantly formed and re-formed, giving and receiving in patterns of inter-action, in a flux of becoming. And when, in exchange of heat with the chill of space itself, the vast thing cooled and separated itself into identities recognizable even by scientific ignoramuses, the exchanges did not cease. The original rocks were gradually worn down and surrendered their particles to the separated waters, whose own chemistry was thereby changed, and in the process changed and re-ordered the rocks into what were to be younger rocks. The shapes and layers of rock, sands, clays and waters kept, and still keep, a vast, slow dialogue of giving and receiving, each changing and being changed, without pause.

The dance of the shaping earth is echoed by the dance of exchanged life in the cells of living bodies. In them, life is exchanged and finds new ways of love. To use the word 'love' in such a context is in no way to draw an *analogy* with human feeling; rather it is as accurate a *description* as we can manage of the nature of reality at two different levels. But the understanding of what the word 'love' indicates *about* that nature can only be drawn, first of all, from human experience, because we are using our human minds to explore the reality and so it is only from human experience that we can get the concepts which enable us to do so.

This is equally true *whatever* model we use. To make use of, for instance, 'mechanistic' models is just as much a use of human experience to interpret reality as it is to draw on 'love' as description. It just feels more 'scientific' because machines operate outside ourselves and are not supposed to have emotions. But to envisage reality by thinking about machinery means the exclusion of enormous areas of human experience as 'unreal', since these will not fit into the model of reality we decide to be sufficient. To use love as model is to exclude *nothing*. Even machines are the product of vastly complex exchanges of raw 'natural' material, human inventiveness

22

and labour, and all the kinds of mental, chemical, spiritual and chronological permutations of exchange which are involved. If all this makes one dizzy in trying to think of it, that is because reality is indeed beyond the scope of the human mind, whence the desire to reduce it to manageable proportions by making it a 'machine'. The model of exchanged life, whose name is love, helps us to conceptualize but leaves open the way to sheer dazzlement, which is a proper reaction to the unimaginable complexity of reality. It is comparatively easy, too, to make the mental shift from 'model' to verification because human love, as seen and expressed, is so clearly a matter of exchange of life, giving, upholding, renewing, responding, reaching out; a constant flow of energy which is actually the experienced nature of relationships of all kinds.

But we notice also that the exchanges in nature, as in human love, seem to press towards a point at which they 'need' to break through to 'something else'. The breakthrough from non-life to life is the most obvious and dramatic of these, only equalled, perhaps, by the breakthrough from 'instinct' to self-conscious awareness, and crowned by the mysterious point at which the human thing becomes capable of God. In each case a new sphere of experience has been entered, and each deserves an epic – an epic prayer.

Among the more exotic subjects for possible epic prayers is, for instance, the example of breakthrough suggested by some scientists in connection with the famous 'Black Holes' in space. Black Holes are formed (it seems) when the mass of a dying star collapses into a kernel of matter of inconceivable density and of minute size and having a gravitational pull so great that nothing in its range, not even light, can escape it. Black Holes draw in and annihilate all matter and energy within reach. At the heart of them is a region physicists call (with reason) a 'singularity', where the density is so enormous that all the laws of physics break down. Nobody can guess what goes on in there, but some scientists have allowed themselves an imaginative leap worthy of any poet or mystic, and suggested that the 'singularities' are the passages by which energy and matter sucked into a Black Hole might emerge into another universe. This is not the kind of hypothesis most people expect from scientists, but it has a character of imaginatively straddling categories of thought which we shall find to be typical of 'breakthrough' considered as a necessity of reality as exchange.

The model of Exchange, then, seems to require, as part of its language, the concept of breakthrough, and with it another concept, that of 'spheres'. It is used to express the sense of a passage from one area of experience to another through some kind of barrier or obstacle, however insubstantial and transparent.

This use needs explaining. The 'spheres', in this sense, are modes of apprehending reality around us. The word itself is not uncommonly used in this way, but my particular use of it was partly inspired by reading Dante's *Divine Comedy*. In his journey towards the ultimate truth—the Trinity—the poet passes through sphere after sphere, and these 'spheres' are the transparent concentric globes which, in medieval cosmography, moved within each other round the earth, and on them the planets and fixed stars turned in their grave and hieratic dance, crying out, as they turned, the 'music of the spheres'. But this concept of successive spheres, each one nearer to God as it was higher from earth, was reflected in reverse in a concept of created life which was also 'layered'. The categories of being, from the angels downwards, were wide but distinct. Human beings rose above the beasts, who had 'soul' but not the spiritual soul of the humans. Below the beasts lay the layer of the 'vegetable' realm, of beings which have life but without consciousness, and below that there lay the realm of inorganic matter. But below that, as the medieval mind discovered it, was yet another 'layer'—one which, in a sense, only exists in the mind that conceives it, for it is the realm of simple 'matter', the 'stuff' of creation yet uncreated—undifferentiated potential. There is nothing 'below' this except nothing or 'hell', which is (as I shall suggest) 'nothing' because it is a contradiction of being. And through all these layers or 'spheres' the human person passes, unconsciously at first and later consciously and by choice. The 'spheres' are the 'layers' opened up by loving response to reality, and they are separated from each other by some kind of barrier, albeit a transparent one— but only transparent to eyes cleansed, as Dante's were, by the water of the river of life. To ordinary human eyes the spheres are opaque, yet they can and do become transparent and finally break.

As I have used the word, the 'spheres' include the areas between each barrier, since this is the way we normally use the word as image. We naturally operate in several different spheres, in this sense, yet there is a definite transition whose nature we can evoke

24

by the idea of passing through a kind of separating 'membrane'. For instance, we all know that behaviour, clothes and habits of speech which are appropriate in our 'everyday' homes and places of work are not appropriate when we move into a 'sphere' we can call 'celebration'. When we give a party or celebrate Christmas or a wedding, life feels different, and we expect different things of it. Even time seems to change its quality. We 'live through' much more in a shorter time when we are celebrating. The sphere of experience which is entered by people in love is yet another and deeply important one which I shall be discussing.

But Dante's medieval 'spheres' were further away from the level of everyday human life as they were nearer to God. The complementary insight is that the nearer we get to God the closer we get to the centre of ourselves, and vice versa. And a lovely modern version of this, which expresses very exactly the notion of 'spheres' which I want, is provided by C. S. Lewis in the last of his 'Narnia' books for children, called *The Last Battle*. In it, the children, who had once been Kings and Queens of Narnia, and their friends the Talking Beasts have been defeated by their enemies and imprisoned in a small and squalid stable on top of a hill. The Stable Door proves to be the door to a fair and sunlit land. But then, looking back through the door at the bidding of Aslan, the divine Lion, they see the End come upon the world of Narnia, as all their beloved land is engulfed in darkness and the icy sea of chaos. Turning sadly away from the door, they hear the call, 'Farther up and farther in!', and they begin to travel, faster and faster, towards the mountains, and as they go they realize that all around—hills, river, trees—is familiar, yet different. 'More like the real thing', says one, and someone replies, 'Narnia is not dead. This is Narnia.'

Having passed through the 'barrier' of the Door, the 'world' in the new sphere is indeed the same, yet utterly different because 'more like the real thing'. But the children go on and on, towards the heart of their world, and come at last to a walled garden at the summit of a high, steep mountain in a hidden valley. Here, Lucy (Lewis's favourite heroine) looks back over the wall at Narnia far, far below (but Narnia as known 'beyond the Door') and then, her back to the wall, turns *inwards*, to look at the garden. Presently she speaks to her companion, the Fawn, Tumnus:

25

'I see now. This garden is like the Stable. It is far bigger inside than it was outside.'

'Of course, Daughter of Eve,' said the Fawn. 'The farther up and farther in you go, the bigger everything gets. The inside is larger than the outside.'

Lucy looked hard at the garden and saw that it was not really a garden at all but a whole world, with its own rivers and woods and sea and mountains. But they were not strange; she knew them all.

'I see,' she said. 'This is still Narnia, and more real and more beautiful than the Narnia down below, just as *it* was more real and more beautiful than the Narnia outside the Stable Door! I see . . . world within world, Narnia within Narnia. . . .'

'Yes', said Mr. Tumnus, 'like an onion, except that as you go in and in, each circle is larger than the last.'

Here are Dante's 'spheres'—but the travel is 'inwards', 'farther up and farther *in*', penetrating farther into the 'real reality' of the sphere of everydayness, towards the centre. The heavenly spheres of Dante's *Paradiso* become here the layers of a homely onion, but in both there is movement *through* the 'spheres' on the way to God. So 'exchange', 'breakthrough' and 'spheres' are related concepts in the model of reality I propose.

To use such a model is to alter our whole way of thinking and feeling about 'life', about ourselves, about our relationships. But to 'use' in this sense means to make it part of one's basic experience, and that does not just happen. That it may cease to be purely theoretical and become part of the daily and personal apprehension of reality, I draw on one kind of human experience which is common yet not ordinary, and deeply important—personally, socially, historically. It is an experience which is, itself, an example of exchange and of breakthrough in exchange, that of Romance.

The images of passion are images of love in action, but especially of some kind of breakthrough to an encounter which is perceived as difficult. This difficulty must be overcome, and the overcoming involves an event, a 'moment' at which the 'overcoming' happens and an encounter can take place. These images therefore imply a sequence of events, a story.

The idea of 'love' need not imply 'story'. It can convey a state of being, an experience of communion as in John Donne's ecstatic lovers, lying silent and still on a grassy bank through timeless hours, feeling no need even of the language of physical love. But at the end of the poem they are emerging from that trance of being-in-love and asking, 'our bodies why do we forebear?', for they must go on with the story. The story will be about passion, and 'passion' implies, by its evocation of a moment of breakthrough and encounter, a before and after. But it is a story about love, a story of the breakthrough of love, in fact a passionate love story, a 'Romance'.

This puts the whole affair in a context whose concern is the articulation in story of passionate love. The French word *roman* came to mean a story, originally one in a 'Romance' language, specifically and originally a story about love, but a special kind of love celebrated in the 'Romance' literature which originated in France in the eleventh and twelfth centuries. It was preoccupied with the phenomenology of passionate love, and it expressed this in poetry because that was the only way it could be expressed.

Therefore the language of Romantic passion can provide the kind of concepts, images and language tools which can enable us to articulate the theology of exchange, for it is a paradigm of Exchange. It is familiar and therefore verifiable and observable, yet it is also mysterious. It involves every level of human being; it touches the earthiest of earthy experience at one end of the spectrum and the heights of mystical love at the other. It can help us, therefore, to understand exchange and breakthrough in inanimate matter, and in God. It can help us, above all, to 'see' Incarnation, and the Church which is its outcome.

Later parts of this chapter, and much of the next, will be devoted to exploring the theological meaning of Romance, but in order to do this properly I must first look at the nature of the 'material' world we live in, in which Romantic passion happens and which is altered by it.

This is really to approach the business of employing a 'new' model and language from a different angle. I am asking my readers to take part, in this book, in a dance of the mind and heart which involves some strenuous and unaccustomed movements. We are so stiff in our categories, so laced up in corsets of eighteenth-century rationalism, that we can scarcely bend, and even normal breathing is difficult. So what follows is intended as a mental un-lacing, so that we can get a full breath of reality. It tastes odd, at first, but it

27

is our world, and it *is* odd—much odder than we have been inclined to believe. We live, in fact, in a universe whose behaviour is stranger and less predictable (predictable, that is, according to the only categories of possibility we usually admit) than our familiar models of reality allow. This is why it is so necessary to become free enough to admit the possibility of things, events and experiences which we have been accustomed to rule out, not because there was no evidence for them but simply because they did not fit our models.

I have called such things 'odd', because it is a reasonably neutral word. There are other ways of describing the things that happen or are observed, and which do not fit the models we normally use to handle reality. 'Weird', 'strange', 'other' and 'uncanny' are a few. But phenomena so described can also, for our mental comfort and convenience, be labelled 'incomprehensible', 'incredible', 'fantastic', or even, at one period, 'mythical' or 'romantic', and by such words we indicate, one way or another, that these things are 'not real'. Yet whatever may be the category into which we finally push things thus described they are at least this much 'real' that they have occupied and do occupy people's minds, sometimes to the point of obsession. Therefore they need to be considered if we are claiming to make use of a conceptual model which excludes no kind of human experience from its scope.

There are first of all things at the level of experience only just beyond the purely 'everyday', such as telepathy, 'prophetic' dreams and 'coincidences' unlikely enough to challenge credulity, and also the physical changes which take place under the influence of, for instance, violent personal emotion or mystical experience. People know what is happening to someone else, far off and out of touch. They 'see' things that are not going to happen until next week. They can become, under certain conditions, free from the normal need for food or sleep, or they can fall into a trance-like sleep because some event is taking place (such as a birth or death) which has tremendous psychic significance but with which the person is, at that stage, unable to cope. None of these things is precisely 'everyday', but they are sufficiently often recorded and explainable to be acceptable to most people, so they scarcely stretch the category of everydayness. In this category also belongs (for instance) the strange interaction between architecture, musical sounds and the human body. The builders of some Indian temples, and also the

28

Cistercian architects of some twelfth-century churches in France, built them so that the chants used in worship induced what can only be described as a kind of mystical experience in the worshipper. Connected with this is the fact that certain musical intervals are known to produce physical changes which enhance spiritual awareness, and religious chants (including plainchant) use these intervals, though most people who use them now are not aware of the fact. Linked to this again is the impact of the Baroque, especially German Baroque, a style in which architecture, painting and sculpture use space and decoration in such a way as to 'unsettle' visual categories and give the mind little to hold on to, so that it easily soars into the painted heavens whose earthly 'edges' seem to have disappeared. Here, music also becomes so much 'part of' the place in which it sounds that one can talk of the soaring angels' wings of the music and of 'sonorous' repetition of arched spaces.

The next category is that of readily seen but quite 'inexplicable' phenomena, commonly dismissed as fabrication or illusion. I can only refer to a few examples, and among the weirder ones are 'rains' of unlikely articles such as fish, nails or frogs, recorded at different times and places by reliable (and understandably angry or frightened) witnesses. There are cases including several contemporary ones of bodies found totally burned up, but with clothes (even stockings) or nearby furnishings unharmed and even un-scorched. There are cases of people being reported seen in two different and distant places simultaneously. Possibly 'poltergeist' phenomena should also come into this category, since they often involve the moving around or smashing, or arbitrary disappearance or appearance, of objects. 'Levitation'—the capacity of people in certain mystical states to leave the ground and float around—is another in the same category, and also violent changes of temperature, so that some mystics have felt (and been felt to be) so hot as to be painful to touch, while sudden extreme cold often accompanies the appearance of ghosts, or is experienced by itself as a type of 'haunting'. Some people have given off intense light, and by no means all of these were mystics. Evidence for these and many other incidents is plentiful and accessible. This does not mean that all must be accepted, but it does mean that unless we continue to reject such evidence as *necessarily* false we have to admit that the world is a great deal odder than we normally recognize, and that it is odd not in purely arbitrary ways but according to certain patterns which can be traced, although they do not correspond to the pattern of everyday expectation. Various explanations of such phenomena are offered from time to time. I am not suggesting any particular explanation here, but only noticing that such things do (if *any* evidence is reliable) occur.

A further category concerns things which are seen but are, in a sense, 'not there'. Rains of frogs and levitated mystics are definitely *there*, however outrageously novel their mode of being there. A ghost is not 'there' in the same sense, nor are 'visions'. They may or may not be seen by more than one person, and even when the seeing is shared it is evanescent. The things or persons seen in such cases cannot usually be touched, though this is not always the case, for some 'visions' do seem to involve physical contact, but in the area of 'oddness' it is impossible to be quite clear about where boundaries come. It is arguable, for instance, that the visions of certain saints who not only saw but touched the person of Jesus were in the class of seeings of things that are *there*, so there may be a confusion of interpretation, rather than an actual difference of category.

The volume of supportive evidence for seeings of ghosts by very sane people is great, though of course never conclusive if one refuses to admit that such things *could* happen. Some ghosts seem to be simply people going about their daily avocations, but in another time. (These are the ones who walk serenely through walls which when they were 'alive' were not there). Some seem to linger in a place where they have been very unhappy, as if the place had absorbed the imprint of their misery. More rarely, great happiness seems to have done the same thing. Others seem to have a purpose in mind, such as righting a wrote done during life, or preventing a wrong among the living, or just plaguing people. Some ghosts are malevolent, more are well intentioned. Again, I venture no theory as to what ghosts are, I only say that they have been *seen*.

It seems possible that many people who have visions do not report them, partly because they risk being put in hospital, but also because the things they see just do not demand to be 'published'. The little girls at Cottenham who saw fairies in their garden only became famous because adults, overhearing their conversation, challenged their veracity; they offered to prove the existence of their tiny friends by photographing them, and did so, producing pictures

30

which no amount of expert fake-hunting has been able to prove to be other than authentic. So perhaps the fact that we think of 'visions' as mainly bearers of messages for others besides the visionary is misleading. In any case, not only saints or mystics have them. Mentally ill people have them, and most mediums do, and people who are 'fey' get momentary ones. And they vary among themselves enormously, for some are distinctly visual and others are impressed on the memory by what Dame Julian of Norwich called 'spiritual sight', though expressed in visual terms for purposes of communications. Some seem to be 'straight' encounters with recognizable human beings, however exalted; others are encounters with beings in categories which do not have any everyday equivalent, and so have to 'take' an earthly-imaginative structure in order to communicate. Of such are visions of angels, or the strange theophanies of Ezekiel, and of such, I would guess, was the encounter with a faun in the botanical gardens in Edinburgh, and later with the great god Pan himself, by one of those involved in the remarkable explosion of 'nature spirits' associated with the beginning of the famous Findhorn Community. At that time also this community was able to grow vegetables and flowers of a size far beyond the normal, which boggled the minds of local gardeners and was confirmed by eminent and sober horticulturalists as being quite inexplicable in terms of the natural nourishment available from a soil at first so poor and salty as to grow nothing but coarse grass. This aspect of the Findhorn experience is one of the best attested contemporary examples of things which are undoubtedly 'there' but inexplicable in terms of ordinary cause and effect. (That was in the days before Findhorn became 'respectable' and before the effects of a gnostic type of theology, possibly associated with 'white' witchcraft, had time to become evident.) The visions were 'seen' in a fashion appropriate to the cultural idiom of the seer, hence a professor with a classical background saw a 'faun'. This applies whether the vision had an explicit purpose and message, or whether it was a private experience, such as those which sometimes happen to very sick people, or apparently just for fun like the Cottenham fairies, whose clothes and hair-styles were so disconcertingly 'in period'.

Beyond all these categories is that of experience which is described in terms of 'seeing' only because it is unclassifiable in terms of normal sensory experience and can only be communicated in quasi-visual paradoxes of bright darkness and dark knowledge, or 'unknowing' which illuminates. It is stretching a point to call it communicable at all, but as an experience it recurs over and over again in the writings of mystics, though not, so far as I know, in any other context.

The categories of 'odd' experiences I have described are not exhaustive. I have not mentioned the category into which many of the miracles of Jesus fell, as well as many other 'healings', which is that of obvious physical change without normally explainable physical reason. Healings are quite a frequent occurrence, now as then, and some are done by direct physical contact and some at a distance, some by 'faith' (of the healed) and some apparently without. Not all are 'religious'; there are healings by magic, and some people simply 'have the gift'. There are such things as the multiplication of food, or the alteration of shapes of things (a grave that is never the same length on successive measurings, for instance).

Another kind of evidence of oddness which has become much better known recently is the witness by people who have clinically 'died' and come back to life. The experiences recalled by these people fall into recognizable patterns and sequences. Not all go through the whole sequence, but there is one, which commonly includes the experience of being out of, and looking down at, one's own inanimate body. People who have experienced this can often recall the conversations of those working on resuscitation, for instance, but also found themselves able to move out of the room and follow other people. If the experience continues long enough it seems to come to a 'beautiful country' of some kind, but also to some barrier in it, a river or other division, beyond which, possibly, is the point of no return. Carl Jung recorded one of the most elaborate of these experiences, and he, like many others, *decided* to come back, for the sake of those still living who needed him. These accounts are from so many different kinds of people, varying in age, intelligence and religion, many of whom did not know that anyone else had ever had such an experience, that it is hard to dismiss them. They raise questions about, among other things, the relation of 'soul' and body, for over and over again some kind of *physical* being is experienced in distinction to the sick or injured body which is 'dead'. The stories of people who have had telephone conversations with a person later discovered to have been dead at the time of the call are another weird question mark about the nature of bodies, 'dead' or alive. (We can also slip in here the fascinating results of historical rummaging which shows scientific discoveries made many centuries before their conventional dating, and alchemical theories relating accurately to nuclear physics and other matters.)

There is one source of evidence about the 'oddness' of the world which is not so much a distinct 'category' as a way of approaching what may turn out to be the same or related phenomena. We hear of particles describing curves which have no tangents, about numbers greater than Infinity, about the universe being supported by sound vibrations, about anti-gravity and anti-matter. Scientists draw on symbolic and even poetic expression, devise 'models' and diagrams which they assure us anxiously are 'not really at all like' the thing they 'explain'. Such scientists do, in fact, precisely the kind of thing that anyone dealing with really strange experience does, including the New Testament writers: they describe one kind of experience in terms of another kind which, in default of any more direct way, might help to convey to those who have not actually shared the experience something of its reality and significance. Together with all the other evidence of 'oddity' in the physical universe, this kind of thing helps to provide a more realistic context for considering the significance of the life of Jesus of Nazareth than if we insist on regarding the strangeness in his life as either peculiar to him or invented by the evangelists.

Allied, however, to this search for poetic image in order to convey some sense of the reality encountered at the furthest limits of scientific research is the suggestion by some scientists that the very basis of traditional science—the possibility of 'objectivity'—is ultimately misleading. Archibald Wheeler, of the University of Texas, is emphatic that we have to stop thinking of nature as a machine that goes on independently of the observer and to realize that we ourselves 'make' reality by the way we respond to it. There is (to use my terms) an exchange of life between the observer and the observed. To help this realization he has proposed a kind of mental 'experiment'. Imagine a game in which one player leaves the room while the others are supposed to choose a word for him to guess. Subsequent questions and answers, to discover the hidden word, suggest the way we usually suppose that scientific research works.

But, says Wheeler, suppose the people in the room change the game. They do not choose a word at all, there *is* no pre-existent answer. All each will do is to answer 'yes' or 'no' as he or she pleases, provided he or she has a word in mind which fits both the reply given and all the previous replies. The outsider, asking questions, assumes there *is* a word, but in fact the word is coming into being as he asks. Finally, he makes a guess and is right, because he or she, and the others, have created the concept out of their dialogue. In the same way the physical world as we apprehend it emerges from the 'questions' we ask about it. If the player asks different questions he discovers a different word, and if a scientist (or any one else) does different experiments and pursues a different line of research he will evoke a different kind of reality. Thus, 'observation' can be thought of as a giving and receiving of energy in exchange, and at the intersection of that exchange a phenomenon comes to be. Its individuality is the point at which all those converging energies meet and break surface.

The important thing about all this is not whether or not any particular 'oddity' can be 'proved' but the way in which our mental picture of reality is modified once we take seriously the possibility that such things do happen, for all of them contradict one assumption or another about reality. They especially bring in question our assumptions about the human body. The basic image which governs assumptions about our bodies is that they are defined by their skin. At this point, our physical being stops; or, conversely, our physical being and all the emotions and thoughts which it makes possible are 'contained' in that skin. Communication with other bodies— human or not—can only be by touching them or speaking to them (directly or indirectly). But all the oddities of ESP, ideas about 'auras' which can be perceived around people, and the current jargon about good and bad 'vibes', as well as those out-of-the-body experiences, bi-location, not to mention powers of healing, imply detectable and quite concrete relationships between bodies which are not verbal or tactile, as well as powers of bodies to do, and be, things which are not explainable if my skin is where I 'stop'.

If we admit such ideas, or even the possibility of them, we posit a different kind of world. If such things do or can happen, we cannot use a mechanistic model, nor an 'archetype' model; neither can we use a process model, and we cannot, I think, even use the 'exchange of life' model I have suggested, just as it stands, but only with the help of the extra concept of 'breakthrough'. For the first version of the exchange 'model' I suggested was at least observable as *sequence*. We could see how it happens, at least in outline, even if the sheer complexity of the actual operation defies imagination. But 'oddities' do not fit into this vision, they are not part of a sequence imaginable in such terms.

The name for 'exchange of life' is *love*, and one of the manifestations of love, the one in fact from which this book takes its title, is Romantic passion and is precisely a break in some kind of sequence which seems opposed to love. It is therefore 'odd', in precisely the same sense as those other things. Its oddness, like their oddness, does not imply that there is no sequence or general 'pattern' of exchange, but rather that, somehow, the pattern as we perceive it is in some way inadequate to 'carry' the full flow of the exchange of life which we call love. There is, in fact, 'something wrong', and the strong tides of exchanged life are deflected or distorted in various ways to compensate for this. These 'tides' must find a channel, and the one they find, or make, takes routes which are strange and even 'impossible' according to normal patterns. With the temerity of the truly ignorant I would venture to suggest, here, that the notion of curved space is an example of this. The path of light through space is not a straight line but is distorted more or less by a strong gravitational field. Gravity is a 'field', like a magnetic field, and the 'magnet' is matter itself, which creates the gravitational field by distorting the space around it. Gravitational fields not only 'bend' light but slow it down, measurably. It is not so long since such an idea would certainly have been dismissed as 'impossible'. We cannot easily describe gravity as 'something wrong', yet perhaps it is. Perhaps the 'differentness' of matter is a distortion of the ultimate reality of its relationship with energy. But since the distortion is there we have to discover how the 'flow' of exchange actually behaves.

A strange consequence seems to follow from such reflection. To use the 'exchange' image very concretely and naively, let us image a stream flowing between banks which become dammed, suddenly, by falling rock from the hillside. The flow is stopped, the water builds up to form a lake. Two consequences follow. One is that there is now a lake, and in it may grow fish and weeds, and by it may grow trees, and animals may drink and flourish which otherwise might not have been able to do so. The other consequence is that when the new water level reaches the top of the dam, or encounters stone or earth loose enough to be pushed out of the way, it will flow over the top and fall, with much greater force than that of the original flow. This can produce results which would not have been possible when the stream was undisturbed. It will wear away the rock below much faster than before, but also it can be used to generate other kinds of power—to pump, to drive engines, to light a town.

This suggests that the fullest energy of exchange of life, which is love, becomes available *because* something is 'wrong' with the situation. Love, in fact, is experienced not only as peaceful creativeness but as violent breakthrough; it becomes Romantic passion. But the energy of love also issues, for parallel reasons, in the oddness observed in material phenomena. To throw out a few unimportant guesses at random, it seems possible that 'ghosts' may happen because something called 'death' blocks a communication between people which is (for reasons not always clear) essential. The energy of exchange, unable to flow in 'normal' channels, finds other and 'odd' ways, using what seem to our narrow experience bizarrely disconnected aspects of physical reality in order to do so. And it may be that food is multiplied (and there are modern examples of this) very simply because there is acute need for food in conjunction with the kind of person who *is*, in some sense, a 'breach' through one of those blockages I mentioned. Through that human breach flows the power of exchanged life, and, since there is no possibility of satisfying the acute human need in 'normal' ways, this intensification of power takes abnormal channels.

All this is guesswork, but the imaginative model on which it is based is extremely suggestive. It suggests, among other things, that an essential element in the operation of oddness is some kind of breach in the blocked exchange. Such a breach in nature occurs, of course, wherever the mounting pressure of frustrated energy finds a weak spot. And this can be thought of as either accidental or deliberate. The rising water will fall over the dam whenever it can surmount the lowest rock, or displace a wobbly one. But the creation of a weak spot could be (as in a real dam) done deliberately, so as to direct and exploit the released power in the best way. Left to itself, the released power can be destructive rather than beneficial, and this may account, among other things, for such horrid phenomena as those charred corpses in uncharred rooms, or for the apparently motiveless 'panics' which seize people, or for destructive poltergeists. A weak spot, therefore, does not imply a failure, but simply the place where circumstances, random or planned, make it possible for the interrupted flow to break through.

The whole phenomenology of Romantic passion is a direct result of the fact that love is experienced not as natural exchange of life as in plants or in ordinary human sexual feeling, but as concentrated at one point, where it is enabled to break the highly defended barriers between two conscious and complex human beings.

There are, however, various possible weak spots which can be thought of as somehow powerfully evoking, by *their* nature, the nature of the exchanged life. One is physical beauty. All images of 'heaven' or of ultimate Good take beauty for granted as an accurate reflection of the truth they seek to evoke within the mind and heart of the listener or see-er. Beauty *is* heaven, in some way, and beauty of face and form are capable of evoking recognition of the nature of the inner and inarticulate 'experience' of exchanged life which is oneself.

The Romance writers took this for granted and delighted to describe such an occurrence. In one of the 'Lays' of Marie de France (one of the many women—some of whom were actually 'troubadours' or *trouveres*—whom the Romance movement empowered and inspired), there is an account of the arrival at Arthur's court of 'the flower of all the ladies of the world' whose mission is to rescue her misjudged and endangered knight.

> Passing slim was the lady, sweet of bodice and slender of girdle. Her throat was whiter than snow on the branch, and her eyes like flowers in the pallor of her face. She had a witching mouth, a dainty nose, and an open brow. Her eyebrows were brown, and her golden hair parted in two soft waves upon her head. She was clad in a shift of spotless linen, and above her snowy kirtle was set a mantle of royal purple. . . . As the Maiden rode at a slow pace through the streets of the city there was none, neither great nor small, youth nor sergeant, but ran forth from his home, that he might content his heart with so great a beauty. Every

man that saw her . . . marvelled at a fairness beyond that of any
earthly woman.

And when the imprisoned knight hears of her coming her says: 'It
is small matter now whether men slay me, or set me free; for I am
made whole of my heart just by looking on her face.' Thus beauty
can often be the 'place' where breakthrough happens. Another is
some kind of shared enthusiasm or commitment, which is in itself
a 'place' where the flow of exchanged life is seeking outlet and
destination. Another is simply a shared image of love itself, as when
Paolo and Francesca, reading a tale of love together, found the
barriers between them suddenly breached—in their case, to their
doom.

Another kind of human experience which is a natural weak spot
is death—not only the actual experience of dying, but the idea of
it. The knowledge that oneself or a loved person is suffering from
a fatal illness notoriously shakes people loose from preoccupations
which previously seemed very important and confronts them with
a deep truth. Death is often associated with Romantic passion
because passion is 'timeless', it has no 'history', it is a kind of death
to everydayness. There is a fittingness about the romantic preoccupation with death, even if it easily became sentimental or morbid.

Romantic passion, then, is *itself* precisely the kind of breakthrough
of exchanged life, at the vulnerable point in some 'barrier', for
which I have tried to provide an adequate imaginative model. But
there is something else about it which throws light on the notions
of exchange and breakthrough in history. For just as people live
meaningul sequences—that is, have a story—so communities, nations, cultures also have 'histories', in which traceable sequences
display the exchanges which build up an ethos, a religion, a whole
culture, with the significant breakthroughs which characterize that
process. But the term 'Romantic passion' conveys to us a particular
interpretation of certain human emotions because, at a certain point
in history, a type of perception developed which enabled the importance of the experience itself to be recognized.

The word 'Romance' derives from 'Roman'. The Roman con-
quests took with them all over the subjugated territories the Latin
language, expressing Roman law, ideology and culture. It was a
sophisticated, flexible and highly logical language, rich and lucid

and self-confident as the culture it articulated, and equally unaccommodating to the twilight areas of human experience, to the allusive, mostly orally transmitted culture and religion of the northern peoples it subjugated. Yet, as conquered peoples became Romanized, and as the 'barbarians' drove westwards in wave after wave of conquest and were themselves assimilated more or less to Roman ways, the Latin language changed. First it lived side by side with a number of other dialects and languages—Celtic, Norse, Germanic and later Arabic—and then gradually in each place the 'barbarian' languages affected the spoken Latin, itself already a much more 'popular' language than the classical Latin familiar to people who read Virgil or Horace (or even Augustine). It was different in each place, of course, and no two were alike in the ways the languages related to each other. In some, the two coexisted for a long time, in others they gradually merged. In Italy, homeland of Latin, a recognizable Romance language—Italian—was slow to develop. In northern France (land of the Franks), where there was growing cultural self-confidence under Charlemagne and his successors, the development was comparatively fast and distinctive.

The flow of exchanged life pushes onwards, breaking down barriers, and it breaks through at the weakest point. Roman culture was not 'Romantic' in our sense about human feelings. (It was sexy but it deprecated taking passion seriously.) Yet, by the time all these linguistic changes were taking place, the Latin culture had carried with it over Europe the theology of Christianity, and Christianity had been adopted (more or less) by the 'new' Europeans also. So we have a situation in which the explosive force of Christian awareness was being carried around in vessels of Latin, whose models of reality were quite unsuited to contain the stuff. Latin theological concepts boggled, and Europe was torn by heresies as people tried to make sense of Incarnation and Eucharist in language basically unsuited to the purpose. But Christianity is a lived thing, and as it was lived it was changing people's lives and ways of thinking and feeling, bypassing the incapacities of language and producing in the process a remarkable loosening up in Latin itself. Finally, however, this was not enough. New nations, whose experience of life was quite unlike the Roman one, were also absorbing and modifying and being modified by the new religion. The climate of feeling about life was being changed—not, of course, just by the new religion, but by this combined with the need to adapt to a more settled way of life, to be 'cultured', to articulate law, and also to incorporate the remaining and still strong Latin influence.

In the south of France, towards the eleventh century, there developed a language, the Provençal Romance language, the *langue d'Oc*, which was peculiarly suited to a cultural breakthrough because it was a kind of weak spot, linguistically and socially. Provence was recovering from the collapse of Charlemagne's empire and subjected to the influences of returning Crusaders, their imaginations full of the sights of foreign cities and strange and richer lands. Its language, while clearly 'Roman' in much of its skeleton, was full of words to do with country life, a life *essentially* rural, much concerned with the seasons and growing things and human reactions to these experiences, whereas Latin was the language of an essentially urban culture, imposing even on country life the organizational attitudes of the city. But Provençal culture was also now deeply interested in clothes and ornament, in festivity and heroism and beauty and food. Its language was that of a society in transition. Social divisions were fluid, aristocrats and ragged *jongleurs* could write and sing the same kind of poetry, and people could and did come quickly to prominence in the little uncentralized courts with no long tradition behind them. So there emerged a language of many diphthongs and triphthongs, a liquid, incantating language, but one with the hard 'c' at the ends of some words which gave its name to that part of France, the Languedoc. It was a language of surprises, light and stimulating, not sonorous or impressive like Latin.

I stress the crucial importance of the actual sounds of the language people have to use when they are trying to communicate ideas. It is at the basis, for instance, of Tolkien's writing of *The Lord of the Rings*. He wrote it, he said, to provide a context for the language he had been inventing, or rather adapting, from Norse languages, as a 'linguistic experiement' or a 'philological game'. Some critics said this proved the book was unimportant, a 'mere' fairy tale, but others held that the book could not be 'part of any game, philological or otherwise', since in it 'the heart of the author is laid bare', as one of them put it. 'No one ever exposes the nerves and fibres of his being in order to make up a language.' Maybe not, but nobody could make up a language without exposing the nerves and fibres of his being, however unintentionally. Conversely, it is only when the right language becomes available that certain 'fibres' can be revealed at all. The *need* to uncover and communicate 'pushes' the existing language towards change and, as change begins to be felt 'under the surface', attention concentrates at that point, it is 'rubbed thin' by experiment and desire. In the end something breaks through, as in Provence, and a new dimension of spiritual awareness becomes possible.

So in this new language men and women were finding ways to say things that had not been said before. They were saying things with religious roots, but not religious things, for the theology possible in Latin language could not 'feel' the spiritual impulse of the time and place and people.

To put it another way, the Christian demand, implicit in even the most crudely presented version of the teaching of the New Testament, was for a free response of love, a fervent giving and receiving, an openness, in fact an exchange of life which had to be, somehow, physical-yet-spiritual. But the available language of the Church and the customs and laws adopted by the Church had been shaped in a fierce school of conquest and compromise and the control of unruly crowds and unruly emotions. Rich and self-confident, Rome had said, 'We know it all; this is all there is to know.' Challenged and forcibly adapted and displaced by the new nations, Roman language and culture still said the same things but, under that pressure, said them with a cynicism and harshness uneasily balanced by a tolerance of what it could not prevent. None of this allowed the Christian feeling for life to say adequate things about itself. It could say nothing in *Christian* terms about real human love, about sex (except negatively), about bodily experience as spiritual. Its whole attitude to the physical was suspicious and grudging at best. But the 'feel' of Christian being was, by then, in the mind and heart of Europe. Inarticulate, it pressed towards words. Homeless, it searched for 'a local habitation and a name'—if not in a religious context, then in a human one that fitted it. If it could not use Christian words then it had to have human words which could carry that kind of impulse.

The impulse found its 'weak spot' in time and space, the only possible one in the course of the history not only of Christianity but of humankind, for the linguistic and cultural breaking of the dam which occurred in eleventh-century Provence affected, in the long

41

run, every culture in the world, as each one reaches the point at which the articulation of this different experience of reality becomes necessary.

Through the 'weak spot' in the dam it came, at first a trickle, then a stream and finally a river that widened and engulfed France, Spain, Germany, England, Italy. As European culture spread, other languages and cultures felt the ripples touch them and the water creep upwards over their territory, sometimes on stony ground where it simply stood in pools, and sometimes over soft land that soaked it up and where it was fed by native streams. So at last the great freshwater sea of Romance, by inlets and along stormy coasts, has touched every human culture, encouraging the growth of strange fish and of luxuriant plants on newly watered shores and providing, also, a way for the exchange across its surface of strange and exciting ideas which, in that exchange, grow and develop.

That is Romance, but it began in Provence and it began with a language which was capable of communicating love. It did not communicate *amor* or even *caritas*, it communicated *amour*, which sounds quite different, and specificially it communicated *amour courtois*, courteous or 'courtly' love—love as developed in those little, excited, newly leisured courts, where people had time and desire to explore new ways of relating and of thinking about relationship, because old social patterns had broken down and new ones had not yet hardened. The word 'court' gave the adjective *courtois*, courteous—with all that the word implies for us of disciplined yet sensitive and deeply respectful care for another. 'Courtly love' is the notion and practice of love which grew in the courts of Provence: a brief flowering, but rapid and very intense, and it was a new flower. This newness cannot be exaggerated. As C.S. Lewis said in the first chapter of his classic work on Romance, *The Allegory of Love*:

There can be no mistake about the novelty of romantic love; our only difficulty is to imagine in all its bareness the mental world that existed before its coming—to wipe out of our minds, for a moment, nearly all that makes the food of modern sentimentality and modern cynicism. We must conceive a world emptied of that ideal of 'happiness'—a happiness grounded on successful romantic love—which still supplies the motive of our popular fiction. In ancient literature love seldom rises above the levels of merry

42

sensuality or domestic comfort, except to be treated as a tragic madness, an ἄτη which plunges otherwise sane people (usually women) into crime and disgrace. . . Plato will not be reckoned an exception . . . . In the *Symposium*, no doubt, we find the conception of a ladder whereby the soul may ascend from human to divine love. But—you reach the higher rungs by leaving the lower ones behind. The very first step upwards would have made a courtly lover blush, since it consists in passing on from the worship of the beloved's beauty to that of the same beauty in others. Those who call themselves Platonists at the Renaissance may imagine a love which reaches the divine without abandoning the human and becomes spiritual while remaining also carnal; but they do not find this in Plato. If they read it into him this is because they are living, like ourselves, in the tradition which began in the eleventh century.

Lewis did not try to guess *why* this new thing appeared. Bold in my unscholarly status I have made such a guess, for this is not a matter of scholarship but of recognizing (tentatively but with delight) the characteristics of that phenomenon of breakthrough which will occupy much of this book.

We may be able to grasp the nature of this cultural 'weak spot' and how influential can be a 'breakthrough' at such a point, if we consider a parallel case near our own time. 'Blues' music is a musical 'language' which came into existence out of an extraordinary congruence of circumstances. Enslaved and uprooted, cut off from their cultural traditions, the black people in the American South had a strongly artistic and intuitive character and a spirituality deepened and strengthened by the stress of the need to resist the natural tendency of the enslaved towards apathy and servility. Music is the one art-form which is literally 'free'. It does not require materials or education or even time, because people can sing as they work, and as so often the art of the poor was in the music of the human voice. It was in that special kind of voice which is rarely found except in black people, especially women, that a new 'sound' broke through, with its use of particular musical intervals, of odd irregular rhythm, of syncopation, 'slides' and tremolo in idiosyncratic but characteristic combinations. This sound expressed—indeed made it possible to express—a range of human feeling which

43

had not been culturally 'available' before. The characteristic mixture of melancholy, endurance, controlled yet passionage longing and at the same time a quality of human and energetic earthiness, and all this somehow shot through with a certain quality of mystical wisdom: this is 'blues' music. It changed the Western musical 'scene' permanently and flowed over into the whole culture in some degree. Its influence has not been as powerful or as available as that of Romance, because it is a musical, not a verbal, language and therefore lacks the possibility of such direct and explicit assimilation, but the kind of thing it was and the way it happened display the same 'rules' for the occurrence of Romantic breakthrough which I shall be examining in the next chapter.

There is a need to examine them precisely because this book is not about Romantic love, except in so far as Romantic love is part of that greater whole whose 'pattern' it illustrates on a scale and in a manner which is very accessible to us. In preparation for that we need to ask, here, 'What is it which broke through? What is so special about it? What *is* Romantic love?'

It has no relationship, as Lewis pointed out, to the experience of human sexual love as the ancients understood it. Nor has it anything directly to do with sacred sexuality, though this is as old as the oldest religions, and sacred prostitution has been regarded as a form of worship and union with the god or goddess in many times and places. In some of the 'mystery' religions a ritual involving sexual intercourse with a priestess or priest of the cult was part of the initiation process, and a ritualized royal 'mating' of sacred kings and queens was also (it seems, though there is much argument around this) part of some fertility rituals. In all these, the act of physical intercourse was itself the central fact, though the psychological effect on the worshipper might be regarded as important in varying degrees. In contrast to this, the peculiar thing about the Romance idea of love is that it is not primarily a matter of physical intercourse at all, yet it is definitely and unambiguously bodily sexual love, directed to the whole person of the beloved, not just to her 'soul' or spirit. It is, therefore, not 'Platonic' love, a union of minds only.

Romantic love, as its high medieval exponents presented it, concentrated on the experience of passion, the release of spiritual power in, and between, a man and woman through their specifically sex-

44

ual, but not primarily genital, encounters. Passion, they proposed, was the means whereby men and women might move into a different and more exalted sphere of experience. It might, in due time, be expressed in physical intercourse, but this was in a sense tangential to the central experience. There were different schools of thought about this, as the exponents of 'courtly love' elaborated, commented and endlessly argued about the nuances of the great doctrines of ~~saving passion,~~ but all this elaborate and—in the end—trivializing debate stemmed from the tremendous discovery, by poets and story-tellers and lovers, of a fundamental fact of human experience, that of the significance of the 'breakthrough' of spiritual power and vision occasioned by the encounter of passionate love. The cultural breakthrough of 'Romance' came about in order to allow Christendom to celebrate the fact of spiritual breakthrough between men and women, whole, bodily and in love.

'Courtly love' began in Provençal, and soon French courts, and not in the huts of peasants, and has therefore been dismissed as a trivial aristocratic game. It was a game, and it was courtly, but then the educated and (reasonably) learned at any period are usually those who have time to develop ideas and spread them. And the most serious human preoccupation may be, in one aspect, a game, with 'rules' and purposes. But this discovery, which began in the small world of the Provençal courts, proved to be so obviously true-to-experience that it spread in a time remarkably short (by the standards, that is, of a world with limited social mobility and slow communications) to other countries and to other spheres of society.

It even spread outside Christendom, to the Persian court, but there it did not penetrate beyond the courtly world, and that for a very good reason: it was not, in Islam, rooted in theology, but was simply a fashion of human love. So also we find in many other cultures beautiful 'romantic' stories, but they are not articulated as a 'theology'. In Europe Romance was, very precisely, rooted in Christian theology, even though it seemed to take the form of a revolt against the rule and teaching of the Church about marriage.

The fact that Romantic love was first elaborated in terms of an explicitly non-married devotion, one which was indeed openly and proudly adulterous, was in a sense accidental; it was a reaction against a Christian Church that connived at, and profited from, the degradation of marriage to the level of a commercial transaction for

45

the sake of dynastic or financial profit, or (among feudal depen-
dants) to suit the convenience of the overlord. Little genuine love
or even respect had a chance to grow in such unions contracted in
such a climate, and the Romantic revolt was fully justified. But it
was a revolt based on an insight which could only have developed
in a milieu deeply impregnated with the Christian ethos. We shall
see this when we turn, in the next chapter, to the greatest writer in
the exposition of the meaning of Romantic love, the Florentine
Dante Alighieri.

It is often the case that one can 'live with' an insight for a long
time and then one day some further experience will illuminate it to
such a degree that all before appears to us as sheer blindness,
though at the time it seemed sufficiently clear. We need the Romantic experience to understand what Charles Williams, who disliked
Latinisms, called the 'Flesh-taking', even though that fundamental
statement about reality had been lived with, and lived by, Christians
for eleven hundred years before the doctrine of Romance developed.
We need it *because* it grew from the experience of living in the light
of Incarnation, and could not have developed without it.

For Romance is about the Spirit in the Flesh. It says, loudly, that
love is not a 'spiritual' affair (in the sense of 'unconcerned with the
body'), even when permanently unconsummated. In the vision of
the Romantic poets it was a love which sprang into being precisely
through seeing, and responding to, the physical presence and beauty
of the beloved. It remained physical throughout and expressed itself
in terms of actions of worship and service of a perfectly material
kind, whether in the giving of a gift or a kiss, or the accomplishing
of a quest or the winning of a fight in honour of the lady. It is *bodily*
experience, but an experience of the body as transfigured by the
breakthrough of passion and seen thereby in a new dimension,
literally changed, in the changed world discovered by this breakthrough into a different sphere of experience. Only Christianity,
rooted in the Flesh-taking, could create the environment of thought
and feeling in which such a concept could take root and flourish
and affect all of European culture from that time on, as no other
cultural influence has ever done. Only Christian doctrine teaches
that the divine can be not merely immanent in or symbolized by
material bodies, but actually enfleshed, and only this doctrine could

make such an articulation of experience permissable and therefore possible.

The other thing about Romantic love which could only have sprung from Christian roots (however little the gardeners of Romance realized this) is that the doctrine is essentially dynamic. It is about an energy that smashes through the surface of everyday awareness and makes possible an exchange of spiritual power and knowledge which not only penetrates the lovers through every aspect of body, mind and spirit, but reaches far beyond them to transform other relationships and the very aspect of the material world. It is clear, also, that it does not come *from* the lovers but 'enters' into them, and having done so it demands to be *used*, to be given and taken, to act and affect, to change and be changed. It discovers its meaning in the response to it; it can only be known in being given.

The language of Romantic love is clearly, therefore, a theological language which expresses the sense of reality as Exchange. It concentrates, first, on that point of Exchange where the flow of it, encountering an obstacle, has to find a way through. This is the thrust which leads to the passionate breakthrough. But without the model of Exchange Romantic love does not make sense, for breakthrough happens when there is something trying to get somewhere and being prevented. The passionate breakthrough happens because Exchange is what life and being *are*, and to prevent it is to turn the universe back on its course, a concept which I shall have to examine in the context of the nature of evil. But if it is true that to block Exchange is to contradict the very nature of reality, then it is no wonder that, eventually, something has to break.

2   The Face of Beatrice

In 1209, Philippe-Auguste of France appeared with his army in the
Languedoc, massacred the inhabitants of Beziers and besieged Car-
cassonne. This was one episode in that particularly horrible conflict
known as the Albigensian Crusade, when a number of land-hungry
nobles were delighted to declare their Catholic orthodoxy by de-
stroying heretics and taking their lands and wealth. Centred on the
town of Albi, this heresy was a form of the ever-recurrent Mani-
chean doctrine which regards material reality as evil and ultimately
unreal and seeks spiritual liberation from the flesh, condemning
marriage and adopting, at least among the truly devout, an extreme
asceticism. Since the povety, austerity and mutual charity of the
'Cathari' (the 'Perfect' as they were called in mockery) were such
an obvious condemnation of the cynical worldliness and militarism
of many Catholic clergy, they attracted popular support and clerical
hatred, and the 'crusade' to suppress the heresy involved not just
a few obvious 'heretics' but a great part of the population. In
particular it involved the courts of Provence, where the doctrine
had attracted people whose minds, searching and sensitive to new
areas of feeling, were receptive to the aspiring quality of the 'new'
doctrine in contrast to the gross materialism of the Church as they
experienced it.

In 1213, Count Raimon of Toulouse, aided by his brother-in-law
King Pedro of Aragon, went out to repel the invader, and with
them were the finest of the courts of Provence, Aragon and Cata-
lonia. They met the French under Simon de Montfort at Murret on
12 September and were completely defeated. The French seized all
territories east of the Garonne (that is, most of Languedoc). The
crusade was well pursued, and among the many things it destroyed
was the courtly life of Provence. The troubadours fled to Spain, to
Germany, even to England, but most significantly of all they fled
to Italy.

In Italy, to be fashionable was to be French, and to be French

48

was fashionable. Courtly love and its troubadours and songs, although originating in Provence, had long since occupied the *'Langue d'oïl'* as well and flowered brilliantly there, and when the Italian merchant Pietro Bernardone came back from trading in France he called his baby son 'François' (which is old French for 'French') or, in Italian, 'Francesco'— 'the Frenchman'. François took the imprint, and when he was converted and became possibly the most extraordinary and radiant of all Christian saints, there was converted in and with him the 'courtly love' in which he had soaked himself as a gay and gorgeous boy. About the year 1225 he composed the *Laudes Creaturarum*, a poem written in Italian 'Romance', full of that vernal and delicate vitality, of a passion both gentle and ardent, which is characteristic of the best of troubadour poetry.

In Florence, half a century later, a very different kind of man caught the delightful infection. (He was, incidentally, a member of the Third Order of Franciscan men and women who, while living ordinary secular lives, wished to follow the poor man of Assisi and to belong, in some sense, to the company of his *jongleurs de Dieu*.) Dante Alighieri was the man who renewed the somewhat decadent tradition of courtly love by discovering in it the theology of his poetic insight and the poetry of his theological insight.

In Dante we can find concepts of Romantic love worked through in detail and applied to the actual experience of Romantic love at its most intense and typical. For Dante's love for Beatrice is the archetype of Romantic love, coming as it did as a kind of final crest of articulateness in the tradition of Romance before it took other forms. But Dante is also important for us because he brought a true Christian awareness to his experience of Romantic love and so infused into his understanding of Christianity the light of his romantic experience. It was from the climate of thought and feeling created by the schools of courtly love and the whole luxuriant literature of Romance that Dante drew his original images, but he was both more consciously Christian and more humanly sensitive than many of his predecessors, as well as being a better poet and therefore a more daring theologian and a more accurate lover.

Dante's exposition of the meaning of Beatrice spans the whole range of his poetic achievement, from the *Vita Nuova* to the heights of Paradise in the *Divina Commedia*. From one point of view one can say that his first significant encounter with Beatrice, on a May

49

morning in the streets of Florence, was the point at which he met Love, and that the rest of his life was devoted to exploring and celebrating the meaning of this encounter. From another point of view we can say that it was only when he was capable of writing the *Paradiso* that he was able to experience properly the original encounter, so that, in a sense, he did not have the full experience until that moment. Both these things are true, and we shall see later on, in the life of Jesus, the way in which an incident can anticipate another occurrence which is still to come and which when it comes will illuminate the real nature of the earlier event. When the Gospel writers emphasized symbolic links between earlier and later events, either within the life of Jesus or between events in his life and Old Testament 'prophetic' words or events, they were doing the same thing that Dante experienced and which is indeed observable in every human life, seen from a certain point of view. In every case we can view the link between events either backwards, perceiving the fuller significance of the earlier event in the light of the later, or forwards, noticing in the earlier event the prophecy or foretaste of the later. But whichever point of view is adopted, forwards or backwards, a great deal of varied experience lies inbetween. There is an evident passage from sphere to sphere in Dante's own life. This experience requires to be integrated, somehow, into the understanding of the experience of passionate breakthrough.

Helen Luke says in *Dark Wood and White Rose*, her commentary on the *Divine Comedy*:

> It is a very common experience; everyone who has truly 'fallen in love' has had it, and sex in the narrow sense is not the important thing. It is the recognition of 'our native country' through love of another. We glimpse his or her eternal identity and so also our own, and we know in that moment that we have the freedom of that country forever.

This is the truth grasped by the devotees and students of Romance in the twelfth century. It is the 'passionate breakthrough' to a new life. It is very common and yet, fully lived, very uncommon, and it is only in the fully lived experience that its essential meaning can be discovered; we shall see this much more powerfully in the life of Jesus. In trying to understand the 'structure' of the passionate breakthrough Dante gives the clarity of definition which is needed, because he was not only a great poet, but a great Christian poet (which is not the same as a great poet who is a Christian), and he was writing about a personal experience. Charles Williams, the modern prophet of Romantic love, referred to the 'Beatrician moment', the one when a person breaks through to a wholly other sphere of experience, and the eyes of the lover are both dazzled and endowed with new vision.

In between the first encounter with Beatrice and the full disclosure of meaning lay the normal things which happen to human relationships: misunderstanding, divergence of ways, infidelity in some degree, death—and time. For many people, the passage of time and the events in the sphere of everydayness which time carries are proof that the revelation of that first encounter was a silly dream. Dante, never wholly losing sight of it, entered finally into the fullness of the experience, or at least as much of that fullness as a dweller in time and space can discover. But even in the earlier days he understood so well the nature of what was going on in himself on account of this Florentine girl that timorous ecclesiastical censors altered his all-too-precise terminology. For Dante calls Beatrice his 'beatitude' and even his 'saviour'. He knows that in encoutering her he has encountered that which he will, according to the teaching of the Church, enjoy forever in heaven, the very life of the noble Trinity, and since this is so she is the 'saviour', rescuing him from a half-life of everydayness and introducing him into the vision of glory-yet-to-be. Yet she is these things because she is also, without attenuation, Beatrice, an 'everyday' young woman of most solid earthliness.

When, at the end of the *Purgatorio*, Beatrice comes to lead the purged and aspiring poet to the awesome sphere of Paradise, she appears in a processional chariot, surrounded and celebrated by angels and allegorical figures, all providing a setting in which we would expect the revealing of the eucharistic Lord. Yet when the moment comes it is Beatrice who stands there, very much his own Lady, and even though she is still veiled he responds to her presence not only with awe but with a strong stirring of human desire. 'The ancient flame', he calls it, quoting Virgil's words about Dido's passion. There is no mistaking the kind of 'flame' he is talking about, which springs to life at the sight of her. She is his original

51

and unrepeatable Beatrice, yet she is *also* Christ, also Eucharist, also Mary, the God-bearer, also Church—body of Christ in its human relationship of exchange. For when Dante is finally allowed to look into the 'emerald' eyes of Beatrice ('whence Love let fly his former shafts at thee') he sees reflected in them the image of Christ. In the final and highest sphere of his vision, when he beholds the White Rose of the spirit centred on ultimate Love, he sees Beatrice 'in her glory crowned' and hails her as the one who 'led me, a slave, to liberty'. She is indeed his saviour, the one who can break through the spheres for and with him. But then she turns her head to gaze ever inwards, and he, guided by Bernard, most ardent adorer of the God-bearer, perceives Mary of whom God took flesh; but she in her turn looks towards the Centre, and his eyes, at her entreaty, are empowered to behold the ultimate Bliss itself. So Dante sees Mary 'through' Beatrice and the Trinity 'through' Mary, in a perfect and perpetual and 'courteous' exchange of love given and received, flowing inwards to the centre and outwards in the same gesture, for here, in Paradise, the spheres give way to a constant and perfect energy of exchanged love.

Yet Beatrice does not merely stand as an 'image' of Mary and of Christ and of Divine Love, in the sense of a more or less adequate analogy. Beatrice actually *is* 'beatitude' and 'saviour', 'God-bearer' and 'Christ'. She is these things without ceasing to be her particular self, but by being them *in relation to Dante*, who through her was enabled to break through to the sphere of glory in himself, as he perceived it in her.

Here we see the two aspects of Romantic love to which I referred at first as specifically Christian because incarnational. It is the real, bodily being of Beatrice by which Dante meets God walking in the streets of Florence, and he is changed by that encounter in his own bodily being. Charles Williams, commenting on this scene in *The Figure of Beatrice*, points out the detailed comprehensiveness of the effect of the 'Beatrician experience':

The appearance of Beatrice, her 'image'—'*la sua immagine*'—produces at their first meeting these distinguishable effects which he attributed in the physiological and poetic habit of his day to three centres of the human body ... the 'Spirit of life' which dwells in the inmost chamber of the heart trembled and said

'Behold a god stronger than I who is come to rule over me'. The 'animal spirit' which lived in the brain where all sense-perceptions are known was amazed and said 'Now your beatitude has appeared'. The 'natural spirit' which dwelled 'where our nourishment is distributed'—that is, in the liver—begins to weep and say 'O miserable wretch! How often now shall I be hampered!' . . . the 'liver' is the seat of organic life . . . Dante allowed fully the disturbance to this third seat of his consciousness . . . his sex, like his intellect, was awakened . . . long afterwards he was to cry out: 'The embers burn, Virgil, the embers burn' and the fire was general through him.

The second aspect of Romantic love is the fact of the essentially dynamic nature of being as it is revealed in Christ. The lover comes to self-awareness in the awareness of the beloved; they are defined in exchange of life. The exchange can and must happen in 'two directions', each person being both lover and beloved, but in Romantic doctrine the relationship is defined in terms of Lover to Lady, not the other way round, so that two lovers, though equal, have a relationship to each other which is not interchangeable. Beatrice, Dante's lady, is the way in which he discovers and is released into the 'sphere of glory'. It is always so, though the one who is 'the way' may be the man in the case. One reason for this is that, in this discovery, the beloved is the 'door' which, being touched, opens the way, so that the lover may enter into the new 'sphere'. It is Beatrice who opens the 'door' for Dante, but from whichever direction one looks at it there are two different roles, even if *both* enact *both* roles.

There is, however, an important reason why the Romance writers saw the roles embodied only one way, in the male lover and the female beloved, and this lies not only in the obvious and traditional sense of the feminine as the 'place' or 'earth' of love, the inner realm where life grows, but—through this—in the feminine character of Wisdom, which makes this relationship more theologically explicit. This is not a consideration which was in the conscious minds of the Romance writers. Yet the more one considers the images of Wisdom the clearer the relevance becomes. In the central chapter and towards the end of the book I shall have occasion to study the concept and being of divine Wisdom at much greater length. Here I can only sketch briefly the relevance of Wisdom to Romantic passion, and so establish a link which can be taken up later.

Wisdom, in both canonical and deutero-canonical 'Wisdom' books of the Old Testament is not merely a personification of human wisdom, nor even of God's wisdom; she *is* herself divine. As a hypostasis she is the one who creates and holds all things in being, not commandingly 'from without' but dynamically from within, *moving* in them. She 'penetrates all things, reaching from one end of creation to the other', in the depths and the heights. All things are made 'through' her, and she 'enters into holy souls and makes them friends of God and prophets'. The word used by Charles Williams to describe this relationship, which he discerns as a basic mode of divine action and being, is 'co-inherent'. Wisdom inheres in creation, and creation inheres in her divine activity. As divine, Wisdom has authority, but it is exercised from within as she forms and teaches and guides. Wisdom is, therefore, a fairly exact theological explanation of why the 'Lady' of Romantic love is the one in whom, and through whom, the sphere of glory is entered and experienced. When the lover encounters the beloved, what he sees is the feminine Wisdom who is the radiance of the eternal God, and he sees her in the very flesh of his beloved. So for him and in him the human woman becomes the God-bearer, the 'Mother of God', but also Christ, for whose role and nature Paul, and the writer to the Hebrews, and John, could find no better images than those once used to define divine Wisdom herself. All this is so not in spite of but precisely in virtue of the fleshliness of the human woman, the 'Lady', which she shares with the Word made Flesh. In this role of 'saviour' she is identified with him, she *is* what he is, but not by imposing one reality over another to the obliteration of one. The two things can be true at one and the same time because they exist only and always in the movement of exchanged love.

In order to take this experience and make it available as a theological 'tool' in the rest of the book it is necessary here to take it apart in some detail, and then to see how it works out in the life of Jesus. Romantic love is not simply sexual attraction. The language of our culture in relation to sexuality and love is so restricted in what it will allow sexual feelings to 'mean' that what might have been a transforming 'Beatrician experience' ends up as nothing much but satisfied desire, hung around with unsatisfied nostalgias.

54

But 'genuine' Romantic love does occur, in spite of the culture, because it is too basic a human occurrence to be altogether denied or explained away. And however it may be subsequently weakened or corrupted through lack of knowledge or courage, it has certain characteristics which are significant.

These characteristics are the following: 'particularity'; 'singleness'; a capacity for changing the 'face of reality'; a kind of 'halo' of obscure glory; and, also, painfulness. It has also a great potential for corruption, though this is less a characteristic than a possible direction of the entire experience. (There is also a final, but actually primary, thing to add about Romantic passion, which is what one *does* about it.) These characteristics need to be clarified.

The very obviousness of *particularity* can make its importance less noticeable. Because the Romantic experience is a fully physical experience, it is particular. It happens through one person, not just in relation to 'humanity'. It is this particular girl (whose hair and eyes are a special colour, who smiles just so) who is the gateway to a universal glory. She provides a direct encounter with a basic reality of the universe at a level far deeper than the intellectual but, by that fact, illuminating and strengthening the intellect which itself is rendered sensitive to such awareness by the experience.

Singleness is a less obvious characteristic. It happens once, with one person, but other encounters of a comparable kind may come later and raise problems which must be resolved. This does not alter the fact that, at the point of encounter, the passionate breakthrough is not only particular but single, for the whole energy of the lover is concentrated on this single point. There is a curious kind of proportion to this, whereby a relationship with more opportunity for the couple to meet and 'get to know' each other tends to have less violence of emotion. Common-sense advice given to parents whose children have fallen in love with the 'wrong' person is, often, to 'let them see more of each other', because this will probably dilute passion with experience, while opposition may make the lovers even more obsessed with each other. This is so because the passionate breakthrough does not, in fact, indicate any great degree of compatibility between two people. All it means is that *something* in one is able to release that in the other which, at that time, has reached the point at which the breakthrough is required if spiritual growth is to be possible. It will force a way at some

55

point, and the concentration of the impulse at the single point of encounter, through lack of opportunity for wider acquaintance, actually gives it its 'passionate' character, though it also makes the chances of developing a full everyday relationship more remote. From the point of view of the Romantic encounter this does not matter, though there is another aspect of Romantic doctrine, that of fidelity, to which it matters a great deal. But at the point of encounter intensity matters, and intensity is increased by narrowness and by obstacles, as a river running through a narrow gorge is faster and stronger than one meandering through meadows.

Once the breakthrough has occurred the waters so released rapidly flood the mind and emotions. People in love may look different, they have a 'glow', they walk more lightly, move more delicately. But also the face of reality is changed, the world looks different to them. All kinds of people seem more lovable or more interesting; compassion is more easily aroused, generous and tender feeling is so near the surface as to be painful. There is also, often, a sense of daring, a longing to undertake difficult things for the sake of the beloved, even without her knowledge. And not only other human beings but other material things acquire a sense that they embody a secret which is so near the surface that it is about to become apparent. (The Romantic poet or artist, of course, tries actually to make it apparent.)

Everything, from the face of the beloved down to the neighbour's cat, acquires a greater and more precise reality, but at the same time, apparently contradicting this, there is *the 'halo' of glory*, Dante's 'stupor', a sense of not being able to perceive clearly what one sees. The clarity of things seen is set within an ambience of felt ignorance, a sense that there is a more inclusive meaning, which *should* be understood but cannot be. It is not a feeling of general 'mystery', but rather a nostalgia for something which is precise in its nature yet elusive because un-remembered, like the atmosphere of a dream which flees as one wakes.

Finally, the Beatrician experience is *painful*. Even in its joy it has a quality of longing for a completeness which is not achieved nor, the lovers feel, even possible. The oneness which is experienced is, they feel, only a glimpse of an experience which is closed to them. Something gets in the way, and although this 'something' may present itself to them as other people's codes of behaviour, or the necessities of everydayness, these are mere symbols of the essential barrier within. The barrier has been breached by the thrust of passion, but the opening is too small and something which was before unseen can now be seen through the gap. That hurts, with a sense of ineffable 'wrongness', yet that 'wrongness' is the indication of something so 'right' that to be rid of the hurt would be unthinkably worse than bearing it.

All these characteristics of the Romantic breakthrough are matters of experience, though temperament, circumstances and above all the attitude of the particular culture, filtered through the mind that experiences passion, alter the proportions. For instance in some the experience may be so deeply happy that the lovers would be surprised to hear it suggested that it was painful, yet there is a pain which they accept and expect: of separation, of failure to understand each other totally, of need to be concerned with other things. Again, people whose character is very 'action-oriented' may not experience the changed 'look' of things in any appreciable way because they have little awareness of 'things' except as a field for the expression of love felt as a call to caring. But, intensely or barely felt, these characteristics are present.

Among human experiences Romantic passion is peculiarly open to corruption, and this opens up the discussion of the whole 'problem' of evil. The associations of the original Romance movement with gnostic heresy (and even with Satanism in some of the backwaters of Catharism) is not due purely to the fevered imaginations of celibate Inquisitors. The popular linking of the Romantic revival in the nineteenth century with 'decadence', opium, occultism and a cult of sensuality for its own sake is also an indication (however exaggerated by the suspicious) of the kind of path that passion can take. Recently we have seen an unprecedented flowering of interest in the occult, a renaissance of serious witchcraft, and finally the rise of the cult of a kind of sexual licence so idiotically degraded that it seems unsure whether to collapse into a ludicrous banality of adolescent viciousness or to take a hopeless dive beyond tragedy. There is something so extremely nasty about what happens to Romantic passion when it 'goes wrong' that it is not very surprising that Romance itself has generally been viewed with suspicion by both Church and State, and indeed by 'all sensible people'.

The last element of Romantic doctrine is so important that it

57

should have been placed first, except that it could not make sense outside the context of all the rest. It is the element referred to in the French of its originators as *amour voulu*. To them, Romantic passion might seize on human beings unawares, but simply to submit to be swept away by emotion was unworthy. They had as profound a contempt for such *amour fol* as they had for the false lover, because the lover who betrayed love was not only one who was calculating or shallow but the one who was self-indulgent, surrendering not to *love* but to *emotion*. In contrast to this they asserted that the only proper response to the *revelation* of love was a *commitment* to love—absolute, unconditional and permanent. The painful and often humiliating 'service' rendered by the sworn knight to his Lady was the working out of this in practice. 'Let him who has found a constant lover prize her above rubies, and serve her with a loyal service, being altogether at her will,' admonished Marie de France.

Amour voulu is a 'giving back', in free but completely uncompromising dedication, of that which has been freely and undeservedly received. This concept, strange to a culture which sees Romantic passion not as 'willed love' but as 'dominating emotion', leads us to understand what Jesus meant when he spelt out the meaning of love not as mystical invasion but as acts of practical service. It is the basis of both mysticism and moral theology.

All these characteristics of Romantic breakthrough are part of a total human development. Therefore in order to understand the event itself as a theological paradigm, it is necessary to see also *how* it occurs. Why with *this* person? Why *then*? Why *thus*? These are questions which will have to be answered in detail in a number of different contexts throughout this book, and here it will be enough to establish a kind of sequence of events for Romantic breakthrough, to indicate what occurs, and why, and leave illustration to the memory of the reader. It must also be said that the sequence I describe here is established by hindsight only, and that the three questions I asked cannot, even then, always be answered with more than 'reasonable' assurance, for no human person or situation can yield all its elements to the outside observer.

The sequence goes like this: a *remote preparation* creates the situation in which an *immediate preparation* can make or discover the 'vulnerable point' for the *breakthrough* itself. Once the breakthrough has occurred it requires something else in order to be effective—*a language*.

The *remote preparation* means a probably lengthy process in which the person is inclined, by circumstances and by 'education' (conscious and unconscious), to recognize and *want* something at least vaguely corresponding to the Romantic experience. This is both likely and unlikely in our culture. We are culturally sodden with Romantic expectations, and the young are showered with the perfume of it regularly. But it is a less than authentic brand of Romance, too heavily scented with purely sexual connotations, so it may distort the experience when it comes.

There has to be this 'remote preparation' or nothing happens. (There are plenty of people around to whom, visibly, 'nothing' has happened.) Adolescence itself is such a preparation, and this shows that there is a process, not just a state. If 'nothing' happens in adolescence it is because growth has been, somehow, arrested. Growth happens under the influence of cultural expectations, and adaptations to them, which produce a variety of behaviour and ideas but within certain limits of personal spiritual 'reach'. Yet this reach is increasingly felt to be too narrow. There is a restlessness; obscure desires stir but are still obscure. So the remote preparation is 'inward' and spiritual, reacting to and with the 'outward' and cultural—but I say that with reluctance, merely to make clear two aspects, for in practice the distinction is false. The 'outward' activates and indeed 'creates' the inward, yet the 'inward' of each, touching other 'inner' persons, is what creates the culture which in turn bears so heavily on the developing 'inner' consciousness. I have put this account of 'remote preparation' in terms of individual people, yet it will have been clear to anyone who has read the previous chapter that the things which went on in France towards the end of the 'Dark Ages' provided just such a restlessness, a sense of obscure need, a grabbing at trappings of luxury or heroism or sensuality, expressive of a desire for something or other, without any clear notion of what is desired.

In this situation occurs the *immediate preparation*, something which creates a 'weak spot'. Something happens which shakes the person loose from normal expectations and settled attitudes. It can be a book, or a vacation, or a disaster, or simply an intensification of the influences which have created the 'remote preparation'. It can be, in practice, the encounter with the person who will be 'the' person, but in whom the 'Beatrician experience' has not yet appeared. It can be something quite small and apparently trivial, such as suddenly catching sight of one's face in a mirror. There is no longer simply a vague sense of need but a definite expectancy, which may be somewhat fearful. There is within the person *something* which is, as it were, on the lookout for *itself*. It cannot 'come out' until something opens the door, from 'outside'—and when something does open it, there is an immediate sense of recognition. All is new—yet this is 'home'. Is it fanciful to see in eleventh-century Provence elements like this? The strangeness of Crusading experience, the sudden increase in the status and influence of women, the comings and goings of landless knights living on 'chivalry', and of poor, bold, exciting *'jongleurs'*, the influence of a persuasive and officially abhorrent heresy? Any one of these might have been enough to challenge the 'new' love to recognize itself.

The response to this recognition is passion: the thrust of the whole personality towards the strange 'home' it perceives. It is accompanied by intense emotion, which varies in quality according to temperament from a gentle but strong and certain joy to a desperate violence which is afraid of losing that which is perceived. But something very odd precedes this: I can only describe it as a kind of 'gap', in which there is no feeling or 'movement' but a timeless instant of oneness. It is an experience of recognition so complete and profound that it is impossible to say what is recognized. That is why it is experienced as a 'gap', and it can be so content-less that the person recoils and takes refuge behind a hastily closed door. Passion, therefore, is the thrust which leaps that void; it is a leap of faith, without guarantess or even knowledge. The leap is, therefore, not primarily emotional, but powerful emotion is released by it. The breakthrough of passion is this self-giving towards a wholeness intensely desired, but across a gap of 'un-knowing'. This is what makes it passionate—it is difficult; it is, as we saw, painful.

When the breakthrough has occurred, all depends on something quite simple: What do we do about it? *Amour voulu* must have some guidelines if it is to do more than flounder. What people do *about* the passionate breakthrough depends on what they understand to have happened, and in consequence what their expectation is of

60

themselves. Clearly, the reaction of a person who has learned that Romantic passion is a disgraceful lapse from proper emotional direction will be quite different from that of a person who views Romance as the high point of human experience, or again from that of a person who has been taught that it is a fleeting though exciting experience, to be indulged and enjoyed but not directed. So what a culture or group 'says' concerning the breakthrough event is obviously of quite crucial importance. On this 'language' depends whether the experience is to be fully lived as *amour voulu*, or dismissed as trivial, or rejected as sinful, or wallowed in, or surrendered to without thought, or evaded, or greedily grasped, or perverted.

'Language' is communal, it means a society. The breakthrough cannot be 'private' since its results depend on a shared 'language' about it. This is the origin of religious and spiritual movements. The desert Fathers, the Franciscans, the Lollards, the Jesuits, the Separatists who went to New England, the Shakers, the Salvation Army and modern communes and religious sects are (to name a few out of thousands) examples of how the passionate breakthrough in one person's life is articulated in a language which becomes that of a group who also respond to the vision they perceive in the founder. Hence the passionate breakthrough leads, somehow or other, to *community*, and also (if it is fully lived) it creates and re-creates the community within which it is understood, illuminating for others, as well as for the lovers themselves, the reality which each has encountered. (This is as true of a community for evil, such as the Hitler Youth became, as of a community of love.) Clearly, Romantic passion did create a community in its historical beginnings. The 'language' we now use to understand and live it was made possible by that community and re-created by it.

Romantic passion, then, is of all 'normal' human experience the one with the capacity for the highest soaring (even to Paradise, if Dante is to be trusted) and the deepest degradation. It is certainly true, as many have pointed out, that as a doctrine and cult with a real influence on the morals and behaviour of a culture it has been confined to Western culture, and that only since the high medieval period. But as an undefined (and therefore comparatively un-influential) experience it has been an 'underground' movement in every culture of which we have record. It has sometimes been cultivated as an élitist pastime, sometimes covered up or excused as a social *faux pas*; it has been ostracized as an aberration, recounted in story or drama and used as material for myth-making and tale-telling, from Homer onwards. But until it surfaced in European cultural consciousness in the twelfth century it was not considered an event so significant in human life that its implications might be of literally eternal importance. The fact that the ecclesiastical censors deleted references to Beatrice which directly suggested that she was, in some senses, 'God' to Dante shows that this notion was there and was shocking to them—but shocking as ridiculous, not as serious enough to be dangerous. If they had taken it seriously they would have been obliged either to accept it or to denounce it as heretical. They did neither.

Yet the experience of genuine Romantic passion is of quite central importance in understanding the nature of human beings as God-created, God-directed, and God-centred, not only as an *analogy* of human-divine relationships but as an *example* of it. Through it we may be able to understand much more clearly the eternal realities which include it, of sin, grace, redemption, resurrection—indeed, of the nature of God. And in the process we shall come to a better understanding of our unpredictable earthly experience, of material reality in all its 'explained' and unexplained complexity.

But if Romance gives us a language which can open up the whole of Christian theology that is at least partly because it expresses itself as poetry and as story, sometimes one and sometimes the other, but at its best as both together and simultaneously. Poetry works by the intensity with which it evokes mood, or place, or person, and in itself is capable of creating a kind of breakthrough, so that the hearer or reader is transported for the moment into another sphere. In the light which flows from that sphere things in the sphere of everydayness are enabled to disclose their own real nature, so that we become aware that the most humdrum reality is, in fact, not 'everyday' at all, but 'the means of grace and the hope of glory'. In that light we see, as Rilke supremely makes us see, that the redemption of *things* is the especial task of human passion. 'Things' are not of themselves capable of glory, but in human response they are:

Are we, perhaps, *here* just for saying: House,
Bridge, Fountain, Gate, Jug, Fruit tree, Window,—

62

possibly; Pillar, Tower? . . . but for *saying*, remember,
oh, for such saying as never the things themselves
hoped so intensely to be. Is not the secret purpose
of this sly Earth, in urging a pair of lovers,
just to make everything leap for ecstasy in them?
                                        . . . So show him
some simple thing, re-fashioned by age after age,
till it lives in our hands and our eyes as a part of ourselves.
Tell him *things*. . . .
                    These things that live on departure
understand when you praise them: fleeting, they look for
rescue through something in us, the most fleeting of all.
                                        (Ninth Duino Elegy)

Children, and saints, see 'things' that way in any case, because
they do not demand of them that they be 'useful' or bestow prestige.
We, who lack that humility, need the poet's vision to show us the
face of reality. But we have then to transform his vision into action,
we have to choose and be faithful and so we need stories which spell
out for us the proper response to the vision granted to us in virtue
of the poetic imagination. We see in them people dealing with the
reality of 'things' as glimpsed in that vision and know that, ultimately, 'everydayness' *is* the 'category of glory', but only when we
have learned to live in that sphere ourselves.
    A story has, as Alice pointed out, a beginning, a middle and an
end, and if one of these is missing it does not make sense. It is about
actions and consequences. But Romance is a story about poetry, a
sequence of cause and effect in time which happens because of the
breakthrough of something which is timeless. And it is also, in the
end, poetry about story, an eternal moment in which the experience
worked out in time and causality is seized and known, yet never
possessed, because its nature and purpose is simply to create the
means of 'exchange' with another category. Romance is truly
(though I doubt if Eliot would have liked this idea) a 'moment in
and out of time', a doorway between worlds, which is why this book
is a Romance, story and poetry: the story of God's love for human
beings and the poetry of that experience, in its effect on people, but
also in its effect on the context of people, which is the whole material
universe. It is also the poetry, and the story, of the effect of people

63

on God. It is this because the gospel story itself is a Romance in the strict sense. It has a beginning, a middle and an end (and this is true though there are a number of possible beginnings, middles and ends which can be arranged to make the story). The evangelists, and St Paul, are also writing fantasy, or 'poetic story' in the sense that they are using certain imaginative categories to evoke the fuller and deeper meaning of the events they narrate. But, unlike 'ordinary' fantasy, which has to invent non-realistic situations in order to evoke the deeper meaning of those we experience in 'real life', the Gospels are about life at a point of realness which only needs to be properly seen in order to disclose its meaning and so to create a new world. Coleridge said that the Secondary Imagination, the human power to evoke reality by symbols, is an 'echo' of the Primary Imagination, which is 'the living power and prime Agent of all human Perception and . . . a repetition in the finite mind of the external act of creation in the infinite AM'. The breakthrough of the creative act of secondary imagination, in story or poetry, is the work of Wisdom, and Wisdom 'rejoices' in creation. The intense joy of that experience is truly Romantic and we shall see, in some incidents in the Gospels, this joy at work, and also the painfulness of the Romantic experience. 'Having joy set before him, he endured the cross', but the joy is there on the way, as well as ahead, and I want next to study an example of this. In order to do that I shall be using the kind of language I have been describing, the language of Romantic passion, based on the model of reality called Exchange. It is a language of fantasy, designed to evoke the deeper meaning which underlies 'everydayness', yet also it is *about* everydayness, about the most ordinary, earthy things, but seen in the light of the sphere to which Romantic passion gives access.

Equipped with this language, I shall be able to move towards the centre of the book, of theology and of all things, which is the ultimate Exchange and the one essential Romantic breakthrough: the incarnation of Christ, leading to his death and resurrection. But before I can dare to think about the transformation of reality which is referred to by the word 'resurrection' it is necessary to see Exchange, and passionate breakthrough, going on in this unique life in other ways, as it does for all human beings. Jesus is 'the passionate God' supremely at that moment which turned all of living and loving inside out, which was his death and resurrection. But if he is that then, he is that always, and we have to see the passionate character of incarnation working out in his life as it moves towards that end. At the end, also, we shall see the ultimate encounter with evil, and so this will have to be understood more clearly in the rest of his life before we can understand the nature of the final struggle between life and death. If the progress seems slow, I would ask the reader to have patience. Possible short cuts would bring us to our destination, certainly, but we would approach it from an angle which would make it impossible to see it properly. The way I propose to travel is comparatively slow and steep but the viewpoint it obtains is really necessary.

I want to consider the idea of 'passion' (in the sense given to it so far) in the context of the life of Jesus as a whole, and see how the phenomenology of Romance helps us to understand him. But our whole human life is not an even progression but rather a series of cycles of growth, consisting of episodes of breakthrough to new levels or 'spheres' of being, with stages between of using and 'exploring' the new sphere, until a time comes when further breakthrough is needed if development is to continue. I have chosen to take one especially important moment in the life of Jesus in order to discover that interaction of the things I referred to in terms of 'exchange of life', 'barrier' and 'breakthrough' which I have explored in connection with natural forces and in the phenomenology of Romantic passion.

The episode I want especially to consider from this point of view is the one we call the transfiguration, because, among other reasons, this incident shows us the human Jesus apparently quite at home in a sphere which certainly does not belong to 'everydayness'. Some kind of major transition is shown to a sphere which is quite strange to us, and 'strangeness' is, as we have seen, something which cannot be simply brushed off the surface of our world-picture by the dusters of those efficient cleaning ladies, Reason and Science.

It is important to distinguish between the strange and the unthinkable. The strangeness of the life of Jesus does not lie in the idea of God becoming human. That is not strange, it is literally 'unthinkable'. This is because there is no way even poetic language can compass imaginatively a statement whose two terms split to show an intellectually unbridgeable gap. All credal statements are really poetic images, intended to define the 'edges' of the gap, but it is easy to slip into using them not to define the gap but to obliterate it, and when we do that we are falling into heresy, no matter how orthodox the actual statements. (It is, none the less, always worth while to *try* to define the edges of the thinkable in this vital area, with apophatic theology providing a healthy corrective to such efforts.)

Strangeness, however, is thinkable. It is not beyond the scope of our imagination and reason, but it does odd things to them, and because this is uncomfortable we try to reduce strangeness to everydayness, yet also we crave strangeness. We do not want too much of it but we want *some*—hence the attraction of travel in far-off places, in the 'time-off' from everyday work, but hence also the hoary old joke that the British abroad demand tea and fish-and-chips and Americans demand ice-water and hot showers. Familiarity is demanded, to temper the strangeness. But if we do not want too much strangeness in daily living we do want it somewhere in our lives, and we get it through science fiction or in art or poetry or scientific discovery itself. The craving for strangeness drove the sales of Tolkien's *Lord of the Rings* into the millions, for his kind of strangeness was, like foreign travel with fish-and-chips, the ideal blend of the earthy and recognizable with the utterly strange. But Tolkien wrote fiction, and we experience vacations only as pauses in 'real life'. It is a very different matter to claim that strangeness is a clue to essential reality. This is why I have chosen to 'begin in the middle', in several senses, and to try to 'see' the effect and meaning of the strangeness of the flesh-taking in this central incident of the life of Jesus.

The story of the transfiguration is 'in the middle' in the obvious sense that, chronologically, the three synoptic Gospels put it about midway in the public life of Jesus, not in terms of length of time (we cannot know precisely the actual time involved anyway) but in the sense that it formed a kind of watershed in the career of Jesus, as Luke makes particularly clear. It is inbetween the foreshadowing and the fulfilment; it is neither one nor the other. It is an anachronism, and has often been felt to be so. And it is 'in the middle' in the sense that it takes place not in one sphere or another but across the 'boundaries', releasing one into another in the oddest way. To some extent *all* 'strange' events do this, but it is useful to

66

observe it in this 'acute' form, for it opens up questions with which the rest of the book will be concerned.

In the accounts of the three synoptic Gospels the transfiguration is an incident which takes its place in a course of events whose sequence is reasonably clear, even if the dating and exact order is not. It is also an account of something which, as a 'happening', could not be fully described within the category of everydayness. Recounting this story required the poetic recourse to words which are not so much descriptive as evocative of the precise nature of the experience, because that is the only way in which it is possible to say 'what really happened'.

The four writers (if we include the Letter of Peter) tell us about what we call the 'transfiguration' by using concepts and symbols evocative of relevant themes in the history of the Jewish people. This does not mean they are 'really' only exploring the inner significance of the mission of Jesus at this point in the story. No such spectacular incident would be required to illustrate the fact that the death of Jesus, which he had begun to prophesy, was the essential work of redemption, one which (as their early Christian hearers knew) was to issue in triumph over death. The writers are, rather, telling us about something which was important because it had a 'crisis' character in relation to what came before and what came after.

The transfiguration is quite different in kind from anything else in the Gospel accounts. It is not like an account of a healing or any other miracle and it is not like any of the accounts of resurrection appearances. Some scholars have indeed suggested that it is a 'displaced' account of one of these, but they do not suggest convincingly (to me at least) why it should be so different from all the others, nor why it should have been 'displaced', since it serves no particular didactic purpose which could not be served without it. It is simplest to suppose that the writers were doing what they said they were doing—giving as clear an account as possible of something that happened in the sight of three men, who afterwards recounted their experience to others as well as they could. But because of the nature of the experience both the witnesses and those who wrote down the story used images which give it precision by reference to other experiences, from the past, which are recognized by hindsight as belonging to the same sphere. This is poetry, and it is theology. It

67

is, in this case, sheerly romantic poetry, a poem about a passionate breakthrough in the fullest sense.

In the four texts (two of which are almost identical) is a record of an experience which concerns chiefly a person to whose normal physical presence all three witnesses were accustomed. But it also concerns two other people who had died many centuries before and who, therefore, could not have been recognized in the ordinary way by the witnesses. At some point, however, they knew, or were told, that the two men they saw conversing with Jesus were Moses and Elijah, men who were themselves the symbols of 'the law and the prophets', Israel's twin pillars on which her whole self-consciousness as the chosen of Yahweh depended. The way in which this strange encounter struck the witnesses is evoked in terms which deliberately recall the great theophanies of Israel. The bright 'cloud' which covered the tent in which the Lord made his dwelling among his people is a familiar image for God's presence in power. It is a word which indicates the inability of the senses to interpret what is happening, and it occurs also in the works of mystics of many faiths. The brilliant light, and the 'tabernacles' or 'booths' which Peter wanted to construct, are linked to this in the imagination of the witnesses and of those who recounted their experience, for the 'tabernacles' were those that Peter had been helping to build since childhood. They were shelters of interwoven leafy branches decorated with flowers and fruit, in which everyone lived throughout the yearly 'Feast of Tabernacles' after the harvest, to remind the people of the time when they had no land to plant and harvest but dwelt in tents in the wilderness, wholly dependant on the Lord's bounty. And among those earlier tents had been the gorgeous 'Tent of Meeting' on which the Lord descended to dwell with his people, in a bright cloud of glory, from which Moses emerged with face so brilliantly transfigured that he had to veil it before anyone could bear to look at him.

But in the evangelists' accounts the elements of everydayness and of strangeness, explicitly related to earlier experiences of God's 'dwelling' with his people, seem to succeed each other in a definite sequence. There is everyday reality, a mountain (people argue about *which* mountain; the very arguments assume it was a particular mountain and in principle identifiable), and there are four men going up it and one of them going a little apart to stand and pray,

68

which is a thing he has often done before, and often, too, on mountains. But then another sphere of experience is entered, for the praying figure acquires a radiance, a 'glory'. His face, says Luke, was 'altered'; it 'shone like the sun', says Matthew, and his clothes also became dazzlingly white; 'as light', says Matthew; 'glistening, intensely white, as no fuller on earth could bleach them', says Mark. This is 'seeing' in the most precise sense, but it is seeing something which 'couldn't happen' in everyday life, as Mark's comment makes clear.

Then, together with this radiantly transfigured Jesus (but still, clearly, the Jesus they knew) appeared the other two figures, not familiar to them except from the stories of their people, but somehow identifiable. It seems as if, at this point, the experience moved into yet another sphere, in which time was somehow by-passed. The two visitors 'belonged' in another time. (There is no suggestion that they were 'glorified' as Jesus was. They are encountered as, in some way or other, their earthly selves, yet out of sequence.) We are told nothing of what they looked like, but it is clear that their appearance was not vague but precise; they looked solid enough for the idea of making 'booths' for them to seem, if not sensible, at least appropriate. And, just like ordinary people, they were there for some time, long enough for a real conversation to take place, which Luke tells us was concerned with the 'departure' of Jesus, that is with the accomplishment of his death, in Jerusalem. Whether actual words were heard, or whether the import of the conversation was known in some inner way, or whether Jesus told them about it later on, we are not told. We are also told by Luke that the three witnesses were 'heavy with sleep' but 'kept awake', and this bemused condition is borne out by the rather wild nature of Peter's suggestion about building 'booths', made when the two visitors seemed about to withdraw. And it was at this moment that the most awesome part of the experience occurred, when they entered, or at least perceived, a final sphere. Vision failed and the figures disappeared in the 'bright cloud'. A voice came to them: 'This is my Son, the Beloved, listen to him'. It was only after this, so they said, that the witnesses fell on their faces as their ancestors had done in the wilderness of Sinai.

Then (how much later we are not told) it was all over, and a familiar hand touched them, and a familiar voice said: 'Rise, and have no fear'. When they looked up it was 'only Jesus', the everyday, the usual, but to whom now they could never relate again in quite the same way.

Such a tremendous and complex experience cannot happen by chance. It seems only reasonable to suppose that some very strong necessity must have brought about an event so extraordinary. The suggestion that the whole thing is a displaced resurrection appearance attempts to explain it by moving the whole episode into a context with seems (superficially) more consistent with it. Events in that context are not *expected* to be 'normal'. But the difficulty about the transfiguration accounts is that the thing occurs 'in among' events which, though sometimes marvellous, happen on one predictable level of experience. Even the multiplication of loaves or walking on water, though fantastic events, do seem at least to have been visible in the ordinary way. But if we refuse to let ourselves off the hook by pushing the incident into the category of 'resurrection appearances' then we want to know, or at least feel entitled to ask, 'Why then?', 'Why to those?' and 'Why thus?' This necessarily involves a certain amount of imaginative reconstruction of the incident and others which preceded it. In the light of what I have already said about 'models', about 'oddity', and about 'ringing true' as a critical criterion, it seems proper to do this, making due allowance for the non-biographical nature of Gospel as a literary form.

It is difficult, realistically, to suppose that the evangelists treated the accounts of witnesses, and the available collections of stories and 'sayings' of Jesus, as so much inert material to be pushed into a convenient didactic shape. Such a treatment is not consonant with any sense of the uniqueness and power of the events being dealt with, and no author of ordinary integrity would use it, still less a convinced and converted follower of the Jesus celebrated by these writings. Certainly the 'material' is shaped and carefully pointed, the mood is frequently that of poetry rather than of journalism (though there is some of the latter especially in certain episodes in the fourth Gospel). But this material *is* the actions and words of Jesus; the writers' talent and skill is used to make these actions and words—that is, the man himself—as clearly visible as possible; and it is possible from (not in spite of) the way the material is presented to discern a full human development.

This development of the life of Jesus is, like all growth, a passage

70

from stage to stage, the stages initiated by some event which seems to make available, in the light of a new sphere of experience, knowledge and strength gained obscurely in earlier months or years. The 'crisis' nature of these transitions in all human life is sometimes more, sometimes less apparent, but major and minor 'alterations' in life can themselves be the 'immediate preparation' for a much greater breakthrough to a new level of personal awareness.

What I want to suggest here is that the sequence and nature of the events in the life of Jesus which led up to the event we call the transfiguration were of a kind which 'expected' some further breakthrough, and moreover that this had to be one which must go beyond what could be contained within the category of everydayness, even though we admit that this category itself is neither so interiorly consistent nor so obviously understandable as we like to think.

Such changes from one sphere to another were not, as I have suggested, unique to this unique life. Jesus himself never claimed that the things he did were possible to him alone; in fact he said quite explicitly that his followers would do the same 'and greater' things. Also he constantly 'played down' the significance of his healings, not because he did not consider them important (he clearly did regard them as proper signs of the sphere of experience he called 'the Kingdom') but because people were treating them as indications of his role, whereas it was, rather, the person and mission of Jesus which gave them significance. The same applies to the different kind of strangeness exemplified in the incident of the transfiguration, and indeed not only to this and other events in his life but to the whole 'event', the 'breakthrough' for human kind as a whole of this one human life. He was to be the 'firstborn' into the sphere of glory, not the only one to make that passage.

The sequence of previous events moves through recognizable stages. The earliest stage covers a period in the public life of Jesus during which it was only just beginning to be 'public' at all. He deeply impressed the individuals he met, and some chose to drop every other concern in order to go with him. They recognized him as in some sense 'Messiah', but the content of that title as applied to their new teacher and friend is unclear; indeed its meaning was fiercely argued about then, and has been since. It was not a role which they chose to follow but a compelling and unique personality.

71

At the end of this period, according to Luke, he visited his home-town of Nazareth and, reading the appointed Scripture in the synagogue, used Isaiah's prophecy to assert its application to himself. Here we have an indication of the 'dialogue' nature of Jesus's self-discovery. The reading of the prophecy seems to have revealed itself to him with a fresh absoluteness as the description of his own role, and the account of his announcement of it to the assembled town, suddenly and out loud, reads much more like an irresistible impulse to share a discovery than a pre-planned manifesto. The reaction of the neighbours was mainly negative, which was predictable, and to suppose that he (after some thirty years' experience of these people) had planned it that way suggests a lack of concern for the right moment to reach people which is out of character. But it may well be that, once he had made this revelation of himself, he found himself inevitably launched into the next stage. He had already begun to heal and teach, as the people in the synagogue pointed out, and the familiar passage from Isaiah revealed itself newly to him *in their reaction* as a description of the significance of what he had begun to do.

At any rate we find him very quickly plunged into the most completely public part of his public career, a period characterized by the great 'sermons' given to huge crowds and also by innumerable healings, a handful only of which are reported in detail by the evangelists. The teaching began in synagogues and moved out into the open partly because of the size of the crowds which came and partly because of the resentment of the leading Jews, which was already becoming apparent.

That he should teach was inevitable, once his self-discovery had reached the point exemplified by the incident in the Nazareth synagogue. This was what he discovered he had come for; his work was, at least in part, 'to preach the good news to the poor', yet we take this for granted too much. Public preaching need not have been his method. He could have taught a select few, or perhaps he could have sought a role more completely expressed in terms of the 'servant' symbolism of Isaiah, which he clearly knew to be crucially important. But preaching did become one of his main activities in the first half of his public life, and I have suggested that we can see why it did.

The healings, on the other hand, seem to have taken him by

72

surprise, and Luke suggests that it all began because, when he was teaching in the synagogue at Capernaum, a 'possessed' man began to cry out at him, recognizing him as 'Holy one of God'. Jesus, knowing what kind of breakthrough *this* represented, silenced him abruptly by dismissing the evil spirit from the man. Again we have a sense of the discovery of meaning *evoked by* the stress of a situation. Everyone present was amazed, naturally enough, and the report spread like wildfire. Meanwhile, he had gone a few doors down the street to his lodging with Simon's family, and at once they asked him to heal Simon's mother-in-law, who was feverish.

This is what one would naturally expect them to do after the synagogue incident. It is in Luke's account and I would be inclined to accept Luke's chronology fairly closely, not only because he claimed to have taken much trouble to get his account 'orderly' but because it makes sense psychologically. Matthew puts 'teaching and healing' all over the country together in one sentence to introduce the chapters in which he picks out important examples of each. That arrangement suited his purpose. Luke, however, tells us in his account of the early days after the baptism that Jesus 'taught in the synagogues and was glorified by all', but he indicates quite clearly that the great period of healing miracles began after 'something happened', specifically the encounter with the demoniac in the Capernaum synagogue. It seems reasonable to suppose that Jesus's own response to this led to the further reaction of the people, to which in turn he had to make the response proper to his growing self-knowledge. The response to his healing of the demoniac was, predictably, that people with all kinds of sickness, mental and physical, gathered round the house at sunset of that day (when the Sabbath rest ended). And he healed them because, in a sense, he could not help it. He was that kind of person, though he must have realized even then the basic misunderstanding to which this would give rise. He 'would not permit the demons to speak because they knew him', but everyone else, of course, talked and talked. And of that strange, chaotic and epoch-making evening in the street outside Simon's house Luke reports that afterwards, for the first time recorded, 'A great while before day, he rose and went out to a lonely place, and there he prayed'.

The new and overwhelming development of his mission drove him to seek solitude in order to wrestle with the knowledge it

73

brought him of what he was, and must be, and must do. By the time his disciples found him and told him that 'everyone is searching for you' he had evidently come to terms with it. He told them, 'Let us go into the next towns, that I may preach there also, for that is why I came out.' Yet he had apparently intended, up to the previous day, to settle in Capernaum for a while at least. It was, presumably, soon after this that the incident in the synagogue at Nazareth took place. Otherwise why did he say that 'this text is fulfilled as you listen'? This is possibly why Luke, whose sense of literary construction is superb, uses the Nazareth incident to introduce this period.

For, after this, the ministry of Jesus was a double one, of teaching and healing, in a completely public and 'available' way. But this had the inevitable result that the healings were what people came for; inevitable also was the mounting distrust of the wealthy and influential and pious. Already the pattern was forming which had his death as its meaning, and he must have known it, even as early as this, and with increasing clarity as the months passed.

We find him, very soon, choosing twelve from among his followers, for special training in carrying out his work. This also seems to arise from the necessities of the situation. Sheer compassion for the people who flocked to him drove him to heal, as well as to try to convey to them the reality of the news of the Kingdom among them. And compassion also required that he get help in doing these things, for he could not personally reach all of those who needed him. Luke says that he 'appointed twelve to be with him and to be sent out to preach and have authority to cast out demons'. This seems to have happened in two stages, for the 'sending out' actually came somewhat later. At first they were with him and helping him, and all of them were, it seems, so constantly besieged by crowds of the sick and of the 'hungry and thirsty for righteousness' that normal life became impossible. 'They could not even eat', and his relations not unnaturally concluded that he was out of his mind and needed to be shut up until he calmed down. We get a picture of a man driven by such an urgent sense of the need around him that reason and common sense were set aside. At the same time he was being followed and harrassed by critics, many of whom were no doubt sincerely worried about the implications and possible political results of his activities, and who voiced fundamental questions about the way he was carrying out his mission—questions which echoed

74

or perhaps provoked those in his own mind. And so he answered them, with growing assurance and clarity.

He responded to situations and so discovered his own meaning. If healing were needed he healed sickness, but what of the healing of sin? Sinners came to him and so he told them they were forgiven. Then came the obvious question, 'Who can forgive sins?' The answer was obvious, too. And so we find him deliberately associating with people whose sins needed such forgiveness as he found it in himself to pour out. Thus he aroused even more criticism and anger.

It seems to have been towards the end of this period of the great preaching tours of the country that Jesus crossed over into the district of Tyre and Sidon, which was 'foreign' territory, possibly to let the opposition die down for a while, and perhaps also for a much needed rest from the crowds. It was there that the odd little incident of the 'Canaanite' woman occurred, which shows more clearly than most the way Jesus tried to obtain the answers to questions he was asking of himself through the responses of others. Not only was this yet another demand for healing, in a place where he might have hoped for a respite, but the demand came from a foreigner. The demands had hitherto come from his own people, God's chosen people, the 'lost sheep of the house of Israel', and this was proper and inevitable. The question of how foreigners related to all this simply had not arisen; the whole climate of thought made such a consideration literally 'remote', even if he and his friends had not already been driven to the limits of their capacity by the existing demands.

It is clear that it did not even occur to the disciples that he would cure a foreigner. 'Send her away', they begged him. But because of his basic attitude to people, already hammered out in his dealings with other 'social outcasts', to him it did occur. So he had to decide, there and then, how to respond, but the implications of accepting what the woman clearly felt to be her *right* to healing for her daughter were staggering. So he asked *her* for the answer, provoking her to respond by a kind of desperate half-teasing rudeness which was made 'fitting' by her evident confidence in his ability to help, and in the fittingness of her request. (It was clearly a meeting of two strong people; there is a strange kind of 'camaraderie' about this brief conversation.) The response he got gave him a 'way in' to what he longed to do, and he did it, and broke through to a new

75

level of awareness through a kind of dialectic, which seems to me to be characteristic of the way Jesus's understanding of his mission developed. In this case the 'immediate preparation' may be the strange people and context, in itself extending the available 'language' by which the event could later be understood.

Luke does not record this incident. He tells us, however, that at some point during the Galilean ministry Jesus finally sent out his disciples in pairs to preach and heal without him, and that when they came back both he and they needed a holiday, not only for a rest but in order to have some peace to talk over their experiences.

Matthew's version suggests that it was after he had received the news of the death of John the Baptist that Jesus retired across the lake, perhaps implying that this shocking event demanded time for prayer and reassessment of the situation. In any case he was looking for quiet for himself and his tired followers; but they did not have it for long, for the crowds followed them round the shore of the lake to the place which Jesus and the Twelve had reached by boat.

This 'lonely' place, therefore, was the setting for one of the most controversial of the miracles reported in the Gospels, the 'feeding of the five thousand'. Matthew gives two separate accounts of multiplication of food. Arguments about whether it really happened twice, or whether there were in circulation two different reports of the same event, cannot be finally resolved. (Matthew's 'four thousand' come at the point where Jesus was travelling 'abroad' and the crowds praised 'the God of *Israel*' which may indicate that these were non-Jewish or semi-Jewish people across the lake. This would make sense, placed as it is after the first *healing* of a foreigner. But both accounts are relevant here.)

Remembering that reports of the multiplication of food are not confined to the Gospel accounts, nor to the remote past, but that apparently reliable reports of such things are available in contemporary and near-contemporary instances, we still have to ask 'Why?' The simplest answer is the obvious answer: the people were hungry. Yet he could have done as the disciples suggested and sent them away to buy food. He had been teaching and healing them for some time—one account says 'three days'—and their hunger was predictable. But apparently he neither did anything about it nor showed signs of being aware of the problem until his disciples (who presumably had expected the initiative from him, or they would

76

have spoken sooner) pointed it out to him. Once more, he was wrestling with a demand whose implications were enormous, and he needed some response which would free him to do what seemed to be required of him. So when the disciples said 'send them away to buy food', he did not reply, 'No, *I* will feed them', but 'No, *you* feed them'.

In John's account, Jesus himself asked Philip, 'How are we to buy bread, so that these people may eat?' This emphasizes the point I want to make. He knew that the people needed food, and John says 'he knew what he would do', but said this to 'test' Philip. He needed the response he got, in order to act with assurance. In all the accounts, the disciples protested in half-joking exasperation that it was impossible to feed such a crowd with the only food available, which was the equivalent of, at most, two or three people's picnic meal. It was only *then* that he took the loaves and fish, and blessed them, and there proved to be enough to feed everyone, and some over.

If we want to know more deeply why he did this, we can discover the answer in John's account, which gives us psychological clues to the whole development as I think John often does. The people were hungry, they needed food, and it seems possible, indeed likely, that the challenge of it had been growing in the back of his mind while he was teaching and healing them. These people, out there in the 'wilderness', were so obviously just like their ancestors, dependent on the Lord's bounty, ignorant and bewildered yet hopeful. If he did not send them away to get food before they reached the point at which they ran the risk of 'fainting on the way', it could have been because the sight of them and its associations (with the manna, and with the hopes of the 'messianic banquet') were driving him imaginatively towards the action he in fact took. These people, as much as their ancestors, needed 'manna from heaven', and he knew that he who was indeed Messiah, though not in the sense in which they understood it, had the power to satisfy them—physically, certainly, but the further implications were even more startling and not easily accepted. So it was not for some time that he found it possible to face the implications fully. In the end he needed, as we have seen, the articulation of the problem which he obtained in his dialogue with his disciples.

So if practical compassion had been the simple and sufficient motive, to respond to its demands inevitably opened up a path whose end was only dimly visible. But by the time the crowds had eaten, Jesus had, it seems, reached a point at which he was taking a firm hold of the immediate significance of his own action, especially (at this point) with its connection with the idea of the messianic banquet, and his instruction to the Twelve to gather up the leftovers seems designed to underline the extraordinary nature of the event, rather than to slide over it or play it down as a possible distraction from his main purpose. He must have known very well that the wonder would provoke a near-frenzy of messianic expectation in the crowd, but this partially misleading interpretation seemed to him a worthwhile price to pay.

John gives us the deeper answer to 'why' in the 'bread of life' discourse, which he says was given next day to the excited crowd of the miraculously fed. It opens with a condemnation of the people who had come to him 'because you ate your fill'; it has an undertone of warning, and it shows us that the hunger of the people—hunger for food, but also for security, leadership, hope, forgiveness—opened up for Jesus a further meaning in his own mission which had earlier been only implicit. The actual development of the 'discourse' shows this, for it is presented as a dialectic leading further and further into discovery of Jesus's own meaning. The announcement of himself as 'living bread' is shown to us as the *conclusion* he was reaching, not as the premise from which he began. There is a development which is real and 'organic'; it is not a systematic 'explanation' of a thesis developed beforehand. And it is soon after this that the synoptic Gospels place the strange little discussion in which Jesus asked his friends to tell him who he was supposed to be, by public opinion, and by themselves. And when he had evoked from Peter the reply (which no doubt surprised Peter himself very much), 'You are the Christ', he was then able to articulate in concrete terms the realization which John's account of the bread-of-life discourse shows taking shape symbolically—the fact that his career was bound, if he continued to do what he knew he had to do, to end in torture and death, yet already with an obscure but definite assurance of what lay beyond.

This is the immediate prelude to the transfiguration in all three synoptists. I have described this development at length, because it shows over and over again that we are dealing with a real process

78

of personal discovery which had to be made, as all such discoveries are made, through crucial exchanges with other people, whether in direct dialogue or through acted-on response to need or to criticism. And each major development comes about with a 'breakthrough' quality. There is a sense that the dialectical process reaches a point at which the conclusion required takes the whole process into a new level of living. This happened at Nazareth and with the Canaanite woman and at the point at which Peter made his profession of faith, and many other times. But in particular it happened in contexts in which the needed conclusion pushed its way into an area of experience so unusual as to constitute a breakthrough to a new sphere, not only in the sense of a 'transition' for Jesus himself but in the sense that his making this transition forced open another sphere for other people also. Of this kind are the beginnings of healings at Capernaum and the feeding of the crowd in the wilderness.

The transfiguration happened very soon after the feeding of the crowd and the acknowledgement of Jesus's identity as 'the Christ' with the passion prophecies which followed that. When it came it was not a dialectical progression in the sense of an explicit discussion, but rather the acted-out dialectic of a truth so shattering to the normal capacity of the human imagination as to force the barriers of everydayness entirely. It was not just the operation *within* the categories of everyday sensible experience of a power beyond the normal; it was an actual, direct experience of the life from which that power might be supposed to come.

It seems clear that the three disciples saw, and Jesus experienced briefly, that life of resurrection into which he had 'not yet' entered; it is as if the extreme need of the moment somehow 'anticipated' the proper order of events. (Such things happen, not infrequently, in less spectacular ways. I have seen, for instance, a ten-year-old child experiencing a genuine passion of romantic love and being thereby introduced into a realm of experience 'normally' expected considerably later. Usually the 'ordinary' closes around the 'anticipated' experience, seemingly isolating it, yet it has its proper effect on the person.)

This makes sense in the life of Jesus if we can try to experience imaginatively the build-up of expectation, fear, hope, longing and uncertainty which must have been going on in his mind. And it was not possible for him to share this explicitly with anyone. He could

79

'prophesy' his coming death and rising, but we are told over and over again, by Mark especially, that the disciples did not understand. Peter's incredulous rejection of such a disaster was probably his own typically outspoken kind of reaction, but the general one among the Twelve must have been similar. Yet the need to communicate, to share this growing knowledge in such a way as to come to terms with it, must have been well-nigh intolerable.

It has been plausibly suggested, on the evidence of accounts of their behaviour later on, that the women around Jesus had a better 'empathy' than the men, but they necessarily expressed this by attitudes and actions rather than by words. Mary of Bethany's symbolic gesture of anointing the feet of Jesus is this kind of silent indication of a comprehension of the whole situation. Jesus recognized it at once, but the Twelve were evidently incapable of this. Of its nature this kind of sharing was mute and limited; to Jesus it must have been deeply important, but it could not provide the fully articulate sharing he needed.

Doctors and nurses who work with the dying have tried to impress on others that to refuse to talk to a dying person about the approach of death is not 'kind' but the deepest cruelty, because most people do 'know' that death is approaching and desperately need to talk about it in order to cope with it. If no one will acknowledge the fact of imminent death this relief is denied them, and this agony was many times multiplied in the case of Jesus, first by the knowledge that what must come was both an essential aspect of his mission but also (in principle) still escapable, and second by the fact that it was his own people who would bring it upon him, people with whom he lived but whom, step by step, he was being driven to alienate. His references to the fate of former prophets show what was in his mind, as well as parables like the one about the owner of the vineyard whose servants were ill-treated and killed and who finally sent his son to die also. But he was unable to share this insight. He could not press on these young and very vulnerable men a knowledge which would either drive them away in anger and fear or impose on them a burden so heavy as possibly to lead to breakdown.

Yet such things must always be shared—mirrored, articulated through another—if only imaginatively. Artists and writers do it in their work, and we recognize what is going on when, for instance,

80

we make allowances for 'poetic' temperament whose emotional violence (needed, in the artist, to break a way through certain conceptual and imaginative barriers) overflows at times into other aspects of life. No such release was possible for Jesus, or rather his kind of poetry had to break a barrier more apparently impregnable than that of any other poet. He could not, on the other hand, allow himself to 'overflow' in erratic moods or even take 'time off', when his days were saturated by the sheer quantity of human need. But in any case what was creating such a pressure in the person of Jesus was unique, so that he could not have shared it in any adequate way with even the most courageous, loving and stable of human friends. No relief, none of the absolutely necessary sharing, was available in the category of everydayness. The breakthrough to another sphere altogether was required by the nature of the case, for there was no easier or more 'ordinary' way.

The picture we get is of one more occasion on which he went off by himself to pray, because of the need that was in him, only this time he was not quite by himself because his sense of vulnerability and loneliness was such that even the presence of uncomprehending affection and loyalty was some comfort. And then it happened—not 'planned' but of sheer necessity. The power broke through, the doors between mortality and immortality were blown open by the force of his longing. The mortal body disclosed its proper yet still unattained being. And the doors of time, also, swung loose in the gale of that explosion of power, and men separated by centuries found each other in the contemplation of an experience which was, for each, the explanation, the dénouement, the ultimate meaning of human life. So he, the one about to die, was able to share with those who had died in expectation. His own fore-knowledge became, in the process, lucid and assured, and he took hold of it with all the power of a personality in which no psychic energy was locked up in the maintenance of defensive devices.

At this moment the witnesses were in the presence of that from which all else took its being, and it acknowledged the meaning of what Jesus had just done. 'This is my Son, the Beloved—the one who has taken on himself the final deed of love, because his being is itself the exchange of uttermost love with Me, in the Spirit whose very name is Love.' No wonder the barriers were breached, no wonder the light shone from him, no wonder the glory of resurrec-

81

tion showed through before its time, since at that moment the death which was to release that glory was embraced, absolutely and irrevocably. And no wonder that the evangelists, striving to convey the quality of this experience, wrote poetry of an intensity only rivalled by that which celebrates the high moments of encounter with the risen Lord. It was soon after this, as Luke tells it, that 'he set his face to go to Jerusalem', to do and to suffer that which he had undertaken on the mountain.

Examination of the transfiguration in this way shows that the extraordinary things which happened to this man happened in the same kind of way, and for the same kinds of reasons, as more ordinary but crucial transitions happened to him and to others, and which happen, notably, in the 'model' breakthrough of Romantic passion. Each breakthrough in human life releases the person into a new sphere of his or her own personality, but also into a capacity for deeper communion with others. ('The inside is larger than the outside'.) The extent, and therefore the power, of the potential thus made available depends on two things: the greatness of the need to break through, and the willingness to 'be broken'. In Jesus we have, because of his unique calling and responsibility, a need so great that it could break any barrier—if he were willing. And his willingness was total, he had come only to 'do the Father's will', so nothing else counted. Hence, although the nature of the process of breakthrough is familiar in the life of any human being who is aware of and responsive to the pressure towards 'something else', yet in Jesus the degree of both need and willingness produced a difference not just in the significance or 'size' of the breakthrough, but in kind. His need, and willingness, made him free in a sphere of power and knowledge to which other people do not attain. Yet it was only in the final breakthrough of resurrection that he smashed a barrier through which absolutely no one else could break. In the episode just studied we see the foretaste of this, yet at this stage it is still not completely unique as an experience. Even in the transfiguration, as well as in such things as the healings, the multiplication of loaves, walking on the water and so on, we are hearing about things which are very unusual, but not unique in kind, and they are not even always 'good', as we shall see. Even in the culminating moment the great Voice speaks words which are unique to this one man, yet the Voice itself has been heard before, in other times and places. If we are trying to understand both the meaning of Jesus—incarnate God, one person totally unique—and also to realize the intimate and ultimate meaning of the flesh-taking for all of material reality whose nature is exchange of life, we shall have to pay close attention to the method, nature, effects and significance of the 'breakthrough' events in his life, not because their strangeness proves *his* strangeness but because his experience of these spheres has unique significance.

There is another and vital aspect of this incident which I have touched on already. The witnesses were three only who, from that time, were frequently singled out to be involved in important crises in the life of Jesus. Why did he take them with him? He was not given to displays of power for anyone's benefit, and I have suggested that in any case he did not expect what happened, although it seems likely that, as is often the case, he knew that 'something' was near the point of breakthrough. It seems much more likely that, as I have already suggested, he took them with him because he needed their company. Knowing that, once more, he must 'go apart' to wrestle with the appalling inner necessity of understanding and accepting his own meaning, he found that this time he did not want to be entirely alone. Perhaps it 'felt' more crucial than at former times, or perhaps he knew by then that whatever they could or could not cope with consciously just then, it was vital to them and to him that they should be involved to the limit of their capacity in the meaning he was discovering. This was not a situation in which a 'leader' could simply give orders and plan. The whole project was, he knew by then, a shared one. And the sharing did not consist of merely 'training disciples' in the usual sense, but of empowering people to *be* what he was, and therefore to do what he had to do. (In saying this I am using hindsight, as the evangelists, indeed, always did in their accounts. It seems legitimate to discern the implicit presence, at that time, of what became so clear later on as a basic theological principle operating in the actions of Jesus, namely, their relationship with himself not just as followers, but as the Church, his 'body'.) So his need for companionship and their need for involvement came together, as such things do. It was 'natural' for him to take his closest friends, and, to reverse the idea, it was natural that it should be his closest friends whom he took.

These three had a special relationship with him which the rest of the Twelve did not have. Once this evidently caused friction, when James and John, through their mother, seemed to be demanding special privileges, but on the whole the difference seems to have been acceptable to the rest, to whom, perhaps, a closer relationship at this stage might even have appeared as threatening. It is easier to be a disciple than to be a friend, and it was only at the end that Jesus was able to address all the Twelve as 'friends', precisely because, by that time, they had 'been through' experiences with him which had served to break down barriers within them and make them capable of such a relationship. But the three who were given the (from a 'normal' point of view) dubious privilege of being closest to Jesus were men who had already crossed one of the usual human barriers. Really to be a friend is to lower one's defences, to be vulnerable to the demands of love. A secure childhood, an adventurous temperament, previous generous response to suffering or joy—these are among the things that dispose to that kind of openness. They dispose to it; they do not create it. There is still the need to create the conditions of immediate preparation, and we can see in the Gospel accounts the ways in which, over and over again, Jesus set himself, in his approach to people, to 'loosen' them, to shock or shake them into a condition of ability to 'hear'. In the story of the Samaritan woman, of Nicodemus, of the 'rich young man' and many others, we see him using appropriate tactics to do this and then to try to break through, but not always with success. The response is free, there is nothing fated about it. Yet it seems that in some cases he had to do no more than just be there and invite response. Whatever their previous history, the inner pressure towards breakthrough in these three young men was such that the presence of his love was all that was needed to set them free. 'And they left their nets and followed him', with an ease and abruptness which are among the most moving of all the evidences in the gospel of what kind of person Jesus was, and is.

When it happens like that there is no going back. It seems to be one of the 'laws' of spiritual development that the greater the openness the faster things happen. Things certainly happened fast to Peter, James and John, and the experience on the mountain was necessary for them, however hard. Just as *he* had to share and articulate his foreknowledge, but could not do so with them, so *they* had to become aware of what kind of relationship they were involved in. Afterwards, he warned them not to talk about it, 'until the Son of Man is risen from the dead'. To make the knowledge public just then would be to distort it, because it would only make full sense in the light of what had not yet happened. But even though the three could not fully understand, they had undergone a necessary initiation which prepared them for a fuller sharing.

It must, among other things, have created between them and the rest of the Twelve a kind of a 'gap' which would, however, make them not less but more sensitive to the needs and difficulties of those who had been called with them. This is a familiar experience. Spiritual 'privileges', if they are real, only isolate the privileged person in the sense that he or she has an increased and incommunicable knowledge of the depth and responsibility of existing relationships. In a book by Ladislaus Boros, he says this of the poet's need for 'withdrawal' in order to discover a new and more intimate relationship with reality:

> An essential pre-requisite for the salvaging of the truly real from among its surrounding confusion is that the individual existence should know about both the reality and the confusion. Accordingly poetic activity can only occur in a frontier position . . . The spirit . . . takes itself afar off in order to be nearer the world. The nearness of things is made really near only through their remoteness . . . Only in this dialectic of the proximity that is realised in remoteness can the phenomenon poetry occur . . . We abandon things, we give up all idea of seizing and grasping. That liberates the world and makes it possible for mysterious and transcendant realities to rise up.

The isolation into which the three had been drawn released in them depths of awareness, obscure but working, which could only come through such a painful yet exalting experience. To be seized by God in this way means to be thrust to a greater depth into the mystery of incarnation, and this is precisely what happened to the three young men on the mountain.

But for Peter, James and John with Jesus, this was not just a breakthrough to another sphere, but an 'exchange' of spheres. When a 'barrier' is broken there flows through it the energy of love as passion. But the energy is not just in one direction. This cannot be

85

expressed in the simple terms of the river and the dam, because that is a one-way flow. The dynamic suggested by the phrase '*exchange* of life' is a two-way one, but the image has to be 'stretched' to suggest something about what 'exchange of life' (which is love) can mean when it occurs in the context of a breakthrough such as the one I have described, whose 'once for all', crisis nature is obvious. (This applies not only to such a 'supernatural' event as the transfiguration but to any human crisis of major spiritual significance.) If this is an exchange on the Romantic passion model, what happens to the two 'sides' of the 'barrier'? Is the effect all 'forward' into the new sphere of experience, or does it also operate 'backwards'? The use of the model of 'exchange' suggests that there must indeed be an exchange of spheres, not just a passage from one to another. In some sense, the experience of being which is entered must be modified by the entrance into it of a new consciousness. The person has added to what is in any case a *shared* sphere of being something unique, which then becomes shared, without losing its personal origin. A person who goes to live in a beautiful house, for instance, may bring to the care and embellishment of the house many previously learned tastes and skills, and not only the newcomer but all who live in it will gain by that coming.

But the sphere *from which* a person moves to break through must be somehow affected, and this seems more difficult to envisage. To use a very homely illustration, it might be something like what happens when a person opens the door to a kitchen where onions are being fried. When the door was shut, people sitting around in the other room were unaware of onions. But if one of them likes onions, and gets to know there are onions through that door, and gets up from his armchair and opens the door to the kitchen and goes through it, then the smell of frying onions comes *out*, in the opposite direction to his movement, thus possibly creating a longing for fried onions in other people in that room, who might otherwise never have considered onions at all! If some dislike onions, of course, the smell would irritate or nauseate them. We shall have occasion to consider this reaction in the next chapter. (I am reminded of St Paul's more elegant but similar image of the double effect of the 'smell' of the 'knowledge' of God; we are, he says, 'Christ's incense to God for those who are being saved, and for those who are not, for the last, the smell of death that leads to death, for the first, the sweet smell of life that leads to life' 2 Cor.2:15–16.)

This, roughly, is what I want to suggest by the phrase 'exchange of spheres' as an extension of the image suggested by 'exchange of life'. Both are modes of love, but one operates in situations where some kind of psychic obstacle or barrier stands in the way of the needed flow of exchanged life. Romantic passion is this kind of exchange. The lover's impulse of love touches a vulnerable point, breaks through into a new sphere of experience. This experience is characterized by a 'different' look, a kind of vision of the essential bodily being, and also by acute 'obscurity', which descends on the senses under the impact of the experience. We saw both of these things happening to the three young men on the mountain, who also suffered the painfulness of Romantic passion, for the vision could not be made to last, the bliss glimpsed was withdrawn. This event in the life of Jesus is, in fact, not altogether beyond us imaginatively; we can and do 'know what it feels like', though in a minor way. And so we know that all such experiences are a kind of breach between two worlds, by which each affects the other. The lover takes into the new world of vision his or her kind of awareness of life, and the poetry made will be personal and particular, never general. And those who read this poetry will be changed too, challenged in some way. The door between the worlds, opened with pain and glory, can never be completely closed again, and there is a traffic through it, however modest and unnoticeable. Also—and this is important—this happens in *time*. There is a story, a before and after, something is going on which continues and grows. What this implies I want to explore later, but there is a more important question to be answered first, and that is the question of why 'spheres' exist at all.

A universe, a reality, whose basic nature is exchange, and which is characterized at every level by the phenomenon of breakthrough from sphere to sphere, is the 'given' context in which Jesus lived and did the work for which he was sent, as we live and do our work. It is the 'flesh' of his 'flesh-taking'. But the very fact that the passage from one sphere to another requires violence, the thrust of Romantic passion, raises the fundamental question which the believer has to confront: how can it be that the one who took flesh in an 'ensphered' and 'opaque' universe can also be said to be constitutive of that

87

universe? No wonder it seems less blasphemous to reject the whole notion of incarnation than to try to make sense of that.

Therefore the questions we have to consider are those I raised earlier and which are implicit in all the preceding studies: Why are the 'spheres' opaque to us? Why is passion necessary? What went wrong? What, in fact, is 'sin'? If the ultimate reality is Love, how did sin get there? What is evil?

3   The Refusal of Exchange

If the breakthrough to an experience of glory is possible to human beings at all, why should it be so difficult and so rare? A capacity for this kind of experience there must be or it could not occur at all, and in Christian teaching the experience of glory is in the end the only proper one. Yet even the little 'everyday' breakthroughs of life are problematic and costly, and the capacity for glory in the fullest sense is recognized by few and experienced in their earthly lifetime by only a handful. What prevents it?

Even before we consider the obvious fact that there is (and always has been, as far as we know) 'something wrong' with creation, in the sense that destruction and waste seem to be inherent in it, it is a puzzle that creation should have what I called a 'passionate character'. All the development we know of, natural and human, physical and psychological, goes in 'jumps' or 'breakthroughs' with periods of consolidation and slower growth inbetween. After the production of its fruit the tree changes its reactions and ways of growth; after the chick is hatched the hen's behaviour changes suddenly and drastically; after the first visit to the theatre the stage-struck child is never the same again; when a nation has suffered invasion, or experienced a major revolution, its whole system of social relatedness breaks through rapidly to new patterns and can never recapture the lost ways of exchange.

Breakthrough has (as the word implies) an element of violence about it; the energy of the exchange thrusts, hard and painfully, at the weak spot in order to rediscover itself beyond, so even before considering the nature of evil we come up against this notion that there is a kind of resistance to exchange. In the next chapter I shall be thinking about the meaning of incarnation and redemption, which have to do with a sinful situation, but there is an old theological tradition in Christianity which held that God would have taken human flesh even if there had been no such thing as sin. Why should this be so?

89

I think we may suggest that this idea has to do with the Christian instinct that God's love is essentially, and not merely accidentally, 'passionate'. But how can there be 'passion', in this sense, in the exchanged life of God, in whom there can be no resistance, no obstacle, to love? I think we may suggest that there must be, in the dynamic of divine love, something which has that quality of head-long givenness which we associate with passion. Indeed it seems inevitable that even by the wavering and feeble light of human imagination we should discern some such quality, if the doctrine of the Trinity is to have any meaning.

I showed this happening in the context of Romantic passion, which is not about cause and proportionate effect, but about events followed by reactions in a different category of experience. It is not about gradual complexification but about sudden transformation. It is not about a process, however beautiful, but about *exchange*. It is not about a plan but about a love affair.

If Romantic passion is indeed the human paradigm of the nature of all reality then we should expect to see all this verified at other levels, and we do. In the origin of life, for instance, it seems that the 'remote preparation' would be the increasing availability, in high density, of those chemical elements which are required if life is to occur, but which do not necessarily *produce* it. The immediate preparation might be, perhaps, some 'disturbance' of the *status quo* which moved the elements of the situation into a different relationship with each other. What happened then? The only possible answer is that *love* happened. This is the answer of poetry, because no other language is accurate. People with the appropriate scientific knowledge can describe the composition of live cells; they cannot tell us why life happens. Only poets can do that, and did so in the book of Genesis, and in the books of Wisdom, and in the introduction to the Gospel of John, and in the Scriptures of other religions also. So when we consider this moment of creative passion we can properly use the language of Romance and find that it does have the characteristics, as well as the sequence, of Romantic passion.

It is particular: the chemical-physical circumstances which made this breakthrough possible are precise. We may not be able to tell exactly what those circumstances were, but we can be sure they were precisely right, and could have been no other way. It is 'single', and unrepeatable for the particular form of life to which it happens.

90

This new life may go on to need, and achieve, further break-throughs, but this one is over. At this point, of course (as we can see in human Romantic experience), the whole process of growth may fail and then disintegrate gradually, as a romantically initiated relationship may simply disintegrate if those involved do not 'claim' the experience explicitly and live out its implications consciously. At the level of unconscious being, this means that (assuming the breakthrough to life for non-life happened millions of times) there must have been many occasions on which that was all that hap-pened. The circumstances did not open a way to further definition and complexity of exchange, and life broke down into non-life.

Perhaps we may also discern the quality of 'obscurity' about this kind of breakthrough, in the Romantic sense that the event is, *in our minds*, an example or glimpse of something greater, and indescrib-able. Even the most rigidly 'scientific' description of the origins of life is dealing with a reality whose wholeness is beyond our mental capacity to grasp, so it can only try to evoke an awareness of its nature by analogy. There is, too, the element of painfulness, for in every breakthrough to a new level of being an earlier simplicity, which had its own kind of perfection and beauty, is lost forever. We can, perhaps, think of that love which creates this breakthrough 'suffering' in it, because what has previously expressed love has died in order that the new love may be born.

If we think of the beginning of conscious response to God in creatures, it is even clearer here also that the exchange of life works by Romantic passion in creation. We can evoke a sequence, from obscure hints in many cultures, of something lost, long ago. There was some change of circumstance, some condition of challenge, for which existing humanoid responses were inadequate. And 'some-thing happened' which we cannot observe, yet which we can im-agine without enormous difficulty because it has the same 'character' as that familiar experience called falling in love. We can perhaps conceive of it as a moment when Divine Wisdom appeared to a potentially but not actually human creature and presented to that dazed being the face of Beatrice, the face of the one 'by whom all things were made'. In that moment he and she, what Charles Williams called 'the Adam', was indeed made, in the image of love itself, in the exchange of being with God. Love in the potentially human thing leapt to encounter love, in a thrust of passionate

91

response, and the barrier was broken, and humankind walked in Paradise, knowing all earth as newborn, which indeed it was, though it had existed for aeons.

Afterwards, through countless unrecorded centuries, there was a need, as there always is, to know what had happened and to decide what to do about it. The new earth must be described, names given, patterns of understanding established and patterns of behaviour discovered. *Amour voulu* must succeed the breakthrough of irresistible passion; commitment to the human task must interpret the obscure glory of human consciousness. This task is the unending service of humankind to, but also as part of, creation, by understanding and promoting its inter-relationships, by celebrating and loving them; but in order to carry out this task the 'paradise consciousness' of undifferentiated oneness with God and with all creation has to be surrendered, though the 'memory' of it persists in those hints of something lost long ago.

We are already edging to the consideration of sin, it seems, but we must not jump too quickly. To carry out the human task in this way involves a distinction, a differentiation, which has the same kind of painful quality I described just now, of leaving behind forever something which is perfect in its own way in order to respond to the demand for a higher experience of being. There is pain, but the pain is not, I think, essentially connected with what we have to call sin—that is, with what 'went wrong'. Here, 'before' sin, we may discern something which we can perhaps think of as 'pure' grief, a joyful sacrifice of one good for the sake of a more intensely glorious and passionate gift. The beauty of the unconscious simplicity of the animal, of love expressed in un-free but perfect exchanges of life, nourishment and care, must give way to the perilous delight of the divine Romance of God with humankind. And it is precisely at this point that for the first time real tragedy becomes possible; there can be a refusal of love, a refusal which is free, willed and absolute. The possibility of such a refusal is the price that love pays, and is willing to pay, because no price is too high for a love whose very nature is limitless gift.

This is the language of Romantic passion. It is the only language which can accurately bring to our minds the reality which it describes. These are descriptions, then, of the exchange of spheres, of those crucial exchanges we call 'ecological' and of those others we

92

study under the headings of psychology, religion, anthropology, as well as of palaeontology, chemistry and more. These can give us the circumstances, they can show us the materials of transforming passion in creation, but they cannot evoke the creative *event*. Only theology, in the form of poetry, can do that. It is a work for divine Wisdom herself.

Thus it is inevitable and necessary that this headlong love which is the being of God poured out in the creative act and working in the medium of matter will encounter, if not precisely obstacles, at least something which I called 'spheres'. As created matter becomes more differentiated and more complex it has to 'leave behind' previous forms, losing something as well as gaining something. But the spheres of life are not in themselves 'something wrong'; they are the way in which the exchanges of divine love can become even more complex and marvellous as love gives way to, and supports, and is supported by, yet another kind of being in the dance of divine Wisdom.

Differentiation is not evil, for in order that love be aware of itself as love, the lover has to be differentiated from the beloved. There can be no love, in any recognizable sense of the word, where there is merely oneness, as opposed to union. Even if I say that 'I love myself' I can only mean anything by that if I have a concept of myself which I can consider as lovable, and it would be more accurate to say that I perceive, and somehow share in, a love first *given to me*. This is true theologically (as St John points out in his first letter), but we know it simply from experience and in practice, as it works in people. It is the love given to me which makes me know myself as loved. Children deprived of love cannot value or love themselves, and until someone else does they are 'empty' and warped in their whole growth. If we remember the words of the second 'great commandment', in which we are bidden to 'Love your neighbour *as yourself*', we realize that this deeply ambiguous phrase must mean, in one aspect at least, that love is known only in exchange, between one-and-another. If this is so, there has to be 'another'.

One can only be said to 'experience' something—that is to be consciously aware of it—if it can be set over against something else. (I would never learn to *experience* being white unless I met a black peron, and vice-versa.) Oneness cannot be *experienced* as oneness from within. It can only be experienced when it is *union*, and it cannot be that unless it has known separation first, yet this necessary separation feels unnatural and we resist it. The small child does not want to separate from his mother and constantly returns to her for reassurance, so risky does the big, new world seem, even though it fascinates and draws him. It is hard, too, to leave home, and the young woman or man on the edge of adulthood needs to have a sense that 'my home' is still there to come back to if the challenge of difference is to be faced. Without this security the risks seem too great. Perhaps we should not 'read back' such human states of mind into the processes of unconscious life, but we can at least see that there is a kind of inertia in nature, which means that changes only take place because circumstances make them essential. The natural thing (if I may so phrase it) is not to change—that is, not to discover new and different ways of being. It is the pressure of external forces, changing the environment so that the old state becomes impossible to sustain, which produces differentiation.

But in human beings differentiation cannot, at the conscious level, simply happen. The circumstances may lead to *separation*, but for real differentiation in a free creation there has to be conscious choice. The choice is not between 'good' and 'evil', for we are speaking of a situation in which, hypothetically at least, there is no 'evil'. The choice is between a known good and an unknown one, and the unknown is presented simply as the choice of love, as response to love. Yet the known, also, is the work of love. The crucial point is that, as we have seen, reality exists (and only exists) in exchange, and to refuse to go to meet the unknown is, in effect, *to refuse exchange*. It is refused in favour of a known good, but that 'good' is only good as it came into existence in the exchange of life. To refuse to leave it is, in a sense, to change its nature; it is to turn it into something which is held to exist *for itself* and not in the flow of exchanged life, given and received. It ceases, therefore, to be loving. So we can see that differentiation is essential to love, and true love is what reality *is*; there can be no question of simply being part of a vast 'process'. For conscious beings choice has to be real and it has to be loving, and it is in such choosing that creation continues to take place. In this way, consciousness actually creates.

This difficult concept can be illustrated to some extent by the example of recent teaching about the conduct of childbirth. The

Leboyer school of thought about the conduct of labour emphasizes the fact that the very rough reception often given to the newborn inhibits and may even prevent the good relationship with the mother on which the child's psychic health and growth depend. The baby emerges from the 'oneness' of the womb life by way of an experience which is, in any case, difficult, since the child is propelled, willy-nilly, through a passage only just wide enough to allow him or her to pass, and experiences extreme and certainly painful pressure on the sensitive head. Feelings of panic and anger are likely, if not inevitable, even in a perfectly 'trouble-free' birth. Once emerged, the child's untried senses are exposed to bright lights and loud voices, and the cord is cut at once, which means the child *has* to breathe immediately and deeply in order to stay alive, and so the lungs are expanded suddenly and under stress and the child cries from the shock. The newborn, after being hurriedly examined to make sure all is well, is then probably weighed, wrapped up in a blanket and put aside until later while the mother is attended to. After all this, it says a lot for the emotional resilience of babies that they do, usually, establish a relationship with the mother when they are eventually given a chance to do so, but it is not surprising that their first reaction to life is a loud, angry and frightened crying and their further reaction to the mother's breast may be either refusal or angry, rapacious grasping.

In contrast to this, the whole process of separation and re-union can be gentle and harmonious. The baby is welcomed as gently as possible into a room whose dimmed lights and lowered voices will not assualt the unaccustomed senses. As soon as the body has emerged completely the baby is laid on the mother's stomach, face down, with the cord still uncut, and in this situation of almost womb-like proximity and warmth is allowed to take the first breath at leisure and gently. Once breathing is established, the cord is cut. After a while, when the baby has become accustomed to the new environment, he or she is given a warm bath, again continuing the womb experience but with a difference. Photographs taken during this process, and when the child is finally at rest, show the contrast between on the one hand the wary, withdrawn look of the shocked but finally quiescent infant, getting over the horror of abrupt and painful separation, and on the other the smiling face, serene in its openness yet with an oddly 'detached' look, of the baby whose

95

experience of birth has been respectful of the stages of readiness, and carried out with tenderness.

Separation there has to be, however. We can easily understand that the violently-born should be resentful, vengeful and resistant in establishing relationship, but we have also to ask: is the gently separated child fully differentiated? Is that Buddha-like smile perhaps a sign that full differentiation has not been achieved? *Can* it be achieved except by some degree of violence? On the other hand, can it be simply that the demand for union in love, presented to the newly differentiated, encounters in a gently handled baby not the resistance of fear and anger but the resistance of a quiescence, of staying in 'known' good or oneness rather than union, in this way 'refusing' the gift? It would need a great deal of close study of the subsequent development of babies born in this way (with all kinds of imponderables in the environment making assessment difficult) to formulate even intelligent guesses about the difference this makes, but it does seem possible that the risk of the differentiated entity refusing the self-gift of exchange, and desiring rather to be self-sufficient (drawing to itself what it needs from without) is very real, yet it is a risk worh running, because the 'gentle' birth allows for an un-fearful and 'free' response.

I have used this earliest possible example because it is a situation in which we can see that no *guilt* is involved, yet there can be a *wrong*. For whether there be an angry grabbing and grasping or a placid acceptance of what is 'good for me' as of right (and anyone who has watched tiny infants being fed has probably seen both these patterns), there is a tendency in the necessarily differentiated personality to claim autonomy, rather than to exchange.

As St Augustine pointed out in his acid comments on the evil tendencies apparent in babies at the breast, even they exist in our sinful situation. We cannot expect them, therefore, to provide us with a model of 'paradisal' responses. But the description of a 'perfect' birth can help us to *imagine* a situation in which differentiation could take place as freely chosen, but without fear or pain. The spheres of experience would be real, but in their rich difference capable of a more complex and beautiful pattern of exchanged life. To choose difference would be to choose to go forward in the great dance of creation, with Wisdom as choreographer, from oneness to difference and so to the possibility of true union. It is the choice which matters. We can perceive, perhaps, in the scriptual description of Paradise the evocation of an environment designed to support and assist the human choice towards love. The articulation of the human task as that of caring for the earth ('to till it and keep it') seems to express the demand for a loving response, a differentiation leading to, and existing for, the purposes of a deeper and fuller union.

But in practice the choice of differentiation comes to us as risky. When the un-free aspects of human life (that is, the inevitable processes of growth) cause differentiation to take place anyway, as at birth and adolescence for instance, the newly differentiated may be choked, oppressed and frightened by the new separateness to the extent that they become paralysed and refuse to move further. They therefore choose an 'impossible' autonomy—'impossible' because reality is exchange, and the choice of 'autonomy' *depends* on the existence of continuing exchange in all other spheres. And this is an indication of the nature of sin.

In a previous chapter, the attempt to understand the nature of the 'passionate breakthrough' in human life was illuminated by studying its occurrence in an incident in the life of Jesus, because his humanness, more completely human than any other, tells us things about ourselves which we could not otherwise perceive, except very obscurely in symbols and myths. In him we see the symbols and myths in historical, concrete fact. So in struggling with the question of the nature of evil we can find help in the encounter of Jesus himself with evil.

The whole life of Jesus was, in a sense, an encounter with evil; indeed its purpose was explicitly to rescue humankind from the paralysis of sin. He encountered evil in those who hated him for various reasons, and in the form of sickness and death among those who sought his help, and he finally encountered it in his own suffering and death. But in the incident of the Temptation we are shown evil presenting itself to him, in his own person, an encounter undiluted by the complexities and ambivalences of ordinary human motives and circumstances. It is, in a sense, quite untypical of normal human encounter with evil, yet in another sense it is at the root of the matter. By examining this, we shall be able better to see how evil works in human life; that is, we shall see evil as *sin*, a whole situation in which the human world is involved.

Two things about the accounts of the temptation of Jesus are immediately apparent. One is that the encounter was regarded by the early Church as of great importance; all three synoptists give accounts of it (though Mark's is so short as to seem to be a 'reference') as they do of the transfiguration, and John, who does not describe it, throws light on it from a different angle, as we shall see. The other thing we can see at once is that, since Jesus was alone throughout the experience, the account of it can only be in some way derived from his own revelation of it at a later time. It must have been a difficult thing to communicate, and the expression of it is necessarily a poetic one. (I repeat, with emphasis, that 'poetic' does not mean *extra* to any fact; it means the only way certain kinds of facts can be accurately communicated.)

The way the experience of the Temptation is expressed is very precise and unambiguous. It is recognizably in the same style as the terse but vivid detail of the parables, or the almost brutally practical (poetic *because* practical) instructions given to the disciples going on a mission, or to would-be disciples. It is generally quite clear when Jesus was using images as comparisons to convey his meaning, for instance in the parables, or when he asked the crowds if they expected John the Baptist to be like 'a reed bending in the wind', or likened discipleship to carrying a yoke, and when, on the other hand, he was giving exact information about facts, however peculiar. He did this, for instance, when he told Nathaniel that he had seen him 'under the fig tree', or the Samaritan woman that she had no husband, or the Canaanite woman that her daughter was healed, or when he revealed to the Twelve his detailed foreknowledge of the manner of his death. The accounts of the Temptation do not read like metaphors intended to convey an inner experience; they read like reports of actual experience, however unusual, and necessarily using sharp images to convey what happened. The reason why many people assume that these accounts are a vivid way of conveying a purely subjective experience is that, as I said before, we have ruled out, without argument, the possibility of any such experience as 'objective'. It *cannot* have happened because such tings *do not* happen. And in this case incredulity is compounded by reluctance to take seriously the possibility of a 'devil' or 'Satan' as a 'person' in any recognizable sense of the word. We are so hung up on the imagery used to evoke this 'person' in medieval art or literature that we cannot get past it. We are also influenced, still, by remains of eighteenth-century enlightenment prejudice, which could just about stomach God (within well-defined limits) but was nauseated by survivals of medieval peasant superstitions such as belief in 'spirits', who were indeed, in popular imagination, easily lumped together in a category including not only angels and devils but goblins and ghosts.

We need not be so simple-minded as our ancestors in our rejections (though a degree of level-headed skepticism is always proper in dealing with accounts of the 'supernatural'). I suggested, in discussing the transfiguration, that the importance of the incident lies not in the fact that these things happened to Jesus, but that it was Jesus they happened to. So here, also, there is plenty of evidence that 'evil spirits', or something we can designate in that way for convenience, do speak to people and can carry them around. Levitation and instantaneous 'travel' are well attested phenomena which occur in a context of evil as well as of holiness, and a great many people have 'seen the devil' and felt 'his' grip.

To say this does, in one way, beg the question of interpretation. Assuming we can accept that people really do, physically, have these experiences of seeing and hearing and touching, and being gripped and even transported by some power beyond 'nature', there remains the question of whether the 'power' was properly described by them. Naturally, existing religious ideas would provide a vocabulary for description which might make it all too glib to be particularly valuable as evidence. On the other hand, there are reports of similar experiences by people who found it hard to explain what had happened because they had no ready-made language in which to do so, yet what they did say tied in with the descriptions of those who firmly attributed their experience to 'Satan'. And this goes both for those who were appalled at, and resistant to, the power of thier 'visitor', and those who wanted and welcomed it. There is considerable literature available about Satanism, much of it quite recent, and through it all 'Satan' comes through as very definitely personal, with defined wishes and commands to convey and with enormous power over matter and to a lesser extent over human minds. All this ties in with the experience of Jesus as reported by Matthew and Luke. But if we can assume that it is possible to think of the evil power as 'personal', we still have to wonder about the implications of the whole account for understanding the nature of evil, which was what Jesus was up against.

In what follows I would want the reader to bear in mind that in using words like 'person', or even pronouns like 'he', to refer to the 'other' element in the encounter with Jesus in the wilderness we are stretching language beyond what is, in a sense, permissible or sensible. We do not know, really, what weight to attach to such words in such a context. We simply have to try to keep at the back of our minds the awareness that, in a sense, we cannot 'mean what we say' but that in order to say anything at all about this question—and we must do so—we have to use such words. The same thing, of course, applies to all theological language, but some of it is so familiar that we do not notice the strangeness. We have domesticated it. Thereby we run into a great danger, but still we do have to use and re-use and indeed re-discover such words, and we have to do so now in the context of the nature of evil. So I shall use words like 'Satan' and 'evil power' with no further apology, but aware of the danger of misunderstanding which all poetic language runs as an occupational hazard.

If we say Satan is 'evil', what do we mean by that? If he has 'evil power', what kind of power is it? Where does it come from? This raises the question of what we mean by talking of 'evil spirits' and what, or who, it was who 'tempted' Jesus. The scriptual references to such beings are both strange and enlightening, and they are, after all, the ones which shaped the mind of Jesus on this subject.

The life of Jesus, like all human life, is situated in a 'sinful' context, and we are asking what this means and how it got that way since, as we have seen, it 'need not' have been so. The 'Fall' of humankind and with it the fallen condition of all creation (which St Paul calls 'futile') is attributed only indirectly to such an 'evil spirit'. The story in Genesis speaks only of 'the serpent' who tempted Eve and Adam. It does not suggest why a 'serpent' should have wanted to subvert their loyalty to the God with whom, until then, they had been on intimate terms. But other stories throw light on this.

The Apocalypse, following Jewish mythology and legends, identifies 'the serpent who had deceived all the world' with 'the great dragon . . . known as the devil, or Satan'. Satan is a strange figure in Scripture. The name means 'accuser', and in the book of Job he is the 'Counsel for the Prosecution' of Job, trying to prove him only virtuous because it pays to be virtuous. He is, here, the agent of the Lord for the testing of Job's disinterestedness. But he could be the agent of the Lord without wishing to be, and the New Testament shows Satan as 'tempting' humans for his own reasons, putting evil ideas into the heads of people like Judas or Ananias and good at disguising himself as an 'angel of light'. Sometimes he is simply the immediate cause of evil experiences such as sickness, although it is clear that he works only within God's 'permission' even though he does not acknowledge that permission. Jesus called him a 'liar' and a 'murderer', and deception and destruction are his basic occupations; they are, in fact, his 'being', since we are talking of an 'angel', and whatever else is meant by that concept it must certainly mean that 'being' and 'doing' cannot be separated as they can in human beings.

But one important concept emerges from comparison of the various and very ambiguous scriptual references to Satan, and that is that the coming of Jesus made a crucial difference to the 'status' of Satan. In the Old Testment he is described as under God's control, yet human beings can do little about him except hope for rescue. But over and over again in the New Testament Christians are assured that they can resist him, even overcome him. Jesus said that he saw Satan 'fall like lightning from Heaven', on the occasion when he welcomed the return of his seventy 'other' disciples who had been travelling through the country preaching the coming of the Kingdom, healing and 'casting out devils' (Luke 10). 'Even the devils submit to us when we use your name', they told him. The meaning of his exclamation is not perfectly clear, but it does at least seem to mean that something very drastic had happened to the power of Satan. In a sense that power had previously been a power for evil but one not clearly differentiated from human experience of God's action as his 'anger', and of his power to punish. Now, it seems there is a sharp separation. Satan has 'fallen from Heaven'; evil can no longer be experienced as something to be submitted to, rather it must be *attacked*. And this conviction is forcibly and very clearly expressed in the poetry of the Apocalypse, in which Michael, the defender of God's people, with his angels 'attacked the dragon, and drove him and his angels out of heaven and *onto the earth*', which is the realm of human beings. And it is human beings who are now going to deal with Satan, by dying. 'They have triumphed over him by the blood of the Lamb and by the witness of their martyrdom, because even in the face of death they would not cling to life.' The significance of this in relation to the death of 'the Lamb' Jesus belongs in a later chapter, but here its importance is to give us a hindsight only available through this specifically Christian theological development into the meaning of that sinister but unexplained 'serpent' in Eden. The serpent, if he is Satan, is the one whose whole being consists in an attempt to destroy the links between creator and creature, the web of exchanged life. Why does he want to do so?

If we transpose the poetic imagery of Scripture into the terms of the model of exchange, we can perhaps say that one Being among the great Receivers and Givers of exchanged love wills to receive but not to give, wills to turn the energy of divine love—poured into him without limit—back into himself. He claims autonomy, he refuses the exchange. By doing so he, in a sense, concentrates that energy behind the 'barrier' of his own differentiated nature. He makes it 'his', to use as he wills.

Among the best imaginative evocations of this 'turning back' of divine energy by appropriating it and using it to dominate is to be found in novels by Charles Williams. One is called *Shadows of Ecstasy* and its theme is that of exchange and refusal of exchange. This theme became more subtly developed in later books, but this first one, crude in many ways, pins down very precisely what it is that gives to the strange figure of Nigel Considine power over minds and bodies, to the point of almost over-running Europe. Considine is in a sense 'anti-Christ', and therefore very like Christ. His doctrine is that all experience, painful or blissful, must be directed 'inwards': '. . . the business of man is to assume the world into himself. He shall draw strength from everything that he may govern everything . . . by the transmutation of your energies, evoked by poetry or love or any manner of ecstasy, into the power of a greater ecstasy.' He intends to conquer death by driving into himself all the power of life and possessing it. He 'feeds', therefore, on the ecstatic deaths of his possessed followers, as well as on his own past experiences of desire and of beauty. All is turned back into himself. 'I have poured the strength of every love and hate into my own life and what is behind my life', he tells his followers, and bids them not to 'spend'

102

their energy, but use it to 'overcome'. Love must not be *given*: 'It's a waste to spend on the beloved what's meant to discover more than the beloved.' He tells them: 'Put away all desire but to be fulfilled in yourselves.'

This is an evocation of a human (almost a superhuman) being, living by the refusal of exchange. Considine's power is enormous and growing. Williams was right to express this choice in terms of a human being, for that is all we can do. Attempts to evoke imaginatively a non-human power must fail; all we can do is work analogically and be aware that that is what we are doing. But, by analogy, we can 'see' in Considine the nature of the choice made by the Adversary of humankind. In C. S. Lewis's 'space' trilogy, which begins with *Out of the Silent Planet*, the power of evil encountered by the hero, Ransom, in both the 'angelic' being who took to himself the divine power given him for service and the human or other created beings who have free will and use it in that way, are described as 'bent', and so are their resulting actions. Lewis, whose model of reality was basically Platonist, was here employing an image which does not fit the Platonic model but does strikingly fit the model of exchange. 'Bent' is precisely what evil is; it bends back to itself the power of divine energy, deflecting it from its true purpose. So this Being refuses exchange, yet his 'being' is itself created out of the 'stuff' of the divine exchange. He, the Adversary, *is* exchange; he cannot 'be' without renewing his being, therefore he needs to reach beyond autonomy in some way. If he will not do it as giver, then he must do it as conqueror, taking into himself yet more of the energy he has to have, and craves, but cannot accept as a gift. The Gift by which he exists is to him (having refused to acknowledge exchange) an intolerable insult, since to the one who refuses to love, love can only appear as in itself a conquest, a domination. Refusing to acknowledge Gift, he craves conquest, and if he cannot as yet conquer the Giver he can, at least, seek to conquer, control and deflect to himself the energy of other created beings. But the choice he himself had originally made of refusing exchange could only be repeated by another being whose giving and receiving were also in freedom. Therefore the loving responses of un-free creation were beyond his direct reach; he had no foothold in those categories of being which could not but give and receive, in and through and between their kinds. There remained, therefore,

103

two points at which he might hope to deflect to himself the energy of exchange, and these points were in the nature of other immaterial free beings, or in those material yet aspiring creatures to which the Giver had also imparted freedom. At these two points he was, so the poetry of Scripture tells us, successful. With the perversion of other 'angelic' beings we are less concerned here, for in a sense it makes little difference to our earth-centred minds whether the damage to the material universe was wrought by one being or by millions, and in any case the validity of talking about numbers at all in such a context is questionable, since the concepts of unity and multiplicity, though valid, must have an altered significance in the context of the 'purely' spiritual, which our imaginations cannot grasp.

The Apocalypse describes this perversion by saying that the dragon 'swept a third of the stars from the sky and dropped them *to the earth*'. The acutely relevant point for us is Satan's attack on *human* minds. The poetry of Genesis does indeed show the approach as being through the mind, which is what we should expect since, as I suggested, un-free physical reality could not be *directly* affected. The human thing was, we are shown, moving towards the destined perfection of embraced love, for which it must reach through the spheres, unimpeded yet governed by the proper measures of exchange. Nearing the scope of its own potential freedom, it encountered (besides the constant and patient and urgent wooing of the divine Lover, awaiting the response of freely given love) another kind of suggestion.

Charles Williams developed the idea that the temptation of 'the Adam' was to desire to perceive differentiation 'as God' perceives it. We saw, in considering babies, that the choice of love leading to union presents itself to beings in time and space as a demand to leave the known good for the unknown. The point is that *both* are good and —in the being of the Creator—remain good. But in order thus to 'be' with the Creator, the free time-and-space creatures must move from one to another. If this is done then the movement is experienced as one from good to good. But it is only when this movement is made, when the self is given to the exchange, that *both* can be known as good. There is another possibility: to experience the unknown good while still holding to the known good, since that is (in a sense) what God does. If the choice is viewed in this way

104

the demand that the known good be relinquished appears as a *deprivation*, either of that which is known, or of that which is unknown. In other words, the choice appears as one between good and evil, for it is an 'evil' to be deprived of what one knows as a deep need. The two things appear as incompatibles, not as points in the flow of exchanged life. The 'good', here, is to see as God sees, the 'evil' is to be obliged to make the choice of exchange.

The point I am trying to make here is fundamental, because it is about the actual origin of sin in human life; it is 'original' in the sense of being 'at the origins' of human life as such, and also 'original' in the sense that this is the basic pattern of all sinful choices. It may seem a delicate argument, and rather obscure, and I think this is inevitable because we are dealing with a reality which is obscured for us intellectually and imaginatively by its own effects. That is, our imagination is itself conditioned by the sinfulness we are trying to understand and is resistant to this kind of clarification. So there is, I think, a tendency to reduce the description of an 'original' sinful choice to a failure in some kind of arbitrary test set up by God, because that makes it all 'exterior' and manageable. The idea that sin is somehow concerned with choosing our own proper nature is hard to 'hold on to' because we do not, in fact, experience our nature as 'proper' at all. Even in trying to *think* about original sin we are actually tending to choose a way of thinking which enables us to *blame God* for setting things up that way and depriving us of a privilege to which we have some kind of right. I know this is a circular argument—which is exactly how the Adversary wants us to move, in a circle with no outlet towards trust, surrender and love.

This notion of the kind of choice we have means that we see 'good' as the ability to see as God sees and 'evil' as an obligation to make the choice between known and unknown—i.e. to be 'deprived' of 'being as Gods'. This is what the power of deflected Spirit desires 'the Adam' to see, for if, seeing this choice as 'contention' and claiming 'divine' autonomy, they too refuse exchange, then they must share Satan's voluntary self-restriction. They, too, will be confined within their own sphere, refusing the return of love. In that state, manipulated by him, they would become his, to feed his craving for that very energy whose acceptance as love he rejects and

105

being therefore in a state of intolerably maintained rejection of that by which he exists.

Once the suggestion was accepted, and exchange refused, the spheres became indeed what 'the Adam' had *willed* to see by perceiving the choice in that manner: spheres closed off from each other, opaque barriers to love. Unable to perceive, as love would have them perceive, the sphere of glory as one with which they were invited to exchange life, they perceived it instead as the 'enemy', that which had deprived them of autonomy. Indeed they could only conceive of it in images, since they had refused direct perception. They were 'cast out' even from that state of un-free perfection of exchange to which their physical animal nature adapted them, because freedom, once entered, differentiated them, and as different from animals they remained, for good or ill. If they would not accept exchange in freedom they must be subject to the vision they had chosen, the vision of contention, a world-picture of enemies above, below, before or behind. The way back to undifferentiated innocence was cut off by a barrier so absolute that it 'burned' them when they encountered it in the form of other created but un-free beings. These, therefore, seemed to 'the Adam' to be rivals as incomprehensible in their way as the sphere of glory to which he and she had refused to give themselves and which, because of that refusal, they could not understand. God was their enemy, nature was their enemy, and the only advice they could hear, to enable them to deal with either, came from the one who had himself refused Wisdom. The power which Satan has over human beings, it now appears, is the power given to him by human beings themselves. Without their free recourse to him he could not touch them in their freedom.

There is an extraordinary poem by Rainer Maria Rilke, about the raising of Lazarus. It shows Jesus acutely aware of the way in which human choice has closed off the spheres from each other. By refusing the invitation to pass freely from one to another, humans make evil what is good and turn differentiation into separation. In the poem, Jesus at first is distressed because even Martha and Mary are not able simply to know, without proof, that he is Lord of death; and as for the crowds, 'not a soul believed him'. Rilke shows him as full of anger at the implicit demand that he make such a breakthrough thus and then. He feels he is being asked to respond not to

106

faith but to lack of it. I am not sure whether this particular interpretation rings true, though Jesus did, on other occasions, act 'out of order' for compelling reasons. It is what follows which interests me:

> ... But not a soul believed him:
> 'Lord, you've come too late,' said all the crowd.
> So to peaceful Nature, though it grieved him,
> On he went to do the unallowed.
> Asked them, eyes half-shut, his body glowing
> with anger, 'Where's the grave?' Tormentedly.
> And to them it seemed his tears were flowing,
> as they thronged behind him, curiously.
> As he walked, the thing seemed monstrous to him,
> childish, horrible experiment:
> then there suddenly went flaming through him
> such an all-consuming argument
> against their life, their death, their whole collection
> of separations made by them alone,
> all his body quivered with rejection
> as he gave out hoarsely 'Raise the stone'.
>   ('The Raising of Lazarus')

It is 'their life, their death, their whole collection of separations made by them alone'! The sense of fear we have when we are 'asked' to move from one sphere to another (to life through 'death' in leaving behind the known) is the result of the refusal of exchange, which has warped our imagination so that we cannot see the demand as simply loving. It is not the cause of our refusal of exchange, except in the sense that the world-picture we have (created by sin) makes fearful what is inherently life-giving. And we can see more easily, after an encounter with the urgent physicalness of this poem's evocation of 'separation', that the refusal must have more than 'mental' effects. It must be experienced through the whole physical being. Through human bodies other bodies receive and are changed by and pass on one to another the effects of their fear and enmity.

'In Adam' indeed all die, for at whatever point in the network of exchange a refusal is made there the deflected energy, now become 'evil', distorts the whole process. It seems impossible to tell whether

107

the 'Fall' was single or multiple. It makes little difference, since a single refusal can spread death to an infinite number.

How did it first happen? There is no way we can tell that either except in poetry, which is what the writers of Genesis did, very accurately, as we have seen. We know from experience, however, that this is how it happens *now*. We can see, any day, the way in which each small refusal of exchange can and does set up a response of like refusal in another person. The abused child becomes the depressed adult, refusing exchange because exchange feels too dangerous, and in the process inducing responses of anger or fear in others. One refusal makes the next more likely. Yet, always, the evil that is done claims to be good. It justifies itself, claims reason, claims to be 'really' doing the right thing. The cry of Milton's Satan, 'Evil, be thou my good', is accurate, because evil is never acknolwedged *as evil* by those who do it. He or she may *call* it evil, using the available vocabulary, but it is not *felt* to be evil as long as it is positively willed. It is only when the wrong is repented that it is recognized as evil.

A contemporary example of this can be observed in connection with the growth of the nuclear industry. Whatever one may think of the possible justification for continuing the building of such pontentially (and in some cases actually) lethal installations as nuclear power stations and nuclear fuel 'dumps', even the most ardent advocates admit that they require an enormous apparatus of security, including screening of employees and their families and associates and a whole 'nuclear police' to guard the sites against possible terrorist use of the materials as well as to see to enforcement of safety regulations made ever more stringent, until human patience cracks and evades, as at Three Mile Island. The complexity, extent and expense of the security apparatus and precautions escalate constantly, because as the safety precautions are intensified the awareness of risk increases. More and more actual failures occur and have to be hushed up, safeguards become more sophisticated and so do the 'criminals' envisaged by the computers which estimate the degree of terrorist risk. But the disturbing thing is that, far from deprecating the need for such measures, some nuclear scientists actually welcome them, for the power they give over human lives is enormous. And it is the power which is at the heart of the matter. The need for all this control is proof, to them, of the worthwhileness

108

of what is being done. The sheer danger of it, and the never-ending battle to combat the danger, gives a sense of dealing with tremendous powers, with which it is necessary to 'live dangerously'. A recent book by Robert Jungk, *The Nuclear State*, documents not only the things that go on in the planning and running (and frequent unannounced failures) of nuclear power installations but the speeches and letters of those most influential in promoting them. The author mentions one, the German Professor Häfele, as representing

> the new type of reckless but influential initiator and promoter of major technical enterprises. These 'project swingers' are no longer like the patient, modest, responsible and scholarly researchers of the old days, to whom science owes its status in the world, but scientific enterpreneurs and impresarios who know how to manipulate the administration and the economy for their hazardous mammoth systems. They imitate and associate themselves with those tycoons and leaders who are interested only in power . . . advocating the crazy idea of building fast breeders on the edge of Austrian alpine glaciers, or indulging his dreams of a centralized world state in which 'a new technology and a new social structure would enter on a symbiosis' . . . . his grandiose comparison of the nuclear power constructors with the builders of the great cathedrals, his resounding conviction that this hazardous high technology is concrete evidence of the genius of our age, has—as someone who listened to one of his tirades confided to me—'positively intoxicated our scientists. A new Führer who wanted to arise today would have to talk just like that, combining emphasis on technical progress with a *mythical sense of mission*' [my italics].

We are very close to Williams' fictional anti-Christ, Considine, when we consider what power the great cathedrals were intended to symbolize and serve. The energy of divine love, received by human beings and given back to God in worship in those constructions of human skill and devotion, is explicitly made equivalent to constructions devoted to an energy received by and controlled by human beings (quite a small number, ultimately) for their own ends, which are only incidentally the supply of electrical power: the real power is that over human lives. In order to gain and keep this,

109

any amount of minor and major deception about the degree of danger to people and environment is routinely used, there is bribery on a huge scale, and intimidation of employees small and great is normal, common, and well documented. There is even a strong suspicion that assassination of people who know too much is acceptable, as the case of Karen Silkwood suggests, though absolute proof seems unlikely. 'Evil, be thou my good'; another more clear-sighted scientist, Alvin W. Weinberg, though still advocating and working for the nuclear industry, referred to the 'Faustian' bargain that the atomic scientists offered humankind. But Jungk adds in *The Nuclear State*,

> In his simile, Weinberg sees himself as a tempting Mephistopheles, but in the long run he seems to have felt quite uncomfortable in the role, for on the occasion of a discussion at Luxemburg in 1973 he said he knew a version of the drama in which Faust made his deal not with the devil but with God. Certainly this was meant only in jest, but it reveals something very significant about the mentality of leading scientific experts. Even though they would never admit it, nearly all of them are more or less obsessed with the idea of being able (or having) to play God.

It is not about 'leading scientific experts' only that this reveals something. It shows us once again, though in a form more acutely and enormously dangerous than ever before, the perennial temptation to yield to the intoxicating feeling of 'quasi-divine power'. This is a very old story. 'You shall be as gods'; 'all these will I give you, if you will bow down and serve me.' Evil is done with the utmost conviction of righteousness, and opposition must be crushed because it is futile to oppose what is obviously, in the eyes of the 'bent' person, the necessary and inevitable way to do things.

Sin is a complex notion, connected not only with what we usually call 'moral' evil (that is, interior choices of wrongness) but with other kinds of evil, such as sickness, defeat in war or in business, natural disaster, and death. The close connection of all of these in Hebrew thought is perhaps a little easier to understand if we consider the example I have just given, in which the notion of sin in the context of nuclear technology involves the inextricable interaction of moral attitudes such as those described with the hazards of radiation accident in the plant, long-term sickness, genetic effects, pollution of water and soil, and death of people and other living things resulting from any of these.

Paul makes a close link between sin, sickness and death, for we are dealing with the refusal of exchange by, and *in*, physical beings. Human beings can choose to refuse exchange, but they are involved bodily in the complex exchanges of the natural order and so here, too, sin is at work. Unlike evil 'spirits', humans cannot 'be' pure choice. Their choices affect, and are affected by, their physical being in all its involvements.

The whole question of sin in the body will be discussed in a later chapter, but here we already have to recognize that sin is physically experienced. The perversion of exchange, like the great breakthrough of love, changes people all through. It does not always do this in an obvious and predictable way, because the situation is complicated by the fact that human beings are capable of becoming accustomed to, and producing compensations for, quite drastic damage. For instance, people can 'absorb' for years and years the damage caused by eating particles of lead, and seem perfectly well. The symptoms of mild lead poisoning are ambiguous, and a case can be made for attributing them to some other cause. It is only when large numbers of people are seen to display the same symptoms and the common denominator is apparent that the nature of the illness becomes clear, and even then they may refuse to recognize it. In the same way, habits of resentment or ambition or lust change people physically and can be perceived in the way they move and speak, but a mild 'case' is quite easy to live with and will tend to be unrecognized. Such people appear, and feel, normal, so much so that those who do live in the fullness of exchange seem strange and eccentric, much as a person in fullness of health is rare and seems rather peculiar and even slightly repulsive! For us, sin *is* the normal state of affairs, and we show this when we say, 'I'm human, after all', and mean, 'I'm sinful'. Sin's effects are so widespread that they are the condition of our lives, and its effects are physical, mental and spiritual.

The exact relationship between spiritual and physical health is not fully understood and possibly cannot be, but it is certainly much more intimate than we have been accustomed to think. In fact it is misleading to talk of 'spiritual' and 'physical' as if they were exclu

111

sive categories, for to experience them as separate is itself a result of sin. Moral sin, in most cultures, has been closely associated with physical illness, and although we need to avoid the more simplistic kinds of cause-and-effect explanation we can see that, in some senses, the moral act of the refusal of exchange is bound to have physical effects. To take a very simple example, a woman who (because of insecurity—a passed-on result of her parents' refusal?) refuses to make to her husband, children or neighbours the response of compassion, attention and generous care which she 'has it in her' to give, must, in each instance of refusal, go through a complex process of self-justification, suppression of guilt and compensating expenditure of energy on other things (to provide excuse for non-involvement). All this uses psychic energy, so she is often tired, and the need to resist involvement makes her tense; she cannot relax, needs tranquillizers, has backache and headache. Tension and fatigue also lead to digestive problems, and possibly to long-term effects on the spine and heart. Because she is un-relaxed her breathing may be shallow, leading to lung trouble later. Also she is likely to smoke or drink or develop some other 'comfort habit' which compounds the condition. There is nothing mysterious about this; it is all very familiar, and the name of the game is sin.

In the same way physical sickness often affects the 'victim' of sin; the person who tries to respond to impossible demands suffers from tension and fatigue also, and so has a lower resistance to infection, may 'break down' nervously or physically, or both. And 'social sin' above all is a creator of disease among the innocent. Adulteration of food for profit, bad labour conditions, inadequate wages and all the techniques of social and economic exploitation are sinful and lead to sin in body and mind and spirit. This sequence needs no underlining; it is too well known.

Yet, however the sequence works (and some of it is quite opaque to us) and however blatant the evils involved, we can still see quite well that even at this visible and tangible physical level evil has no 'independent' being. Much physical 'disease' is the body's attempt to rid itself of alien elements—catarrh, sepsis and 'fever', for instance, are the result of mechanisms of *healing*.

Sin is 'in' human beings, in their total being, and it is, in every form it takes, basically a refusal, a deflecting back into the particular being of the energy of life whose nature is to be poured out. The

112

very energy of sin, its power and malevolence, is in its origin the power whose nature is Love, the Spirit. There is no other source. Even at the level of un-free creation sin is present, not so much in what we call 'natural disaster' (which is generally only 'disastrous' to human beings) as in disease in plants and animals, due often to human misuse through greed, pride and laziness, but also to drastic changes in the environment, leading to changes in available nutrients. There is 'something wrong' here, too, but we may guess that minds powerful enough to do what human beings are capable of doing could, if they were moving fully in the flow of the divine exchanges, enter into and direct other forms of life for good. Magical powers are essentially 'appropriated' powers, yet if this deflected and therefore at least potentially 'evil' power can affect natural forces and human bodies (and the evidence that it can is considerable), this does at least suggest the potential power of human beings to guide un-free creation into a greater and more complete harmony. But it also suggests that we may be more responsible than we realize for 'sin' in 'nature'. The web of exchange is intimate, and it seems impossible that such a drastic event as the deliberate refusal of that by which all things exist, a refusal which has become *habitual* in the human sphere, should not drastically affect all other spheres of created being. In Adam, indeed, all die—men and women, birds and beasts and fishes and plants.

For death is the 'proof' of sin. It is the displaying, in physical fact, of that divorce between spheres of life which results from the refusal of exchange. Flesh and spirit, intimately bound together in the dance of divine Wisdom, are, by sin, alienated from each other. Like people living willy-nilly in the same house who say of themselves, 'We aren't speaking', they live together but do not communicate. Finally, they cannot 'hear' each other. The body is gradually or suddenly withdrawn from the exchange of life with the spirit, an exchange already rendered limited, awkward and painful. Death, then, appears not only as the final end but as a dark power reaching out into the daylight world of human life. It grabs people by the heel as they walk by, it threatens and hovers, it is the inescapable, the one thing human beings cannot deal with, the 'last enemy'. But it is important that humankind should not seek a solution to this by grabbing at physical immortality, because in this context that simply annexes to an already narrowed and paralysed 'life' a larger span of that 'life'. It is still *their* life, *their* death', it is not a destruction of death but rather a consolidation of the power of death by making it, as it were, a permanent wall reaching so high that nobody can look beyond it or even speculate that there is a 'beyond'. This would indeed be the destruction of the last hope of breakthrough, and it is better for the Adam that they should be cast out of Paradise by their own fears than that they eat of the other tree, the tree of Life. Thus does the refusal of exchange spread fear, suspicion, isolation and 'their' death through the cosmos, as each individual lives in exchange.

So we see that if the great Refuser could not conquer the beings of unfree exchange in any direct way, he could infiltrate them indirectly. The exchange of spheres would continue; the 'doors' between different levels of being in the 'upward' reach of exchanged spheres were open, therefore, in the exchanges of life (feared and un-understood though they were). Energy flowed from one sphere to another. But this energy was now an energy not of love but of desire for domination and possession. The force of perverted angelic energy reached far into the spheres of unfree material being, by way of the material being of those who were free, but confused, afraid and confined by their own refusal. That refusal drove them, as it had driven their Adversary, to seek to grab what they craved, not perceiving that it was being freely offered to them in love. The exchanges became exchanges of their death, one thing only coming into being by the destruction of another.

For this is our situation: we live in a cosmos whose being is exchange of life, yet at every turn we experience this exchange as both creative and destructive. There is no escape. The spheres voluntarily closed are breached by the thrust of passionate love, and also of passionate desire to dominate, through magic or sexual manipulation, for instance. Yet they are only breached, not laid open to each other. It is all quite senseless, because what we grab is ours for the loving, if only we would accept Wisdom. But that we will not do, indeed we cannot, because we have minds now become incapable of perceiving her, or wanting her. The initiative has to come from her.

This is the irony of the situation, that the very power of the energy of exchange, by which all exists, can be used to refuse exchange as love. Exchange there has to be, but it becomes exchange as dominance and enslavement, forcing the surrender of that which is needed for existence, and surrendering in fear that which should have been given in tenderness. This applies at the level of nature, when plants and animals get out of balance and destroy themselves and each other, and much more at the level of freedom, where human beings destroy other creatures by greed and ignorance and pride (as well as from a need created by mutual 'imbalance') and destroy each other even more thoroughly, as races and as communities and as individuals, by forced and blinded exchanges which cannot endure. Yet through all this the sheer power of the principle of exchange persists in making some kind of sense out of it all, and the opportunity of passion is always there, the possibility of breakthrough, driven by the intense necessity of discovering the thing that is missing. Wisdom has been defined as the ability 'to know the relative disposition of things', and that 'disposition' is constituted by the dynamics of love as the very essence of reality. The wise person, the sage, is therefore one who has 'a profound grasp of the obvious', yet it is only 'obvious' to one who is willing to live in exchange. The 'obvious' reality, the true 'relative disposition of things' is completely hidden from one who refuses to love. Knowledge there is, but it is a mechanistic, manipulative kind of knowledge.

We cannot, of course, talk about the knowledge, or Wisdom, of non-human creation except in a very limited and groping way. Sentience is, we now realize, more widespread in nature than we had imagined, but if it has 'knowledge' in some sense it certainly does not have self-consciousness, and it does not 'have' Wisdom, though it lives by her. And in this situation of the opacity of spheres human beings themselves can have only a very limited knowledge of 'how it works' because their own 'working' is so limited and distorted by the refusal of exchange in themselves. They are creatures whose being operates essentially in several different spheres, including the sphere of glory, but who are not able to perceive this except at 'odd' moments (in both senses). Human beings are not able, then, to 'use' the spheres whether for good or evil ends, by their own knowledge and power, except to a very limited extent. But they are aware in some obscure but persistent way that this ignorance and powerlessness is unnatural and wrong; they want that, wisdom, they itch and crave to know. Hence, through all recorded history, the urge to religion, and side by side with that (and often intertwined with it) the urge to probe the darkness by means of magical or near-magical operations. Although it is not possible to disentangle motives completely we can say broadly that the difference between religion and magic is that the one seeks wisdom and the other seeks knowledge. And the difference between wisdom and knowledge in this context is that knowledge is seen as a possession, to be used at the will of the owner, for good or ill, while wisdom is a gift, to be received with gratitude and recognized as part of the exchange of love. It is not for nothing that 'Wisdom' is the word taken up to define the nature of the Incarnate Word. Wisdom *is* exchange of divine life, love received and given back.

Without Wisdom there can be no full understanding of *why* exchange is the stuff of being. It *can* only appear as material for the exercise of power by the possessors of knowledge, though frequently the possessor of such knowledge fully intends, at least at first, to use it in order to 'do good'. This is why, for instance, 'white' witchcraft is so attractive. Healing power and divination are gifts which can bestow great benefits, but they easily slip from serving to dominating, since they are treated as 'possessions', and so the only criterion governing their use is the personal judgement of the person concerned, which is subject to all the hidden fears and cravings which influence human decisions. But the power is as great in the abuse as in the use. And this perhaps helps us to understand the enormous power of evil. The energy of love is *turned back on itself* and so ceases to be love, but remains as powerful as ever. It must be, in a way, even more powerful, because love is of its nature non-coercive. Love seeks a return of love which, since it must be free if it is love, cannot be extorted but only desired and invited. But the energy of the refusal of love has no such inhibition in the exercise of available power. It will use any means to get what it wants, which is more and more control. 'It' (or 'he' or 'she') fully believes that this *is* what is 'good', for there is no other. Love is strictly meaningless to such a will.

This is, of course, its limitation. The refusal of love means the impossibility of receiving wisdom, and so the refusal restricts the vision of reality to an extent which actually presents reality quite 'untruly'. What is seen is true but is only a small part of the truth, and even that part from a point of view which alters its whole

116

meaning. If, for instance, you try to interpret the behaviour of people who are genuinely in love while disallowing the possibility of genuine love then you are bound to reach some very odd conclusions about human motives; and any action based on those conclusions will be aberrant, from the lovers' point of view, though strictly logical and obvious from the point of view of the non-lover (Romeo's and Juliet's parents, for instance). This is true of all reductionist psychological and sociological theories which exclude precisely the elements which are most significant to the actual people they describe—and manipulate.

This kind of basic misunderstanding is precisely what we find Satan labouring under in the accounts of the Temptation. However we find it possible to think of the power of evil, Jesus must have represented a formidable challenge to it. He was not yet widely known, but the incident by the Jordan, when John baptized his cousin, was of a breakthrough kind (and one on a unique scale), and it must have created shock waves of awareness in minds sensitive to such things. Witches, and people who take the occult seriously and work at it, do become sensitive to events which have spiritual significance. This sensitivity can also be the result of a mystical gift associated with holiness, for instance in the case of the old man Simeon who recognized the extraordinary nature of the apparently very ordinary baby brought to the temple by his obscure parents, but it has no necessary connection with goodness. Some people are naturally and permanently sensitive, but some become sensitive for a while; for instance some kinds of mental illness are accompanied by powers of clairvoyance and of disconcerting thought-reading; also people under stress of danger can have this kind of awareness. But those involved in occult practices, or those who have fairly deliberately surrendered themselves to any kind of impulses they cannot control, will also be strongly aware of the presence of a 'contrary' power which is unnoticed by other people who lack this sensitivity. Such people may react with violent loathing to the presence of the energy of divine love in human beings or between them. (At the end of the last chapter I quoted St Paul's remarks about differing reactions to the 'scent' of holiness.) If this is so we can see that the underground 'seismograph' of spiritual reality must have registered that something quite extraordinary was going on around the young man from Nazareth. But, Satan needed

117

to know, what *kind* of thing? The state of mind of many in Israel was one of acute expectation, but the reasons and hopes associated with this expectation varied from those of pure longing for a kingdom of love and peace to thoughts of conquest and vengeance. The available interpretations in contemporary human minds of the nature of the power present in one who might be 'Messiah' were therefore ambiguous. 'Reading' through human minds, Satan recognized power in Jesus, on a scale he had not hitherto encountered. The idea that it could be the power of love was ruled out because love does not exist for him; therefore it must be the kind of power he recognizes and understands very well: the power to dominate and manipulate—to 'manage' the entire system. Satan does not, of course, 'manage' it as totally as he thinks, because there is this other element in the situation which he is incapable of seeing—the element of love. In encountering the phenomenon of Jesus, he necessarily interpreted the evidences of love as will-to-power gone wrong.

In the first Temptation, the tempter knows that the 'Son of God', the Messiah chosen by God, would have power to 'make these stones bread'. It is the kind of thing that Jesus actually did do not long afterwards, at Cana. This is one of the breakthroughs from one sphere of experience to another, and a Messiah can be expected to do this, but it need not be damaging to the grip of the power of evil if Satan can make sure that there is no *exchange* of spheres. If the power returns on itself, if the spheres, though breached, are kept separate, so that the 'everyday' world (where loaves of bread and stones reside) is simply plundered by a superior power for its own benefit, then no change will take place, the control will be unbroken. Such a 'Messiah' would pose no threat to Satan's dominion. He might even be a valuable ally.

The other two Temptations have the same character and purpose. Luke locates the last Temptation in Jerusalem, perhaps because he wanted, as usual, to emphasize the 'Jerusalem-oriented' nature of Jesus' career. In any case, although the supreme temptation summing up the others is clearly the one to world domination by worshipping the one to whom 'it has been committed', we can credibly read Luke's order of events as indicating that when this attempt had failed there was still the possibility of reducing the impact of that (from Satan's point of view) disastrous resistance.

118

This could be done by making sure that the inconvenient Messiah should at least establish his identity and mission in a way that would maintain an autonomy, a refusal of exchange.

But Jesus would not make stones into bread, nor make a spectacular descent from the Temple roof to conquer and reign as the heaven–sent and expected Messiah, nor seize the vast political power available to him; and to Satan's mind the reason for these refusals must be that he was not as powerful as he seemed. To the blindness of evil, evil's way must be the best, indeed the only way. So whatever scheme Jesus might be supposed to be hatching (he *must* have some scheme, after all, even if he would not admit it!) he could not possibly be a serious rival. It was important however to know what that scheme might be, and Luke tells us that 'the devil left him' but only 'to return at the appointed time' when, perhaps, the sense of a greater threat to the dominance of evil than Satan had supposed possible was becoming apparent.

There is nothing in the accounts to suggest that the tempter on any occasion felt a need to use guile. He does deceive, but only because he is necessarily self-deceived. He is not, on this occasion, pretending anything; he is asking Jesus to act on known facts: 'You *can* do this, it's obviously sensible, so do it.' Even in the vision of 'all the kingdoms of the world' and the offer, 'Worship me, and it shall all be yours', he is not promising what he cannot perform. All this *has* been 'committed' to him, and he can 'give it to anyone'. He is stating a fact and drawing an obvious conclusion—obvious to him, that is. He can see no other sensible way to act on the facts, because he himself can only see created things as means to reinforcement of the power that is naturally his. He quotes Scripture, not to deceive, but because, for instance, the text about protection by angels fits in very well with his own notion of the only proper use of the power present in the higher spheres.

The way I have described this makes Satan sound very 'human', or at least 'personal'. This is how, in fact, the 'Prince of this World' is presented to us, in these accounts and also in many direct references to him by Jesus, especially in St John's Gospel. Jesus finds the poetic form needed for the truth. Satan comes through to us as very much a personal adversary, one to be reckoned with, even though he is, in the event, completely overthrown. His hold on the cosmos, claimed so bodily in the Temptation account in Luke, is to be broken precisely by the one thing he could not envisage, which was unconditional love. Jesus had good reason to know the force of evil intimately, not only through the temptation but through all his healing ministry. And if he himself habitually talked about it in these very personal and poetically precise terms, then we do well to take him seriously. It is certainly inevitable that he would use to describe the experience of evil the language of poetry culturally available to him, but there seems to be more to it than that. There is a sense of intimate personal encounter, rather than of customary expression, in the terms and images used by the evangelists about Satan as Jesus experienced him, and it seems unlikely that any modification of Jesus's words by the writer would take this particular direction. We might expect them to formalize a little, to put obscure references into language more meaningful to contemporaries, but we would not expect them to insert that note of immediacy with which, for instance, John has Jesus say that 'the Prince of this World is coming soon', during the discourse at the last Supper. This sounds like an inner knowledge of a very precise kind, similar to the foreknowledge of his passion which he had tried to communicate to his un-hearing followers. Just as he foretold his passion because he knew it *had to be* that way, this is a knowledge of how death 'works'. It is confirmed by modern studies of the dying process. One kind of refusal of exchange is the refusal, or denial, of death; but to be open to death is to be open to evil, for death is evil. By going knowingly to death Jesus was, in a sense, commanding death, that is, commanding the coming of Satan. This 'Prince' was 'coming soon' because he had no choice, but he was coming to his destruction.

There is, after all, no other evidence than the words of Jesus as the evangelists give them. We can, if we choose, explain them away without too much difficulty, but the fact remains that the New Testament takes for granted the existence of a category of being which we have traditionally referred to as 'angelic', and which is understood as a powerful and significant part of the eternal exchanges by which God communicates his life to his creatures, and they to each other, and to him, with him and from him. There seems to be no reason whatever except prejudice why we should not accept this and go on to ask, as we must, searching questions about what and how and why—knowing, of course, that most of

120

them are unanswerable. But if we can accept the fact, without being thereby tied down to particular interpretations of it, we shall find that it makes sense of many quite usual phenomena, as well as of the New Testament references to angels and other spiritual 'powers'.

We can, however, build on the developing theology of Satan in Scripture already referred to and suggest (only suggest) one possible way of understanding the 'evil one'. In earlier writings, as we saw, evil happenings are attributed to the anger of the Lord, and even the evil wills of men are under his order, so that in a well-known instance the Lord is said to 'harden the heart of Pharaoh' against the Israelites. Later, Satan becomes a 'delegate' of the Lord, to test or punish human beings. Finally, in the New Testament, he is an active and personally malevolent 'adversary', who is to be cast out of heaven and overcome. It seems there is a differentiation occurring *in human minds* in this development, and it parallels Paul's description of how 'Law' and 'Sin' are related. 'Sin existed in the world', he wrote to the Romans, 'long before the Law was given. There was no law and so no one could be accused of the sin of "law-breaking", yet death reigned overall, from Adam to Moses'. In the same way, the 'evil one' is not recognized as a 'separate' being for a time. The source of the power even of evil is known to be the Lord. There are no 'other gods' opposed to him as his equals, so all must derive from him. It is at this stage of moral reflection in a pagan milieu that we can perceive Pan or similar 'nature gods' as necessary and beneficial even in their erratic and destructive aspects. The great and uncontrollable powers of nature are numerous, and they have their equivalent in the 'a-moral' impulses in human beings which are creative and demand outlet beyond social norms, as, for instance, in the Dionysian cults. Death and destruction are the work of the gods also, and in the Hindu pantheon Shiva is both creator and destroyer. But in Jewish minds, in a culture whose experience of divine power is unique, the notion of a 'separated' evil develops gradually. They observe and reflect and find it increasingly impossible to see evil events and people as manifestations of the will of the Lord who has saved and guided them, whose care for them is so 'personal' and intimately loving. And the more acute becomes the sense of God's communicated Being as love, the more it becomes clear that the 'evil one' is a perversion, is 'opposed' to God, and so must be opposed by the true servant of God. Satan is 'driven out'

121

of heaven, he is no longer a 'delegate' of the Lord, nor even the Accuser; he has no part in heaven any more. There is a legend that, when Jesus died, there was a cry through the world of the old gods: 'Great Pan is dead!' The coming and death and resurrection of Jesus made it impossible any longer to experience the powers represented by Pan as divine or 'worshipful'. They were, and are, important constituents of the psyche and cannot safely be suppressed, but neither must they be treated as gods, as many people in our time are trying to do. If they are so treated they soon become 'devils', and so Pan gave us our favourite devil image. But they must be brought to consciousness and identified, and may then be 'converted'. This stage of response to evil is now becoming culturally, as well as individually, possible, and I shall have to return to this.

This is what happens in people's minds, reflecting on the notion of evil. But is there more to it than this? It seems possible to suggest that this development in human intellectual, moral and spiritual response to evil both reflected and brought about a change in the 'evil one', whatever 'he' may be. We have to be careful not to think of Milton's kind of Satan, a superb and very 'human' kind of being. We are thinking (or trying to think) of something utterly non-human, not existing in human categories of space and time at all, and not necessarily having the kind of 'boundaries' of personality by which we recognize human beings as distinct individuals. Is it imaginable that a 'being' could 'choose itself'? Could an 'angelic' being take its nature as love, from the love which made it a 'chooser', and so 'become' itself, and become so more and more, eternally, in unimpeded exchange with the infinite Exchanges who are Love? Might such beings perhaps also become *more* 'themselves' by sharing in the exchanges between the love of the Creator and those physical creatures who also are the overflow of that Love? If so, could not this happen (in reverse) for evil also? If it be 'angelic' nature to be 'chooser' of its own being, there could be a choosing of refusal, as I suggested. But this would not be a 'finished' situation. The choice *is* the being and must continue to choose itself. But if it cannot (having refused to do so) choose the love which gives it being, the choice of refusal means that it is always 'hungry' and will 'eat' (that is, 'choose to be') anything that is not love. The speculations of human beings about the nature of the power of evil in the world are articulations of a deep struggle *within* the psyche, the struggle first to differentiate and then to cast out evil. Could these 'unconscious contents' be the 'food' of the power of evil itself? If so, the two processes would complement and reinforce each other. As human beings strove to understand evil, especially their own evil, and to 'deal with' it intellectually and spiritually, so Satan 'ate' the psychic energy created in this way, and in his turn brought to bear on the human psyche this increasingly defined energy of malevolence and of a huge hunger for perverse being.

In Charles Williams' novel *War in Heaven* there is a passage in which three kinds of evil will are concentrated on a person in the story, and they form a progression, for the first is simply the perversion of genuine religion, a desire for power in order to reach the ultimate secret and sacrifice to It. At this stage,

> It trembled with desires natural to man . . . not by such passions was hell finally peopled and the last rejection found. But . . . it was controlled and directed by mightier powers . . . There impinged upon him the knowledge of all hateful and separating and deathly things: madness and tormenting disease and the vengeance of gods. This was the hunger with which creation preys upon itself, a supernatural famine that has no relish except for the poisons that waste it. This was the second death that cannot die, and it ran actively through that world of immortalities on a hungry mission of death . . . the third stream of energy passed over him. . . . This was no longer mission or desire, search or propaganda or hunger; this was rejection absolute. No moral mind could conceive a desire which was not based on a natural and right desire; even the hunger for death was but a perversion of the death which precedes all holy birth. But of every conceivable and inconceivable desire this was the negation. This was desire itself sick, but not unto death; rejection which tore all things asunder and swept them with it in its fall through the abyss.

This rejection, the refusal of exchange, desires only what it has to have to keep it in being, but that being feeds on destruction and must destroy: that is its self-chosen being. This 'explanation' does at least suggest why the Tempter was so eager and persistent in his

123

approach to Jesus, for here was potential 'food' of an unprecedented quality. He left him, then, but only to 'return at the proper time'.

It follows from all this that the knowledge which the Evil One has is bound to be always inadequate and misleading, since his choice of sources of being is limited to those areas where love is absent. (There can be *neutral* areas; but since 'Great Pan is dead' even in such apparently harmless things as astrology and 'table-turning', the innocent but muddled mind may be very open to the gradual infiltration of evil through what are potentially obsessive 'hobbies'.) And his power, therefore, is limited in the same way. Evil spirits must be limited by their ignorance of that love the refusal of which makes them what they are. They have to work *within the limits assigned to them by love*.

So when Jesus went into the desert he went deliberately, 'led by the Spirit' in order to be tempted. It was necessary to him to encounter this other power. Love required it, and so love provided the setting in which Satan could work. If we look at it from this other point of view we can see that this was, for Jesus, another of those experiences of breakthrough. It came immediately after he had been recognized by John the Baptist when he, with many others, came to the Jordan to be baptized. This recognition, signalized by the Baptist and awesomely articulated and confirmed by the coming of the Spirit and the Voice of the Father, was overwhelming in its impact. Things had, no doubt, been stirring in his mind before that. His thought and longings drove him to seek baptism, and to accept his cousin's reluctance to baptize him not with surprise but with acknowledgement and quiet authority. The awesome response to his action made it impossible, for the time being, to resume life in the category of everydayness. He was led or driven by the Spirit into the desert because he now required the experience of utter loneliness. It was necessary that he should penetrate, at this early stage of his mission, to the roots of life where the deeper exchanges take place, where human passion embraces and is embraced by God in the joy of differentiated love. But this is also the place where the power of evil—that is, of perverted exchange—is strongest, because (the conscious mind being powerless in this region) it is not rationally recognizable and manageable. He fasted, because he was (we may fairly guess) physically changed by his experience in the Jordan so that temporarily the body was not the primary medium of love, but subordinate to the intense need to be aware of an encounter in which the physical as such was unable to help. It seems likely that 'he was hungry' at the end of it because he was 'coming out' of this condition. (This is certainly what happens normally when a tremendous spiritual change seems, for a while, to have suspended ordinary physical needs. After a time, they reassert themselves.)

Perhaps it would be nearer the truth to suggest that the experience of the temptation was a continuation and extension of the breakthrough by the Jordan. It was a discovery by experience of some of the scope and meaning of that tremendous naming: 'This is my Son, the Beloved'. If he is the Servant, as Isaiah prophesied, if he is the Anointed, the Chosen one, then what follows? Satan also wanted an answer to that question. He and Jesus found it out together, but their answers are different.

Perhaps we may guess that for this breakthrough the remote preparation had been the news of the Baptist's preaching as it percolated through the gossip of Nazareth, bringing to the surface the obscure hints and longings of years. And so it seems the final challenge and response came in two stages, the Jordan experience only finding its meaning in the desert. In that wilderness, isolated from the past, from other people, from everyday consciousness, Jesus entered willingly and urgently into a loneliness so absolute that only two things could touch it: love, and rejection of love. Loneliness and temptation go together, and if you want to encounter temptation pure, then the desert in some form or other is the place you have to go, which is, of course, why most of us avoid it 'like the devil'.

The little bit of information we have is no doubt only the tip of the iceberg. Luke says Jesus was 'tempted for forty days', and there is in any case a terrible timelessness about this kind of experience, which must be measured by intensity rather than by time. (But time, also, is an element in real loneliness, for time isolates. Only a neurotic person can be very lonely in one day.) The little bit we know makes clear how the temptation was used, and I prefer the word 'used' to the word 'overcome' to describe what Jesus did with it, because if we seriously accept that he was led by the Spirit to this encounter, then he needed it and had to work with it.

All three of Jesus's answers to the tempter's very practical sugges-

125

tions amount to saying, 'Yes, that's perfectly possible, but there is another element in the situation, which forbids it.' This other element, which of his (and its) very nature Satan cannot recognize, is love. God's being is love, he is only known in his total self-giving 'within' the divine nature and through and in creation. Creation, therefore, in its turn can only truly come into being in responsive self-giving, as I suggested in the second chapter. Jesus, incarnate God, makes that response as a fully physical human being in, and as, and with, creation. His being, therefore, is 'by bread' but not 'by bread alone'. Bread only makes sense as gift; if claimed 'alone', as a right, it is no longer life-giving, it only feeds what Paul calls 'the body of this death', the thing destined to destruction by its own refusal.

In the same way, total dominion is offered to Jesus in return for the rejection of love, for the demand to worship Satan means to be subservient to his principle of action. By such a denial, the servant of Satan can share in his master's power to manipulate and 'feed on' created categories, unhampered by any considerations except those which serve his own ends, at least until it becomes apparent (as it must) that there can be no final sharing in the exercise of this kind of power. In the end, the servant of Satan must either beat him at his own game or be swallowed up by him. But meanwhile the possibilities are dazzling. To this suggestion, Jesus's reply is the same one: true worship is return of love, it is pure gift, responding to pure gift. To serve God alone is, in fact, to be filled with his Spirit, because that is the kind of 'thing' love is, but that love claims nothing, possesses nothing. To claim or possess is to kill what one claims and possesses.

The final suggestion—one which, in one form or another, was to be made to Jesus all through his public career—was that he might use his proper and necessary power of living 'across' the spheres in order to impress people with the reality of his mission. Since it was what nearly everyone seemed to want, including some of his best friends, it caused him great agony of mind. His dilemma was, often, that even to do things out of pure love would *appear* to be a demonstration of power of the kind Satan was suggesting. To heal, and feed, and teach are proper signs of the kingdom, as his message to John the Baptist in prison explained. But what kind of kingdom would these things indicate to the spectators? Over and over, the

126

answer was that the kind of kingdom people wanted, and thought they saw offered to them by Jesus, was Satan's kind of kingdom, in which bread is not gift but possession, and power is power to dominate and to manage and to punish enemies, and supernatural power is a weapon of war against unbelievers. Jesus's answer, in the desert and every other time, is, 'You must not try to manipulate God'. You cannot *use* love as a means to an end. He is End and Beginning and also Exchange between beginning and end, since he is love.

After it was all over, Matthew says, angels came and ministered to him. The spiritual power which refuses love gave way to the messengers of love, the agents of Exchange. The all-too-familiar wilderness of 'realism' blossomed into a garden of exchanged love.

Finally, from John's Gospel, we have a comment on the results of the ordeal through which Jesus had passed in his days of loneliness and temptation. For it seems that, leaving the wilderness, Jesus came back to the Jordan area, near the place where the Baptist was still at work. There he 'hung around', unattached, still disoriented by his experience, perhaps, and not clear about the manner of any renewed contacts with the world of everyday, since he himself was so deeply changed by his period of initiation. He seemed to be waiting for some signal. The Baptist was his only possible 'contact', because John understood to some extent what it was all about, but even John was remote. John, however, did understand, intuitively. Seeing Jesus 'coming towards him' (but it seems he never actually got there), he told those nearby, 'Look, there is the Lamb of God'. And then he told them what had been revealed to him at the time of the baptism. Next day the same thing happened, and John repeated the strange title, this time explicitly addressing two of his own disciples.

John clearly intended these two to do what they did do, which was to follow Jesus, and so to set him off on the beginnings of his public life. Perhaps John knew that he needed that 'trigger', but the words he used to announce the identity of his successor who, as he said, 'existed before' him are words which have echoed through Christian liturgies from the beginning until now: 'Behold the Lamb of God'.

It was clear to John, seeing Jesus newly returned from the wilderness, that something had happened to him which made him not just the 'chosen one of God' but one chosen in a special sense. He was the suffering Servant who would be, in Isaiah's image, 'pierced through for our faults', 'like a lamb that is led to the slaughterhouse'. This is the one, says John, who 'takes away the sin of the world', and the image links up with the image of the Passover lamb, whose blood on the doorposts of Israel ensured the people's salvation in the day of punishment. The Passover lamb was the symbol of freedom, of that great rescue from the evil power of Egypt, the 'house of bondage' which is sin. 'Behold the Lamb of God' who has already taken on that role which will lead him to death. Already he knows, though perhaps only obscurely, where he is going, and he knows it because he has entered willingly into an intimate struggle with evil in its most pure form, at the point at which its power is most clearly a *divine* power, poured out by divine Love which cannot help giving itself because that is its nature. The power of love is constantly poured out, so the rejection of love continues to be possible. If it were not so, there would be no possibility of the acceptance and return of love, either. So in encountering the tremendous majesty and knowledge of Satan Jesus was encountering that which was most intimately his own, the very love which was his life, his own Spirit, the Spirit of Love herself. It was necessary that, there in the desert, he should make the choice of absolute love in the face of absolute rejection, both of them real possibilities. In his case this was infinitely more so than for any other human being, since in this man the possibility of love was literally limitless; therefore also he experienced to the uttermost the possibility of the rejection of love. What that meant to one who said that 'my food is to do the will of my Father' and told his dearest beloved that 'the Father and I are one' we cannot even begin to imagine. But it shows us well enough what we mean when we talk about the problem of evil, evil which is so obviously real, and powerful, and yet *is not*. It *is not* because there is no such thing as evil in itself. As Dame Julian tells us, sin is 'no thing'. It is the perversion of love, no more and no less than that. And it was the work of Jesus to make evident in his own body the ultimate unreality of evil.

4   Resurrection

This chapter is the centre of the book from which it takes its meaning. All the rest depends on it, for here we are at the heart of things, and at the crucial point—and both those images are meant with all possible literalness.

The centre (and the beginning, the end and all in between) is Jesus, the Christ. It is the divine flesh-taking, and at the heart of this is the concrete mystery we refer to as resurrection, which reaches out, and is reached to, by things that I have to put in other chapters. The 'passionate' character of all reality was shown to us in the mysteriously familiar example of Romantic passion, yet it is not Romance which gives meaning to the flesh-taking, but the other way around. The 'Way of Exchange' is the nature of all being, but just how it is spiritual and eternal as well as cultural and ecological we could only know by seeing it in the person and work of Jesus. This is why I used an incident from the Gospel accounts in order to discover the way of exchange, and of breakthrough, going on in his own life. And the strangest question of all is the one everyone asks, implicitly or explicitly, in every human age and society: *Why is there evil, and what does it mean?* This question is posed concretely and fully, and answered concretely and fully, in the life of Jesus who is our redemption, but in order to talk about redemption there has to be some language about sin already available. Therefore that chapter had to come before this one but linked to it by its use of the experience of the temptation as the 'way in' to an understanding of sin and evil.

The chapters which follow this one are also 'concentric' to it. We need to follow up some of the implications of the sheer fleshliness of the flesh-taking and think about the human body under the impact of that event: Christ's body, in all senses. Not really separated from all this are what are called the 'last things', though 'last' must mean not only chronologically 'last' but ultimate and eternal, coming under the heading of eschatology, and what that tells us of the nature of the Church now and baptism as somehow the frame of all this. These things derive their being and their meaning from the supreme and constitutive instance of passionate breakthrough which is the flesh-taking itself, and so do the activities of people who are the Church, in the area of 'morality', prayer, politics and vocation.

Is it possible to see the wholeness of the life of Jesus according to the dynamics of passion already discussed, and having those same Romantic qualities? It is always too easy to read back into history the things one wants to see. 'History' is, in any case, the pattern of past events as laid out by the historian in order to give meaning to the present. In the case of Jesus of Nazareth we have a more bizarre situation than in that of any other historical human being, because of the claim that he not only occurred in history but was also the meaning of history, backwards and forwards. But in considering the flesh-taking as 'passionate' it is best to take the categories and characteristics set out in the context of the Romantic experience and simply see what emerges. This procedure helps us to be precise, and precision is what is needed, so that we may be at least in that respect not too unworthy of the very precise and practical character of the actual message of Jesus as it is given to us by the New Testament writers.

The chronological sequence is required to provide the context, both before and after, for any passionate breakthrough. There is no problem about this. The remote preparation is clear. The history of the Chosen People known through its own historical records, its stories and myths of origin and its prophets, had more and more seemed to point forward to some event, or person, or probably both, which would somehow 'fulfil' all that had gone before. By hindsight, as is always the case, the hints and guesses look much more prescient than they can have seemed when they were preached and pondered and written about, but it is clear that they were recognized very early to be hints and guesses about something of ultimate importance to the whole people. As time went on it was seen that they concerned not only the people of Israel but all people, and finally that they involved, somehow, the whole natural order as well. The images of the Messianic Kingdom are a late development in the literature of Israel. The experience of invasions, and finally of the destruction of the kingdom and of Jerusalem with the long

130

exile which followed, raised the chosen people's expectations to a plane of universality because that was the only level on which they could survive once the hope of worldly peace and prosperity had been dashed. This is clearly not at all unlike the process by which the vague longings of adolescence are focussed at first on a pop-idol, a journey to some exotic place or a motor-bike, which later show themselves to be inadequate to symbolize the increasingly important but still obscure longing for an experience of meaning which will change everything. There follows, typically, the stage at which poetry, or music, or religion, is the means by which the deep longing is both expressed and fed.

But none of this is enough, however intense the longing may be, and in Israel it was indeed intense, as even the most superficial reading of the later prophets shows. But the stage of immediate preparation has to consist of some experience which dislocates the person, shaking up habitual ways of thinking and acting, creating one of those weak spots at which the demand for breakthrough to the new and prophetically promised life can be experienced. Without this no real change can occur, although a person or society, under pressure of such need, can produce from within itself some convincing counterfeits of genuine breakthrough. 'Falling in love with love is falling for make-believe', said a popular song, and it is common enough. Social panaceas preached by demagogues, packaged 'fulfilment' via meditation or sexual harmony, the 'peace and joy' of the kind of religious movements which flourish in troubled times and invariably concentrate on inner states: all these and many others are ways in which the longing for eternal life (for a time and after a fashion) satisfies itself with something which is not genuinely a breakthrough because nothing has broken, all is being manufactured *within* the state of imprisonment, making it tolerable and therefore even strengthening it.

The real breakthrough comes to the one who is vulnerable, whose self-confident enclosure has been worn thin or loosened by the impact of some disturbing experience. For Israel, this experience was the Roman occupation. To be conquered was not new. The Jewish people had known invasion and oppression and slavery and managed to make theological sense of it. What they had not known was the combination of subjection with comparative prosperity and the right to the free exercise of their religion, but only by permission

131

of their foreign rulers. Rome did not, normally, 'oppress' conquered people or destroy their laws, and the Jews found themselves, as a nation, probably more prosperous than they had been since the time of Solomon. Roman rule was severe and its justice rough and swift, the poor were heavily taxed and suffered accordingly, but the nation as a whole had the advantage of Roman trade and communications, and even the poor were better off under the Roman judicial system than they had often been under their own unpredictable rulers. So the Jewish people under Roman rule were humiliated yet not oppressed, prospering under a peace they loathed, practising their ancient faith by favour of, and goaded by, pagans who regarded Yahweh as just one more tribal god.

This was an experience for which nothing in their religious culture had prepared them. They could not integrate it into any of their categories of thought and behaviour, and as a result there were successive and interacting episodes of anger, despair, obstinate hope, apocalyptic or transcendental religious cults, occasional violent revolts and constant minor 'resistance' movements. There were attitudes of passivity or of cynical opportunism. This is what we should expect; it is what we see in individuals under similar conditions, though naturally in the individual one single type of reaction tends to predominate, according to temperament, whereas in a whole nation many kinds of reaction coexist at one time and none predominates.

We can say with some certainty, from the available evidence, that this was the case in Israel, and we can see at once that this was exactly the kind of experience which creates a weak spot at which breakthrough can occur. It always occurs at one particular point, even though the thing itself is potentially 'total' in its effect and in practice quickly affects the whole situation. But it has to start somewhere, and the 'somewhere' often looks (and in a sense is) quite accidental. Dante might have encountered a different girl, or he might have got himself romantically embroiled in the feverish political causes of his time, or he might have gone off on pilgrimage, fired with a vision of Jerusalem through the eloquence of a popular preacher. In fact, he met Beatrice, and so 'it' happened in and through her, for which after ages give thanks.

In Israel, the weak spot was a also a girl. It was a particular Jewish girl, of royal descent but of otherwise obscure and ordinary

132

family. In the web of exchanged life many threads crossed at this point. Some are clear, some are conjecture. The influences on the nation as a whole I have sketched. They worked with especial force on a sensitive and ardent temperament such as we can discern in even the scanty scriptural references to Mary of Nazareth. She was a thoughtful and 'interior' person, evidently, but her thoughts were the thoughts of her people, its prophecies and hopes and hates.

In his book *The Virgin*, Geoffrey Ashe has speculated that Mary's family drew its spirituality from one of those religious movements in Israel which were based on the messianic expectation. Since in Judaism body and spirit are one person, to meditate ardently on the hope of salvation was to speculate when and where the Messiah would come and, no doubt, of whom he would be born. In such an atmosphere (and the existence of such a mentality at the time is not in doubt), the development of a girl who was spiritually gifted and temperamentally highly wrought would be rapid and extraordinary.

But to this soul, as to all who are to live, the decisive moment of breakthrough had to come, the one which is not necessarily final and not necessarily complete but in virtue of which all that comes after becomes possible. It seems that the moment of breakthrough for Mary was also the beginning of the breakthrough of salvation for all creation. What was the 'immediate preparation' for her? We can only guess. Perhaps it was the imminence of marriage, a concrete and practical reality which challenged a spiritual development so intense and unusual as to be, necessarily, very private and very solitary. Perhaps, even, she was actually in love, for this also would shake up the tendency for concentration on the inner vision which we might expect in such a girl. One kind of breakthrough prepares the way for another kind. This is a law of spiritual development, as we saw in the study of the transfiguration.

Whatever the nature of the sequence in her, a moment came at which a unique demand was made on her. The uniqueness of this demand matched the uniqueness of her need and preparedness, as the transfiguration occurrence matched the uniqueness of the person and the moment, and as the multiplication of loaves happened because of the same kind of coincidence of person and need. Her response was a self-giving so total that she was, as it were, subsumed in that giving. It *was* herself. But the event we are talking about is

133

the conception of a baby, which is above all a bodily event. The perfection of exchange in body and spirit is evoked marvellously by Charles Williams in a passage from his novel, *All Hallows Eve*:

> It had been a Jewish girl who, at the command of the Voice which sounded in her ears, in her heart, along her blood and through the central cells of her body, had uttered everywhere in herself the perfect Tetragrammaton. What the High Priest vicariously spoke among the secluded mysteries of the Temple, she substantially pronounced to God. Redeemed from all division in herself, whole and identical in body and soul and spirit, she uttered the Word, and the Word became flesh in her.

Mary, mother of the Word, had much to learn, later. She made mistakes, she did not understand, she suffered. But from that time her being, her very body, was the Being of the One to whom she had assented.

Anybody *could* have been the God-bearer. Somebody, some particular body, had to be and was. She is the perfect image of exchange, the 'gate of heaven' through which sphere after sphere of concentric glory is opened, and excluded human kind may once more come to its own proper source and end and self in the giving and receiving of love in the Trinity.

> O Virgin Mother, Daughter of thy Son,
> Lowliest and loftiest of created nature,
> Fixed goal to which the eternal counsels run. . . .

prays St Bernard in Dante's hymn to Mary, but the 'fixed goal', the point to and from which all the history draws, the trysting-place of divine love, is in reality not fixed but is rather the point of exchange, the weak spot at which human pride and self-sufficiency was breached and the floods of the Spirit flowed through the gap. Charles Williams' compactness of imagery brings all to the same point when in 'The Founding of the Company' (*The Region of the Summer Stars*) he considers how those who know the exchange are:

> . . . each alone and none alone,
> bearing and borne,

134

as the Flesh-taking sufficed
the God-bearer to make her
a sharer in Itself.

For Mary is alone, as all are alone, yet she only becomes her
most personal self as she comes to a point of knowing in the acceptance of being given and received, 'bearing and borne'. In the willed
exchange of love the divine *amour voulu* is laid on her and expressed
in her, and so she is never alone, for she is the door between the
worlds.

There is an extraordinary ambiguity about the figure of Mary.
Apart from Jesus himself there never was a concrete historical
personage so bedecked with interwoven images. It is significant, for
instance, that as soon as the developing liturgies of Christianity
began to differentiate the cult of Mary and celebrate her Son in her
at separate festivals they drew on the imagery used to refer to the
feminine Godhead, divine Wisdom Herself. There is an interesting
counterpoint in the way in which this imagery is applied to Mary
and the way it is used in the New Testament to describe the nature
and role of Jesus, the Word and Wisdom of God. It was a misplaced
and needless fear of magnifying Mary at the expense of her Son
which caused the compilers of the revised Missal and Offices of the
Roman Rite to remove almost all the Wisdom passages from the
liturgical celebrations in honour of Mary. Poetry is of its nature
allusive, one image reinforces another, or complements it, or strikes
sparks off it, and two images may gain in significance by contrast.
The poetry of Wisdom can often illuminate the breakthrough of the
flesh-taking by the way it describes the role of Mary, to whom the
human body of Jesus owed its existence and its actual physical
characteristics. The fact that both Mary and Jesus can be evoked
by the same image seems only appropriate.

In the old form of Matins for feasts of the Blessed Virgin occurred
the magnificent poem from the book of Proverbs, describing Wisdom as co-creator. The Greek translators, as well as cautious modern ones fearful of a feminine creator, translate the Hebrew as
'Yahweh created me . . . before the oldest of his works', but St
Jerome's Latin, bolder than they, translated the word as 'possessed',
which makes a great deal more sense, whether one thinks of Wisdom
as a 'quality' of God or as his Image and active power. Also, that

most unambiguously Trinitarian of all the Fathers, St Athanasius, was quite clear that the references to Wisdom as 'created' did not alter the fact that the description referred to the pre-existent Word of God: 'Because his form and likeness is created in God's work, he says as though of himself, "The Lord created me in the beginning of his ways in his work" ':

Yaweh created me when his purpose first unfolded,
before the oldest of his works.
From everlasting I was firmly set,
from the beginning, before earth came into being.
The deep was not, when I was born,
there were no springs to gush with water. . .
(Prov. 8:22–4)

In the 'Little Office' of Mary, the Matins reading is from the deutero-canonical book of Ecclesiasticus (Sirach), describing how Wisdom, coming forth 'from the mouth of the Most High', was sent to pitch her tent among God's people. Viewed in a certain way, this is a poem about the search for, and the discovery of, such a weak spot in the human race as might enable divine love to be recognized, and so to enter into the human world and be one with it:

I came forth from the mouth of the Most High
  and covered the earth like a mist.
I had my tent in the heights
  and my throne in a pillar of cloud.
Alone I encircled the vaults of the sky,
  and walked on the bottom of the deeps.
Over the waves of the sea and over the whole earth
  and over every people and nation I held sway.
Among all these I searched for rest
  and looked to see in whose territory I might pitch camp.
Then the creator of all things instructed me
  and he who created me fixed a place for my tent.
He said 'Pitch your tent in Jacob
  and make Israel your inheritance.'
From eternity, in the beginning, he created me,
  and for eternity I shall remain.

136

I ministered before him in the holy tabernacle,
  and thus was I established in Sion.
In the beloved city he has given me rest,
  and in Jerusalem I wield my authority.
I have taken root in a privileged people,
  in the Lord's property, in his inheritance.
I have grown tall as a cedar in Lebanon,
  as a cypress on Mount Hermon. . . .
I am like a vine putting out graceful shoots
  my blossoms bear the fruit of glory and wealth.
Approach me, you who desire me,
  and take your fill of my fruit,
For memories of me are sweeter than honey,
  inheriting me is sweeter than the honeycomb.
They who eat me shall hunger for more,
  they who drink me shall thirst for more.
Whoever listens to me will never have to blush,
  whoever acts as I dictate will never sin.
          (Ecclus. 24:3–13, 17–22)

Poets seldom fully know what they are writing about, at least at
the time of writing. The writer of this poem certainly could not
guess that, centuries later, his word would proclaim with unique
force the turning-point of history. But if all life is exchange, through
all the spheres, then the images of poetry are not confined to the
categories of meaning which are consciously in the mind of the poet.
He, indeed, receives them from conscious and also from deeply
unconscious sources, and so he gives them, and from him they are
received by others, and again given, changing and growing as they
are thrown from one to another through many themes and ages, as
the underlying reality is rediscovered and recreated. And ambiguity
is of the essence of poetry, since it must speak at many levels and
stir the depths of the mind in ways that words of single value—
prose words—cannot do.

So here it is indeed possible to read these passages, among others,
to express the reality of Jesus, and clearly he recognized this himself,
for there are obvious echoes of this particular passage in the words
of Jesus as John recreates them. But these words also express the
theological reality of Mary, in whom Wisdom found her place, the

137

woman from whom he took human life; neither will be confused with, or distracted by, the other, but rather each illuminates the other. In these and other passages (but these two must suffice me) in which poets echo and re-echo an awareness too great for any to handle alone we come closest to grasping the reality of the coming of Christ, the Word and Wisdom of God.

For Wisdom is also the 'Word' of God. She is his self-utterance, the exhalation of his very being in a total giving of love. So Paul, trying to express the incredible reality of Christ, took up the imagery of two different poets of divine Wisdom. He did not simply reproduce them but, as a poet should, created from them a new poem, giving to the older images a new precision and depth of meaning. 'I was by his side, a master craftsman', the author of Proverbs makes Wisdom say (further on in the passage quoted earlier). Wisdom, who was 'possessed' in the beginning by the Lord, comes (in the book of Ben Sirach) 'forth from the mouth of the Most High, and covers the earth like a mist', which penetrates every reach and detail of creation, the depths of the sea and of human minds. And the greatest of the poets of Wisdom is sure that 'alone she can do all', because she is 'breath of the power of God, pure emanation of the glory of the Almighty . . . she is a reflection of the eternal light, untarnished mirror of God's active power, image of his goodness'. So, with utter conviction of the rightness of it, Paul defined the meaning of Christ, not as king or victim, as healer or teacher, but simply as exchange, as the 'place' in and through which divine love is poured out, to create and then to redeem, and so to give back to the Father, 'reconciling' everything in his own being, whose only definition is love:

He is the image of the unseen God
and the first-born of all creation
for in him were created
all things in heaven and earth:
everything visible and everything invisible,
Thrones, Dominions, Sovereignties, Powers—
all things were created through him and for him.
Before anything was created, he existed,
and he holds all things in unity.
(Col. 1:15–17)

138

So far it could be simply Wisdom, as the old covenant knew her, that Paul described. But Paul knew Wisdom in another way, which thrusts the poem and the experience it expresses and the fact itself into a different category, the category of fleshliness; not just as 'penetrated' by Wisdom but as herself, as a body, 'planted' in a people. In that people she grows in and through them as the point of exchange in such concrete and ascertainable ways as we have seen, until the final breakthrough makes possible another kind of bodily being. 'The Church is his body', says Paul, astonishingly carrying on the passage as if this statement were the most obvious corollary to what he had just said; and to him it clearly was:

> . . . now the Church is his body,
> he is its head.
> As he is the Beginning
> he was the first to be born from the dead,
> so that he should be first in every way
> because God wanted all perfection
> to be found in him
> and all things to be reconciled through him and for him,
> everything in heaven and everything on earth,
> when he made peace
> by his death on the cross.
>   (Col. 1:18–20)

The transition from 'the Beginning' of creation to the one 'born from the dead' is one movement, yet it is abrupt, it is not a smooth or effortless movement. This 'reconciliation' is not effected by the serene sway of Wisdom in creation. 'He made peace by his death on the cross.' This is the passionate breakthrough, by which his body, the Church, comes into existence. This 'body' is a *conscious*, known and knowing organism of exchanged life, so that the Church is nothing other than the *amour voulu* of Jesus at work in individual, concrete men and women, evoking in them a response to the love which 'made peace by his death on the cross'.

But in the transition from the gracious self-gift of Wisdom to the uttermost extreme of passionate sacrifice there has to be a 'medium of exchange'. There has to be flesh, .human being; but Love does not 'take' body, it requests it, it avows neediness, it waits upon the

139

reply of the beloved. And this cannot be a generalized one; again, there is need of the particular response. Mary's *fiat* is indeed the response of creation to its Lover, but it is that because it is her own, her personal und unique response of love. And once her reply is given she becomes, herself, uniquely the place of exchange, the gate of heaven by which much traffic must pass in and out. But she is not merely passive, hers also is *amour voulu*, a willed and conscious co-operation in the work of recreation. How else could hers be the reply of all bodies—of all life—to its creator and redeemer? She *must* be co-worker, or she does not make human sense. She, the body in which his body is formed, must then be able to say, in her own different and distinct way; 'From eternity, in the beginning, he created me, and for eternity I shall remain. I ministered before him in the holy Tabernacle, and thus was I established in Sion.' She must say, with absolute assurance: 'Yahweh created me when his purpose first unfolded.'

Mary is the 'handmaid', the slave of the Lord, she is one of the poor, the *anawim* of Yahweh, and so she is the weak spot where God's Romantic passion for human beings, and through them for all creation, could break through. She is earth, body, 'medium of exchange', yet she is all three (because otherwise she could not be these) as conscious and fully willed, as active and sensitive, as a real human life. It happens because of a real woman's courage and doubt and joy and bewilderment and deep pain and utter fidelity.

In a sense, Mary *was* the incarnation, the flesh-taking, because for a while that simply was the situation. Historically, biographically, Mary knew more about it than Jesus did, for some years. How much was intellectual knowledge, and how much intuition, we cannot tell. That she did 'ponder' we are told, and we also realize that the result of some of her pondering was an interpretation of her son's role which, on two occasions at least, clashed with his, and thereby perhaps helped to clarify his own discovery. She was a particular and recognizable human being. She was, it seems clear, strong, intelligent, dedicated and (I would guess from her abrupt disappearance from the apostolic scene) a born leader, capable of being a focus of resentment and misunderstanding and being, therefore, partially rejected by the young Church. She was, in fact, very like her son, *figlia del tuo figlio*, as Dante pointed out. As human, as this mixed and intense woman she as it were 'held' the moment of

140

divine breakthrough, as the action of a movie is sometimes suspended at a moment of dramatic tension so that we may observe, oddly enhanced, the elements of a scene which is essentially in motion. The stillness of the held moment does not prevent or even check the movement, it only allows us to experience it more intensely.

This was the 'gap' of romantic love, the leap into the darkness and ignorance of flesh, of being time-bound and culturally conditioned. All this Jesus 'got' from his mother, and all this he took as his own being; and it was with him and in him as he went on to discover and live the further and final meaning of his manhood. She was 'in' him as he went up to Jerusalem, and so, therefore, were all the other beings with whom she formed one vast web of exchanged life. So when it became necessary on the historical 'other side' of the passionate breakthrough to find a language to express this coinherence of all humanity in Christ, Mary became the language. The images of the Church are images of Mary, and images of Mary are images of the Church; the 'Beloved' of the Song of Songs, the Bride of Christ, the heavenly City in which God dwells, Ark of the Covenant, the Woman of Revelation who bore the child who was caught up to heaven, the very Body of Christ.

Singular, particular—the flesh-taking is clearly these. It is communicated by one and one: by divine Messenger to Mary, by Mary to Elizabeth, by the Spirit to Simeon, and he to Mary, by John to Jesus and Jesus to each of his beloved, and they to each other and all others. It is present in the acute particularity of human bodily being, the body of a young man from Nazareth who looked like his mother. And it changed lives, and life, at the point of breakthrough, as we have seen that Romantic passion must do. When Jesus said, 'the kingdom of Heaven is among you' or 'within you', and when he told stories about that 'kingdom', he was evidently referring to something very precise and quite ascertainable, something with 'edges'. There is a border to be crossed, a reality to be 'released' from within, a new sphere of being to be experienced. Whether you enter it, mix it in the dough, eat it, dig it up, release it, plant it— whatever way you treat it, 'it' is not vague nor remote but a here-and-now power experienced in the very nature of things, and it is immediately recognizable. It changes each person, but this change is experienced as *between* people. They immediately 'see' each other

141

differently. What they see is, he tells them, God's reality. So, of course, they must act according to this new and accurate vision of the proper nature of life. They must behave as lovers do; they must serve one another with complete fidelity and humility, and also with a kind of joyful unreason. They must forgive to an exaggerated extent, give beyond the demands of common sense, cultivate an attitude to property and career which most people will regard as thoroughly irresponsible. This is how lovers are, and theirs is the Kingdom of Love, in which they also are to rule. But to rule, here, means to put on an apron and wash people's dirty feet. It also means to die for them.

There is one other effect of the breakthrough of Romantic passion which is very obvious throughout the Gospel accounts of the career of Jesus. It is the element of obscurity—a kind of dazzlement. The concrete and observable events, the healings, the changed lives, the challenges and encounters, are lived in a context of mystery, not because they are at all hard to perceive but because their unmistakably concrete nature seems always to be what it is in virtue of a 'something else', unstated, unseen, yet with a frustrating sense that it *ought* to be seen and stated—whatever 'it' is. The nostalgia without obvious reason, the sense of 'something lost' and unattained within even the most satisfying love, is familiar in the poetry of Romantic love. The same thing is evident in the Gospel accounts. The disciples' love for Jesus was immediate, devoted and sufficiently unreasonable to satisfy all the canons of Romance, but clearly it was often a baffled and hurt love. Just when they thought they were getting to understand, they found themselves dropped into helpless bewilderment.

Why could they not cure the epileptic boy? They had done all that he had told them, but nothing happened. His reply to their puzzled question was cryptic and unhelpful. 'This kind' required prayer and fasting before healing could occur. Which kind? They did not know. And when they had done all that he bade them, they would be still 'merely servants', he told them, all their enthusiastic service dismissed as no more than a matter of duty. He said, too, that they were to be like children. Something in a child's response was what he wanted from them. Why? Children were, after all, silly, messy little creatures who got in the way of sensible people. He often snubbed their enthusiasm and brushed away their suggestions and questions, sometimes almost angrily, yet the next minute he would be urging them on, almost begging their understanding of the urgency in himself. He cured their relatives and told them to 'hate' those same relatives. He gave the people bread and then blamed them for wanting it. He broke the law and upheld its holiness. Altogether he seemed to operate according to some apprehension of reality which they could not share; it always eluded their grasp. The glory which their love shed around them clarified, and yet dazzled. They felt themselves moving in a mist which closed them in blindness and ignorance, and then parted to reveal a landscape of such jewel-like intensity of light that the everyday world seemed, afterwards, ghost-like. But once more the mist would close in. They returned from the feeding in the wilderness to the plots and suspicions and doubts of the town. They came down from the mountain to frustration and the growing sense of impending doom.

Those closest to Jesus evidently suffered most from the sense that they were always on the edge of discovering the vital element in the situation and never quite doing so. Peter comes through to us as the one who was most constantly trying to force his way into this central mystery and most often getting thrown back, but the others felt it too. Philip's naive request, 'Show us the Father', really sums up what they all wanted: the key to the whole thing. But it was not to be obtained in that way. The only way they could come to know what it was that seemed to be always just about to show itself (but never did) was to do what Jesus himself did when he 'went up to Jerusalem' for the last time. The painful obscurity which surrounds the experience of even the most idyllic love can only be penetrated by the thrust of total gift. It is in the *Liebestod* that Wagner's Isolde finally breaks through beyond nostalgia, finding the fulfilment of love only through death.

We may understand this better if we look again more closely at one particular element in Romantic love. It is hard sometimes to distinguish that baffling and unidentified nostalgia which surrounds Romance from the element of sheer pain which I identified as one of the essential marks of the passionate experience. The two things are not identical, for some of the pain will have quite obvious reasons, such as absence or misunderstanding, or practical obstacles to the relationship. But behind all these is the reason for the essential pain of Romantic love, which is indeed closely allied to that name-

143

less nostalgia, itself painful. For Romantic love creates a situation for itself which is, in a sense, 'artificial'. It *deliberately* excludes certain elements of the 'wholeness' of the natural experience of human love. For a time at least the complete satisfaction sought in consummated physical love is excluded. The intensity of Romantic passion which creates the breakthrough of the spirit into a new kingdom comes about, it seems, because of a deliberate refusal to do what is 'natural' and proper about the perceived good in another human being. This concentration of the full energy of exchanged life in a narrow channel forces a way through yet more barriers between the spheres of reality, instead of immediately allowing it to spread sweetly throughout the realities of a satisfied everydayness. Romantic love is here, as I noticed at first, both 'everyday' and 'strange'. It includes all kinds of delightfully and poignantly every-day things such as the discovery of shared tastes or having a meal together as well as the experience of physical desire, but in the Romantic experience all this is caught up and in a sense dissolved in a deeper and more painful desire and a more intense delight which takes the whole thing beyond the sphere of everydayness. The cost is high, and the complaint of the ill-used physical and emotional nature is intense, and in a sense proper and right. Such a restriction is, as critics of Romance have pointed out, an outrage on nature, which she has not deserved. Only the conviction that this is, somehow, the way to the innermost kingdom of love justifies such a perverse treatment of good gifts. Yet the notion that it is worthwhile to suffer this, if not permanently then at least through postponed satisfaction, is at the heart of the Romantic doctrine. And even when there is physical union, in marriage or not, it never fulfils all that it seems to promise. There is still pain, still a sense that something essential is missing, or lost.

We may come, by this way of considering the marks of passion, to the heart of the mystery of the flesh-taking, by which the flesh taken was destroyed and transformed and became something new, and yet the same person; but a person in whom not merely some but all of the barriers to exchange between the spheres of experience had been destroyed. We come to that part, or aspect, or meaning, of the life of Jesus which is normally called by the word which describes his whole mission.

If we can say that the passion of Jesus shows us most clearly the pain of the kind of love which can break barriers, then we can also understand why such love is painful, wherever and in whomever it occurs, not accidentally but essentially, and this because of that reversal of the flow of exchange which is the nature of evil. If the way I have approached other events in his life has validity then we should expect to find in the final acts of the life of Jesus the kind of necessity and urgency which created, for instance, the experience we call the transfiguration. We do find precisely this.

A sense of urgency is increasingly clear from an early stage in the public career of Jesus. It is an urgency which certainly includes the feeling that time is short, because the mounting hostility of authorities of various kinds makes it clear that they are not going to continue for long to allow him to challenge and disrupt their carefully constructed political, psychological and spiritual enclosures, but there is another kind of urgency which has little to do with time, as such; it is the urgency which the lover feels in seeking a return of love. He may be prepared to take a lifetime for the job, but every moment of that lifetime 'contains' the full force of his longing desire.

The evidence of all this is not hard to find. The 'training' of the Twelve, for instance, is pushed ahead in a way which seems, from a common-sense point of view, to be asking too much too soon. A group of young men who could get into an acrimonious discussion about precedence in what they evidently thought of as a very earthly kind of 'kingdom' do not seem to be, in any obvious way, sufficiently mature psychologically or spiritually to be able to cope with the vision of the kingdom which Jesus was presenting to them. If Luke is reliable (and I suggested that his ordering of events usually makes psychological sense even though it is not a strict chronological order), the incident in which Jesus took a small child as a lesson in humility to the status-seeking disciples was completely lost on them, at least for the time being. John 'answered' by congratulating himself and the others on having rebuked a man who was healing in the name of Jesus but was not 'one of us'. We can hear the resignation in the reply of Jesus: 'Do not forbid him, for he that is not against you is for you.' He answers John, but makes no attempt to take up again the lesson previously ignored.

Jesus was demanding of his Twelve, and indeed of the crowds, a degree of understanding and faith which we may well feel to be

145

unrealistic. He was doing what people in love so often do, which is to have such faith in the vision of essential beauty and life in the beloved that peripheral qualities are ignored, yet it is these peripheral qualities which may well determine the response, limiting it or suppressing it altogether. The sense of urgency is such that it seems at times that good pedagogy and even affection had been sacrificed in a risky attempt to break through to minds all too well defended against love. And the outbreaks of bitterness—cursing the unresponsive towns and ruthlessly snubbing would-be disciples who show more complacency than dedication—are precisely what one would expect when the passionate plea of love is repulsed.

The amount of sheer warning in what the evangelists record of the words of Jesus—against failure to 'watch', against unfaithfulness, against complacency or worldly preoccupation or even family relationships—is often overlooked, for we prefer to remember the lessons on the mercy of God and his fatherly care. The whole feeling of this very marked aspect of the words and attitudes of Jesus is summed up in the double cry of longing, for the end and for the necessary means: 'I came to cast fire upon earth, and would that it were already kindled! I have a baptism to be baptised with, and how am I constrained until it is accomplished!' The very word 'constrained' (RSV—the Jerusalem Bible gives 'how great is my distress') gives the sense of pressure, of frustration and pain at the intolerable restriction of love, and the passage which follows is a promise of stress and division for those who would 'catch fire' and so suffer the same 'constraint' of not-yet-consummated love. But the 'constraint' is part of the movement of passion itself, pressing through the narrows towards freedom and joy.

The accent in all the references of Jesus to his coming suffering and death is on the necessity of it all. 'The son of man *must* suffer . . .'; 'Let these words sink into your hearts. . . .'; ' . . . everything that is written . . . is to come true' (Luke); 'Jesus began to make it clear to his disciples that he *must* go to Jerusalem and suffer'; 'The son of man is going to be handed over . . .'; ' . . . the Son of Man is about to be handed over . . .' (Matthew and Mark almost identically). And in several places these prophecies are coupled by the evangelist with the comment that the only way to be a disciple is to 'carry his cross' after him. It is scarcely surprising that the Twelve 'did not understand'. The inner logic of Romantic passion

146

does not appeal to minds whose familiar images are those of conquest and rule.

The necessity of passion, the 'must' of the lover, is self-evident to him, baffling to others. The Twelve continued to the end to refuse to believe that the failure and degradation of which he continually warned them could really occur, and when it came they were utterly demoralized. Living among them in those last months Jesus had to be alone with the knowledge of that necessity, unable to share it with them because they could not accept it; yet they were the nearest to him, the ones most likely to be able to share. Beyond this inner circle were other disciples, men and women, and many more whose hearts had responded to him, who had been healed and changed. Beyond those were the thousands who had heard him, or heard of him, and been encouraged, at least momentarily, and beyond those again were the ones who distrusted him, the majority of the powerful and influential. Step by step, he had alienated them all. Many of those who had been thrilled by what they thought was his message had become discouraged by his strange words and forbidding manner; others had, after the days of the great healings and crowds ended, shrugged cynically and laughed at their own hope. Others again felt betrayed and resentful. The disciples were doggedly faithful but increasingly puzzled and even angry; the Twelve were edgy, frightened and withdrawn. Finally, he was alone with the driving sense of necessity, an urgency narrowed down to his own single-minded dedication to the thing his Father was asking of him, by which alone love could have its way.

There is a quality about the behaviour of Jesus during his passion which sets it apart from any other kind of heroism. In a sense, it is not heroism at all, because a hero is intent on *being* a hero, on making clear to everyone his moral superiority and his indifference to the worst that his enemies can do. Jesus did not behave in a heroic way. His attention was, at every point on which we are informed, not on himself but on others, ready to respond in whatever way was needed. There is a detailed attentiveness, an extremity of compassionate awareness of the nature of others' reactions and needs, which we easily overlook because we have heard it all so often. From his concern in Gethsemane for the wounded servant and for the fate of his own followers, to his plea for the men who nailed him to the cross and the assurance of salvation to his fellow

147

sufferer, the impulse of his whole being is a love poured out in detailed, personal care as it was poured out in the gift of his body to destruction. He did not merely surrender to death; he gave himself away, body and mind and human heart, all one gift.

What was it that he had perceived as 'necessary'? What, in all this, was to accomplish the purpose of his love? His whole being was directed to this purpose. Clearly and more clearly it appeared to him as the way he had to go. And he knew it not vaguely but in detail; he walked knowingly to a death accompanied by contempt, betrayal, public degradation, rejection by his own people and desertion by his friends. He 'set his face' towards not only the worst of physical torture but the total destruction of dignity and meaning even in death.

It was, moreover, in everyday terms a useless, an unnecessary death. He could have avoided it, many must have felt, without compromising his ideals. He could have continued to teach and guide his friends in their search for truth and love, he could have been still the healer and consoler of the poor. By thus walking into the arms of death he might be said to have shown a callous disregard for the people who had turned to him and needed him. He was abandoning them, in their trust and longing, to the worldly, cynical powers he had so often denounced. By any reasonable imaginative assessment of the situation the death he chose—and 'chose' is the only appropriate word—involved the loss of everything that could give coherence to a human life. It undid that life. It gave way to incoherence, asking of Meaning itself, 'Why hast thou forsaken me?'

The scope of this destruction can only appear if we look not only at the human circumstances but at the nature of the person to whom this was so necessary. The unique force of this passionate breakthrough arises not only from the degree and extent of the destruction, but from the ability of the person to be affected by it. He was, he always had been, more intimately aware of the power and meaning of evil than anyone else could be. In a sense it lived 'closer' to him, in himself, than it could live with any other human being, just because that self was of the same 'stuff' and intensity as the perverted energy one of whose names is Satan. He knew his own being in this utterly alien use. (The tempter had, after all, recognized not so much an enemy as a potential ally.) Every impulse and evasion of evil was known to him with an immediacy which

148

caused him, all his life, to respond with what was by normal standards a quite disproportionate force and urgency to the human need for release from it, whether he encountered it as sickness or as sin. The only thing that had, until then, kept him from destruction was the fact of his own purpose, for he knew what evil could not know: the point in time at which there was a coming together in the network of exchange of many things to a centre. Historical circumstances, human purpose (for good and evil), and his own human readiness as his self-discovery reached its love-accelerated completeness—all had to flow together. Until they did so there was no 'permission' to the awaited clawing attack of evil, designed to annihilate this rival who had refused alliance or service.

This unique scope for the attack of evil, which we saw in the Temptation, made possible the unique significance of this passionate surrender. Evil had never had an opportunity for such a total conquest, because never had it been presented with a victim so undefended by those thick layers of ignorance and rationalization which human beings, under the pressure of the presence of 'wrongness' in material reality, have developed to protect themselves. Jesus was aware of and lived fully in depths of humanness which are accessible only to the Beloved of the Father, the divine Wisdom who penetrates all things. In those depths he suffered the intimate onslaught of evil to which the sheer horror of physical and mental pain and spiritual desolation had laid him open.

The paradox of passion is that the thrust of love seeking love consists in being vulnerable. It is the undefended self being offered, the naked appeal of the absolute person for the gift of life. It is taunted, sometimes, as shameless and undignified, and so it is. Only when shame (in the older sense of reticence or modesty) and dignity are set aside can the extreme of love show itself, yet shame and dignity are the necessary defences of human nature as yet unready for passion, and so properly avoiding it. There is no dignity, or shame, in the naked suffering of the passion of Jesus. There is only utter vulnerability, a giving which is so absolute that Christian imagination has all too often been at work to mitigate the horror, either by supposing that the Son of God had evacuated the condemned body of Jesus at some point sufficiently beforehand to leave scope for majesty, or simply by sentimentalizing the thing into a kind of divine heroism. It is not heroism; it is simply love.

But this love is, in the flesh-taking, essentially and inevitably painful. At this point we can suddenly see *why* redemption involved suffering. We can be precise in saying exactly what it was that made the suffering of Jesus so much greater than that of any other human being. Suffering—any kind of suffering—means that something which should be 'complete' is somehow prevented from being complete. A cut finger hurts because the wholeness and function of skin and muscle is broken; hunger hurts because the stomach lacks food; bereavement hurts because a person who was 'part of my life' has been taken away; mockery hurts because my 'self-respect'—my sense of who I am—is reduced; betrayal hurts because someone I relied on, who 'held' part of me, has taken away that part, leaving a wound. But all these various kinds of incompleteness which hurt us are only partial. They are part of, and also images of, the incompleteness which is separation from that intimate, inmost 'self' where (the inside being 'larger than the outside') we encounter God and are united with him. We truly do 'hunger and thirst' for righteousness, as Jesus said; and that hunger is blessed, it is the human soul's ultimate hunger, the longing for God. If, then, these smaller incompletenesses hurt us so much, how much more must the lack of God hurt? Yet we do not, usually, feel this. We are protected from feeling it by layers of ignorance, and we know it only indirectly, and muted by acquired defences. The name of those defences, in Paul's theology, is 'the flesh' (σαρξ in Greek), by which he meant not just being bodily but the human state of being conditioned by physical existence, shut into an unlovely isolation within and between ourselves and unable, therefore, to exchange life freely. It is the 'body of this death', and in this condition we do not feel the longing for God, we only feel hints of it in our failures to be, even in small ways, what we are obscurely convinced we ought to be.

The great refusal of exchange is indeed part of our inheritance; it is the whole structure of 'the world', whose function is to enable us to relate to each other and work together without seeming too much to threaten our carefully built-up defences against the forces of desired exchange.

But in Jesus these defences were absent. He felt the minor hurts of human life, but he knew them for what they were—the images of the frustration of that deepest and ultimate hunger, the longing

150

for God. He who is the Beloved, whose real Being is to give love back to the Father in the fullness of joy, was prevented from that completeness of gift by the human nature he fully was, and must be for love's sake. We know a little of what that meant, because those human beings who have even for a moment broken through to spheres of experience in which he lived have suffered a longing for God so painful that it seemed, at times, that human nature could not support it. Even those less terrifyingly gifted, yet called to share to some extent in his awareness, can testify to the quality if not the degree of that pain. It is the pain of sheer love, a longing so simple that it penetrates every aspect of the person, for it is a longing for that which *is* the person. There is no pain so great as the pain of the soul's longing for God. In it, all other pains are included and drawn to a point at which it is impossible to distinguish between pain and love. This is the urgency with which Jesus moved towards death, in the full impulse of passionate dedication.

But such a simplicity of love is unimaginable to the evil will, because it is not attached to anything. Attached love, even the purest, can always be twisted to *look* like selfishness, if one wishes to believe that there is no such thing as love. But simple love and longing for God is something which evil cannot touch because it cannot 'see' it.

It is because it is simply love that the self-gift of Jesus is redemptive. Since love is the one thing evil cannot compass, either imaginatively or really, it evades the grab of evil. Therefore the power of evil—'natural', human or diabolic—did indeed succeed in doing precisely what it set out to do, which was to destroy the enemy it perceived, a foe of tremendous and baffling strength, capable of healing and converting human minds as well as material elements. The huge power in Jesus, which had refused co-operation in what the Great Refuser saw as the only obviously sensible use of power, was (inexplicably, but opportunely) vulnerable to 'the Prince of this World'. And into all the channels laid open by love the power of destruction thrust itself, to seize the very citadel of that power. It found nothing there. All was destroyed except love, and love is 'nothing' to the intelligence and grasp of evil.

But the very being of Jesus is love, and when he had accepted into himself the fullness of the thrust of evil there was no more it could do. The Christian assertion, repeated liturgically again and

151

again, is that by dying he 'destroyed death'. This is literally true, because the power of death is sin, and sin is that 'defendedness' of human nature which keeps love confined. Where there is no sin, death finds nothing to 'grip'. Love is exchange of life, and sin, which blocks that exchange, is the place where death can hold on. In dying, Jesus, as it were, released the grip of death's power *to be an evil*.

In order to realize the scope of this we have to remember how the model of exchanged life displays for us the infinitely intricate and intimate coinherence of all reality. Jesus was (like all human beings) inherently related, physically and mentally, to all of creation. And this man, Jesus, is the Beloved, the one in whom the Father's purpose (necessity, the 'must' of passion) is to 'unite all things in heaven and on earth'. Therefore when the impulse of love drove him to make himself vulnerable to the worst that evil could do (could do, that is, not merely to *a* human being but to *this* human being, whose capacity for suffering was necessarily unique because he was God), the effect of the ultimate impotence of evil in him spreads outwards also to every being with whom he is enmeshed 'in heaven, on earth, and under the earth'.

This could not but be so. Reality is exchange, and if this thing happened in reality, then all of reality is affected by it, radically, intimately and permanently. But material reality, from which the spiritual is not separable but only *distinguishable*, exists in time and space, and the exchange of life is therefore an exchange in and through time and space, even though in certain circumstances these categories of experience may be twisted or by-passed. Therefore the full effects of this irreversible event are not apparent immediately, but only (as the 'nature of things' would indicate) little by little, as and when the flow of exchange carries the message of freedom— fastest by human will and choice, or mediated more slowly, and as Wisdom enlightens, to other forms of created being.

It will be necessary to consider the element of time in the transformation wrought by the passion of Jesus in other contexts. Here, it is important in considering the way in which the meaning of this destruction of death became apparent and operative. This is the aspect of the matter which we call the resurrection. The resurrection is the thing which actually happened in the death of Jesus. It is the moment of breakthrough, the explosion of fully reciprocated love which knows itself free of all restriction. Whereas the 'Beatrician moment' of human love experiences the reality of divine love only fleetingly and within the confines of earthly life, the resurrection is divine love unlimited, or at least it is that for Jesus himself, the one who is 'firstborn from the dead'. Others have still to follow him, but he has opened the way.

We may sum up the event thus far: the nature of God is love, and the origin of love, the Father from whom is life, pours himself out in total giving in the Beloved, who, in his human nature, receives the outpouring of love, and receives it *as human*, that is, as coinherent in all human life and in all creation. Therefore (since sin is the condition in which created life *is*) he receives it in a condition which 'blocks' the flow of love in return. It is the work of incarnate Wisdom to make that longed-for return possible.

The cry of Jesus on the cross at the very end was, therefore, the cry of awareness that all was indeed accomplished, brought to its consummation. He knew that he could, at last, give back to the One he loved the unshackled fullness of love, and in so doing *carry with him* on the surge of that passion the love which is the essential being of all creation. This is, in a sense, the moment of resurrection, or rather it is the moment at which that process begins, for the resurrection is not a single event but the ever-extending 'outflow' of the energy previously dammed up by the power of sin and death. This out-flow of love to the Father from whom it came operates, as I said, mostly in time, and time is involved in the sequence of events we know as the resurrection. The period of time during which the body of Jesus lay in the tomb is part of this sequence.

I want first to consider this sequence in Scripture and in history, so as to get an idea of the workings of it outwards through human lives and all creation. After that I want to come back and consider more closely the single and personal being of the risen Jesus. This may seem to be the wrong way round; I want to do it this way because the consideration of the strange way in which resurrection is actually found to work raises questions and offers a challenge to the would-be disciple, and the only way to discover some answers and learn to respond to the challenge is then to see how it begins to work in Jesus himself, who is the model for the disciple. As always the personal experience of Jesus is constitutive of all that we

153

mean by Christianity. Incarnation is first of all an experience, only subsequently and inadequately a 'doctrine'.

The extraordinary change wrought by the passion was at work, but not all at once. It was, it must be emphasized, a material change, and material changes take place in time. What exactly these changes were we cannot tell, though the strange evidence (still incomplete but very suggestive) provided by experiments on the cloth of the shroud of Turin corresponds with oddities in the gospel account of what happened. There is, for instance, the fact that the grave clothes were found in place as if wrapped round a body, but the body had gone from inside, and the report that the guards were knocked to the ground by some mysterious force. These things at least strongly suggest that, as we would expect, there was a radical change in the 'molecular structure' of the body, which at a certain point passed a barrier at which 'quantitative' became 'qualitative' change and produced violent effects in the environment, scorching the grave clothes in inexplicable ways and knocking the guards insensible.

This was not the end of the process of change, for another barrier of some kind was passed at a later time. The one we call the 'ascension' is even harder to discern since its chief characteristic, to the outside view, is that Jesus became invisible to his followers, yet he assured them that he had not left them and that he would be with them in a definite but indescribable way, by the power of his Spirit. The third stage in the process of resurrection, which occurred some ten days after the 'ascension', produced definite physical and emotional effects, and these were observable not merely by those to whom 'it' happened directly but to others who saw and heard them under the impact of this strange experience. The mighty wind and tongues of fire of this 'Pentecost stage' of resurrection are yet another indication that something very fundamental was happening to material reality.

What I am suggesting is that if we take seriously the claim that God became human then the consequences must be expected to be observable in material fact, but not in matter as isolated from the 'spiritual', because the whole point of the doctrine of exchange is that material creation reflects and is constituted by the exchange of life in the blessed Trinity. To become spiritual in the Christian sense is not to become *less* material, but rather to become, as Jesus

154

did by his passionate self-giving, *more* material. In the resurrection matter becomes fully possessed of that perfection which it can only otherwise experience at odd moments, such as the 'Beatrician' moment. But since it is occurring in the total material universe this process takes place according to the conditions of that universe. It works by exchange, but like all exchange it occurs in time and through space, and its occurrence in time and space is modified by the effect of conscious, living decisions—as all occurrences are since humankind appeared on the earthly scene. In this process—the process of exchanging the new life of resurrection 'outwards' from Christ the firstborn—a great deal must depend on actual human communication of the event itself and its implications, by word and by physical action. The latter takes place as part of a communication which is not purely conscious and operates at the level of unfree, natural exchange also, but under a kind of pressure which produces changes analogous to the changes which originally took place in the physical body of Jesus. (This is the same kind of pressure which, as I described it earlier, pushes the everyday experiences connected with falling in love into a different sphere, thereby in a sense leaving out the everyday quality itself, but only so that the beauty which is exemplified by everydayness may be rediscovered in its own fullness 'on the other side'.)

'In Adam' all died, for once the process of sin had been initiated it *could not help* including all of material creation, since all is co-inherent. But since evil is inherently self-contradictory its power depends on the deflection of an energy whose 'proper' tide is towards exchange. In that case there must be a *progressive* build-up of 'frustrated' exchange. The pressure is not a fixed weight; it must increase, with time and with the human responses and choices involved. If we remember that the energy of exchange is the very being of God—that is, of love—and that this love by its very nature *cannot help* pressing towards all possible gift, then we can see that the pressure and the resistance must both increase, in human minds and in the rest of creation, until they reach a point where one or other has to give way.

To put it naively, either God had to 'give up' or the deflected current of evil had to be reversed and the energy released. But God cannot 'give up' without ceasing to be God, so no dualist interpretation of the struggle is possible. Only there had to be a way to get

155

out of this impasse of locked tensions, and it came at the only point at which it could come—that is, by a will *within* the situation of sin, a will locked into that tension, yet not conditioned by it. We have seen a little of how it happened just then, historically, but there is one consequence of taking material reality seriously on the plane of both sin and redemption which might not be immediately obvious as a result of resurrection.

The process of resurrection has to work in time and space, but the pace of this can be altered by the conscious decision of human beings who offer themselves to the process and become, therefore, very powerful 'points of exchange' of resurrection. But they, too, are bodily, limited by time and space, and cannot reach out to give the message directly to all human beings, nor does the process proceed far enough in a normal lifetime for any one of them to have a very great impact, as points of exchange, in the non-human creation. *Some* effect they do have, in the degree of their own changedness, some being more changed than others in ways that are obviously physical. People who can heal, communicate with birds or live without food are comparatively rare, and these oddities are no criterion for judging the person's total 'degree of resurrection', only for seeing how far the process has been able to reach at the purely physical level. Remembering always that love (which is the sole energy of the 'process of resurrection') cannot coerce, it follows that the build-up of the tension of sin-and-grace in creation does not actually cease at the *historical* point of the resurrection of Jesus himself.

The tension broke *at the point of greatest tension*, which was when the faith of Israel reached its own peak in Jesus. But if it reached a peak *there* and *then*, it does not follow that all of creation had reached a comparable degree of tension: in fact we would expect the opposite, for the tension in Israel had been 'deliberately' heightened by the passionate nature of divine love, as is indeed the nature of passionate love, and the story of this heightening is the whole history of the Chosen People, its tales and poetry and prophets and agonies. If this deliberate heightening took place at a certain point then all the rest of creation was, by contrast, still comparatively— and variably—in a state of much less uncomfortable tension. This is one reason why non-Christian religion and non-Western (i.e. not Christian-influenced) cultures often seem much more integrated and at peace with the human condition than is Christianity. As Paul put it, 'I was once alive apart from the law. . . the very Commandment which promised life proved death to me' (Rom. 7:9–10). But the process of the progressive heightening of this tension of sin and grace must go on chronologically *after* the historical point at which the great reversal of evil began to operate. We would expect, then, that the presence of evil as a felt and operative thing in human society, and in the indirect effect of human society on natural things, would become gradually more and more obvious as time went on. We do seem to be witnessing such a process, and it is, as we would expect, exponential in its growth.

Thus we get, at points all through history since the point of incarnation, very evident encounters between the two thrusts of energy, of a kind which would not occur before. We get not only the expected conflicts between good and evil (with Christianity as 'good' and atheists or pagans as 'evil') but something much more baffling to our moral sense. We witness the encounter of still barely corrupted cultures, such as those of some North American Indians, with a kind of culture in which the impact of the message of resurrection has *itself* produced that heightening of tension *before* the breakthrough which occurred originally in the history of the people of Israel. Before the breakthrough there is an embattled resistance, as there was resistance to Jesus himself, and it is this structured resistance in a human society to something alien and threatening in the middle of it, heightened and strengthened by the sense of the presence of challenge, which seems to turn the energy of a whole society to conquest and subjection in its own territories and elsewhere. There is likely to be more, and more obviously malevolent, evil in a society in which Christianity is preached than in one which has not heard the ambiguously 'good news'.

This happens because in only a small number of people will the message of resurrection be fully accepted and at work. And some will (according to the nature of evil) in their degree deflect the energy of the knowledge of Christ in order to reinforce their own resistance to the reality of his demands, just as, in Israel, the old Covenant was misused to reinforce resistance to its own fulfilment in the new one. By forced exchanges such a society will seek to assimilate to itself the power of goodness (material wealth, beauty of things or ideas) which it encounters in groups or societies which

157

are still uncorrupted, and to impose its own values on the culture it has robbed. 'Spiritual imperialism' is one of the more horrible crimes of our era, but it is exactly what we would expect to happen if I am right about how both sin and redemption are at work.

The things which have happened to the culture of the Indian sub-continent are a good example. It began with ordinary imperialism, that is with a desire for wealth from a fresh source, as European businessmen discovered tremendous possibilities for trade and gradually controlled and later took over the political scene in order to safeguard trade. At this stage there was at least an explicit and theoretical (and often more than theoretical) commitment to care for the well-being of the conquered peoples. But the forced exchange of goods became a forced exchange of culture, as an already largely self-sterilized type of Western education was introduced as the price of acceptance into the world that mattered. The ancient webs of social, cultural and religious exchanges in the sub-continent were broken, and although quite large bits survived they lacked connections and could not function well. The old social and religious systems, though often brutal and (by real Christian standards) lacking in compassion or a sense of the absolute value of human beings, did work and give meaning to life. But Indian art and culture and religion, taken in isolated bits and out of context, were exported with enthusiasm to the West, where also they had no context. Eventually, Western people disgusted by the self-obsessed quality of much Western culture picked up clues from Indian cultural exports and went off looking for salvation in India. A few, who had the good fortune to meet teachers whose roots were long in the surviving and genuine spirituality of the East and whose minds were aware of the problems, found something real. But many found the trappings of religious techniques whose life-stream had been cut off by the break-up of the ancient systems.

This is one example among many of how a culture which has assimilated some elements of Christian moral insight can combine it with the desire for security and domination and persuade itself that its Christianity justifies all its actions. And there will be just enough real Christian 'feeling' in individuals to make the whole process tolerable to the dulled consciences of the public in the oppressing society. So the real religious genius of an older way is adulterated, enfeebled or obliterated, and the quasi-Christian society is even more convinced of its own inherent moral superiority. Its openness to the genuine exchanges of resurrection is therefore minimal, until such time as its hypocrisy becomes so blatant that a substantial number of its own people can no longer be deceived by it, and this is what seems to have happened in Europe and in America. We are in the next stage, of demoralization, anger and doubt, but there are signs of a further step, and I shall look at this later on. Another aspect of this progressive heightening of tension can be seen in the way in which much technology and scientific discovery have been used. The desire to dominate other forms of life, and to use them in any way which tends to produce more wealth, is the basis of 'factory farming', in which animals are treated purely as food-sources, not as living beings at their own level. The concept of science which allows people to pursue a line of research for its own sake, because it is possible and without regard for (or even awareness of) repercussions in other kinds of life or environment, is also typical. 'Science for science's sake' is a devilish formula and has devilish results, just as 'Art for art's sake' became a formula for an eventually debilitating approach to art. Yet both of these were attempts to ensure that human talent was not used simply as a tool for other ends, whether political or religious. But talent serving only itself is as thoroughly corrupted as talent serving someone else's ends. In either case the flow of exchanged life is turned back, and the pressure builds up until a breaking-point is reached, which may take the form of political or intellectual revolt or religious 'revival'. In all of these there is an element of genuine spiritual breakthrough in individuals who are truly 'converted', yet the final effect is merely a different kind of corruption. The reason is that the customs and words and rituals which are used to express the new awareness of life in the revolutionary situation are, for most people concerned, not a *result* of their converted experience seeking expression but merely an alternative behaviour pattern, another kind of 'law' by which to protect themselves from the implicit or explicit demand that they die and rise again, and thus become, in their turn, points of exchange for the new life in all creation.

So it happens that the very message of life can be used to prevent the exchange of life which the message demands, and many great saints and reformers have known this and wept because of it. In William Blake's little, bitter poem 'The Garden of Love' he speaks

159

for all those who have seen religious language, morality and ritual as a blight, a destroyer of life and of joy in exchanged love:

I went to the Garden of Love,
And saw what I never had seen:
A chapel was built in the midst,
Where I used to play on the green.

And the gates of this Chapel were shut,
And 'Thou shalt not' writ over the door;
So I turn'd to the Garden of Love
That so many sweet flowers bore.

And I saw it filled with graves,
And tomb-stones where flowers should be;
And priests in black gowns were walking their rounds,
And binding with briars my joys and desires.

This kind of religion—all too recognizable in all Christian traditions—is the deathly parody of that sacrificial constraint, that fervent direction of will in the service of love, which is the *amour voulu* of the passion of Jesus as it is carried and lived by those who are 'in' him.

But this parody and paradox seem to me to be an inevitable result of the fact that resurrection is being exchanged, in a world in which sin is also being exchanged. There must inevitably be a greater and greater likelihood of direct encounter between the true and the false, and in this struggle the older, less consious and in many ways beautiful patterns of religious exchange are destroyed, instead of being allowed to reach their fulfillment gradually. Sooner or later this heightening of tension must lead to open confrontation, and I shall be considering this in the chapter about baptism and death.

Yet the beginning of all this is the single fact of the resurrection of the man Jesus. For all the moral ambiguity of its results, which Jesus himself foresaw and warned us about, it is a matter for joy, a *Liebestod* tragic and yet triumphant.

'Having joy set before him, he endured the cross', but the joy was not merely in the future, it underlay the whole experience and made

160

sense of it. And Paul's great poem of praise and blessing (Ephesians 1) makes the pattern apparent and shows us that what Williams called 'the One adored Substitution' is the place from which a whole intricate growth of 'substitution' takes place, so that we eat, work, suffer, pray and rejoice in and for each other, in so far as we do these things in and for him.

> ... he chose us in him before the foundation of the world
> That we should be holy and blameless before him
> He destined us in love to be his children through Jesus Christ
> according to the purpose of his will
> to the praise of his glorious grace
> which he freely bestowed on us in the Beloved.
> In him we have redemption through his blood. . . .
> (Eph. 1:4–7)

His grace is given 'in' Jesus, and redemption, the 'bringing-back', is 'through' his blood. The crossing point is his death on the cross. But a little further on the task is, as it were, laid on those who have thus been loved and redeemed. 'We who first hoped in Christ have been destined and appointed to live for the praise of his glory.' As Jesus lived, so must his faithful ones live, realizing 'what is the immeasurable greatness of his power *in us* who believe . . . which he accomplished *in Christ* when he raised him from the dead . . . he has put all things under his feet and has made him head over all things *for the church* which is his body, the *fullness* of him who is all in all.'

This is first of all the personal experience of the man called Jesus. It is *because* it is his own personal experience that it is all the other things. We must avoid the tendency to dissolve the experience of Jesus into a generalized experience of resurrection. There is no such thing as generalized action by God, rather the particular experience of each (human or non-human) is exchanged with every other, through time and space, and thus becomes shared and common— but never general, always particular.

I want to end this chapter by considering the Gospel accounts of the resurrection appearances, which need to be read side by side with the theological reflections on the same event of Paul and of the writer to the Hebrews and of John. They are poetry, striving to

161

evoke accurately the nature of what actually happened, to Jesus himself and to those first witnesses. This is the foundation for understanding what happens to others who are brought into contact with the experience, and so become themselves points of exchange of resurrection. If they are to do this with real dedication, and with comprehension of the paradoxical nature of the undertaking as I have explored it, the fullest appropriation of this experience is essential.

One of the first things which is noticeable in the four accounts—and it is equally noticeable in all—is that the man who appears to his friends after death is recognizably the same person as the one they knew before. The whole experience is so strange that it is easy to overlook this. But not only do they recognize him (though not always immediately), but the style of conversation is recognizable too. The odd mixture of ordinariness and authoritative wisdom is there. 'Have you anything to eat?' has all the poignancy of remembered familiarity. 'Was it not ordained that Christ should suffer?' is the voice of the Teacher of old. The sternness mingled with deep love is there, and even the frustration at incomprehension. 'You foolish men!' he cries again, and 'What is that to you?' is the loving rebuke to preserve reality. He greets Mary by name, very simply, with the directness of an old and profound relationship, and his question to Peter cuts through to a tried and basic devotion: 'Do you love me?' 'Be not faithless but believing', he commands, in that familiar tone of urgency.

We might, of course, say that the writers who gave accounts of the earthly life of Jesus would use the same style in recounting the strangeness of those later days. But on reflection it seems more likely that, in default of evidence to the contrary, they would transpose the style of speech into something more nearly in accordance with what they might expect of such an event themselves, an event unique and altogether unfitted for any known literary category. The odd thing is the note of practicality and the insistence on physical presence, whether in the explanation of Scripture or the cooking of breakfast. Even the final episode of the ascension seems to be designed to emphasize the physical reality of a body which can be seen, and then suddenly can be hidden altogether. This is so natural (and yet the point is not laboured or underlined, but merely 'appears') that it seems impossible to invent. It has all the concreteness

162

and immediacy of real poetry, which makes experience available by giving it a context in which we can make sense of it.

Another aspect of the resurrection stories which is significant is the time-sequence. The speculations which thought of the forty days as merely an image of a waiting period referring back to the forty years of Israel in the wilderness and having no reference to any actual space of time seem to overlook this. What is being evoked for us in the accounts of the resurrection is not a single event but the beginning of that process in time whose further implications are made clear by quoting the words of Jesus himself when he sends his followers out to 'preach the Gospel' and also from the reflections of Paul on the incorporation of all humankind and all creation in the process. But it begins with the death of Jesus, and from this moment the great undoing of the power of evil began, affecting first of all the person of Jesus himself.

In the imagery of the 'harrowing of hell', Jesus, after his death, was able to set free the spirits of the righteous who died before his time. This is a sign of the awareness from early times that even before the moment (whenever that was) of bodily resurrection there was something going on which indicated an unprecedented power at work in creation. This 'descent to the underworld' is actually, if it means anything, an 'interference' with time. The 'adored Substitution' reaches back to men and women long dead to change history from within. The accounts of the transfiguration lend some support to the idea. The possibilities and problems raised by such an idea are too large and too unsupported by evidence or even realistic guesses to be leaned on or discussed at length, but it does suggest interesting avenues of speculation.

More concrete and definite is the indirect evidence for the kind of thing that happened to the body of Jesus at a certain stage. It seems that the 'making' of a glorified body could not be immediate but took time. The evidence of the Shroud of Turin, to which I have already referred, bears out the evidence of the few indications given by the evangelists. Something very basic had happened to nature at that point. If the death of Jesus actually did what Paul said it did, it destroyed sin and death in him, and that meant it destroyed the inner barriers of resistance to the exchange of life, at first at this one point, and it is plausible that the earthquake which occurred was a reaction to this, a shock wave spreading outwards from the body which still hung on the cross. But the results in the physical being of the risen Jesus are more verifiable.

We really have to stop thinking of the resurrection accounts in the Bultmann manner as simply ways of recording inner experiences which the disciples had. Inner experiences of that magnitude do not, in any case, just happen; they are caused by something which has an impact commensurate with the effect. But in any case to think of it in terms of spiritual experience is to miss the whole implication of the flesh-taking, and all of the thrust of Paul's theology of redemption. Jesus was the eruption of God into creation, not just as immanent but as explicit, human fact. This is not a reversible process. It could and did have effects both backward and forward in time, but it could not *retire* from time. To 'return to the Father' did not mean that Jesus, having finished his work, simply went home like some tired commuter. A human body, a human person, is *in* creation—enmeshed with it totally—and Jesus was, from the moment of his conception, *in* creation in that sense. By being in it, he altered its composition radically and permanently, and the moment at which the effect of that alteration became operative was the moment of his death.

There are indications of the nature of the change and the stages of it. The earliest stage seems to have produced very violent physical effects, as we have seen, but the obvious characteristic of this stage is the clear physical, visible and touchable presence of a recognizable person. After a certain time, another stage was reached at which it became possible for him to be present to his beloved in a different way, and in more than one place at a time, therefore no longer physically visible in the same way. Yet all the things he said about this later kind of 'presence' sound just as concrete and definite as the ways of presence with them in his earlier life; in fact the implication is quite clear that he was to be in some senses *more* present than was possible before.

Again, there is a time-gap. Between his disappearance from view and that explosion of divine energy by which he swept the persons of his most intimate friends into his own new life there was a period of waiting, as there had been between his death and his coming from the tomb, and between that and the ascension. Why these particular time-spans were needed we cannot guess, but that they were not merely arbitrary we may properly conclude. The final and

164

greatest time-span suggested is that between the coming of the Spirit and the final Coming of the Lord, and it is hardly surprising that the earliest Christians expected that it would be short. The whole thing up until then had been at high speed, and also they had no way (as we have) of realizing the complexity of the processes of exchange in nature and in its human dimension, which must slow down the process of resurrection. The expectation was intense, and much of Paul's theology of resurrection, as well as references in the Gospels to shortness of remaining time, is developed in relation to this expectation.

Yet the reasons why this stage of the process had to be, in practice, vastly longer than anticipated is implicit in Paul's theology. The famous passage from Romans 8 about the travail of creation towards new birth contains one reason why resurrection had to take a long time to reach the next and final breakthrough, as I have suggested. But this is clear also in all the passages in which Paul wrestled with the fact that Christians were still, in many (maybe most) cases, very far from fully living the life of Christ to which they had dedicated themselves in baptism. It is an intractable problem with which all theology and all Christian life has had to struggle ever since, and it has been among the most fruitful sources of heresy. On the one hand it leads to thinking of human beings as powerless in the grip of divine process and on the other hand to making them morally independent of God and able to reach perfection by sheet effort of will or (in a modern version) by knowledgeably manipulating the unconscious mind. Both of these tendencies are attempts to simplify the process of resurrection and make it more understandable. But a process begun and continued according to the dynamics of exchange can only work by the way in which exchange actually does work, that is by passionate breakthrough at its many levels and countless occasions, in individuals, in groups and in whole cultures. So Paul's theology is relevant even when his time-scale is not, and I shall have occasion, later, to consider further a strange idea which is implicit in so much of what Paul says about the expectation of the End, but which the second letter of Peter makes explicit. It is one of those 'throwaway' lines of Scripture in which the most staggering theological concepts are referred to in passing. Here the idea is that the *timing* of the End of all things depends on the activity of the Church, especially in prayer.

165

'What sort of persons ought you to be in lives of holiness and godliness, waiting for *and hastening* the coming of the Day of God?' asks the writer. The point of this quotation is to help me to pin down immediately one aspect of the exchange of resurrection which we can see going on, and it has to do with the reversal of that dire result of sin which is the 'separation' of spirit and matter, not only in concepts but in experience. Our own inability to come to terms with our physical being, our ignorance of and lack of control over its processes and especially over the 'last enemy', death, is one of the most distressing and obvious results of sin. Again, there are signs that in 'primitive' cultures the sense of oneness of body and spirit has not been destroyed, though it is partial. It is under the pressure of deep religious and Romantic longing for a fuller truth that the body becomes the focus and symbol of all that gets in the way of enlightenment. This was true in the world into which the Church emerged, and the Church itself inevitably absorbed this anxiety and even intensified it, as it waited for the Lord with a passion becoming increasingly anxious, bewildered and frustrated as time passed and 'nothing happened'.

But we can see in some very everyday occurrences that the intended exchanges between spirit and body can become actual if there is a sufficient motive, that is a sufficient thrust of passion. Doctors and nurses are familiar with the fact that a person so sick that he or she 'ought' to be dead will stay alive until some beloved person has come or some plan is accomplished. The person will then quite suddenly 'decide to die', and it often happens within minutes. Conversely, a person who is medically as good as dead may suddenly 'decide to live' and make a rapid and complete recovery, because of an intense need to finish some task left undone.

There is a real alteration in the usual relationship between body and spirit. But if this really is 'exchange of resurrection' at work, changing creation towards its end, why do so many disciples of Christ in all centuries seem to have had even more than the usual share of physical illness, instead of being unusually 'at one' in body and spirit? (The East, in fact, seems to have been much better at realizing the physical possibilities of spiritual growth than the Christian West. But, as before, it is not so much that these things are proofs of the power of Christ but that such power, used 'in Christ' and not for self-transcendence or illumination alone, becomes a way in which his power is effective.) I would suggest, tentatively, that in the West anti-physical doctrines and moods penetrated Christian thought to such an extent that it was, in a sense, impossible for most Christians to let resurrection be effective in this area of experience. Like Adam and Eve, they experienced something good as evil; therefore for them it *was* evil. Consequently in such a person the intensity of divine passion is deflected round that obstacle and instead becomes blazingly intense in mind and heart. But sometimes this intensity 'overflows' and affects the body in violent and *uncontrolled* ways, such as ectsasies. These are involuntary and can even be distressing, because they are not understood and therefore not developed as ways of exchange. Occasionally there are signs that the situation rights itself at the point of death, when weakness of the body makes it cease to seem a threat. Then the flow of divine love is able to penetrate that also, and brings the whole person to a point of evident oneness and peace in perfect exchange with God, on the brink of eternity. This is one of the ways in which we can see how resurrection is exchanged through creation. There are many others, and some will be considered in the context of body-symbolism and sexuality, later on. It is all part of what began on Calvary.

Thus there is indeed a process at work in the whole of creation, but it is one which depends on the free response of human beings for its accomplishment. And this process is intimately and vitally connected with the actual personality of Jesus. It begins with him and spreads outwards from him in detectable ways of exchange, affecting other humans by direct communication, challenging them to do as he did and affecting non-human creation both in the natural ways of exchange which occur without human decision and in the many ways by which natural exchanges are altered by human intervention.

This time-sequence of resurrection is linked to the first aspect of the resurrection accounts which I noticed, that of being recognizably 'Jesus of Nazareth'. This may seem a fanciful conception, but it is worthwhile to ponder and observe and wonder whether the ways in which the transformation of creation takes place do not reflect quite recognizably the personal character of Jesus as he comes through to us in the Gospels. Those people who have lived most consciously and intimately with God, and even those who more erratically relate

167

their lives to him, report that he comes through to them in earthy, everyday ways, which may suddenly give way to the inexplicable and openly marvellous. He is sometimes ruthless in dealing with their weaknesses, but only when they are willing that he should be, and yet he is often extremely gentle, not to say tactful. He provokes questions and gives cryptic and unsatisfying responses. In all circumstances he is unexpected and even outrageous in his methods, and 'speaks as one having authority'. He plays jokes on people which can even be fairly brutal (but only if they are 'up to' that). It all sounds very familiar, and although this sort of subjective assessment cannot be offered as evidence to the unconvinced it is verifiable by the believer, and indeed it is what we should expect to be the case if the incarnation really happened, and if the basis of reality in which it happened is that of exchange of life. The transformation which takes place, in space and time, is a transformation not only originating in Jesus, who is incarnate God, but also continuing to *be* him, and yet only with full respect for the nature of things, human or non-human. There is no coercion, but only patient waiting for the moment at which the passionate breakthrough becomes possible because desired. This is not some 'cosmic process' at work, but very personal love.

The symbol of this strange reality, through the Christian centuries, has been that of the human heart of Jesus. Response to this image in recent times has been made difficult by the interposition of a layer of strikingly sentimental and trivializing devotion to the Sacred Heart, decked out with suitably third-rate art. (This was paralleled, significantly, by the general trivialization of the concept of Romance, so that by now the word itself indicates mawkish escapist fantasy, very unlike the strong, exciting and yet tender and vernal tone of the original Romantic voice.) The use of the heart of Jesus as the proper and adequate image by which the poetry of Christianity could express its awareness of how redemption happened and happens begins from very early times. It looks for its roots in the Gospel of John, in which it is told that 'the disciple whom Jesus loved' leaned against his heart at the last Supper, and in which also the strange incident is recorded of how the side of the dead Christ on the cross was pierced by the spear of a soldier who wanted to be sure he was dead, and from the wound flowed water and blood. The incident is plausible physically, but John's emphasis on it is due to a recognition that this event symbolized a profound truth about the whole redemptive act. For the water of regeneration and the blood of the new covenant came—both, and both together—from the passionate death of the human being, Jesus, and must always find their origin there, or fail in their power to save. This awareness looks back in time and finds its foreshadowing in the Old Testament, so that the liturgy of the Heart of Jesus speaks with the mouth of Hosea:

> When Israel was a child I loved him,
>   and I called my son out of Egypt . . .
> I led them with reins of kindness
>   with leading strings of love.
> I was like someone who lifts an infant close against his cheek,
>   stooping down to him I gave him his food.
> How could I treat you like Admah. . . .
> My heart recoils from it
> My whole being trembles at the thought. . .
> for I am God, not man.
>   (Hos. 11:1,4,8,9)

So it is that Jesus, the man who was God, sums up in himself the kind of love which Hosea expressed. It is the cry of a person in love, desiring love, and Paul's great poem (Rom. 8) of humankind overwhelmed with love knows it all as the deeply personal love of Jesus who is Christ:

> Who can be our adversary, if God is on our side? He did not even spare his own Son, but gave him up for us all, and must not that gift be accompanied by the gift of all else? . . . Who will pass sentence against us when Jesus Christ, who died, has risen again and sits at the right hand of God, is pleading for us? Who will separate us from the love of Christ? . . . Of this I am fully persuaded, neither death nor life, nor angels or principalities or powers, neither what is present nor what is to come, no force whatever, neither the height above us nor the depth beneath us, nor any other created thing, will be able to separate us from the love of God, which comes to us in Christ Jesus our Lord.
>   (Rom. 9:31–2, 34, 38–9)

It is cosmic, yet not dissolved in the cosmos, for the power of this love is that of a properly human love, yet a human love faithful, vehement and absolute beyond any human love, because it is also God's love. So, centuries later, St Bonaventure held together in the essential Christian tension the vast scope of redemption and the source of it all, the love of the human heart of the man, Jesus:

> You who have been redeemed, consider who it is who hangs on the cross for you, whose death gives life to the dead. . . . God's providence decreed that one of the soldiers should open his sacred side with a spear, so that blood and water might flow out to pay the price of our salvation. This blood, which flowed from its source in the secret recesses of his heart, gave the sacraments of the Church power to confer the life of grace, and for those who already live in Christ was a draught of living water welling up to eternal life.

It has been sadly possible to read statements about 'grace' in terms of a static image of some 'thing' conferred on the faithful to make them holy. Bonaventure's words, among many others, present the outpouring of blood as the adequate image of the self-giving of passionate love poured out in exchange.

'O wonderful exchange', the twelfth-century Cistercian Gueric of Igny wrote in his 'Christmas sermons': ' . . . you take flesh and give divinity, a commerce in charity . . . emptying yourself, you have filled us. You have poured into men all the plenitude of your divinity. You have transformed but not confounded' (*Liturgical Sermons*). This is the genuine Christian insight, which brings human beings to union with their God not by dissolving them in him, or him in them, but by bringing them to a glory of distinctness through exchange of love with the 'one adored Substitution'.

St Gertrude, the thirteenth-century German mystic, thanked God above all for 'the priceless gift of your intimate friendship, giving me in so many different ways that shrine of your godhead, your Son's divine Heart, to fill up the sum of my delights'. This is the authentic voice of incarnational spirituality, theologically accurate in its tone of human and romantic love, and perceiving with the immediacy and intensity of true passion the eternal God fully and only given in the human, bodily reality of Jesus.

170

For that is the significance of this great image. The heart is physical and it is the vital centre of bodily being in a person who expresses and experiences love. Julian of Norwich told it vividly, showing us the joy of the lover in his power to give himself so completely. This is a theological statement, the accurate poetry of redemption:

With a glad countenance our Lord looked at his side, rejoicing as he gazed. And as he looked, I, with my limited understanding was led by way of this same wound into his side. There he showed me a place, fair and delightful, large enough for all saved mankind to rest in peace and love. I was reminded of the most precious blood and water that he shed for love of us. And, gazing still, he showed me his blessed heart riven in two. In his sweet enjoyment he helped me to understand, in part at any rate, how the blessed Godhead was moving the poor soul to appreciate the eternal love of God that has neither beginning nor end. At the same time our good Lord said, most blessedly, 'See, how I have loved you'. As if to say 'My dearest, look at your Lord, your God, your Maker, and your endless joy. See the delight and happiness I have in your salvation, and because you love me, rejoice with me'.

Finally, in the seventeenth century, the message of the human and Romantic love of Jesus was sent out once more, through the mouth of a lover whose whole life was a passionate self-giving. More soberly, but with the urgency of the insight of love, Margaret Mary Alacoque shared the message which was the mainspring of her own life, as she (suffering and ardent point of exchange) was bidden by love:

I believe that the reason behind our Lord's great desire that especial honour should be paid to his sacred heart is his wish to renew in our souls the effects of our redemption. For his sacred heart is an inexhaustible spring which has no other purpose than to overflow into hearts which are humble, so that they may be ready and willing to devote their lives to this good will and pleasure. (A letter quoted in *Divine Office*).

171

'The effects of our redemption' is a name for the process of resurrection at work in all creation. It is physical transformation of the limited and enslaved creation into 'the glorious liberty of the sons of God' by 'the love of God which is in Christ Jesus our Lord'.

At this point we are thrown into awareness of the meaning of that ultimate Christian statement about reality—that it is Triune. It is not in considering the origins of created things that we can best catch some sense of what it means to say that God is 'Three in one', nor even in being exposed to Paul's intense vision of Christ as 'image of the unseen God'. In either context the doctrine of the Trinity can be—must be—encountered, yet it seems to me that it is only here, at the most intensely human and bodily point of the movement of redemption, that we receive some faint but real intimation of why it is essential to make such a strange assertion.

For most people, the doctrine of the Trinity is baffling, a humanly meaningless statement one is taught to accept 'on faith', and not all the shamrocks in Ireland can really help. Triangles, linked circles, paintings of two men and a dove or three identical men do not lead into the heart of it, and the marvellous metaphysical counterpoint of the Athanasian creed only makes music in the mind which is already attuned to the mystery. But if we follow the mystics and simply seek to enter as deeply as possible into that which is signified by the human heart of Jesus then we find ourselves also at the heart of the Trinity and see it from 'inside'.

The passion of love which offered itself to be the point at which estranged human kind could receive the torrent of divine *amour voulu* is the demonstration of the inmost reality of the Three in One. It is the point at which we are enabled to see, in direct and unambiguous human terms, the nature of that which is the very being of God. The love which incarnate Wisdom so longs to give back to the source of his own life is received totally, as it is totally given and returned to its Source and Origin in one unbroken movement of ecstatic joy and thanksgiving, and that joy, that intensity of exchange of Being, is the one called Spirit. That which the Father breathes, speaks, expends is his own being, and it only *is* in being given. Therefore also it only *is* in being received, and the essence of that exchanged being (Exchange itself) is the one who from the generative embrace between Holiness and Wisdom has being as life, gives life and praises life. There is no holding, no containing, but an eternal torrent of exchanged glory which in human experience we have to separate out and call 'love' to distinguish it from other human exchanges. But it is 'love' because it *is*. This is reality, whose nature is indeed love, totally given, totally received, totally given back. All else that we call reality is 'made of' that, and creation is the natural exaggeration of a love which must always love more.

That is why the refusal of the Exchange is unimaginably Nothing, a contradiction inconceivable, yet it happens. And because it happens there are no lengths to which love itself will not go to restore the broken communion with, through and within those who have broken it, and themselves. Resurrection is the restoration of 'all things in Christ', so that 'all things' may be what they are in the movement of the dance of divine Wisdom. ' . . . And the Church is his Body', because that is where it is known that this incredible fact is the answer to the question people ask each other, or try not to ask: 'What is life all about?' But we know the answer, the nature of reality, the meaning of things, only because we are drawn to experience it, in the particularity of the flesh-taking, at the point where the heart of Jesus marks the centre of all the Exchanges of the passionate God.

5   The Body of Christ

The title of this chapter is deliberately ambiguous, yet precise. The body, the physical being of Jesus of Nazareth, living, dying and risen, is—as risen—still present in various ways which are equally real, maybe more real than his 'ordinary' presence on earth. The body of Christ is the Church—and what is the Church? The body of Christ is the eucharistic food—and what is the Eucharist? The body of Christ is every human being, and indeed all creation, for he is the beginning and the end of all. And all these meanings are one meaning, ultimately, yet they are distinct. What is the relationship? How does it work?

We need to grasp the sheer *literalness* of the way the phrase 'the body of Christ' is meant by St Paul, from whom we gain our most precise understanding of the whole strange affair, though this same emphasis is found differently but complementarily expressed, in John's Gospel and letters. As John A.T. Robinson says, in his admirable little book called *The Body* (quite the best study of Pauline concepts in this area that I've ever read), 'It is almost impossible to exaggerate the materialism and crudity of Paul's doctrine of the Church as literally now the resurrection *body* of Christ'; and the same applies to the other ways in which the phrase 'the body of Christ' is used. We are not using a metaphor or a symbol (in the usual, weak sense of 'symbol') to help us grasp a different kind of reality. We are simply saying this (the Church) *is* Christ's body; this (the consecrated Bread and Wine) *is* Christ's body; this (the human and risen Jesus) *is* Christ's body. To 'incorporate' someone in Christ is for that person literally to be, in his or her ultimate reality, Christ—not by mystical experience or even by evident holiness, but just by accepting to be what he calls each one to be. At this point we should, perhaps, recall what I noted in the first chapter, the fact that an unprejudiced view of accounts of 'oddness' in the material world persuades us to modify our assumptions about the nature of bodies, in particular about their 'limits', and to con-

174

sider seriously the imaginatively difficult idea that our skin is a misleading symbol of the limits of our physical selves. It is a useful way of 'wrapping up' certain important aspects of our physical being, a wrapping which, because of sin, has become a kind of prison.

The best way to approach this mystery is, as before, to see how it all begins in the actions and words of Jesus himself: the body of Christ is no other thing than the body of Jesus, and the body of Jesus is the person of Jesus. It is perhaps necessary to make clear, once more, why I continually ask the reader to enter into imaginative reconstruction of the personal experience of Jesus. This is not an extra, a kind of background or light relief, nor an aid to 'devotion'. This whole book is based on the idea that theology must spring from taking seriously the fact of incarnation—and this really does mean the *fact*, not just the *doctrine*. The incarnation was, and is, a personal experience which happened, first of all, to one man. Therefore all that happened in it, and grew from it (resurrection, eucharist, church) are also his experience. We really cannot hope to understand these huge things at all unless we can perceive their beginnings in the actual human experience of Jesus.

We saw in earlier chapters how it seems that Jesus broke through to new areas of experience of himself and of his Father's kingdom (both at once), not because he planned it but because obedience to his Father's will required some action of him which, in practice, had extraordinary material concomitants. The thrust of the need to give love in a particular way broke through the normal behaviour of material reality because that was the only way for the Father's will to be done.

I suggested, earlier in the book, that the impermeability of our 'spheres' of experience is the result of sin. Jesus lived in this sinful state of affairs and worked with it, but the love that was his being was bound by its very nature to change that situation. Centrally, he did this in his death, but his living of a human life did not follow a planned progression towards that moment, any more than any other human life does. The very thrust towards that moment required him, often, to follow what one might call detours round the granite rocks of human blindness and ignorance, but also it required the breaking down of obstacles around which a detour was impossible or inappropriate. Among these events, a few seem to have the

175

character of anticipation, as if *time itself* were the obstacle. They manifested the effective power of the resurrection to which he had 'not yet' attained in his flesh.

In a sense all he did was that kind of anticipation. The way he loved people, and their response to him, was an introduction for them into 'the kingdom'. They were experiencing that in him which was 'not yet' and yet which could not be wholly contained within the imprisoned servant status which he had taken on. It was there and it showed and people responded to it. Sometimes it showed more strikingly and created a furore, but it was always there. So all his teaching and healing and indeed all his many relationships were, theologically, the 'anticipation' of the resurrection life (his own *and* ours) which was 'not yet'. But there were a few occasions of which we can use the word 'anticipation' in a more precise sense, and the transfiguration was one of them, but it was brief; he did not stay within that sphere of his being. He returned to the outer spheres, yet the needed change and development had been accomplished. Something had happened to *him*, to his own personality, his own bodily self, which affected others also, though at that time both the number of those affected and the extent of their realization was very limited. But the point is that things could and did happen to Jesus, in relation to those he loved, which changed their relationship permanently because it introduced them, and himself, there and then into an experience which 'belonged' to the life of the resurrection, although he was 'not yet risen from the dead'. I am suggesting, now, that this kind of thing is what happened at the Last Supper, also, and that by trying to understand this we shall come a little nearer to understanding what we can mean by the words 'the body of Christ'.

As a preliminary part of this, I want to think for a while about the other obvious example of 'anticipation', when Jesus changed water into wine, at Cana in Galilee, right at the beginning of his public life, at a time when his direction and role were still surrounded by questions to which he had, as yet, no clear answers, and when he himself said that his time had 'not yet come'.

This incident gives us, among other things, the clearest indication we have of the kind of relationship Jesus had with his mother. This is important because, as we saw, his physical relationship to her gave her a special place in the network of Exchange, in the sense

176

that his most direct and simple involvement in the human race was through her. Yet she was not simply an instrument. She was God's 'door' because she was a very remarkable woman and her particular qualities developed in relation to the calling to which she responded. So it is not at all surprising that on the first occasion on which we are shown Mary and the adult Jesus involved in something together this involvement should have the nature of a conflict.

Commentators, especially Catholic ones, try to play down that conflict, yet it seems a proper one. Jesus had just been through his wilderness ordeal, a process of discovery of a kind which must have shaken up and brought into question everything he had up to that time learned and thought and hoped and feared. When he was 'given back' himself afterwards, everything that he had taken with him to the time of temptation was restored to him, but changed. It was so changed that it was like walking in a new country. By the time he came back to Galilee and joined the wedding party at Cana he had had time to work out a few things, but nothing was ever going to look the same as it had before, and all had to be re-learned and newly interpreted, step by step. But his mother had not shared that experience. Her own 'desert experience', we may guess, had been during the time when Joseph was trying to make up his mind whether to marry her or not, but other such experiences had to follow, for there were big changes to come in her life which were linked to what must happen her son. During his growing-up years she had no doubt shared with him much reflection on the meaning of the prophecies of their people. We can never know how explicitly they dared to articulate even to themselves the 'role' of Jesus himself—child of mysterious promise yet so normal in his daily life up to that time. But it was inevitable that they would 'ponder in their hearts' the meaning of it all, together or separately. And we can detect, I think, a definite parting of the ways. Luke's evocation of Mary's self-understanding in the 'Magnificat' shows an interpretation of God's action as saviour in terms of revolutionary change in social relationships. She saw herself as the one who stands, humble but exultant, at the gateway of the reign of God, the messianic kingdom of justice and peace. And among the things that God will do for his people is to give them food and drink: 'he has filled the hungry with good things'. The years between had no doubt deepened and refined her vision, but it did not leave her, for

177

it was and is at the heart of the Christian idea of salvation. An interpretation of God's redeeming love in action which fails to see that kind of transformation as integral to the action of the kingdom in humankind is in danger of 'spiritualizing' it out of existence. If God's action in history transforms reality it transforms *social* reality. This Mary knew and Jesus knew. But the further question was, how? And even if we set aside those cruder versions of 'how' which inspired the Jewish resistance movements at the time, we can, I think, suggest that Mary's attitude at the wedding shows that she thought of the 'how' in terms of the exercise of supernatural power when the time was right for it, and it seemed obvious to her that the time *was* right. For what other reason had Jesus gone to John at the Jordan, and then spent all that time in seclusion, and had subsequently already attracted disciples? She seems to have expected that Jesus would automatically share this view, and this is a very normal maternal expectation! Very likely he *had* previously shared it, or at any rate accepted and pondered over her expressed thoughts about it. But he had been through an experience which, among other things, specifically called in question such a notion of 'how' God's kingdom was to be established. In fact, Mary's request (more of a demand, in fact) that he act a 'messianic' part in this simple and obvious way must have caught him on a still raw nerve, for she was asking him to do something very like what Satan had asked him to do: 'Make these stones bread'; 'They have no wine'.

Bread and wine, food and drink, the basic necessities of life, the basic symbols of life. To exercise power over these is a kind of ultimate assertion of sovereignty—but what *kind* of sovereignty? 'You shall worship the Lord your God, and him only shall you serve.' This kingdom can only be itself in obedience, in service, in exchange. And so, coming out of the desert, Jesus had heard John's voice evoking a different, yet equally familiar interpretation of how God was to be obeyed. 'Behold, the Lamb of God', the sacrifice, the Substitution.

If John said that, he spoke out of a deep intuitive awareness which came to him when he saw Jesus newly returned from the desert. John was, at that point also, the 'voice' articulating what was in the heart of Jesus himself. He was announcing not only to his own disciples but to Jesus himself what he was perceiving in Jesus at that moment. It must always be —there has to be a voice

178

from outside to articulate inner conviction. And the shape of this role which John's words evoked was very different from the other one; it was the role of the suffering 'Servant' of Isaiah, the role of undergoing, of helpless yet fully willed suffering and death.

This was the 'title' which Jesus took back to Galilee with him. It made it impossible for him simply to accept the kind of saviour-role his mother, and indeed his friends and new disciples, thrust at him. His rejection of it was, inevitably, in some senses a rejection of her also. 'What have you to do with me?' as the RSV has it. The Jerusalem Bible, trying to be tactful, gives 'Why turn to me?', but the notes to the passage admit that the closer translation of this 'semitic formula' is 'What to me and to thee?' and that it is 'intended to deprecate interference or, more strongly, to reject overtures of any kind'. This, it seems, was precisely what Jesus was doing. He was 'deprecating interference' and 'rejecting overtures'; specifically he was rejecting the role offered him, but his reason is odd: 'My time has not yet come'. This 'time' or 'hour' is the 'proper' time for the kingdom to be manifest. It is the hour of his glory, the hour of resurrection, in fact. If he knew anything certainly at that time it was indeed this—that his hour had 'not yet come'.

But his rejection was not a simple rejection of the kind of messianic power implied, as if he had to choose between two alternatives. The implication is that it was inappropriate *then*. And we can see why, for at that juncture it did indeed appear as a contradiction of all that was implied in John's recognition of him as 'Lamb of God'. Yet, when the 'hour' did come, the two seeming alternatives would be reconciled, indeed they would be seen to be one, for the transforming power is released in the moment of passion. But that lay far in the future, in a knowledge still obscure. 'My hour has not yet come.'

In that case, why did he turn all that water into very good wine? Perhaps it is not fanciful to suggest that we can see here an example of the process of separation leading to the possibility of real union, to which I referred before. If so, we can see that it sheds light upon the later event, a stranger and more powerful 'anticipation', when union could only be brought about by a defining of separateness. The child in the womb, still one with the mother, is fed directly by her body. It is only the separated individual who can actually be

179

given and receive food and drink. It is necessary to differentiate, even violently, before there can be the deepest union.

This happened at Cana, and it happened in the upper room. Jesus rejected his mother's demand, which was in a sense an unjustified demand, of the kind that mothers do often make on their children. It showed a lack of respect for the proper separateness of the child now adult. It was made suddenly, under pressure of real compassion and desire to help, and therefore allowed no time for the 'pondering' which might have modified it; and so it expressed very directly and simply the strength and weakness of the relationship. It did not 'ask too much' but it asked wrongly, and to obey would have been to accept a wrong relationship, disrespectful to the reality of her as the making of it had been disrespectful to the reality of him. So he rejected it, he separated himself strongly and clearly from any simple identification with her wishes or ideas. In that differentiation they were able to rediscover each other, newly and beautifully.

Mary had, in her impulsive demand, given to her Son the clarification he needed in trying to understand his own direction. And he, in rejecting that kind of authority in her, gave her a tremendous insight into who, and what, he truly was. We can see that in what followed. She did not renew her request, rather something happened to the character of the request itself. It became something which she had *given* him, and she left it with him; she took her hands off it, as it were. She simply bade the servants do whatever he told them. It was an act of trust, of homage even, but with no hint of servility. And it set him free. It set him free in relation to this particular situation in which there was a real, human need for precisely that action which she had demanded. There was a need for it, and therefore it was appropriate that he should fulfil that need, and her action made him able to do so, because it broke a barrier for him. Because she 'gave' him this, it was no longer the kind of suggestion that Satan had made. To respond was to respond in love, to liberate into this particular bit of the world of sin ('sin' being, here, the lack of wine, and the social humiliation and personal hurt for the family that such lack involved) the power of exchanged life which it was his whole mission to pour out on earth. The time was 'not yet', but love and need could bypass time. To meet this simple, real, human need the love of the risen Lord—Messiah, the

180

saving God who feeds his people, who 'fills the hungry with good things'—could go ahead of itself. Divine Wisdom could indeed say, as she had come to do, 'Come and eat of my bread and drink of the wine which I have mixed.'

There are elements in this extraordinary encounter and its result which are a help in approaching a more crucial encounter and its infinitely more far-reaching effects. The note of 'anticipation' in response to a need not otherwise to be met I have already referred to. It is important to notice that the 'need' was not merely for a given quantity of wine. Conceivably, some wealthy friend might have been induced to buy wine. The need was, more deeply, for an acted—almost a ritual—definition of relationship and role, with his mother, his people, his disciples, in fact with *people*. This is an element in the whole account of the incident which has far-reaching significance. The model of reality with which I have been working, that of exchange, helps us to realize more vividly the 'organic' nature of the actions of Jesus. They are not *applied* to situations and people from outside, as from some divine platform. They *grow* from and to real people, they are exchanges, and always at several levels. In this story we have seen the vital exchange between mother and son by which a new depth of trust and love was reached, and in this and consequent on it an exchange of Wisdom, in word and in action. The thing happened between them; in that exchange of love Wisdom poured out her gifts and they reached to all those who were in the path of that torrent. In the need to give and receive that exchange the sphere of the coming Kingdom was breached and its power released into the everyday reality of a country wedding. And the country wedding was not just a laboratory for a divine experiment. The occasion was a ritual one, and a special kind of ritual, having to do essentially with the most intimate and basic of human exchanges, that of marriage. This is not accidental. The Baptist himself knew Jesus as the Bridegroom, and having proclaimed his coming he was concerned only to present the Bride to her Lover and to disappear. The wedding feast was already begun. The ritual of marriage celebrated by the community of Israel was a celebration not only of the union of one human couple but of God's bridal covenant with his people, a covenant which Jesus was to transform into an explicitness of material fact which could not have been conceived before. The occasion of this 'beginning of miracles', therefore, was as fitting as it could be. The ritual expressed both the immediate human encounter and the wider, symbolic one. And at all levels food and drink were involved, indeed were indispensible. Separation made union possible, wine could be consciously given and received, as an act of love.

We have, then, elements of chellenge and response, of need and response to need, of ritual encounter and everyday encounter. There is a coming together of national history and of personal experience. There is a whole rich complex of exchange, weaving in and out, and all of it meets at one point of breakthrough, when the power of love transcends the restriction of sin and the presence of God becomes explicit. 'And his disciples believed in him.'

At the end, when the time had almost come for the last barrier to be broken, it was the same only much, much more so. In order to try to realize the theology of this I want, once more, to discover as far as I can the human reality which made it happen.

We have to rid our minds, as far as possible, of the view of this supreme Gift which sees it as something which Jesus planned to give as a mother gives a parting gift to console her children if she has to go away for a while. This is a good image, from one point of view, but it is quite inadequate to express the dynamics of an event which was to crack open the categories of reality in such a way that they could never be fully closed again. The trouble with the 'gift' image is that it is static, it evokes an *object* and as soon as we think of the Body of Christ as an object we are on the wrong wavelength and get nothing but misleading signals.

Food, after all, is basically a kind of communication. The sharing of food has always had an enormous significance in human societies. To share food creates a bond so intimate that, in some societies, it is as sacred as a blood relationship. The human instinct is to offer food to a guest, and many people feel unsatisfied and humiliated if they cannot offer what they feel is adequate fare. (Hence, of course, the great worry about the lack of wine at Cana.) To give and receive food is to exchange life, not only because it actually nourishes the body but because it is a language, a vocabulary of quite exact statements about the relationships involved. The kind of food we share is a clear statement about the nature and level of communication which is intended. The bread and cheese given to a tramp at the back door delineates the relationship we have with him as clearly as the roast duck we give to an 'important' visitor. Fish and chips in a newspaper defines the nature of the occasion; so does champagne at a wedding or cake on a birthday. Sharing food also seems to have an inherently spiritual character, and its use in every kind of religious cult seems to us perfectly natural. To offer food to the gods is not ridiculous, it supposes no physical need in the recipient; it is simply the obvious language of shared life. It is exchange, in symbol and in fact. If we begin by holding on imaginatively to the model of exchange in thinking of the nature of food, we shall be closer to its reality. We may put uneaten food in the refrigerator until the next meal, but that does not tell us much about the human significance of food, for it is not as an object on a shelf but as a communication of life that it is at its most real. So this strangest and yet most finally 'real' kind of food can best be thought of as, first of all, exchange. It is a love-gift, but that means its reality is known in the giving and receiving, in its own particular way. But we must then ask, why is it given and received in this particular way? Why did it happen and why then, and indeed what was it that happened?

For this happening, also, is an 'anticipation'. As we have seen and shall see, it is 'proper' to the glorified body of the Lord to be known in being shared. The Eucharist, therefore, *belongs* to the life of resurrection. If it had been instituted during one of the resurrection appearances it would seem fitting, but on this night before his passion he was still as enmeshed in the blocked and inadequate exchanges of a material reality paralysed by sin as he had ever been. Why *then*? There must be a reason. The answers to these questions, or rather the attempt to find them, since there are no final answers, concern not only the body of Christ which is the eucharistic Exchange but the other ways in which that body is given and received in Exchange.

In thinking about this I am drawing on all the Gospel accounts of that evening, including that of John. For John, as so often, gives us the theological and psychological context, the 'reason why'. His setting out of the way in which Jesus talked to his beloved on that night provides the logic of that exchange. I am aware that I am asking much of the reader in following through all the careful and lengthy stages already passed, and still to come, and here I want to say with T. S. Eliot:

I said to my soul be still, and wait without hope
For hope would be hope for the wrong thing; wait without love
For love would be love for the wrong thing; there is yet faith
But the faith and the love and the hope are all in the waiting.
('Little Gidding', *Four Quartets*)

To embark on such a venture as this seems sheer folly, yet we are, after all, only doing what Jesus himself told us to do, when he said, 'Follow me', and to follow this part of his way we have to begin further back, as I did before. We have to recall once more the days and weeks and months during which Jesus and his Twelve had been together, working and walking and talking and eating and sleeping together.

They had no headquarters or regular place to return to, though they had, it seems, a habit of turning up at Bethany for a rest from time to time, and no doubt there were other similar stopping places. But mostly they were on the road, and therefore however many friends they had they were, as a group, very reliant on each other for support and companionship. They could not have that gentle spreading outwards of roots in varied but reliable relationship with their surroundings which is available to people who belong in a definite neighbourhood, even if they are away a good deal. Although all no doubt kept in contact with families and old associates they had uprooted themselves. Jesus himself had done so, and so had those who came with him, and we can see from the many references in the synoptic Gospels to such uprooting from family ties that this was something which bothered all of them and needed to be clarified and justified. The Jewish people are, after all, a very community-conscious people, and while nowadays this necessarily concentrates in the family (at least in the Diaspora), at the time of Jesus it was concentrated in a different way by the alien presence of Rome, in face of which local communities needed to feel strongly their Jewish identity. Therefore to be isolated, as Jesus and his immediate followers were by their travelling habits, was an unusual thing and one which threw them on each other, not only because there was no one else but because they were likely to be surrounded by comparative incomprehension, rapidly hardening, as we saw, into increasing distrust and hostility.

To the Twelve, and to other men and women disciples who were

184

part of the immediate circle of those who travelled with Jesus, the growth of hostility must have been a bewildering experience. It was not what they had expected, and they could not fully understand or accept it however often Jesus told them it was inevitable and fitting. It did not tie in with any of the patterns of thinking they had learned, and although their ideas must have been changing, deeply and permanently, through their daily contact with Jesus, this kind of change takes time. As we have seen in other contexts it does not necessarily break through and take over consciousness until 'something else' comes into the situation. To our way of thinking, the fact of the presence of Jesus should have been just this 'something else', but we have to realize that for these particular people Jesus was the continuity in their lives. They lived with him, and his being and words changed them and shaped them, but at this time mainly as life in a family changes and shapes people. It is only when something challenges or upsets the continuity that the personal depth and reality of what has been learned becomes apparent. So we find that, up to the very end, the disciples—even the closest—displayed what seems at first sight a baffling lack of sensitivity and understanding.

Anyone who has experienced life in a good and loving family or community will know how hard it is, just because of the close daily interaction, to introduce into the normal exchanges of word, act and ritual anything that overtly challenges or is likely to demand a kind of response completely different from the ones by which the group is accustomed to live. If someone in the group, even the most loved, tries to introduce something really new there is a very high probability that one of two things will happen: either the new thing will be rejected without a hearing, and for the time being at least a wall will close around the person who tried to change things; or else, if the person is deeply loved and trusted, what is said will be listened to and then dropped quietly into a kind of pool of non-reaction, while the usual affectionate exchanges hasten to cover over the gap as if nothing had happened.

It seems that this kind of thing is what happened in the group around Jesus. There were many things they could and did consciously learn from him, by word and example, and there was much more which they were unconsciously learning from him, which would only be apparent later. But there were some things which

185

were so out of tune with all that made sense of their relationship with him that they could not hear them. One of them rejected the speaker with the message; he built a wall higher and higher to shut out what he would not hear, until he could not see over it. The others listened, but they did not have 'ears to hear'. They dropped such sayings quietly out of sight and hastened to show their beloved Master how much they loved him, in spite of what he said. And he had to let them do so. There was no way he could get through to them without damaging the relationship, perhaps irrevocably. In that one case it was, indeed, irrevocably damaged already.

So we have the picture of a man moving towards an end he foresees with increasing clarity and embraces with a sense of mounting urgency, but unable to share the knowledge of it in any explicit way. Indirectly, he tried all the time to 'get through'. The form of warning is constant, as we saw earlier. It seems he was trying, in a way, to reach the minds of his friends by way of the teaching he gave to larger groups and crowds. But there was nobody with whom he could 'try out' what he was discovering, nobody who could support him in moments of panic or near-despair, no one who could validate or constructively question his sense of direction. If the need to share had been so great before the transfiguration that it blew open the gates of time, how much greater must that need have been as the last Passover approached.

Yet, as often happens, the very impossibility of full communication probably made the emotional bond all the stronger. The disciples, sensing his moods and his need, could not do enough to show their love and devotion, surrounded as they were by hostility and suspicion and an element of disappointment in the people. Their support was needed and they gave it. He referred to this, later, at the Supper itself, when he said to them, 'You are the men who have stood by me faithfully in my trials.' John says that he called them explicitly 'friends'—that is, people one can share with— and he had indeed shared with them 'everything I have learned from my Father'.

This remark, and its context, suggest that the last months together had been in spite of the tacit exclusion of one subject a time of increasing intimacy and depth of relationship. The discourse and prayer which John presents in the context of the last Supper is no doubt, as we would expect, the kind of thing Jesus might have said

186

on that occasion, but it may convincingly be perceived as a putting together by the evangelist of conversations developed in times and places of comparative intimacy with the Twelve over a longer period. It is not public teaching, and its extreme difference from the style of address in the Synoptic Gospels is easily explained if we imagine the group, as they travelled around the country, taking their brief periods of privacy as the precious things they were, and in them finding it possible to enter together into theological depths which would have been impossible in a more public situation. And we would expect to find this kind of thing presented by John, especially if the author was indeed John-bar-Zebedee (and an increasing consensus accepts this). He was a constant companion of Jesus and one of his three most intimate friends, and the thought and teaching he presents comes to us through a mind probably more closely attuned to that of his Master then any other and growing (as these things do) in a dialectical development.

Ideas, especially such ideas as John presents, are the result of dialogue, one person challenging another to develop a concept or to seize on some thought and heighten or modify it. For a man like John to write down the words of Jesus would be to recall, in that form, the give and take of exchanged thought not only privately pondered over the years but talked over with others who had been present, and with people who wanted to know what Jesus had taught. This process, which is very familiar to anyone dealing with important memories, acts as a kind of filter by which things which are less significant to the person remembering (even though they might have been highly significant to someone else) are dropped, and those things which are most fruitful of further thought—again, for *this* particular person—are heightened and, as it were, 'framed'. So I think the 'discourse' is one man's memories thus filtered, of real conversations, in which Jesus was 'teacher' but in which the response helped to direct and shape the teaching. So the discourse as we have it is, among other things, valuable evidence of the kind of relationship which had been growing between these men.

The relationship was deeply important to Jesus himself. The Twelve and other disciples were not just pupils or listeners, they were friends and lovers. They had to be, for on the quality of this relationship depended the nature of the new thing which they were to become: the Church. Here already we can see that it is impossible to separate the body of Christ as Eucharist from the body of Christ as Church or from the body of Christ as his risen being, which is also, though transformed, the earthly, local, daily-seen and daily-loved body of Jesus of Nazareth. For this one human being represented the final point, the 'remnant', of the scope of Covenant between the Lord and his people. The promises were first made to all humankind, but infidelity and the refusal of exchange had meant that more and more were progressively self-excluded as explicit bearers of the Covenant. A smaller and smaller 'remnant' received that Covenant which God, on his side, would never break. Noah remained faithful and he is the 'type' of those groups who remain faithful to a central insight of Wisdom in the most unlikely surroundings, but Abraham, father of faith, represents the election of one nation as both sign and agent of the unbroken covenant. Yet the chosen people is unfaithful also, and in time is punished, until of that also only a 'remnant' remains. The restored Temple is the sign of God's fidelity, his constant presence, but the people are spiritually disunited and torn by false hopes and misleading ambitions. Only a few are left who are still faithfully waiting 'for the consolation of Israel', for it is becoming apparent to these few that there can be no recovery of the past. If Israel is to be reborn it will be in a new way, as a new people. The new people is moving towards birth, and in the group of disciples around Jesus we see that birth being prepared. But it is still in the womb, not yet capable of breathing the air of the kingdom, and the birth, when it comes, will be (as all birth is) the moment at which a long and infinitely complex process of exchanges comes to a single point of action and passion. Thereafter, the newborn, taking into life all the old exchanges which made it, makes them new in itself and begins a new exchanging, reaching out ever further and further.

Therefore both the love and companionship, and the increasing and final isolation of Jesus within it and eventually from it, are essential. They happened because that is how such human things do happen but, because of the intensity of undissipated love in him, both his sharing and his inability to share produced the most extraordinary effects.

At the risk of being boring I want to re-emphasize that we cannot separate the actual human being of Jesus from the 'theological things' which happened, which means that there have to be real, credible, human reasons for them, arising out of real situations and relationships. We may not always be able to know about them, but we must know that it was so, otherwise we are getting very near to the view of Jesus which sees him as somehow 'inhabited' by God, or worse still as inhabited by a divine plan which he had to carry out. This was a man and is a man, a human bodily person with all that this means of need and possibility.

The occasion was, like the wedding at Cana, a ritual occasion. There is a dispute about whether this was actually the Passover meal deliberately anticipated by Jesus since it was properly to be celebrated after sunset next day. It is not possible to be sure about this, but we can be sure that the way in which this meal and the Passover are inextricably linked by the evangelists and indeed by all Christian writers since is not due to pure muddle. Even if the meal was not, in fact, the Passover, it was just before it, and the time and place were soaked in its symbols by every kind of association of custom and expectation. And in the minds of the early Church the imminence of the Passion is part of all this, for Christ *is* the new Passover.

We are, at this point, in the middle of many kinds and levels of exchanges. We are at the place where an old history ends and a new history begins, at the end of the old covenant and the beginning of the new one, at a place of family reunion and national renewal, in this city, ruled by foreigners, which is the holy city where the prophet has to die. We are at the heart of a ritual encounter which is also a human encounter, and which was 'meant' to have that double character by its nature as ritual.

The Passover is always like this. It is the dialectic of the personal and particular celebration (the place and time and clothes and food, how these particular celebrants are feeling and who they are) with the ancient ritual which draws into itself not only the celebration of the great liberation from Egypt but so much other symbolism— of spring, of a pastoral people at lambing, of dependence and contingency, of sharing, of chosen-ness. Neither side of this dialectic swamps the other. Whether Passover is celebrated under threat of persecution in medieval Spain or in a Nazi concentration camp or in New York or in a Kibbutz in Israel, the particular occasion gives its character to the experience, but it is a character expressed in and through the established ritual and in no other way. And even

189

if the meal which Jesus shared with his friends was not actually the Passover it was set firmly in a Passover context, and that ritual and its meaning were in all their minds. It heightened awareness and yet gave a sense of support and clear direction which made possible an intimacy and depth of encounter rarely possible when the setting for encounter has to be newly and consciously devised.

So we get a situation in which it was possible for the group to reach a new level of intensity of presence to each other. All the circumstances heightened it: the uncertainty and hope and fear of preceding months; the tumultuous public encounters of the last few days, contrasted with the sudden privacy and isolation of the upper room; also the sense of some impending crisis whose character was not clear. They were in just such an inbetween, unsettled state as is required for a breakthrough, and they were wanting it. Above all, Jesus was wanting it. He was reaching out to what was to come with all the urgency of passionate love that was in him, but at the same time and in the same thrust he was longing and needing to communicate with his beloved. 'I have longed to eat this Passover *with you* before I suffer' (Luke 22:15).

Many scholars have puzzled over Luke's mention of two cups of wine, the first one clearly not the cup of the Christian Eucharist, but associated with the saying which is coupled, in Matthew and Mark, with the words of institution: 'From now on I shall not drink wine until the kingdom of God comes' (Luke 22:18). But the Passover meal traditionally includes four cups of wine, and even if it was not so clear-cut in the time of Jesus as it became later (and indeed even if this was not actually a Passover meal) to bless and share wine more than once seems quite a likely thing to do. But there is more to it than this. It seems possible that Luke is showing us the outlines of a very credible kind of sequence of feeling and action. For Luke creates a time-gap between that first cup and the moment of institution, and underlines it by saying that Jesus took the cup 'after supper'. Paul, reminding the Corinthians of the essential ritual they were in danger of overlaying, uses the same phrase, and Luke quite probably got it from Paul, but in any case it was part of the oldest tradition. But seeing that this time gap is created, we can most easily suppose that the other incidents of that strange night (the avowal of coming betrayal, arguments over precedence and the washing of feet, the warning to Peter) took place in that gap. Matthew and Mark divide them up on either side of the Institution, and if Mark was actually drawing on Peter's memories it seems likely he has it right. Luke brackets them all together in a somewhat scrambled way after his account of the institution, but his account reads as if he had put the moment of institution first simply because his record of the command to share the first cup provided a context for his account of the blessing of the bread, and of the second cup. John alone tells how Jesus washed the feet of his friends, but seems to show in this the fuller demonstration of the reply Luke gives to the arguments among them about who was the greatest: 'Yet here I am among you as one that serves' (22:2). All of this could take its place before, or during, the course of the main part of the meal. But if we are willing to allow that Luke was not using the two cups as a 'theological device' but rather recognizing the theological significance of something which happened, he provides a vivid insight into the way it all came to a head. For the first sentences, during the meal, refer to a fulfilment of the Passover, They are about the awareness which Jesus and the Twelve shared, that the kingdom of God was about to come—though the Twelve gave that event a different meaning from the one Jesus wanted them to realize.

'I have longed to eat this Passover with you before I suffer, because, I tell you, I shall not eat it again until it is fulfilled in the kingdom of God' (Luke 22:15–16). These are words which the Twelve could understand, or thought they could. Likewise, at the first cup, the words, 'Take this and share it among you, because from now on, I tell you, I shall not drink wine until the kingdom of God comes' (Luke 22:17–18), could well have been the trigger (in the edgy, wrought-up mood they were in) for the argument about 'who is greatest' and so have led to the great act of menial service which sobered them all and brought them closer together. The bits of converstion we have to fit into this atmosphere, and John's discourse, if I am right about this, shows us the renewal and reinforcement, with greater intensity than before, of familiar yet now awesomely heightened teaching. He had wanted to eat the Passover with them. He had shared wine with them as a sign of an end and a beginning. Bread and wine lay on the table between them. Perhaps he remembered other meals, and especially the time when he had shared food among many in the wilderness. Perhaps there returned to his mind the way in which he had struggled to express to the ignorant, longing, needy people just how it was that he was, himself, the food they needed.

Perhaps not much of the discourse which appears in the sixth chapter of John's Gospel on the bread of life was really developed on that occasion, yet the basic idea which comes to us through John's special kind of imagination rings true, growing out of the intense challenge presented to the self-understanding of Jesus by what he had done for the hungry people in the wilderness. So perhaps on this later occasion the symbols of Passover, the words and the actual roasted lamb, brought it all to the surface. Joachim Jeremias proposes in *The Eucharistic Words of Jesus* that these words imply a longing which must remain unfulfilled. Jesus, he suggests, intended personally to abstain from sharing the Passover meal 'until it is fulfilled in the Kingdom of God'. His abstention from the meal he had shared with them in other years would, if Jeremias is right, heighten their sense of a 'gap', of tension and waiting for they knew not what. And although his own sense of what lay ahead and of its essential meaning was strong, it was the event itself which showed him the way to do what he, and they, needed to share at that point, so that the fulfilment might come. As so often, his own words and actions led to other words and actions. He had given himself to them in service; he had told them they would 'eat and drink' at his table in the kingdom. He had warned and comforted. We feel them coming closer and closer together, touching each other physically and emotionally and mentally, with a gradual deepening of exchanged life in this unique atmosphere. But only Jesus knew exactly how crucial this moment was, and so only he was torn by the realization that, even now, they did not understand. Perhaps he had hoped that, at this last moment, they would truly meet him in insight and awareness, but they could not. Yet how was the Father's will to be accomplished unless these, the very life with him of the kingdom of exchanged love, could receive into themselves, *somehow*, the self-gift which was his, and so be with him through it all? There had to be a way. Words had failed, even that great action of service had failed, though it had brought them all so close to him. There they were, together yet parted, around the table on which lay the remains of the long, leisurely, intimate meal—bread and wine. So we can see how, at this moment, 'after supper', it all came together.

We know what he did. He had found a way to share—to *communicate*—the fullness of the love that possessed him. Words could not be an adequate medium of such an exchange, only himself could be that, himself as the one who was Adam, the one who was the remnant of Israel, the one who was drawing all things to himself to make one what had been separated.

They did not understand very much, even then, but it was done and they remembered later. The kingdom which he had spoken of as imminent had broken in before its time, disrupting sequence, forcing its way through impossible barriers.

I suggested in an earlier chapter that when the force of some great experience brings about a breakthrough out of due time it generally happens that the event remains without immediate repercussions. Because the surroundings are not ready for it, it has as it were 'nowhere to go' and ordinary life closes over and around it, at least for a time. Although the time was brief, and the circumstances in fact far from ordinary, this is what happened to the Twelve (or, by then, Eleven) after the Supper. They did not really know what they had been given and had become, and they did not even begin to discover the fullness of it for quite a long time. Their reactions to the events of the next two days show no greater awareness than before of the meaning of what was happening. The salient characteristic of the group of disciples at this time seems to have been bewilderment.

Something had happened to them which they were wholly unable to 'know', for no language had yet been found to communicate it. But as an experience it had, perhaps, made them even less able to bring mind and will to bear by means of older, familiar categories, and so enable them to take hold of events and act with courage or sense. In the garden they slept, and later ran away because their minds had no foothold in what was going on and their feet expressed this fact. The person who did act with decision was Judas, because he had sorted out his categories; he knew exactly what he thought and what he had to do, and he did it. The rest of them behaved indeed like a flock of sheep, in their mindless reaction to successive but unconnected stimuli. They were altogether demoralized, these men who had just shared in an action which changed the very basis of human community.

They could not make sense, and they were right—small choice

though they had in the matter—not to make sense, for the sense which was to be made of it was not yet possible. So they muddled miserably through those two days, appalled, isolated even in their clinging together, afraid through and through, moved passively, only by the sequence of exterior events.

There is this same feeling of passivity in their behaviour during the forty days after they knew that he was risen. It is then shot through with joy, but it is still impossible to 'make sense' and wrong to try. They are like people only half awake. When he is with them they are alive, but between these meetings they go through the motions of daily life peacefully but without any sense of urgency or direction.

But, by hindsight, and with the theological assertion of the facts of incarnation and redemption to inform our view of the matter, we can see that it was inevitable that it should be so. Something was happening to them at a level far too deep for conscious awareness, as yet. That would come in time, but it could not be rushed. This change was not just a spiritual one in the usual sense, which means 'not material'. It was, however, indeed a spiritual one in the Pauline sense that they were being made into a body whose being is the Spirit of Christ, which was to be their spirit. We take such an idea so calmly because we do not grasp, imaginatively and really, what we are saying.

When Jesus died the resurrection began, the reversal of the processes of death which had spread throughout all creation through the refusal of exchange. A different kind of exchange began, an exchange more coherent, freer, above all more conscious and purposeful, than anything possible before. It worked, as it had begun, at every level of reality, for it was a reconciliation of those things which had been at odds. Matter and spirit, mind and body, heaven and earth, the everyday and the glorious—the spheres of reality were laid open to each other, distinct but not separate, interacting with the joyous perfection of consummated love. But in considering the way this worked, and the way those who experienced it strove to communicate it, we have above all to realize that this came about by a change in the basis of relationship in material reality. The outlines of identity—bodily identity, the nature of bodies—faded, not into indistinctness, but in the glow of an experience of identity in which each one, of any kind, came to its perfect self-knowing not

194

by recognizing its limits in relation to some other being but in knowing itself as the unique point of an incredible multiplicity of loving exchanges.

The Eucharist did not occur as a kind of 'bonus', to support and encourage those who were to be Christians, and the Church did not happen because Jesus thought it would be a useful thing to have around, though he could have managed quite well without. (I am not being flippant, merely evoking rather brutally the essential weakness in some kinds of theological thinking.) Rather, the Eucharist and the Church are one thing, which happened *to* him.

We have seen the nature of love, in the human flesh of Jesus of Nazareth, struggling and agonizing and rejoicing and longing, in concrete human situations as they unfolded, and in them always pressing towards the desired goal, that of true union, the re-establishment of the fullest exchange of love. It happened in particular people, in their human circumstances and temperaments and relationships. We have seen the headlong love of the Father for the Son received with a passion of reciprocated giving which caught up in its tide the human beings to, in and through whom that love was communicated. They became a language of love between Father and Son.

That language is spoken by the Spirit, the life of Jesus himself, the divine Exchange in the body of Jesus. It is difficult for our imagination, conditioned to categories of separation, to grasp the extreme physicalness of this. When Jesus picked up some bread from the table and said 'This is my body', and when later he took a cup of wine and said 'This is my blood', and when he gave that to his friends and they ate and drank, their relationship to him was changed. The bodies of the lovers of Jesus were open to the thrust of his love, simply because in that moment they trusted him absolutely, though without understanding. It was one of those spaces of unknowing, between time and below all knowledge, in which the act of creation takes place, and this was indeed the moment of creation towards which all created things had poured themselves. The first bearers of the new life, the new-born people, found their being newly constituted as his own, his Spirit's work and expression. In this eating and drinking of his body and blood their bodies became his, and the Church sat at table. Next day, that same body, the man Jesus, accomplished that destruction of the deathly mean-

195

ing of death which made possible what had 'already' happened: the fullness of personality given and received in and through the fullness of the sacrifice of all that feels like personality. In the body which was the Bread and Wine, which hung on the cross, this change took place which was a change in his new people because they were now his body.

I have already tried to indicate the nature of this change. We easily suppose that the alternative to a circumscribed individual personality must be a loss of personality. But I have suggested that this sense of personality as consisting of existence within limits—to be defended at all costs—is the result of sin. It is a refusal of exchange, or rather it is the rationalization of the state of affairs which results from that refusal. In a sense, the use of static or even cyclic models of reality are ways of accommodating sin, and the experience of isolation and alienation which sin both creates and needs. If we think of individual personalities as 'constructions', however beautiful, we are forced into thinking of redemption either as the redesigning of that construction or as the release from it of some essential reality which has been forced into 'using' it. And if we think of it like that we cannot assign any meaning to personality as more than temporal and even necessarily sinful. To attain the desired state must then mean to be free of that which constrained and distorted it. And if that distorting thing is thought of as what made people personal, then to be saved must mean to lose personality, to merge with the All.

There is absolutely nothing in the New Testament (or the Old, for that matter) to lend countenance to this. The picture of reality which emerges is quite different. Jesus talked to people about eternal life, or life in the kingdom of God, in ways which made it clear that he thought of them as being still and always 'themselves'. They would not 'merge' into the kingdom, they would 'inherit' it, live in it, have 'mansions' in it.

Yet just as all preceding humankind, in its longing and waiting, came to its point of breakthrough in the body of Jesus, so in that body must the new creation find its origin. It was all there, in his body, sitting at supper, hanging on the cross. The people, then, who were to be, in him, the new creation, must come to a kind of relationship with his body which would make them not less but more personal. Yet the way of being that person must be changed.

196

The sinful person, defined by ignorance of and defence against other persons, must come to a kind of being whose personality is defined in conscious and joyful recognition of the exchanges which give itself to itself. These exchanges are, basically, physical, but we have to understand the nature of physicalness in a way which is itself changed by the different kinds of bodily relationships we are trying to discern.

It may help a little to remember that one of the ways of recognizing increasing spiritual maturity is by noting an increase in areas of full consciousness. The spiritual breakthroughs of life always make consciously available areas of personality previously unconscious. In some spiritual traditions it is also expected that the seekers after wisdom will become increasingly aware of, and able to control, previously unconscious physical processes. Also, large numbers of people are able, in greater or lesser degree, to be aware of the state of mind and body of others near them, or even far off, and even to *affect* that state, and it seems likely that very many more people—possibly everyone—could develop this capacity. There are many cases of people who know what occurred in the lives of others who lived long before. These experiences do not, I think, indicate 'previous existences' but simply the fact with which we have been dealing all through this book: that people live as exchanged, in time and place, at various levels of biological and psychological being, and this is so literally the case that the experience of one person can be discovered by another, transmitted bodily in the network of exchange.

If we take all this together, not as a complete picture but as random indications of the kind of thing we are trying to understand, we may find it a little easier to grasp that when Paul says the Church is the body of Christ he is speaking with absolute literalness. But this makes our experience of bodiliness look not normal but weirdly distorted and inadequate, as monstrous in comparison to the perfected body as an anencephalic infant seems in comparison to a normal baby.

I suggested, in the last chapter, that we can see in the accounts of what happened after the death of Jesus a number of distinct 'stages of resurrection'. As compared with the daily intercourse of their journeyings together, the appearances of the risen Jesus to his friends were rare, unpredictable and brief, and after the ascension

197

they did not see him at all. Yet he said he would be 'with' them always, he said he would 'come' to them, he said he would be 'in' them. The language used by all the evangelists to describe his relationship with those he loved after his passage through death is so unambiguous that we must either dismiss it as some kind of obscure hyperbole or else accept it as meaning exactly what it says. He said he would be 'in' them, but not 'in' them as separate individuals. He would be 'in' each of them as the new creation, as the Church—which is his body.

It could only be so. His body is himself. His being is now this group of people, and they exist—their being is defined—in terms of the life which is his glorified body, that life which is the Spirit of God, which is now their spirit also. This is what it means to live in the Spirit. The implications of this require another chapter, but there is a dimension of the subject of this chapter which also provides the setting and the purpose of all the rest. I mean that we know that the body of Christ is not only the Church but all people, and all things.

Something of what this means was discussed in the last chapter, for what we are talking about is part of the process of resurrection. Now, however, we are trying to see why it is accurate to speak of the body of Christ and mean by that not only the glorified humanity of Jesus, and the Eucharist, and the Church, but also all humankind in so far as it is willing to live in exchange, and with it all created things, animate and inanimate.

Here we rely on St Paul's extraordinary theology of how redemption works. When Paul uses the words 'body of Christ' or 'of the Lord' he means the Eucharist, or he means the people who are called and chosen to be the Church, God's new creation by baptism, but he does not differentiate between the Church and people of good will who are not the Church, in the way we do, because for him there is no alternative between accepting Christ and refusing him. To refuse is to refuse life, to accept is to be a member of his body, living by him. There is no neutral condition. Yet it is apparent that his definition of the Church is not, as we would expect, confined to its visible and explicit membership. The implications of this are not worked out, because for Paul there was no need to do so; his theology, like all theology, grew in response to particular problems and situations. Nobody was asking 'what happens to all the other

198

people?' So he did not deal with that question, but the implications of what he did say are clear, and they are particularly apparent, as so often, in the things he felt no need to say because all concerned took them for granted. One of these was, clearly, the assumption that the spirit of Christ was being shared in an outward-spreading pattern of exchanges.

Unbelievers, he says, may be sanctified by association with believers. A husband may be sanctified by his believing wife, a wife by her believing husband, and the children of such a union are holy. There is no suggestion in this passage that the unbelieving husband or wife, or the children, become sanctified by being converted to belief. They might or might not be converted, but the holiness is something they share in, anyway, simply by the relationship, though only if they are content to dwell with the believers, not refusing exchange. They are sanctified in the exchange of life with one who lives in exchange with Christ. The fact that the relationships mentioned are close physical ones shows how bodily is Paul's theology of the Church.

This way of being sanctified is not confined to close relatives or, apparently, to people present to the believers in space or even in time. The odd (to us) practice of being baptized 'for the dead' is mentioned by Paul in passing and without comment. Its precise significance is much debated, but it is at least an example of the way the early community took it for granted not only that the baptized lived in and for each other in Christ, but that others, not yet believers, or even those who had died in unbelief, could be brought into the life of resurrection by substitution. This only makes sense if there is a real identity in the body of Christ, so that the members of Christ can do what he does because they are himself. Since they live by his Spirit, which is another way of saying they live his life, they can do as he did, they can 'die' in baptism in place of another who never knew, in the flesh, what new life was close at hand. The 'one adored Substitution' lived in many other substitutions, for the life of exchanged love made such things not only possible but inevitable.

But if particular, known people could be so brought all unknowing into the dance of divine Wisdom, the matter did not end there. The examples of husband, wife and children show us that this reaching out of the new life was by bodily exchanges; but all created

199

exchanges are bodily, even to the most unseen and unfelt. Yet the sharing of holiness with the unbelievers is not thought of as an unconscious or an automatic thing. Holiness is living more and more in Christ, being 'formed' more and more into Christ. So the 'sanctification' of the unbeliever does not come about because he or she lives in the same house or shares the same bed with the believer. It comes about because the love of Christ is being consciously and willingly given. Thus the believer, as one with Christ, becomes a place where the exchanges of daily life change their character, as the character of the bread and wine was changed 'on the night in which he was betrayed'.

Clearly the extent of this is limited only by the limits of created being. Those who become, through exchanges of life with the risen Jesus, themselves 'other Christs' are the points at which the spheres are exchanged, and the glory which is transforming them becomes present (even though unrecognized) to those to whom the spheres are still opaque. And unfree creation cannot itself refuse, though it can be and is involved in the refusals of free beings.

But if all can and must become at last the body of Christ in its 'full stature', this is mostly an unconscious process. The fact that most people, and all other kinds of created beings, do not know themselves as 'body of Christ' makes no difference to the fact that this is what they are progressively becoming, yet the gradual and unconscious exchanges by which resurrection becomes universal do not happen smoothly and inevitably, any more than the process of evolution happens smoothly and inevitably. It cannot be so, because of sin. The exchanges of resurrection encounter sin at every moment, and no unconscious response is adequate to deal with this. It has to be conscious, it has to be *amour voulu*. The Church, then, in this sense is the body of Christ in his willed and *conscious* decisions of love. The Church does not define the limits of divine love, indeed it may often be that his love is more visible in the 'unconscious' areas of the body of Christ, but the Church's essential relation to love is well evoked in that other image of the Bride of Christ. For a bride is not a woman seized willy-nilly. She is chosen, but she must choose. She recognizes her bridegroom and gives herself *consciously* to him, so that from their union a new creation can be born.

This offspring will begin in the unconsciousness of infancy when it—human and non-human—is inarticulate, and so the Spirit (the

200

spirit of Jesus *in* his Church, his Bride) must speak for it 'with sighs too deep for words' both in its human expression and in those non-human existences with which humans live in exchange. But it must grow, becoming in time capable of knowing itself and express- ing itself as 'children of God' in full and conscious liberty. Those who are the Bride, therefore, in this sense, are those who have consciously chosen to respond to the love they experience by a response which is fully willed, and articulated in language as clear as the human mind can compass. This is, inevitably, poetic language.

A very remarkable and moving book, *Christianity Rediscovered* by Vincent Donovan, gives a modern example of an apostle making the same discovery. The author is a member of a missionary con- gregation who, after being involved for a while in normal missionary work in Africa, reached the highly novel conclusion that the way to preach the gospel might be actually to preach the gospel. He visited regularly the Masai villages who were willing to listen to him and explained as well as he could what Jesus said and did and was. A year later nearly all of them did ask for baptism, but the evangelist learned as much as the evangelized, and among the things he acquired was a deeper insight into the strong bond which is the awareness of exchanged life in the Church. In this passage the poetry of an African people gives a new depth and precision to the older theological symbols:

I asked them: If you do accept baptism as a community, what will you call yourselves?

There was, of course, no notion of Church, or word for it, in their pagan language. I had no idea of how to refer to them after baptism. After some discussion among themselves, a man stood up and said, 'When we are baptized we will be the *Orporor L'Engai*, the age-group-brotherhood of God.'

The age-group-brotherhood, the *orporor*, the most sacred notion in their culture. It was a word that could grip their hearts, set their hearts on fire, the single most important value in their tribe. And they had chosen it as the word for *Church*. Not only was it the only notion of brotherhood they had, but it was one that could not be acquired by birth but only by deliberate, painful initiation. Their original notion of *orporor* was limited to all those initiated within a seven-year span, and those females who married into the brotherhood. Every seven-year time-span had a name which was never repeated. The Orporor of God would not span seven years but would extend from now until the end. It would, because of the message that brought it into being, cross sex lines, age lines, clan lines, tribal lines, national lines. It would be the first universal brotherhood, but it would necessarily still be an age-group brotherhood—of the last age, the final age of the world, reaching to the kingdom. It has eschatological dimensions built right into it. It has come to be called alternatively the orporor (age-group-brotherhood) of God, of Christ, or of the end.

This concept of the body of Christ is founded on actual experience of the exchanges of people so deeply committed to each other that they scarcely exist except as united. These men had deliberately and painfully given themselves to that body, and it seemed obvious to them that baptism could be no less profound and absolute a transition, a dying more complete than tribal initiation, since from it one rose to a world unmeasurably vaster, in which the exchanges are even more intimate and ultimate. In the same way, it is important, even though Paul was not emphasizing this but only mentioning it, that the example he gives of people deliberately substituting themselves for the dead in order to bring them into the life of the body was by being baptized for them. They did not (as we do) merely pray for them. In Paul's theology baptism is the believer's passage, with Christ, through death to new life. Another aspect of this has to be looked at in the context of the 'last things' in the next chapter, but here I am trying to understand not just *that* but *how* the Christian becomes the substitute, the crossing-point of death and life, as Jesus was, for all of creation.

One of the most mysterious sayings in the New Testament is one which seems, at first sight, lucidly simple in its meaning. When Jesus took bread and wine he added to the words defining the gift a command also: 'Do this in remembrance of me' or 'as a memorial of me'. Luke gives the words after the consecration of the bread; Paul in 1 Corinthians puts them after the gift of both bread and cup. They were, in any case, clearly part of the liturgical formula accepted by all. It seems, indeed it is, a command to continue to do what he had just done, thereby recalling and making actual the end and purpose of his life in the most complete way possible. But there is at the heart of this command a simple word which opens up an abyss of meaning. That word is 'this'.

'Do *this* in memory of me.' What is 'this'? What was 'this' that he had just done? He had taken himself in his hands and given himself—but a self immolated, a self poured out in reality, though an anticipated reality. The anticipation made it fully present, and what was made present was himself dying, himself as undergoing death so that nothing was left but pure love. As we have seen, only his death—*his* death—could accomplish this. Yet, he told them, 'do *this*'; if they—and not only himself personally—were being told to 'do this', then they were being told to do what he had done: to *give themselves* to each other. In him, as his body, they must 'do this' and give their bodies to and for 'many'. So when Jesus told his beloved to 'do this' he was telling them that they, like himself and *as* himself, must die the kind of death he was about to die, a death in which the power of the refusal of exchange, which makes death happen, would be turned around by the total acceptance, in love, of the onslaught of that refusal. Only by doing so could the meaning of the Eucharist as body of Christ begin to come true.

Paul's famous passage in the eighth chapter of the letter to the Romans indicates the way in which obedience to the command to 'do *this*' is the way in which, in fact, creation is 'giving birth' to the 'children of God' who are one with the first-born, Jesus. They are his 'images', which as we have seen does not mean a 'reflection', a separate and merely imitative thing, but the point at which the gift of love is received and recognized and given back. And it is clear that Paul (again taking it for granted rather than explaining or defending it) knows that this response of love by which the Spirit 'bears witness' in the Christian is one which works in exactly the same way as it worked in Jesus—that is, by bringing him to death. If we are 'heirs of God and co-heirs with Christ' it is only because we are brought by his Spirit to 'sharing his sufferings so as to share his glory'. And his 'glory' is what I called the 'sphere' of glory, that ever-present, yet—to us—mostly inapprehensible heart of reality which, when broken open, flows out in exchanged life to transform all that it touches. Through the break in the sphere the glory is 'revealed' as it was revealed on the mountain, and 'all creation' feels the effect of it, is touched and enkindled and changed, until it comes at last 'to enjoy the same freedom and glory as the children of God'. 'He called those he intended for this', and having 'justified' them he 'shared his glory' with them. This 'sharing' does not mean giving them bits of it, as one shares a cake. It means that his glory is in them as its proper mode of being and thus reaches out to all creation through the exchange of spheres, as the Father's will is to 'unite all things in him, things in heaven and things on earth'.

John's Gospel has no account of the institution of the Eucharist, yet of all the evangelists John is the one most acutely conscious of the physicalness of the personal and beloved presence from Galilee to Calvary, and to glory. In the last paragraphs (apart from the 'appendix', chapter 21) of his Gospel we see even more clearly that quality of passionate love which gives meaning to the words 'the body of Christ', in Paul's theology also. John's setting out of the words of Jesus on the 'bread of life' and his testimony in his first letter, together with his presentation of the risen Lord, help us to understand this final reality, and he gives us a strong sense of some functions of the Church which later became more explicit.

We can remind ourselves once more than a considerable body of recent biblical scholarship supports the traditional ascription of the Gospel of John (and his first letter at least) to John-bar-Zebedee. The dating of the fourth Gospel, also, has crept back and back, and John A. T. Robinson is not alone (in his *Re-dating the New Testament*) in assigning a very early date to much of its material. Without going over Robinson's detailed arguments it is possible to say that there is plenty of evidence—not undisputed but very coherent and persuasive—to date the writing of the bulk of John's Gospel over a period of about twenty-five years, from some time in the late thirties of the era to the early sixties as the work was gradually being written, added to, altered and rewritten. This makes sense, for if the author really was John-bar-Zebedee (and even if he was some other early disciple) he must have been moving around and occupied chiefly not in writing but in the ministry of preaching, with all the varied, complex and unpredictable duties this involved in those turbulent early days of the Church. The needs of converts to whom he could not speak personally would make it natural to write down some of his teaching.

We have to rid our minds of the picture of the Twelve as unlettered peasants. Jewish boys were normally at least basically literate, and at that time many of them (but especially any engaged in selling anything, as Zebedee's family were) spoke 'Koine' Greek as their indispensable second language in dealing with the Romans and the many other foreigners who came and went and settled. And the Jewish tradition was very 'writing-conscious', naturally. So as time passed John would find it proper and natural to write down more and more of his unique personal memories, and also to set out as clearly as possible the teaching of the Lord. If much of this was done in bits and revised at different times and later put together by himself or others (or both), that is exactly what one might expect. One point arising from the evidence is that he probably wrote his extant letters after, or towards the end of, the period during which his Gospel was accumulating and developing, and this also 'rings true' since one gets the impression, in the marvellous first two chapters of his first letter, that he was taking for granted his readers' familiarity with his particular way of presenting the significance of the Lord's earthly life.

If this early dating is correct John's account of the risen Lord and his presentation of the Lord's doctrine of the bread of life are drawn from memories as recent as ten years old or less, and not more than thirty years old at the very most. That is long enough for much thought and development to take place, but it is short enough for memory to be not only very vivid but easily verifiable by others. These are not, as in older theories, the reflections of a very old man on his long-ago youth, but the memory of a young, highly intelligent and perceptive man, dealing with events not only recent but of such unique importance to him as to others that he had thought of little else since that time. And if this is true of the discourses, formally and carefully presented as they are, it is much more obviously true of the 'reporting' parts of the fourth Gospel. The stamp of personal recollection is apparent in the detail, but the poetic talent and personality comes through in his spare yet vivid shaping of each story to create its own impact by the images and allusions which are the language of this deeply personal communication. In John's words, in John's mind, we meet the Lord himself, not less but more immediately than those met him who did not know him as John knew him.

With this in mind we can read John's accounts of the appearances of Jesus to his friends after his death on two occasions which John puts eight days apart, the first being that 'first day of the week' which turned reality inside out. Once more the physicalness of the Lord's presence is one of the most obvious features of this account, but the implications of it are often overlooked. He 'came and stood among them' and greeted them and then 'showed them his hands and his side' and evidently they saw the wounds at close quarters and probably touched them, because this is what Thomas, who had not been present, demanded to do when he heard about it later. John's own later words in his first letter seem to indicate this when he spoke of that which 'we have seen with our eyes, which we have looked upon and touched with our hands concerning the word of life'. This could and probably does refer to the daily intercourse with Jesus during his ministry, but there was no need to emphasize this. The insistent reiteration of the claim to direct physical experience of the 'word of life' seems most of all to underline the witness to the risen and glorified Lord who was still and always present to his people just as bodily.

Then, he 'breathed on them' as he bade them go out 'as the Father sent me'. We have to keep remembering the phenomenology of God's romantic love. This requires preparation, the right conditions, and if the moment of the last Supper had made the Eleven at that point capable of receiving his love in that degree of completeness which began to 'incorporate' them into him, so much more—inconceivably more—were they open to him after the experiences of the next three days.

Every remaining vestige of reliance on older certainties must have been swept away. They had been brought down to the depths of personal incoherence, stripped of meaning and even of identity not only by the death of Jesus but, perhaps even more, by the reports of the body's disappearance and of the vision of angels announcing his rising. None of it made sense, there was nothing to hold on to. Bereavement is painful but it is at least solidly factual; but these men were not even allowed that basis of fact. They were rocked with impossible hope which could not let them take refuge in despair, though the dismay in which they were clothed refused to allow them to turn their faces fully towards hope. When he came to them they had nothing to hold on to except his presence, and so his presence was all. They might almost want to disbelieve (Luke nearly says as much: they 'thought they were seeing a ghost' because that was more bearable than the truth), but they were not allowed to.

On a previous occasion he had asked them, 'Will you also go away from me?' and, as if almost reluctantly, Peter had admitted on their behalf that there was nowhere else to go. On that occasion, also, the cause of their dismay had been the impact of a demand that they accept as a fact the inconceivable intimacy of the physical communication of love which he was offering them. Not understanding, they had yet known that 'You have the words of eternal life'. Now, the literal breath of the word of life was enabled to enter their being in this state of utter vulnerability, changing them as they felt its gentle warmth on their faces. This was an exchange of life; the Eleven received him and in receiving must give.

What they must give, he told them, was that same life, their life, their breath breathed out in forgiveness to others. That was what it was for, and it was to be one of the most important functions of the Church. To forgive in the Spirit of Jesus is to *be* his Spirit, historically, himself, and so to forgive as he did. Such forgiveness is no detached announcement of an arrangement made between God and the one in need of forgiveness; the one who forgives gives himself or herself to another who reaches out for it. That is why the one who lives by the Spirit may have to 'retain' sins, for the one in need of forgiveness may refuse to know that need. 'Forgiveness' is the name of the particular kind of breakthrough which occurs when the barrier to the thrust of God's passion has been the deliberate refusal of it. To receive the impact of the outpouring of love and to refuse to accept it is, as it were, to thrust it back on the giver who must, therefore, 'retain' the thing whose very nature is to be not retained but given. The 'unnaturalness' of such a thing, the pain suffered by the one whose breath is thus 'stifled', is implicit in the phrase. To be (as all the followers of Jesus are called to be) one whose breath is that of exchanged love in Christ is to carry, with him, the weight of others' unforgiven sin. But since it is carried with him it has died with him; in his death it is 'exchanged' and made love, but only because it is brought to the cross, the point of exchange in Christ's death for the one who, in deep pain, 'retains' the unreceived gift.

There is an almost inexpressible coherence of reality to be perceived in the way this works. The breath is the life of the body, and that body, at that moment on the evening of the first Easter day, is defined in the group of people huddled in the upper room. They are the body of Christ, they are his 'flesh' which is 'real food'. As they have eaten and drunk his body and blood and thus 'drawn life from him' as he told them, so (living by his life, breathing his breath, flesh of his flesh) they in their turn must give themselves to be eaten and drunk 'for the life of the world'. If they forgive, that is because they are given—given as food, shared out, given away until nothing is left; but that 'nothing' is eternal life, the giving and receiving of perfect love which is the Three-in-One.

Peter's response to the first promise of that bread which costs the receiver his or her life had been an act of faith not in the teaching (which was quite incomprehensible to him) but in the teacher. 'You are the Holy one of God.' He was the one the Father had sent, he was 'bread from heaven', whatever meaning they could give to that claim. Now, as this time whose distance from that other moment could not be measured in months but only in intensity of love, they received that which had been described to them, and in receiving it they became it. So, when the experience found a spokesman, it took the form of the most explicit statement of the fact of incarnation in the four Gospels.

In reflecting on the encounter of the risen Lord with Thomas, we see once more the elements of romantic passion. There is a particularity about this meeting as John describes it which makes it stand out. It is different from anything else in the Gospels, recognizably peculiar to this one man. It is not foreseeable: Thomas had not been, previously, very noticeable in the Gospel accounts. Certainly we did not expect him to be at the heart of such a theological breakthrough as this. Thus the simple, unique, yet (because unique) archetypal character of it is made clear. But the 'obscure' quality, the strangeness of glory, surrounds it and drives the prosaic Thomas across the imaginative gap in such a leap of theological articulation as no one else could manage. And so through him the relationship of Jesus to his little gathered Church is changed and transfigured by that extraordinary definition. And it hurts. John does not say so, he does not need to, but the pain of that encounter, mixed as it is with unutterable joy, is so keen that it is hard even to read about it. But we need to feel our way into the special quality of that encounter in order to recognize what was happening.

208

Thomas had not been there a week earlier. Thomas had probably not wanted to be there. The others had hung together, through that Sabbath, in a crowd of bewildered solitudes going through the motions of community. Thomas, however, was one of those people whose way of dealing with the unbearable is to draw a line round it in heavy black ink. (He had done it earlier, when Lazarus died.) He knew what had happened, and it meant the end of hope and love. Without those, what was the use of the companionship which had expressed them? So he took his solitude off somewhere and dwelt in it. And when the others came after him, saying, 'We have seen the Lord', he did not move out of it. On the other hand, he did not refuse to listen. He had not cut himself off by rejection, he was only protecting his wounds from abrasion, and he listened to them in spite of this. He consented to go back and be with them, as indeed in a sense he had not ceased to be. It was by virtue of this oneness with them in the body of Christ that he could share the experience of the risen Lord, eventually, for even when Jesus came to people alone, as he did to Peter and (later) to Paul, he did so not to each in isolation but to each as member of his body, even if they were temporarily unable to realize the fact. Thomas, then, remained in his solitude in the sense that he would not accept their witness, but he accepted *them*. He went with them, but as he did so he traced once more the outline of his despair and demanded that the thing they thought they had seen should accurately fit that definition. The definition he gave to his refusal of belief was that of a real human body. If it were indeed the one body which mattered to him, it must have holes in it. *They* said it did, but their eyes were not his eyes nor their hands his hands. There is, in this demand, all the anguish of the rejected lover whose state of twitching vulnerability makes him unable to acknowledge hope lest hope should make possible yet another unbearable disappointment.

Thomas's obstinacy is not that of insensitivity, it is that of the super-sensitive person whose only defence is disguise. He wanted—how he wanted—his beloved. He wanted Jesus himself, for himself. He got him. He got all that he had asked and much more, he received the full flood of that passionate love which longs to respond even, and especially, to such demands as that of Thomas. That is why it was Thomas, and not Peter or even John, who was enabled to utter that cry of faith which was to be forever the greeting of the Bride to her Bridegroom: 'My Lord and my God!'

Yet it does not end there. Thomas had insisted on seeing and touching. John underlines constantly the physical reality of that which they knew, saw and touched, the one who came forth from the Father. Jesus himself had once driven his disciples to the limits of their loyalty and of the intellectually bearable in his attempts to get them to realize the terms of a relationship so physical it must break down the categories of all known bodiliness; and in the neediness of love he had, even before his death, broken the barriers of personal definition in order to create a new order of identity. And so he must, finally and yet again and again and again, make them realize the enormousness (and enormity) of the thing which had happened to them—the change in the fundamental structure of reality, as the exchanged life of God was set free in his body, 'for the life of the world'.

It sounds, to our desensitized and indelibly Cartesian minds, as if the words of Jesus to Thomas about 'seeing' and 'believing' were making a contrast between acceptance of proof by mere physical verification and the deeper and more 'spiritual' union attained by blind faith. But that is not what John is telling us that Jesus said. The point is that what Thomas finally believed, and what 'those who have not seen' are blessed for believing, is exactly the same thing, and that is the fact that Jesus lives bodily, personally, in and by those who receive his love. He is their Lord and God *because* he is their life; he breathes in them, exhaled and inhaled, given and received, eating and eaten. To believe this is to live in exchange, to give oneself to that process of resurrection which must reach little by little to every particle of created being, in an exchange from which none are excepted but those which refuse it, and by this eternal outrage remain suspended, as it were, within the movement of the dance of Wisdom, which holds them in being but in which they will not move.

Nothing in John's Gospel is put there unthoughtfully. We are left, at the end, with that challenge to fully passionate and incarnational faith, but also with a vision of how such faith begins and how it must live itself out.

Thomas wanted and needed to see and touch the wounded body of Jesus. He put his fingers into the holes of the nails, he put his

210

hand—indeed his hand was taken and guided—into the gaping hole made by the Roman spear. This is where faith has to begin, that kind of faith which earns the title 'blessed' for those who embrace it, here, at that place where the human heart of Jesus marks the uttermost centre. It is the heart of a man who has died. It is the symbol of a passionate death, the death of the lover for whom life only has meaning if it is given for the beloved. 'For me', said Paul, 'to live is Christ and to die is gain', because it is in death that all barriers to that life are undone. Mystically, theologically, the body of the man with a gaping wound in his side is where it all begins. It is a real body, a sweaty, bloody, repulsive thing, obviously and judicially dead, as dead as the piled bodies of Jews in the gas chambers of Auschwitz; as dead as the child whose parents have battered her once too often; as dead as a political prisoner in a Brazilian gaol or as the meths drinker who, when dawn nudges the others into reluctant awareness of another day, fails to move, and all these bodies are also the body which Thomas touched, into whose sickening wounds he put his finger, then his hand. If John described this scene in such emphatic detail it was because he wanted those who came after him to have this image indelibly marked on their minds. Better than any words this image would form in them a faith truthfully related to its source, the man Jesus. To believe in him is to be in touch with what Thomas was in touch with. To say, *then*, 'My Lord and my God', is to see reality from that point.

The vision obtained is threefold. The believer who is 'blessed' is simultaneously aware of reality (self, other people, things, feelings, the longing for God) as one who shares food with those he loves, as one who hangs on a cross, and as one who, wounded to life, breathes that life into his lovers. It is an awareness of reality as centred and earthed in the human body which is Jesus, but which discovers there that which extends not only 'to the ends of the earth' but to the imageless bliss of exchanged life in the Three-in-One, yet is also one with all other helplessly suffering bodies who are 'the body of Christ'.

Saint Teresa of Avila, expressing herself in the language of sixteenth-century Spanish courtesy, repeated her certainty that it is only from here that God can be accurately known and even the most ecstatically mystical life honestly lived. 'It is by this door that

211

we must enter if we wish his Supreme Majesty to reveal to us great and hidden mysteries. No other way should be attempted.' The door to all reality is the human body of Christ for, through and in whom 'all things were created'. In him all things begin, because 'in him the fulness of God was pleased to dwell, and through him to reconcile to himself all things, whether on earth or in heaven, making peace by the blood of his cross'.

St Bernard spoke for all Christians who reach this moment of awareness. 'The nail that pierced became for me the key that opened the door so that I might see the will of the Lord. How should I not see through that opening? The nail cries out, the wound opens its mouth to cry that truly God is in Christ reconciling the world to himself . . . The secret of that heart is laid bare through the openings of the body: that great mystery of love lies open.' Through the doorway we glimpse meaning in the futility and perversity of human death, which is now his death. Those suffering bodies are his body, and through him, and so through those who accept to die with him, even unknowing wounds are his wounds, now the wounds of a risen body.

Every inarticulate movement of love is the movement of that body, every impulsive and scarcely noticed self-offering is the pulse of its being. Every overcoming of fear or hatred is the victory of its passionate desire. It does not matter, from one point of view, whether the movement is conscious or not, yet there has to be that moment of conscious recognition when the name of the lover is spoken and the pledge of fidelity given and received. The body of Christ is the measure of all things, it is in all and for all, yet the body of Christ finds its definition only in those who, though bewildered and confused, respond with all the passion of which the Spirit of love itself has made them capable to the command: 'Take, eat, drink—do this in memory of me.'

6   Baptized in His Death

Religions of all nations have always been concerned with what are sometimes called 'the last things'. The scriptural concern with this end time and the Church's credally official refusal ever to give it less than primary importance underline the fact that the Church lives by the resurrection, but it also awaits the completion of that resurrection. There is a sense in which all of history between the first Easter and the Day of the Lord is simply an interval, while we wait for the curtain to go up on the last Act.

The link between these two is baptism, a ritual which, though familiar in other faiths, found with 'the Lord's Supper' a new significance in delineating the self-understanding of the earliest Church. Christians were people who, repenting, were baptized and so died with Christ and rose to new life in him and by him; thenceforwards they expressed and nourished and celebrated that life by sharing in his body and blood, which were their unity and community. So baptism is the best place to begin trying to understand the time between, when we live the reality of the symbols which both express it and conceal it, as our lives both assert it and falsify it.

In George Macdonald's story, 'The Princess and the Goblin', the little Princess Irene discovers in the attic of her home an old woman who, she learns, is her great-grandmother. The 'Old Princess' is by turns a shabby old woman, a radiant girl, a queenly comforter, and always a powerful helper. She is Wisdom, though Macdonald does not say so, old and young, gentle and yet enormously strong, all-seeing, pervasive, loving and yet ruthless. When the little Princess must go, alone, into the dark caves under the mountain to find and rescue Curdie (who is himself her saviour) she goes safely on her hazardous way by following with her fingers the invisible thread which her great-grandmother has stretched for her. She cannot see it, but since the Old Princess has told her it is there she believes her. Putting out her hand she can feel it, and she knows with assurance which way to go. Such a thread, tangible to faith, may be found if we begin with the experience of baptism and follow it through the 'last things' to the 'end'.

Baptism is, from one point of view, an easy thing to hold on to, because it is a ritual which may plainly be observed in any Christian Church or sect, and everyone knows, at a certain level, what it is about. But when we try to see it more clearly we find, like the Princess, that we cannot see it at all. But if we put out a hand in faith we feel it again. We may intend to examine its symbolism of birth and find ourselves looking at nothing, because this birth is really a death. We may try to consider it as a purification by water but find ourselves led into very deep water indeed, drawn onwards to pass through the narrows of birth.

Thinking about baptism, therefore, takes us out of light into caves of darkness and ignorance. It takes us from thinking we know into realizing we do not know. There is little imaginative foothold even in the familiar idea of death, since death, in this context, is a purely poetical concept. It is not the thing we can see when a human being comes to the end of earthly life, for that is a jumble of experience with no necessary shape to it. Death, in the context of baptism, is not simply what happens to a body in dissolution; it is about what meaning can be discerned in all that mess and misery. The fear which many people have of seeking 'meaning' in the phenomenon of death is due to the fact that it is too easy to write *bad* poetry about death and so move it out of the category of last things— august and mysterious, overthrowing complacency—and make it domestic and falsely 'comforting'.

Baptism is essentially a poetic action taking from haphazard and diffused experience of death the essentially significant symbols, so that they become the means by which we can consciously enter into a relationship with the reality we thus apprehend. It is by the sharpness of the imagery of poetry that it focuses the personal vision on the point of breakthrough to strange realms of still obscure glory and terror. If I want to pass through that point, imaginatively, in the hope that from there I shall be enabled to discern ultimate things, I must first look very carefully at the things which are easily seen, the symbolism of the visible ritual.

The significance of baptism only seems simple because we think of it as a metaphor. A metaphor evokes a sense of one thing byre-ference to something other, which is comparable at certain points. It is the 'otherness' which makes metaphor possible and effective. It is the extreme unlikeness in most respects of a rose to a girl's cheek which makes the comparison illuminating. But a symbol is more than a metaphor, for it lives out of the thing it symbolizes; it is unlike and yet one with it, as a hand can symbolize a whole person, and it is just this symbolic character of baptism which is difficult to discern clearly.

How little we see may become clear if I ask a few idiotically crude questions about it; for instance, why does bathing with water, combined with words, effect a change of such a momentous character? (The words, after all, do not tell us much, at least at first sight.) If there is a real change, what kind of change is it: change of mood, goals, ethical direction? Does it bestow mystical enlightenment? Paul teaches that in baptism the Christian 'dies with Christ', but when we look at someone who has just been baptized, what precise meaning can we attach to that extraordinary claim?

These questions are naively posed so as to make clear the difficulty we are up against. If we want to get to the real symbolic links, beyond metaphor, there are two related ways in which I think we can come to a closer understanding of baptism as the entrance (in every sense) into the 'last things'. One is by considering the personal effects which are to be expected (though they do not necessarily follow) from undergoing the kind of ritual which baptism is. The other is by linking this to the basic conviction which underlies Pauline Christology, that whatever happens in or to the Christian happens because of, and in virtue of, that intensely physical and total involvement which is indicated by the phrase 'the body of Christ'.

The first of these ways is clearly linked to the phenomenology of Romantic love. The visible ritual of baptism is the deliberate creation of a situation in which breakthrough can occur. A weak spot can occur accidentally, but also it can be created deliberately, the need for it and the probable effect being foreseen and planned for. Many rituals are intended to create a deliberate weak spot for the breakthrough of spiritual power, as even the most cursory study of anthropology must demonstrate, and the particular kind of spiritual effect desired will be indicated by the kind of ritual language employed. By 'language' here, as in some other places, I mean not only spoken words but gesture and the whole pattern of symbolic communication including its penumbra of associated feelings and ideas. In the circumcision ritual of the Ndembu people (described by Victor Turner in his essay on the subject) symbolic objects and acts are each of them centres of complex and ambivalent association. Turner chooses three of them and says:

> The set of three symbols [examined here] play a dominant role— The symbols are trees of different species . . . . each may be said to represent a stage or 'station' in the novice's passage from social infancy to social maturity. At each of these 'stations' a series of actions are performed by persons enacting ritual roles. Furthermore, each tree is associated with a cluster of symbolic objects. Finally, the passage . . . is regarded as a unitary process, with a simple meaning . . . In the course of this simple process . . . each novice is regarded as having grown up. The implications of 'growing up' are multitudinous.
>
> (*Essays on the Ritual of Social Relations*)

The ritual expresses both this simple, uniting theme and the complexity of relationships, of people and roles and social function finally embracing the whole tribe, its past and future, which are involved in it directly or indirectly. The 'language', like all language, is clear-cut at one level and yet charged with obscure yet vital echoes and associations, for ritual language is a kind of poetry. And the words of such ritual language are not merely indicative or evocative but effective. The 'novices' *do* make the passage to grown-up life. The catechumens *do* become 'incorporate' with Christ. We shall have to see what that means, for the language of baptism is a basic vocabulary which enables people to 'say' what it means to become a Christian.

We can understand this much more clearly if we consider the ritual as it was performed at that stage of the Church's self-discovery at which baptism and Easter (necessarily connected) were the focus of the living of its faith by the body of Christ. This was after the apostolic period, at a time when the immediate expectation of the Parousia had faded and the Church had to find a way of living in relation to the last things while not thinking of them as embodied in an imminent and final cataclysm. But it was before the time

216

when the business of 'converting' huge 'barbarian' populations made baptism something perilously like a magical ritual used to remove the pagan from the power of the old gods and devils into the power of the Church. (And power was very much what it was all about, the holiness of many of the missionaries notwithstanding.) The period of the great baptismal liturgies lasted from about the third to the sixth centuries, when the liturgical life of the people in the 'older' Christian lands (Italy and North Africa, for instance) was housed in imposing great basilicas, each with a separate and usually large baptistry. St Ambrose's treatise 'On the Mysteries', for instance, evokes vividly the feeling of the time about baptism. We can see with his help and a bit of imagination how precisely baptism can be understood in terms of the phenomenology of Romance.

The catechumens who were to receive baptism had often been living as part of the body of Christ for many years beforehand. They could not take part in the eucharistic liturgy, but they had shared in the liturgy of the word with everyone else and had been expected to live by the moral norms of the Christian community. This long period formed the 'remote preparation' for the moment of baptism, and the 'immediate preparation' was quite literally and intentionally just that, for the lenten period was one in which the catechumens who were to be baptized that Easter underwent an intensive 'course' in Christian life and doctrine, punctuated by a series of progressive rituals of exorcism and of stage-by-stage acceptance into the Christian community. A version of these was later squashed into the one baptismal ceremony of more recent centuries, but happily there is now an attempt in many places to reintroduce the gradual instructional and ritual preparation for baptism at Easter, precisely because Christians have become aware of the psychological appropriateness of it if 'conversion', rather than magical transference, is what is desired.

The process of 'loosening' the hold of the catechumen on the old life was assisted by deliberately maintained ignorance of exactly what the ritual involved. Questions were evaded and answers refused and no catechumen had ever seen the inside of the baptistry. At the end of this time the catechumen would be radically detached from 'worldly' concerns and structures, almost de-personalized, ready to receive back personality as member of Christ, living by his

217

life. All this preparation was like what we would now call a retreat. It was intended to open up the catechumen to the action of the Spirit, who would invade him or her in the final moment.

The whole community was involved in this, supporting and surrounding the candidates in prayer (as well as refusing to answer their questions!). On the evening of the Easter vigil the whole congregation was in the basilica, engaged in the night-long vigil of prayer and reading and singing, while the candidates were taken to the baptistry for the final rite of their incorporation. There, the whole setting was designed to reinforce the impact of the ritual. The walls were often decorated with mosaics of baptismal symbols and scenes, and the sunken pool of water was approached by steps downwards, symbolizing the descent into death and the grave. The solemn questioning of each candidate by the bishop and the affirmation of faith, bringing to a point of intensity the requirement for deep self-knowledge as given to Christ, were followed by a startling event: there and then, the bishop unambiguously and tersely commanded the candidates to take off their clothes. Each one was stripped naked, the women by the deaconesses, the men by the deacons.

Physical nakedness has a profound significance, or rather when it has significance at all it is profound. In many cultures it has none, it is simply the way people are, and there is an unconsciousness and 'innocence' about this which provokes guilty envy in more conscious people. But in such a culture there is really no such thing as nakedness. As I suggested earlier, there has to be differentiation before there can be union. To be naked does not mean simply to be unclothed, it means to remove (or to have stripped off) the normal defences and disguises of common life, by which sinful people protect themselves from too much knowledge of themselves or others. It means to be defenceless, intensely vulnerable. Lovers delight to be naked to each other because it expresses their joy in mutual giving, without reserve, but violently to strip off a person's clothes is a recognized means of humiliating and degrading a human being. In Christianity, with its awareness of the significance of the physical, for good or evil, it is not surprising that nakedness has always had a peculiarly strong symbolism. (The anti-physical prudery of some Christian traditions is merely a perversion of the truthful awareness of the fact that bodies are where sin, as well as holiness, resides.)

218

Nakedness, in Christian iconography, has symbolized equally the erotic and the innocent, the extreme of penitent love and the extreme of brazen seduction. Francis Bernardone stripped naked and handed his worldly clothes back to his father, and many religious orders and sects have initiated new members by stripping and re-clothing them, though not necessarily in public. For the Christian, un-clothing is a word of penitence, renunciation and love, and the stripping of the baptismal candidate was a very powerful means of preparing the moment of breakthrough. In a sense, it represents the edge of that gap, the entrance into the darkness of unknowing, which is the way of passionate love.

So, finally, the candidate went down into the water and was immersed in it, really under water, three times. Everyone who has ever learned to swim under water (or refused to do so) knows that this involves overcoming a kind of fundamental recoil from the sense of being stifled and crushed by the water as it presses on eyes and ears and breath. The symbolism of the helplessness of death and also (and simultaneously) of the helplessness of the unborn in the waters of the womb is clear, but my concern is to emphasize as much as possible the effect of the actual physical experience on the state of mind of the candidate. In such a ritual experience the sound of the words of the rite, spoken by the bishop while the candidate was in the water, were so much one with the feeling of the water and the scent of chrism in it and the chanting voices nearby that they must have been almost 'psychedelic'—sound felt and water heard.

The ordeal was brief, for the moment of submersion was followed, as one movement, by the coming up from the font into a totally different atmosphere. In an instruction to the newly baptized in Jerusalem in the earliest times it was said, 'You saw nothing when immersed, as if it were night, but you emerged as if to the light of day.' The new members of Christ were dried and anointed with fragrant chrism. 'Christ was anointed with spiritual oil of gladness', said the author quoted above, 'that is with the Holy Spirit—and you have been anointed with chrism because you have become fellows and sharers of Christ.' They were then robed in a new white garment, the women by deaconesses, the men by deacons, whose job it was also to encourage and instruct them at this moment of joy and bewilderment. They were then embraced formally (and no

219

doubt informally too). When all were ready the newly baptized went in procession, with the bishop and the other clergy, to the basilica itself. The great doors were opened and the congregation greeted their coming with songs of praise and joy. Smelling of scented oils, still damp and vulnerable as newborn babies, they were carried on waves of greeting and thanksgiving to their seats, to take part for the first time in the full celebration of the Paschal mystery. They, who had thus died with Christ, were now celebrating in his body the transformation of death to life in Jesus which also transformed them in him. They shared then, for the first time, the meal of the body and the blood of the Lord in which they knew and received their life in him. The poetry of the Paschal eucharistic liturgy, as well as of the very presence and life of the Christian community, provided the language in which the new members could understand and begin to live by the sphere of glory into which they had broken.

It is impossible, as the last pargraph no doubt makes plain, to describe the reality of such a baptismal ceremony without, finally, using the poetry of theology. Try as one will, any other kind of language ends by missing the point. But we also have to realize that such language can be misleading, because what it describes is the essential significance of what happens, without asking questions about how far the description is true in particular instances. For it is obvious that the impact of all that I have described will vary from one person to another, in degree and in kind. It would take a very unlikely degree of deliberate resistance to remain altogether immune to the effects of such a ritual, but with all possible good will the degree of breakthrough which actually occurs must be very variable.

If this is true of a ritual as powerfully articulated as the one described, the fact raises basic questions about the effectiveness of the abbreviated and often perfunctory, as well as theologically illiterate, forms of baptism to which many Christians have been subjected for hundreds of years, and mostly when, in any case, they were too little to be consciously aware of what was going on. All the same, the thing has this Romantic shape; it is easy to perceive in the rich and sensitive ritual described those characteristics of the Romantic experience which I mentioned—particularity, singleness, a capacity for changing reality (moving into another sphere), also the 'obscure glory' which is particularly noticeable here, and the painfulness, apparent in the experience and symbolism of the actual descent into water. Finally, the fact of taking part in the eucharistic liturgy of the full congregation acts out as well as states the explicit and conscious direction of *amour voulu*, dedicated to a lifetime of service, yet giving that service already in the power of the new life entered in the moment of passionate breakthrough. And baptism has this kind of shape and significance even in its most simplified or routinized form, yet it is hard to make any sense of the theological claims made for it if we are relying only on the psychological effects of the ritual as experienced.

What I am going to say now must be taken to mean what I say it means and no more (and no less). I am not going to explain that 'it doesn't matter' how impoverished the rite may be in form and theological articulation, because the essentials are there. And I am not going to say that ritual baptism must inevitably be the deepest initiating experience for a particular Christian. In practice, if it is not it may well be because the ritual is so inadequately experienced, but in any case it is obvious that for many people the moment of incorporation in Christ, the crucial conversion experience, has occurred in totally non-ritual contexts, and baptism, if and when it was undergone, was more nearly a conscious articulation and direction of what was already known. In such a case it has more of the character of the Romantic vows of fealty and service—the explicit commitment of *amour voulu*—than that of the moment of passionate breakthrough itself.

What I want to say here is that we can never discover the real significance of baptism as incorporation in the dead and risen Jesus by examining only the likely psychological effects. Doing that is very helpful because it shows one aspect of 'how it works', but that examination will only help us to realize how people feel about the experience, not about what has actually and essentially happened to them in the only available terms, which are those of poetry. It is ultimately simply meaningless to say of the baptized, 'he was wet', or 'they were elated', or even, 'she was in love'. The final reaction to such descriptions can only be 'So what?' If we really want to know what happens to a person who is baptized we can only answer the question in the terms in which the theology of it is expressed, and then the way in which it can be seen and felt to happen will become capable, also, of poetic description as essential to the whole event.

The important poetic assertion is that this happening is something which Christ does. In his risen body he is himself in that kind of exchange which is able to express his own unique bodiliness in and through those other bodily beings who are open to such an exchange. By willingly receiving and giving in this exchange they become, personally, Christ. The relationship is a dynamic one which can only be grasped imaginatively (even if clumsily) by realizing it on the model of exchange. Though certainly not adequate it does make it clear that Paul's central assertions about baptism are not metaphorical, and that when he does use metaphor, as for instance when he compared the Christian to a litigant who is discharged because 'the law has no more claim' on one who has died with Christ, he is using it to bring into relief by this means the implication of a fundamental reality which is verified by the lived experience of those to whom he writes. Mostly, even the metaphors he uses are startlingly physical. He talks of Christ being 'formed in' his converts, like an embryo; with a mind-stretching reach of poetic imagery he says that he himself is 'in labour' to bring this embryo to birth, so much does his imagination operate on the basic assumption that there is one person, Christ, in whom both he and his fellow Christians live. And when he uses the image of sexual union to describe the relationship of Christ and Christian he is saying something about the intimate personal oneness both of the couple in marriage and of Christ with his Church and is able, then, to perceive precisely why it is so horrible that this exchange be rejected by choosing intercourse with a prostitute. The actions of Christians are the actions of Christ, 'the body is for the Lord', and so Christ acts in, and only in, his body the Church. This is why, when a person is baptized, he or she is changed in a way which is not brought about simply by the creation of a weak spot for breakthrough. It happens when Christ acts in a person, offering the fullness of love, and the offer is accepted.

But there is more to be said. Christ acts in his body the Church, and in that only. It is by the Church that the new Christian is changed, for the exchange of life in Christ becomes the 'way of life' of the one who willingly receives it. But that means, as we have seen, that it can happen without full consciousness, it can happen

222

(so at least the earliest Churches thought) on behalf of the dead, and it can happen in babies, because babies also (perhaps babies especially) are living in the flow of exchange and are vulnerable to the love which seeks for a way to come to be in a new point of exchange. So all this happens in, and only in, the life of divine love exchanged which is the Church, the body of Christ. But this body is the same one which walked in Galilee and hung on the cross. If it is not *that* body, baptism makes no sense, because the baptized will still be living the kind of body which is 'subject' to death, open to 'claims' by the law, because it is still the body of flesh and in process of death. This is why Paul insists that in baptism the Christian has died with Christ. Christ died to sin because sin, having done all it could, gave up, baffled by something it could in no way grasp. It was only at that point that resurrection became possible. So death, the actual physical death of Jesus on the cross, is what is exchanged by the Church when she receives a person in baptism. He himself spoke of his coming death as the 'baptism' for which he longed, towards which he pressed forward, and this fact gives us the link we need to bring this consideration of baptism to the point at which we can, in the light of it, consider death itself.

There is a progression: Jesus himself chose to be baptized by John; later he spoke of his death as a baptism, and after he was risen he told his followers to baptize others, or at least that was how they understood what he was telling them to do. Taking that backwards, if we read the last sentence of the Gospel of Matthew we find that the command to 'go and make disciples of all nations', by baptism, is coupled with the claim to universal 'authority', and the two sentences are linked by the word 'therefore'. In other words, the kind of authority which Jesus has is properly ('therefore') articulated in the making of disciples through baptism. Mark adds the warning that if to accept the Good News, to believe and be baptized, will lead to salvation (that is, to sharing in the exchange of the living body of Christ), to refuse belief is a fundamentally deathly choice. It is to choose to 'keep out' Christ. Mark makes clear the expressly physical nature of what he calls salvation, for the disciples will have gifts of casting out devils and of tongue-speaking, they will be immune to venom and poison, and their touch will heal. This, says Mark, is what actually happened, and it is what we would expect, because the new life has broken the barriers made tough and opaque by sin, and so it gives to the members of Christ the freedom of the sphere of glory. In this sphere the relationships in matter change drastically, as we have seen. (But it is still important to notice that what matters is not that this happens to disciples of Jesus, but that it is to disciples of Jesus that it happens. Those who refuse Exchange, turning the power into themselves, may *also* be operating in this sphere, but for them what is glorious is experienced as hellish.) In Matthew Jesus says, 'I am *with* you always', and when Paul takes up that word he makes it clear how far from external is the relationship it describes. To be 'with' Christ is the same as to be 'in' him: it is an organic relationship.

Luke, who does not use the word baptism in this context, has a remarkable sentence in which 'therefore' is clearly implied: 'So you see how it is written that the Christ would suffer and on the third day rise from the dead, and that, in his name, repentance for the forgiveness of sins would be preached to all nations.' It is because of his death that the call to repentance and forgiveness (in practice through baptism) could be made. But Luke (in Acts 1) it is who uses the word 'baptism' to describe what was going to happen to the disciples at Pentecost. They were, at this point, to come up from the font after their long immersion, able now to realize and affirm the *amour voulu* of Jesus in themselves.

They could do so, and could get others to do so, because of the death they had witnessed and which had become their own. Jesus saw it that way when he looked forward to his death as a baptism, the moment of crisis at which the situation must change radically and enable him to be to his beloved what he longed to be. This insight may, it seems to me, have stemmed from the experience of John's baptism, after which he had heard the voice of the Father defining his being and mission: 'My Son, the Beloved'. For this calling was already linked in his mind with the poetry of the Servant of Yahweh who, in Isaiah, was 'for our faults struck down in death'—the word for 'servant' and 'Son' being the same. This claiming of Jesus by the Father for the work of passion came immediately after he had undergone the ritual of John's baptism, experiencing (in very different physical circumstances) the same kind of sequence of disorientation and surrender as was to be developed more fully and consciously in Christian baptismal rites. It

224

seems not only likely but almost certain, therefore, that the break-through of Wisdom at that point made it clear to him that this was how it had to be. This is, in any case, how the evangelists understood it. The Father's naming of him was the language of his whole knowledge of himself as dedicated to death. And as the months passed and his vision of it all became clearer he knew that those whom he in turn called his 'beloved' must go the same way.

This way goes from baptism to baptism. From his own baptism by John he learned of, and went to, the baptism of his death. By that death he became able to exchange with his own beloved the freedom from the power of death, through baptism in him, but that is not the end of the matter, for *because* of baptism (because of living in the kind of exchange which baptism opens up) the Christian is called to a further baptism. He or she must also die, as Jesus died, in order fully to share, both by receiving and by giving.

Of all human experiences death is the one which is most clearly a breakthrough, when it is able to be experienced. The fact that we cannot know, in many cases, what it is like as an experience, because it happens so fast, or in a state of unconsciousness, makes no difference to this. Those who have been most fully aware of their death and able to communicate something of this awareness to those about them have made clear the structure of the event, and it does have a Romantic character.

The experiences known as 'after death' experiences, which have increasingly been recorded in recent years, seem to be in practice accounts of what it feels like to be dead when you *did not expect* to be. They are the experiences of people trying to make sense of something whose character they often do not recognize at first. They do not even know they are 'dead' for a while. And of course all of these accounts are from people who have 'come back', some, it seems, by deliberate choice to finish an unfinished task, and some reluctantly, consenting to the will of others to keep them in life. So, in a way, that kind of experience is not the experience of death as passionate; compared with the Romantic experience of death it is rather like an arranged marriage. This may seem contradictory, because an arranged marriage is planned and takes time, whereas Romantic encounter is unexpected and swift. But in an arranged marriage which is lovingly entered into, with no reluctance but no awareness of passion, the reality of the mutual discovery of man

225

and wife takes place; but it is gradual and its nature perhaps only realized by hindsight, whereas the Romantic experience is discovered in responding to something which has, to the new lover, such a strong and immediate inner self-validation that, once recognized, the only proper response is utter surrender. In the same way, the person who dies accidentally or suddenly and not consciously prepared may perhaps go through the recorded 'after death' experience, without realizing the full character of the experience. This character may become apparent, later, to the person who has been 'brought back to life', and there is evidence in some cases that this is precisely what happened. Also the person who has been close to an unprepared death and has been saved or recovered will often reflect on the nature of the experience, afterwards, and in both cases such people realize it as containing a kind of demand, to which they know they must respond with their whole being. This is why such an experience can change the whole sense of meaning and direction in a person's life. It is a conversion experience of a very clear kind, but one which occurs *out of* rather than *in* the experience of dying or nearly dying.

On the other hand the person who is able to prepare for death and recognize its Romantic character (without, of course, using such a term) comes to it as would the courteous lover whose whole training has prepared him to recognize in the face of the Lady Death the ultimate meaning and joy which moves in himself but can only be fully lived towards her. The same kind of recognition comes, also, to one who has never received such training in the ways of love, yet whose living of life has been such that when the face of the Lady does dawn, the person recognizes the call that she is and can be helped very quickly to overcome the first bewilderment and shrinking and to find the confidence and hope which will enable him or her to respond to it as fully as the other. This help is the work of those who assist the dying, and it is crucial. They do for the one approaching death what the deacons and deaconesses did for the baptismal candidates. They lead the neophyte to the font, they help him or her to unclothe, the stand by the neophyte descending into the water, and if they truly understand their work they present the new candidate, in death, to the one in whom death dies and so acclaim this entrance into the body which, having been dead, is now risen.

226

As we begin to see very clearly the links between baptism and death, and to see them both in terms of passionate breakthrough, we realize that both, as passionate, break through to the sphere of the 'last things' or 'end time', and that they are last not because they are remote but because everything is summed up in them. We live, now, the facts of eschatology, which is really about the ultimate discovery of what is going on in all creation all the time, though the organic connection between 'now' and 'then' can only be understood when the whole thing is interpreted by means of the model of exchange and the phenomenology of Romance which shows us the 'how' of exchange in a sin-dominated world.

The easiest way to do this is to use a concrete example of it. In the *Selected Writings* of the great von Hügel there is a description of a death which is so supremely and passionately Romantic that it plunges us deeply into an awareness of 'where' what is called eschatology actually happens. (It is a passage I have quoted before, but indeed it can never be read too often.) In it von Hügel records a story told him in the early years of this century by a priest he met, a good, dull man who was so overwhelmed by what he had encountered that he was driven to share the experience:

He had been called, a few nights before, to a small pot-house on the outskirts of this large and fashionable town. And there, in a dreary little garret, lay, stricken down with sudden double pneumonia, an Irish young woman, twenty-eight years of age, doomed to die within an hour or two. A large fringe covered her forehead and all the other externals were those of an average barmaid who had, at a public bar, served half-tipsy, coarsely joking men, for some ten years or more. And she was still full of physical energy—and of the physical craving for physical existence. Yet, as soon as she began to pour out her last and general confession, my informant felt, so he told me, a lively impulse to arise and cast himself on the ground before her. For there . . . lay one of the sweet, strong, simple saints of God at his feet. She told him how deeply she desired to become as pure as possible for this grand grace, this glorious privilege, so full of peace, of now abandoning her still young, vividly pulsing life, of placing it utterly within the hands of God, of the Christ whom she loved so much, and who loved her so much more; that this great gift,

227

she humbly felt, would bring the grace of its full acceptance with it, and might help her to aid, with God and Christ, the souls she loved so truly, the souls He loved so far more deeply than she herself could love them. And she died soon after in a perfect rapture of joy—in a joy overflowing, utterly sweetening all the mighty bitter floods of her pain. Now *that* is supernatural.

Indeed it is. It is the place at which the full force of divine love breaks in, because one more human being has opened her arms to love and said, 'let it be done to me'. If we consider this story in even the most external way we cannot help realizing that the impact of this experience must have changed the life of the man who was called upon to assist this 'saint of God' at her baptism, to lead her and unclothe her and present her to her Lover. And if it changed him it changed, in their degrees, all the others to whom afterwards it was his work to minister, so that they in their turn might place their lives 'utterly in the hands of God' and be baptized in him, as she was. Her death was the breakthrough to glory, it was cross and resurrection, not only for her, but through her for others beyond counting. It was this because at this weak spot the passion of Jesus broke through into her. It did so not (evidently) for the first time but with an unprecedented completeness, so that she became in him gate of heaven, God-bearer, but also saviour, and very presence of glory.

The coming Christ is made present in such a death. We can set aside (only for now, and not because it is unimportant) the question of what happens to the person who has died. The important thing is, first of all, what happens *because* she has died. The direct and indirect influence on minds and hearts of that bridal surrender is part of it all, but I mean chiefly that such a dying lets into the world of material reality still under the power of sin (the 'body of this death') that power of resurrection which 'releases' that element in death which makes it deathly. Death *as evil* loses its grip, exactly as it did when Jesus died on the cross, and for precisely the same reason—and I mean the *same* reason, not a parallel one. It was Christ in this girl who died to sin, because for years she had been living as incorporate with him, as his body, doing 'this in memory of me'. She was no doubt baptized as a baby and could remember nothing of it. Yet that baby was open to the flow of exchanged life

228

in the body of Christ, and within that exchange there were, as she grew up, those little encounters with love which can be as small as a smile or as great as martyrdom. As a child from a poor home she had suffered, as the children of the poor do; in that home she had been taught (in crude religious language, no doubt, but truly and really) that suffering can be redemptive. What the words could not tell her the lives of others did, and especially the life and death of the man on the cross whose image faced her above the altar in church every Sunday, and in cheap little crucifixes on the wall of her family's kitchen or of her garret in foggy England. Thus was the life she shared enabled more and more to invade her being, and then to reach consciousness and with that to increase its power by an exponential leap, breaking through sphere after sphere. So, finally, she came from baptism to baptism and went down into death with Christ, and rose with him, and in doing so she *was* the 'second coming' of Christ.

This has to be so because the Coming of Christ in this sense is the 'revealing of the children of God', it is the recognition, as complete and perfect, of what is going on now and has been going on since the earth shook and the veil of the Temple was torn and the forms of the loving dead were seen in the streets, and will go on until he in whom it began is 'all in all'. And the way it goes on is in such ways as that girl's death, and the death of thousands and millions of other saints, some acclaimed, but mostly people whom nobody has ever heard of outside their own circle and who were soon forgotten even there. And it is going on in all the little 'deaths' whereby women and men and children respond with passionate openness to the love which, in its terrible poverty, waits for their answer. They 'die' in enduring such things as playground teasing, or the weight of depression, or the long-drawn-out suffering of a life in which there seems no chance of ordinary happiness.

In all this the second coming of Christ is being prepared, but it is only being prepared because it is already there. In a sense, the second coming began when Jesus died, because that was the cross-roads, it was 'the point of intersection of the timeless with time', when that which drove in on him who was the solitary 'remnant' was utterly changed and went forth from him as love, spreading from there by the way of Exchange. It is tempting, therefore, to think of the second coming as a final point of the perfection of this process of transformation, coming steadily and beautifully as a tree grows, or even like Jack's beanstalk, rapidly twining and reaching and stretching itself up to heaven. But all this transformation is taking place in a world—a cosmos—which is penetrated into its furthest reaches by the energy of Refusal, distorting the flow, locking it into stagnant pools or twisting it into deadly whirlpools.

That is a metaphor which helps a little, but it is important to see that what is described in that way can be verified from experience. It takes the metaphor to show us what to look for, but we must then look and recognize. Examples are appallingly easy to find, and what is called the 'poverty trap' is one—the familiar situation whereby cultural and material deprivation destroy the ability or even the desire for anything different. Another example on a huge scale is to be observed in the southern Sahara, where a famine occurred not from natural causes but because the people exhausted the scant pasture by over-grazing, and no suitable food or fodder crops were substituted, not because none would grow, but because all the energy and skill were going to produce peanuts for export to prosperous countries.

On a smaller scale we can see in individuals how the deprivation of love in childhood makes people incapable of responding to love; they may become defensive, rapacious, passive or sometimes insane. They, in their turn, warp and destroy love in others. We live in a world in which the flow of exchanged life which presses towards the transformation of all things in Christ is constantly blocked by fear, greed and apathy.

That is why there cannot be a steady growth towards perfection. There has to be a breakthrough, as we have seen in example after example, in level after level of created being. We can indeed live in and by the very presence of the glory which is to come, but between the real and concrete but limited experience of it and the utter freedom of the whole Christ there is a gap which is not just one of quantity or extent of transformation but rather, I think we must say, a gap which requires a qualitative leap. This is a leap like the one from inanimate to animate being, from intelligence to self-consciousness. It is like the leap of incarnation, and the leap by which the body of Jesus begins to live in those bodies of his lovers. As the body of the resurrection passed through ascertainable barriers, passing in each to a deeper and more intimate kind of cor-

230

porateness, so in time there are perhaps other such barriers; but a final barrier, unimaginable to us, there must be, beyond which an ultimate kind of identity-in-unity is to be achieved. This cannot mean the 'end' in the sense of a cessation of the movement of Exchange, for Exchange is the very nature of the Three-in-One. It must mean, rather, the final release of created being from all that would impede its total response to that Exchange. It is the ultimate victory of the passionate God, in which the 'accidental' qualities of impeded love, which make it passion, give way to the unimpeded outpouring of divine love.

How can we envisage this? It is important that we try, because we are part of the happening of it. Children ask, 'Will the world come to an end?' and look anxiously at the sky. The final cataclysm is a thing which seizes human imagination in every age and culture, and the more a self-confident and sensible culture outlaws such speculations from respectable debate the more they flourish in those corners where the magicians 'chirp and mutter'.

But the 'final' events are already present, and it is the link between present experiences of the 'end' and the total revelation of that 'end' which needs to be explored. I want to do this in two ways, using in one the imagery of a modern novel, in the other an actual contemporary social and religious phenomenon, relating them to each other like the music of two voices in a polyphonic encounter, both working within the mode provided by the pheno- menology of Romance. These two voices are provided for me by the images of the last pages of Walter Miller's *A Canticle for Liebowitz*, on the one hand, and on the other by the very strange and new ways in which the phenomenon of the body of Christ as it lives and works now is actually occurring. Both display very clearly the char- acteristics of Romantic passion, and both illuminate the nature of the final breakthrough of the passionate God.

The theme of Miller's long, beautiful, funny, repulsive book is that, following a nuclear holocaust which has wiped out all but a remnant of humankind (and that remnant subject to horrific mu- tations), the following ages will, inexorably and step by step, repeat the mistakes of pre-nuclear ages, until finally the recovered civiliz- ation once more wipes itself out in the futile encounter of 'powers' which gain nothing but death for themselves and their people by their carefully rationalized onslaughts on each other. It is a grim

231

book as well as a very funny one, and it raises ethical questions which badly need to be faced by more than the valiant company of cranks and misfits. But its significance for my purpose lies in the description of the nature of a particular kind of mutation, caused by radiation but dormant up to that point in the story, which at a certain moment comes to life and proves to be, in some sense, the meaning and end-point of the whole tale.

All three of the 'periods' (centuries apart) with which the book deals are affected by the residual radioactivity from the nuclear war which ended all previous civilization. Monsters are born and survive in deserted places, and less horrific oddities are part of daily experience. In the last part of the book, the centripetal folly of malice in humankind is bringing yet another nuclear destruction on the earth amid a patter of political platitudes so efficient they deceive even the self-elect, and the Abbot of an ancient monastery (whose existence forms the continuity of the book and endures through all three periods) is faced with appalling moral decisions. Already, 'minor' nuclear attacks have destroyed cities and killed millions, but huge numbers are not yet dead but doomed by radiation sickness to lingering torment, and the government has set up mobile units and camps to provide official euthanasia for these victims. The Abbot forbids the erection of a camp outside the monastery and fights (even at one point physically) a doctor sent to examine the site and tell the stricken about the 'mercy' available.

The whole set-up in the monastery reinforces the contradiction between the ethos of the monastic life (roughly modelled on the Middle Ages of our era, as well as dating from the 'neo-Middle-Ages' of this imaginary future era) and the ethos of the world in which it survives. The monks chant the Latin Office and wear cowls and sandals (this was written in the 1950s), but the Abbot's office is equipped with computerized communications and some other sci-fi gadgets invented by the author. It seems as if this gap, which consists of intentional anachronism, is contrasted with another kind of gap, hidden and unplanned, which is developing between 'this world' and 'the world to come'.

There is a garrulous old woman who sells tomatoes to the Abbey. The Abbot (whose name is Zerchi—the names of the three Abbots who span this book begin with A, P and Z since symbolically they span a whole culture from beginning to end) is driven to distraction by her demands on his attention, for she is a victim of residual radiation and has a second head which lolls inert and apparently senseless on her shoulder and is mostly covered with a shawl. The head is that of a child in features but, being as old as she, is weather-worn in complexion. This head the woman thinks and talks of as her 'daughter' called Rachel, and she pesters the Abbot with demands that he baptize her. The Abbot, tangled up in a skein of scholastic argument with himself about the relationship of soul and body, cannot decide whether such a rite would or could make sense and meanwhile stalls her anxious questions and persuasions as well as he can. But, as the story moves towards the foreseen cataclysm, Rachel begins to show signs of life. A kind of smile, a tiny movement, and then—yes certainly, a smile. But still she sleeps. Meanwhile, after fighting the doctor to prevent the 'mercy-killing' of a mother and baby and nearly being arrested, the Abbot is seized by remorse and confesses to his Prior. From this he comes—shamed, shaken, near to despair and very late—to hear the confession of Mrs Grales, the 'tomato woman', who had earlier begged him to 'shrive' her.

There is a curious introduction to this episode when Mrs Grales admits that she not only needs forgiveness herself but feels a need to *give forgiveness to God*—'to Him who made me as I am . . . I never forgive him for it'. The piercing truth of this has difficulty in penetrating the entrenched categories of the Abbot's mind, and he protests that God 'is Justice' and is love, but the old woman, though pleading, is surer than he: 'Mayn't an old tomater woman forgive Him just a little for His justice? Afor I be asking His shriv'ness on me?'

The priest is silenced and disturbed, apparently no more than that. While he is giving her absolution after hearing her pathetically familiar recital, the nuclear attack which had been feared comes at last, with a light that scorches like noon through the thick confessional curtain and makes it smoke. Zerchi knows this is the end but gives his automatic safety instructions to the old woman and hears them 'echoed' in a soft, strange voice; then the woman's own voice trails away to incoherence and ceases. He rushes to take the reserved Sacrament out of church, but as he runs out with it the building falls on him, and when he comes to from a blackout he finds the lower half of his body and one arm pinned under tons of masonry, while the ciborium has fallen to the ground and spilled its contents.

233

During his episodes of futile struggle, of blackout and waiting, he comes (in a delirious conversation with a friend who is not there) to a sense of solidarity with both sin and salvation: 'Me us Adam, but Christ man me' and, later, 'I mean Jesus never asked a man to do a damn thing that Jesus didn't do. Same as why I—'.

And here, at this point of death, and although that which is to be revealed in and through it has not yet disclosed itself, we can suddenly see the shape of it. The mounting sense of doom and the impossibility of reconciling available ways of being-with-God with what the God who is crucified in burned flesh and demented politics seems to be saying combine to create a barrier to love and even to sanity which, it seems, nothing can surmount. Yet the barrier must be passed, if God is to *be*. The nuclear blast which destroys the church is the moment of recognition of *this* God, it is 'seeing God face to face', which none can do and live. It is the face of Beatrice, but she is not to be known as 'beata Beatrice' this time, unless she is first known as Lilith, Adam's 'other' wife in the ancient legend. She must be known and forgiven, and when she is forgiven she is recognized as Wisdom herself. The prone and half-crushed and irradiated body of the man who is a priest is bearing the literal weight of the building which fell on him. This building is the Church, piled up through centuries of devotion and sacrifice and love—heavy, solid and lethal. But he is bearing this in and with Jesus, who 'never asked a man to do a damn thing that he didn't do himself'. It is indeed a 'damn thing', a damned thing, that he bears. He bears the weight of sin, the sin in the earthly body of Christ. Like Mrs Grales, the body has an extra head, and a very ambiguous one. (Is it new life? It sleeps still, yet it has smiled in its sleep. Is that *all* that resurrection has been able to achieve?) So he, Abbot, 'Father' of the Church, is bearing all this pain on behalf of the Father, and that—humorously and scandalously—justifies the old woman's intuition that humankind must forgive God, in whom and by whom all this pain comes, because in him and only in him the Refusal itself subsists and can be Refusal. She has forgiven God for his Justice and for his love, and this, we realize, is what had to be done before the consummation of all things could come.

In Charles Williams' Arthurian cycle of poems, *Taliessin Through Logres*, there is one about a moment of breakthrough by the young Galahad ('Percivale at Carbonek'). Galahad was the child begotten

234

by Lancelot when he lay with Elayne, the daughter of the stricken Grail King, whom through enchantment he took for Guinevere, to whom he was pledged in all passionate yet sinful fealty. Waking to this knowledge of his betrayal, Lancelot ran mad and turned to a wolf, and in his animal frenzy desired to eat his child when it was born, but the child was rescued by Merlin and brought up in the convent at Almesbury. The Child, the 'alchemical infant' who will transform base metal of flesh to gold of the spiritual body, comes at last to Carbonek, the castle of the Grail, where lies the wounded Grail King, Pelles, awaiting this coming for his healing and the reconciliation of all things. But at the gate of the castle Galahad stops, for something must be done before he can go in and begin to reverse the flow of Refusal, which is expressed in the myth by the Dolorous Blow which has brought down both the King and all the land to barren futility:

> In the rent saffron sun hovered the Grail.
> Galahad stood in the arch of Carbonek;
> The people of Pelles ran to meet him.
>   His eyes were sad; he sighed for Lancelot's pardon.
>
> Joy remembered joylessness; joy kneeled
> under the arch where Lancelot ran in frenzy.
> The astonished angels of the spirit heard him moan:
>   *Pardon, lord; pardon and bless me, father.*
>
> . . . The passage through Carbonek was short to the house of the
> Grail;
> The wounded King waited for health; motionless
> The subdued glory implored the kingdom
>   to pardon its power and the double misery of Logres.
>
> Under the arch the Merciful Child
> wept for the grief of his father in reconciliation;
> who was betrayed there by Merlin and Brisen
> to truth; he saw not; he was false to Guinevere.

Galahad suffers under the sin of his father and the pain of the sin against his father, which yet 'betrayed' him 'to truth', the incarnate

235

truth who is Galahad, who is Christ. He craves, he absolutely needs, forgiveness from Lancelot the sinner and from those who are suffering by this sin and who are his own kin. The people who are his people and Lancelot's people are represented by Bors, the wise and kindly father and husband, and by Percivale, the philosopher. They are 'the fallen house of Camelot', wounded and requiring healing because of the web of refusal in the exchange, inextricably tangled: love and falsehood, honour and shame, high purpose and murky expedients. It comes to a point in the burning innocence of Galahad who, because he is the one sent to heal and forgive, so excruciatingly requires forgiveness:

> His hand shook; pale were his cheeks;
> his head the head of a skull, flesh
> cleaving to bone; his dry voice rattled;
>   'Pardon, Lord Lancelot; pardon and blessing, father.'

> . . . Stiffly the Child's head turned; the drawn engine
> slewed to his left, to Bors the kin of Lancelot,
> He said, 'Cousin, can you bear pardon
>   to the house of Carbonek from the fallen house of Camelot?'

> Bors answered: 'What should we forgive?'
> 'Forgive Us', the High Prince said, 'for our existence;
> forgive the means of grace and the hope of glory.
>   In the name of Our father forgive Our mother for Our birth.'

The final overcoming of evil can only mean the translation of evil into good—which is forgiveness. Galahad must be forgiven for *existing*, because his existence is the direct result of much sin and folly and pain, and has led directly to much more. Christ must be forgiven his incarnation because his existence brings to an excruciating point of unavoidable recognition the wrongness which might otherwise have been unrecognized and unpainful. He must be forgiven his passion because it allows humankind no other way to life but through that degraded and incoherent agony. The house of Camelot, muddled and aspiring and despairing humankind, has much to forgive God.

But when that forgiveness has been given—by acceptance of life

236

in the ordinary, dogged everydayness of going-on-with-living in love because love is real—then innocence can come in. God forgiven is God forgiving:

'Sir', Bors said, 'only God forgives.
My lord Sir Lancelot is a lover and kind.
I assent to all, as I pray that my children assent
    and through God join with me in bidding their birth.'

And so Bors, the bodily being, the family, the community of everyday love, goes *ahead* of the saviour, passing through the spheres at his bidding. And Galahad—innocence and mystical vision—follows him, out from under the dark archway:

The High Prince stepped in his footprints; into the sun
Galahad followed Bors; Carbonek was entered.

In *A Canticle for Liebowitz* the dying priest in and of a dying world wakes to rainfall and to perceive near him the figure which represents the peculiar horribleness of that world, that two-headed woman who had to forgive God because others would not. He tries to get her to fetch a priest for him, his mind still moving in the categories of the religion that had served, but all she does is to repeat his words in a kind of gentle chant. Then he realizes that the voice is the voice of Rachel, the second head. She has woken, and the old head lolls inert beside her. Rachel is young, new, just born, she has no words of her own, all she can do is repeat, yet her repetition of the words she hears is clear and not mindless; she means by it 'I am somehow like you'. 'Yet you're different somehow too', the Abbot realizes.

Gradually, amazedly, with mounting awe, he realizes what kind of difference this is. The head of Mrs Grales hangs dying and will, he feels, eventually wither away like an umbilical cord. The body is now Rachel's body; it moves with the suppleness of youth, the very skin seems less wrinkled, it glows 'as if the horny old tissues were being revivified'. With his one free hand Zerchi takes splinters of glass from the bomb blast out of her arm, yet she seems to feel no pain and does not bleed, nor does she seem to recognize that he is in pain, and dying. His common sense tells him she must die soon from the radiation, so he tries to give her conditional baptism with rain-water which has fallen on the rock. (The rain-water is, of course, itself deathly with fallout.) But Rachel pulls away and wipes the water from her forehead and then, with opened hands and closed eyes, enters into a likeness of deep prayer. When she opens her eyes again she immediately searches for and finds the ciborium. Zerchi has the reflexes of a pre-Vatican II priest and tries to snatch it from her, faints again and comes to as she offers him the bread, with a strange mixture of reverence and ease, 'as if by direct instruction'. Then he knows that this creature is the new creation, free of sin, impassible.

But the author and therefore his characters think in theological categories inadequate to deal with the symbols he evokes. Miller suggests that this mutation has made possible the recovery of 'primal innocence' and 'a promise of resurrection'. What he actually evokes is, rather, 'final glory' and 'evidence of resurrection'. Above all it is the body of Christ, but the finally glorified body, confronting the one still under the shadow of death. Not for nothing is the pathetic and repulsive 'mother', whose worn body bears this new thing, given the name of Mrs Grales. Her patient bearing of an unconceived, fatherless burden has brought forth an 'alchemical' infant indeed. This grotesque 'Grail Princess' is as deceived, as helpless and as blessed as Pelles' daughter Elayne. In her maternal flesh she has done more than Elayne, for she has forgiven, on her child's behalf, the 'means of grace and the hope of glory'. So Pelles, the thigh-wounded King in his castle, is to be healed and die. The monk buried under crashed masonry is the sign of the living body of Christ crushed and paralysed under the weight of its own history, but he is especially the visible, 'official' hierarchical Church; it still has one hand free, and with that hand it will try, first, to baptize that which needs no ritual baptism since it has passed through death already, and then, humbly, it will receive from the new-risen Body the gift of the Body, the gift of death. And behind it all the final destruction is engulfing the earth in fire.

This is the symbolic scenario of the Last Things, in miniature yet complete. Here is death indeed, and here is judgement, as chosen and sharpened and made absolute in the face of death as absolute. For this is the crisis of all history, and the word itself means 'judgement'. This is not the external judgement of the one who is unaffected by the doom he pronounces. This crisis is the revealing, in sudden awful clarity, of what has been going on all the time so that it is judged in its own being. In Christ's parable of the judgement the two kinds of people are separated according to the way they have lived their lives, in exchange of love or in refusal of exchange. All of history is judged in the moment of the End, because its meaning is made clear in the flash of the final holocaust, and indeed the real meaning of the word 'holocaust' reinforces this: a holocaust is a 'whole burnt offering' in which everything is consumed, nothing is left over as with other sacrifices to be shared in the world of everydayness. But it is sacrifice, it is a making holy, by judgement. What is revealed as love is wholly taken into the fire of glory, but that which is unconsumed in that holocaust is incapable of sacrifice, of becoming holy. It is hell, the choice of final refusal, still trying to deceive even to the point of annihilating and being annihilated rather than consent to the terror of truth. But in this image of the end there also is heaven, essentially known in one 'mutant' creature, and it is a female creature, un-fathered, virgin beyond any previous meaning of the word, God-bearer.

There is here no progression by organic stages, there is the leap of random mutation. And that mutation itself lies as lifeless as the sleeping beauty, its meaning unguessed, until the final cataclysm kills the comically sad vessel that bore it. That devastation releases the life of the waiting glory. This is the final Romantic passion.

Keeping these extraordinary symbols in mind, we have to make a switch in subject-matter, scale and genre and consider something which is going on now, and within range of our direct observation, for the Body of Christ is, in our time, coming into being in a new way, which can be observed easily but requires for proper discernment symbols of theological poetry such as those given to us by the Abbot and Rachel. And I am suggesting that this emergence of Christ in a Body which looks and is different shows us the nature of the Parousia. I am not saying that the end is at hand, or that in this revivified Body we see the first sign of the End. I do not know, though that is always possible. I am simply saying that, on the available evidence, interpreted by available poetic patterns, this is the kind of change in which the End must show itself.

The visible Church (and by this I mean the major Christian denominations, since small sects operate by a different dynamic) is very much in the position of Abbot Zerchi in Miller's novel. The explosion of new technology, the population explosion, the explosion of revolutionary thought and action, of new social patterns and art forms, and the collapse of older meanings and purposes and social, religious and ethical patterns caused by all this have made the Church do just what the Abbot did. It tried to escape from the collapsing building, hoping still to minister to those dying and terrified. Like the Abbot it had already been more or less discredited in its attempts to grapple directly with false philosophies and destructive technology. It had been forced to acknowledge, in that encounter, its own folly and blindness, its inability to convey the reality of God's love. It had retired a little within itself, to seek forgiveness and to give forgiveness, and was too confused by all the noise and threat outside to be able to discern what was, in fact, already growing within itself, in the obscurity of its own 'unofficial', theologically illiterate, sinful and fearful but living people. We also need to realize something which Miller's description makes clear, that when the more violent explosions came the fall of the building was made inevitable not only by the force of the blast but by the nature of the building—so old that its method of construction was obscure, a vast pile which had been repaired many times and not always skilfully, while new bits were added to cope with new needs, and the joins not always strong or appropriate.

But the sense of what the Church is for, of its essential mission to preach and to feed and to heal, made it seem obvious that what mattered if disaster was striking all of humankind was to be able to go on with the job, and the sense of the Church in its best official thinkers and leaders and writers was to get out of the building and take the Bread of Life to those who needed it in their extremity. But the huge thing collapsed too quickly and the attempt to find new ways, but *according to old norms and definitions*, was pinned to the ground.

This was the situation which began to become apparent about fifteen years ago. The efforts at battle, at repair, at mission had failed or were failing. The sheer weight of centuries, of past thought and holiness and splendour, lay on the frail body. It could not move, or at least it could move very little, though it continued to do what it could, and its first effort like the Abbot's was to gather up as many of the scattered fragments of the eucharistic food as it could reach. This was the heart of the matter, this was what it had to live by and to give.

The reform of the liturgy which has taken place is just such a gesture, presenting this historically rich and many-symboled ritual language in a simple and even banal form, yet without really discovering the dynamic which built up the form. The attempt was motivated by a real sense of proper priorities but was fatally handicapped in the scope of its imaginative movement. So the Church has changed. It has accepted helplessness, it has known itself in poverty and suffering, it has identified itself with those hurt by the powers of Refusal. It has wept and prayed; it has cried out for help in its anguish, but none has come, apparently.

But answers to prayer seldom come in the way we expect. The answer to the anguished prayer of the Church has been given, steadily and unobtrusively, and it is now becoming increasingly apparent to those who are prepared to recognize it. But this is harder than it seems for a Church conditioned to recognize the Lord's coming only in categories established by its own conscious mind. For what is happening is not the result of reform or 'renewal'. (The effort of most kinds of Christian renewal was described to me by a friend as 'like doing interior decorating on the *Titanic*', which is unkind but accurate.) It is not even essentially connected with such things as the charismatic movement, or the recovery of a ministry of healing as a normal part of the Church's mission, or the theology of liberation, or the movement for the ordination of women, or the increasing emphasis on the ministry of the laity, though all these things are symptomatic, even if the symptoms are easily misinterpreted.

What is really happening is that the Body of Christ is living its being and action in new ways, to such a degree that many people will not recognize them. They are not totally different, for this is the same Christ, but he is, as we should expect, behaving in different ways to meet the needs of a radically different situation. The Romantic lover will woo his Lady according to the strictest etiquette of chivalry if that is what she seems to want, but if this proves inadequate and she turns away in indifference or repulsion he will try something else. He will paint his nose red and turn cartwheels if necessary.

What is happening now to the Church is not just a temporary

241

muddle before we find re-formed versions of old ways. The changes that have taken place throughout the world, at every level of living, in our time have had a character which is not that of the evolutionary model dear to the Victorians, whereby mankind (definitely *man*kind) moved with dignity and authority towards ultimate perfection. They have, instead, a Romantic character. The stages of it are not hard to perceive, and first of all there has been the breaking of many barriers in technology and chemistry and physics and psychology and mathematics. These have worked on each other and on the minds that felt them, even if they could not understand. The foundations of the mind are shaken and old thoughts fall off the tree. Wars and disasters are on such a scale and the horror of them so intense and so exhaustively displayed to us that people become numbed or cynical. Fear hangs over everything, and normal life goes on under the thick pall of it because there is nothing else to be done. Few admit the near-certainty of a disaster so total that there is no point in taking precautions or wondering what will happen afterwards.

It is no use pretending that the Church can plod on, heroically unchanged, through all that. The situation is one of such widespread and deeply reaching disorientation of minds and hearts as cannot but make them vulnerable to that which waits for them. The question is only whether the one who appears is to be Christ or anti-Christ, and both Paul and John tell us in vivid poetry that not only must such an 'end' be preceded by huge and unprecedented disaster but that something more evil than mere disaster must appear as part of this situation. This is the final result of that build-up of Refusal, the intensification of resistance to resurrection, of which I spoke in an earlier chapter.

What we look for, then, is not first of all the passionate breakthrough of God into his creation, but that perversion of it which looks so like the real thing that it deceives even the elect, or some of them. The difference is that the false breakthrough is not a response of love but an invasion, a rape. There is no communication, but conquest and surrender. That is what many people are wanting: the luxury of being totally taken over and given rapture without questions or responsibilities. We can see examples of this in the attitudes of the more megalomaniac nuclear scientists and their disciples and worshippers, as well as in those who followed the

242

drug-culture, or went to their hideous death in the jungle of Guyana at the call of yet another self-elected messiah. We can see it in the enormous response to that plump and wealthy young man, the guru Maharaj-ji, promising instant peace to his obedient followers, and in the blissful subservience of the 'Moonies'. We long for safe gods and run after them, and worship them. Under the rule of these new gods, who do indeed do 'all kinds of miracles', there is no way in which the body of Christ can live in truth by its older incarnation.

We live in a world which, under this threat and fear, in east and west and north and south makes all its really crucial choices—political, economic, social, sexual—in relation to values which do not contradict so much as simply ignore the Gospel description of the nature of humankind. But worse than this is the fact that the Church generally behaves the same way, without even noticing the concealed premises underlying its adaptation to the world. Only in a narrow band of specifically 'Christian' concerns do 'official' churches normally display moral indignation or act in ways which offer any contrast (let alone challenge) to the usual patterns of social adjustment. Having lived alongside such a Church for a long time most people (people, that is, whose lives are not bound to that 'Christian' area by emotional need and religio-social pressure) have ceased to be interested in what Christians say or do. They do not even, like old-fashioned humanists, get worked up about Christianity; it is merely irrelevant and smells a bit fusty, though as folklore and folk custom it has a certain interest.

But people still long for God, and God longs for them. The process of resurrection spreads, people exchange with people an inarticulate desire, the reviving body struggles to be free of the deathliness which also spreads through the body with the speed and power given it by the very nature of the exchange which it refuses. If the intensity of obscure longing shows itself in the mushroom growth of cults and sects and of white and black magic and obsession with sex, it also shows itself in the pilgrimages to the East and to Glastonbury, in the popularity of centres and courses for prayer and meditation, in the hunger for justice, the dedication of underground workers under tyranny, of anti-nuclear agitators, and of those who run food co-ops and keep open house in the cities where people are flattened by the hopelessness of it all.

This longing desire makes itself felt most strongly as always in those weak spots—the people whom circumstance and temperament combined have jolted out of the safe routine which protects from too much awareness. And everywhere people who feel this longing get together to find ways to articulate it, to do something about it. The way they do so depends on the place in heart and mind which has become vulnerable, and this is why they may be invaded by evil rather than invited by love.

Love comes in all kinds of ways and may not even look like it at first. One weak spot was provided by an enthusiasm for folk-music. In the sixties, some of the disoriented and 'marginal' people (young, mostly—sensitive, talented, angry and yet optimistic) discovered in folk-song a language which expressed both their disillusion with 'the powers that be' (which have always oppressed the poor, and lovers) and their obscure but definite conviction that there is hope in the very fact of being human. The folk-songs were the expression of very basic human experiences, of love and lust and death and birth and laughter, and danger on sea and land. They articulated the final core of human resistance to regimentation and tyranny. New songs were written in the same idiom, about the hero of a railway crash or a mine-disaster in Nova Scotia, expressing also the sense of the ultimate uncrushableness of the human spirit. And these songs were sung by groups who, together and with their admirers, were also discovering a new way of being together, a sense of community, indeterminate in shape and duration but definite and recognizable in atmosphere and ethos. Most of them later drifted apart, but what they had learned and taught became part of the consciousness of newer communities.

Another unexpected weak spot is simply anger. If it was indignation about battered wives, for instance, which moved them to get into the struggle to discover ways to love for the unloved, then they will get together to tackle that with others who feel the same way, and in the process of sharing work, plans, hopes, failures and achievements—the very experience of exchanged love—they will grow in spiritual depth and vitality, learning from each other, learning more about the bad as well as the good in themselves and each other, discovering a kind of vulnerability and kinds of seeing.

Theodore Roszak described, in an article, what he called 'situational networks' of people who had come together, at first, because they were companions in suffering:

They do not aspire to become mass movements or political parties . . . they insist on being small, autonomous, intensely intimate. For want of a better name, I have called them 'situational networks', loose associations of our society's many victims held together by the bonds of shared suffering . . . . the situational group may be the one sanctuary in our big, busy, bullying world where people can come together to tell their tale, sing their song, and so find full personal recognition for all that they are *as* victims and (most importantly) for all that they are *besides* victims . . . the networks are a means of casting off assigned identities . . . and of asserting oneself as a surprising and delightful event in the universe. . . . these profoundly personalistic groupings are part of a larger, unprecedented political task. Through their defiant celebration of diversity, a powerful new ethical principle enters our lives, that all people are born to be persons, and that persons come first, before all collective fictions, even those of revolutionary movements. And is this not exactly what the planet herself now requires of us? . . . After our long, strenuous, industrial adventure, we are being summoned back along new paths to a vital reciprocity with the Earth who mothered us into our strange human vocation. In a sense that blends myth and science, fact and feeling, the Great Goddess is indeed returning. But she returns to us by way of the deep self, out of the underworld of the troubled psyche.

The 'Great Goddess' will turn up later, but here it is the description of the way people gather which is interesting. 'By way of the deep self' they come together and feel impelled to discover, together, what that is. They learn meditation, they begin to pray. And if they come to pray, as so many do even if they are not Christians and have no religious background at all, then the common experience of this adventure, the support they give each other, the discoveries they confide to each other, also deepen and widen the scope of their human awareness, first of each other and then of themselves as part of a greater whole, many of whose members suffer dumbly and remediably. So, often and often, just as the groups that have gathered for 'social action' end up praying, so the group that is gathered to pray ends up giving service to those in need.

There are those who come together to live in community because

245

they long for more honest, more open, more loving relationships, and soon realize that if these things are to be found it can only be by praying and serving also. There are those who go 'back to the land' out of a passion of conviction that right human living can only grow from right relationship to soil and plants and animals. There are politically motivated groups and mystically motivated groups, and they often end up scarcely distinguishable one from another.

Many of these gatherings die soon, because they fail to make the kind of growth in breadth and depth which I have described. And of those which continue for even a few years only a few take the further and crucial step by which they are able to discover language adequate to express the kind of breakthrough they are experiencing, which will enable them to 'take hold of' their lived exchange and make of it real *amour voulu*. If the gathering, or even part of it, has discovered a word which is a true symbol of what they are knowing together, then something radical happens. The passionate leap across the gap between longing and the word which is made flesh in it breaks a barrier and crashes through into another sphere. And that word, over and over again, is the one we may expect: Jesus. When that name is spoken the gathering of people discovers its own name, it is the Body of Christ, a church, and the Church.

This happened once, at the beginning, in the same way, and how it happened tells us a great deal about what is happening now and what it means. It happened on a certain afternoon, not long after the birth of that turbulent and unpredictable entity called the Church. Simon Peter went up on to the roof of the house in Joppa where he was lodging, because he wanted some peace and quiet for prayer. This is always a dangerous thing to do. The Lord is quick to take advantage of vulnerable moments of quiet and openness, in order to introduce very un-quieting suggestions and requests into our lives. Peter found this to be so, for he was subjected to a thrice-repeated vision (one vision being no doubt inadequate to influence so obstinate a man) which flatly and crudely contradicted some of his most deeply held convictions about what constituted godly and acceptable behaviour. Although he did not yet know what was the purpose of all this he knew he was being asked to overcome a moral repulsion so deep as to be part of himself. He must do the unthinkable, violate his strongest religious and ethnic taboos.

246

That was what it meant for Peter (not only as an individual but as representing the infant Church) to accept the possibility that the Spirit could work just as well among uncircumcised heathen as among the chosen people. These unclean people must even be thought of as chosen also. Up to that time he and the rest of the twelve had been calling to baptism Jews who had heard of it and were in varying degrees prepared for it and willing and eager to listen. In the house of Cornelius Peter encountered a different situation. He was called to a group of pagans, headed by Cornelius, who were clearly under the guidance of the Spirit, and lived a kind of community life of brotherly sharing in prayer and service, and in pondering together the insights they received. We can see this from, for instance, the apparently small detail that when Cornelius wanted to send a message to Peter he did not simply use messengers to convey his request but 'related everything to them'. This centurion was on terms of deep trust in spiritual matters with his subordinates. When Peter returned with the messenger he found the entire group (referred to by Cornelius as 'we') assembled and evidently, as a group, eagerly prepared to listen to what Peter had to say. And when they heard the name which Peter announced to them it came upon their ears with that sense of inner recognition which comes to those whose minds and hearts are open and prepared. And 'the Holy Spirit fell on all who heard the word'.

This happened to the assembly in the house of Cornelius before they had received baptism. Uncircumcised, unbaptized, alien in life-style and culture, those people received the Spirit. 'God gave the same gift to them as he gave to us', Peter pointed out later to the sceptical and critical Jerusalem believers. 'Who was I that I could withstand God?' Earlier, I quoted from *Christianity Rediscovered*, the experiences of Vincent Donovan among the Masai. In teaching these people he learned from their religious tradition. And he learned the same thing which Peter learned:

Goodness and kindness and holiness and grace and divine presence and creating power and salvation were here before I got here. My role as herald of the gospel, as a messenger of the news of what had already happened in the world, as the person whose task it was to point to 'the one who had stood in their midst whom they did not recognize' was only a small part of the mission

247

of God to the world. It was a mysterious part, a part barely understood. It was a necessary part, a demanded part: 'Woe to me if I do not preach the gospel'. It was a role that would require every talent and insight and skill and gift and strength I had, to be spent without question, without stint, and yet in the humbling knowledge that only that part of it would be made use of which fit into the immeasurably greater plan of the relentless, pursuing God whose will in the world would not be thwarted.

Many times, of course, the coming together of people longing for God happens within the context of existing Church structures and traditions. Christians meet to pray or to serve, to form communities or run campaigns, to love and discover and suffer and celebrate. They, too, move together under the impulse of an irrepressible longing for 'something' hidden, even though they know to some extent what it is they seek. They have the language, yet with them also it has to take fire, it has to leap out suddenly at them as if they had never heard it before. And there are two things which distinguish this kind of Christian gathering from other kinds of Christian groups which seem externally very like them. One is that they do not come together because it is planned that they should (though sometimes a planned gathering takes this character in time). They are drawn to each other, and draw each other, because they recognize in each other the face of Beatrice, the face of Love. The other thing is that, although the membership may actually consist of people who are, for instance, members of a parish or religious community, or of one denomination, their being gathered is not in virtue of that but in virtue more deeply of a mutual recognition in Christ.

That is why, in practice, even if they begin as a group of people with the same religious background they usually find themselves very soon including others who may have a different one, or none. And this is the reason why those gatherings which begin from a secular or at least non-religious articulation of the purpose of their coming together find it easy to share with religious people, once some initial prejudice or suspicion is overcome.

One way we can recognize the real nature of what is happening is by noticing the kind of relationships and atmosphere in such groups and gatherings, comparing them with the descriptions of the

248

earliest Christian communities, and considering the qualities which Paul says are 'the fruits of the Spirit'. What is happening is world-wide, and it is growing as much in the secular as in the 'religious' world, indeed what Christians are doing is simply to live out more consciously the inner meaning of what is happening to many others. It happens for instance when people get together to protest against something which they perceive as evil, and as they think together about *why* they consider it evil they discover a common vision and begin to live it more fully. I quoted earlier from Jungk's book, *The Nuclear State*, on the threat to human life posed by the nuclear industry, and the huge and growing protest against this shows us one of the clearest and best examples of the kind of way people come together, what inspires them, and whose work is perceptible in this manner of being together. I quote:

> . . . There has arisen within a few years a world-wide movement, a new international movement that resembles no previous popular protest. Its supporters have been recruited from people of the most varied views, social classes and nationalities. They manage without any centralized leadership or formal programme, and to a large extent without formal organization. Their symbol is not the monolithic block, but the river that absorbs many tributaries and flows round, washes away and overflows obstacles in its path.
>
> There are still those who doubt whether a stream that has arisen so spontaneously can last, whether it can make headway against the rigidly organized institutions of the state, the vast financial resources of the industrial establishment, or the long established apparatuses of the big parties. But nobody can deny that this new political force that fits into no previous pattern of ideas has already made a powerful impact wherever it has appeared. . . .
>
> This 'nuisance value' of the protest movement must not be regarded negatively. It is like pain in the human body which, properly understood, may provide a long overdue and necessary impetus to adopt a more sensible way of life. There is endless discussion between the members of this loose association of protesters as to just what such a sensible life should be, *because many of them are looking for a deeper meaning to life and are willing to*

249

give time and energy to help create a more human future. Opposition has brought them out of their isolation and shaken their everyday routine. Over and above the shared opposition that unites them, they are concerned with their personal lives and values.

Among those I have met personally in this new mass movement are architects, lawyers, doctors, building workers, ministers of religion, peasants, fishermen, pharmacists, booksellers, civil servants, businessmen, journalists, hospital nurses, teachers, fitters, salesmen, actors and printers. The mere fact of making contact with each other and breaking out of their isolation is an important phenomenon.

Among the human needs that are for the first time becoming a political factor today are diversity, creativity and beauty— values neglected in the pre-occupation of industrial society with the highest possible material productivity. It is no accident that the same people who oppose the nuclear state are creating a different style of music, painting, theatre and literature. A new culture is coming into being.

In the new society that is developing human feelings are not hushed up, suppressed or stigmatized, but admitted and given open expression. At political demonstrations that I attended in earlier years, I never saw as much spontaneous *cordiality, fraternity, sincerity and friendship* as are to be observed nowadays at demonstrations.

What Jungk is talking about is a secular phenomenon, but this description simply indicates the misleading nature of such categories, for here is an example of people coming together in the Spirit, as they came together in the house of Cornelius. We can apply the test I suggested. Here are the signs of the Spirit, 'love, joy, peace, patience, kindness, goodness, trustfulness, gentleness, self-control'. (The 'self-control' of non-violent protestors has often been noticed. Most of them are quiet and friendly, in contrast to the verbal and physical bullying often employed by those sent to arrest them.) We have seen, in an earlier chapter, Jungk's description of scientists seized by Faustian obsessions of quasi-divine power. He also mentions the lower echelons of this system, whose supporters are 'half-hearted, bored, showing cold rejection, detachment, a strained "objectivity" and over-bearing behaviour, with no trace of warmth or friendliness'. In higher or lower places, there

250

are echoes of Paul's ruthless description of people who 'refuse to acknowledge God', who are, among other things, 'rude, arrogant and boastful, enterprising in sin . . . without brains, honour, love or pity'.

We are reminded, in these protest groups and in so many similar ones gathered for a number of different purposes, of the earliest communities; 'they shared their food gladly and generously' and 'the whole group of believers was united, heart and soul', and as a result, 'none of their members was in want'. This is characteristic of many modern 'communities', to the great scandal of people who conduct their financial affairs more tidily. (There are plenty of things wrong with such communities, also, as there were with the early Christian ones.) All this, of course, is still a long way from being a recognizable 'church', yet this is how it begins, often enough, as it began among the people who came to the house of Cornelius.

Peter and his companions stayed in that household for some days. To take the decision to accept the invitation was in itself an act of converted humility, a difficult decision which must have been very unsettling and strange to these Jews. Having accepted, they were open to God and to these new brethren in new ways. They must have learned, in their new-found humility, to be grateful for the way in which the Lord had worked in these people. They learned how little bits of the new preaching, hints of hopes, had been picked up by the members of the group around Cornelius, perhaps over many months, and how they had talked and prayed together over them, longing and hoping for something to show them what it all meant, but uncertain where to turn, until Cornelius himself had that vision which, as so often happens, came in to resolve struggles and doubts when these had been handed over to the Lord in faith. There were also, in this group, established moral and spiritual attitudes of long standing, which had made these people sensitive to the new and unexpected movement in their lives. Not only Cornelius himself but 'all his household' 'feared God'. So Peter and his companions found themselves sharing experiences with people who in their own way had been led by the Lord through spiritual discoveries to the moment of revelation, just as the immediate disciples of Jesus had done in their own entirely different way. As much as Cornelius and his household recognized in Peter's message the fulfilment of all they had learned and prayed, so Peter and the

251

others learned to recognize a crucially important message to themselves. It turned their previous assumptions about the nature of the Church upside-down. They were prepared to accept the implications of this—those they could perceive and those they could not yet perceive. Struggles and conflicts were to come as they wrestled with the consequences of that acceptance, but the principle was clear, and it was this: not only would the Lord bring foreigners, of alien culture and faith, into his Church in response to preaching, but he would bring to a point of deep and rich development in the Spirit communities of people who could not yet even recognize what was going on in them. He would not wait for those who knew themselves as his Church to take the initiative; he would require of them only to witness the work already accomplished, to give it a name and so bring it to the flash-point at which a whole new dimension could be discovered.

If we can accept this we can see that the kind of gathering described above cuts across all the usual Christian categorizing. It is neither parish nor religious community, neither purely contemplative nor purely 'social gospel' oriented. It is often neither Christian nor non-Christian but a mixture. It is not even 'ecumenical' because that word means that people are conscious of, and working to overcome, specific divisions regarded as clear-cut, whereas these gatherings, even if they begin the ecumenical way, have forgotten all about that before they reach the stage at which the phenomenon can be properly recognized.

It is all odd, mixed (in every sense) and sinful and uncertain. The degree of what can be called explicit Christianity is varied, from the community that joyfully celebrates the Eucharist as their heart and meaning to the one that can just about say 'Jesus' and know they mean something deeply important. In all this ambiguity it might seem to be impossible to give a name to what is going on, and foolish to try.

Foolish it probably is, but then so is Incarnation. This happening that I have described is incarnation. It is the body of Christ, taking flesh as he can and must, in those who are prepared to become him, to the limit of their capacity.

This is how the Church is happening now. It is obviously not the only way. The older official Church is still alive under the weight of beautiful rubble, and still saving and loving. And that other symbol of the Church, that battered, ignorant, sly and fearful old woman who wants help and does not understand very much, but has insights of such blatant veracity that they sound like blasphemy—she is still there, too. Now, as always, it is the 'marginal' people—poor, harassed, needy—who most easily hear the good news. From her very body, gnarled and aching with toil and life's uncomforted abuses, the new Church finds its own body and comes to life, and the one life gives way to the other. The older one dies, gently and shriven, and the new one comes to birth, not separately but from within the old, which is her grave, the font of her baptism. There is no doubt that this thing which comes up from death is not the old but the new. It is different in its texture, its quality of movement, above all in its eyes, which see a different world. And, as it comes to life, having no language as yet, it picks up and *echoes the words* of that paralysed yet genuine and still living being, who is also the Church. It echoes words grown narrow and heavy and stiff, and as it echoes them they sound different, they become as liquid and yet incisive as Provençal poetry, but they are the songs sung to a child, the cradle-songs of the God-bearer. So the old language is given new life also.

This growth of small Christian communities has been increasingly noticed and documented, especially in the form of the Latin American *communidades de base*, but most commentators have failed to see how this growth is the conscious Christian tip of a much wider growth. It is a universal phenomenon, which bishops and other Church leaders as well as sociologists are having to reckon with. But most Christian commentators assume that these groups are, and should be, a means of revitalizing the traditional structures; whereas they are, at least in embryo, actual new Churches, in the New Testament sense of a small, local, 'house' Church. Each one is wholly the Church, the body of Christ fully present in each gathered community, yet they are also linked to each other as points of exchange in that body, which includes all other Churches and ultimately all created things. As it must, this new (yet so old) Church incarnate in many small, local churches comes into being by baptism.

But the baptism by which it began was the death of Christ; also it has always been the Church's insight that those who die for him are baptized in that death, whether or not they have had time to receive ritual baptism. It is by dying with Christ that we are baptized, and this is the other side of the truth that it is by baptism that we die with Christ.

So, when the Church itself has come to a death (and how else can we describe what has been happening to Christianity?), that death becomes its baptism to new life. But that which goes down into the font is the deathly flesh, that which comes up is the new creation from out of the old, not annihilating it or discarding it, but transforming it. Of course it looks different, moves differently, is incapable of recognizing much that seems obvious to the old. But it is truly the body of Christ. It is young, vulnerable, ignorant. It needs to be loved and tended, but it does not need to be ritually baptized. This is not at all the same as saying that people who discover themselves as this new being of the Church should not be ritually baptized. Many (maybe most) begin as groups of people already baptized and others may or may not come to that poetic vision which is necessary in order to let the ritual express their being as body of Christ. But God's new-risen body does not wait on ritual; rather the ritual effects what it does in virtue of that which the body already is and has done.

We can verify the theological sense of this in St Paul's categories. 'You have stripped off your old behaviour with your old self,' he writes to the Christians at Colossae (Col. 3:10), 'and you have put on a new self which will *progress towards* true knowledge the more it is *renewed* in the image of its creator.' This 'self' is not, as one might think, the 'self' of the individual Christian. It is the 'self' of Christ's body, the Church. Paul never uses this and similar phrases to speak of the individual. To him, what we put on or die into is the whole body, though before that it was indeed individually body, and deathly, separated unnaturally from its own truth. In each individual baptism a new part of the body is saved from 'slavery to decadence'. The whole thing is time-conditioned, happening by stages. 'The inner man' (that is, the new creation, the self 'which is the body of Christ') 'is renewed day by day. Yes, the troubles which are soon over . . . train us for the carrying of a weight of eternal glory' (2 Cor. 4:16). Training takes time, it is a gradual and strenuous process. 'And we, with our unveiled faces reflecting like mirrors the brightness of the Lord, all grow brighter and brighter' (2 Cor. 3:18). That is the Jerusalem Bible version, but the RSV translates more tellingly, saying that we are 'being changed from one degree of glory to another'. This is the Spirit's work, taking the 'inner man' through many transformations, until 'Christ be formed in you' like the embryo coming to birth, and *'We* [plural] shall *grow* in all ways into Christ'. Once we grasp that Paul is talking about the 'renewal' and 'training' and 'formation' of the whole body of Christ, and not just of individual members of it ('members' *means* limbs, parts, inseparably one in the body) then we realize that we ought, in fact, to be *expecting* the Church to go through just such painful and illuminating transformations as we know to be an inseparable part of the Spirit's work in the individual.

Also, therefore, the baptismal symbolism applies to the whole Church. It has died many deaths, it goes down into the font, leaving there its old self with whom we are all too intimately acquainted, and rising a new self, more fully Christ than before. Yet it has not come to the End, he is not yet all in all, though at times of great change it may feel as if it were so, and many revival movements and sects have come to grief because they took the experience of anticipated glory for proof that all was glory. We know, too, that the scope of a transforming experience depends on the degree of 'remote preparedness' and on that kind of dislocation of normality we have now seen so often.

We know, therefore, why it is that all poetic scenarios for the End include unrest, uncertainty, a sense of doom and finally disaster on a scale and of a kind unprecedented in the imagination of humankind. And that is the final baptism, the death of the body of Christ as a Church, which is now still partly unsaved, fleshly and subject to death. When we speak of Judgement and of the Doom, we are speaking of the pre-conditions of that baptism: the questioning, the stripping, the descent into the waters. When we speak of heaven, or glory, or the Second Coming, we are speaking of that which comes from the font, washed and changed, the ultimate 'freedom of the Children of God' which is Christ, when *'we* [plural] become the perfect Man, fully mature with the fullness of Christ himself' (Eph. 4:13) ('. . . to the measure of the stature of the fullness of Christ'— RSV). *This* is the point of breakthrough, when what has been formed over ages becomes apparent with great suddenness and in a quite unexpected way.

When that day comes, the food which nourished the body in the time of growing will no longer be needed. But up until that moment it is indeed needed, yet the way in which the nature of that food is understood changes. The Church's awareness of the Eucharist has changed deeply and more than once, and the kind of consciousness it has of itself under this sign is the kind of consciousness it has of itself generally. When sharing in the Eucharist is regarded as an obligation the Church is a system of obligations. When the Eucharist is enthroned and given royal honours, the Church behaves like a king. When the Eucharist is the food of little ones, the Church is the realm of the little ones. Realizing this, if we then turn back to the symbolism of Miller's story, the conclusion we are faced with is startling.

The gesture which, in Miller's *A Canticle for Liebowitz*, finally convinces the dying Abbot that Rachel is a being of 'primal innocence' is that of taking the ciborium and giving him holy Communion. But the innocence of undifferentiated oneness is that of the unborn, unfree, who know without knowing. 'Flesh knows what spirit knows, but spirit knows it knows', said Williams' archetypal poet and lover, Taliessin in *Taliessin Through Logres*. Unfallen, 'primally innocent' flesh knows, but it does not know it knows, and it is in choosing to know, but not in exchange, that it falls. This gesture of Rachel's, then, cannot be that of primal innocence; rather it grows from the wisdom of glory, which knows in its essential being what it sees and touches, not merely with the limited knowledge of senses and laborious intellect.

The reborn Church gives to the dying one the body of Christ which is the life of both. It is very willing to do so, but the old is less willing to receive it. Often enough it tries, as Zerchi at first does, to prevent what it feels to be an unworthy, even sacrilegious, action. But it learns, as the dying Abbot learns, and in humility receives the Lord of both.

This is true at two levels. At the wider symbolic level the new body of Christ, as soon as it reaches that degree of self-knowledge which enables it to recognize itself as such, wants to reach out and share its life with those whose life is from the older Church. Sometimes it is welcomed, sometimes repulsed. Sometimes those who are of this new body are too ignorant and prejudiced to recognize fellowship, sometimes this is true of the old.

At the level of specifically Eurcharistic fellowship the situation is much more open than many people imagine. The bread is more often broken by the old Church for the new than the other way round, simply because the sheer poetic richness of the eucharistic signs takes time, and living, to realize. The young little Churches which make up this revivified body are often youthfully clumsy in their handling of the mysteries, as indeed were the first little Churches, but the truthful passion in them finds a way. They learn by a combination of imitation and intuition; they celebrate, and celebration forms and changes them and itself. They begin to realize the thing they do and are, then they share the bread and wine, and if the 'old' Church cannot recognize it with them they will 'know him in the breaking of bread' in any case, often without feeling any need for ordination.

This fact of non-ordained eucharistic ministry is also linked to changes in definition of roles, and in particular of sexual roles, in new Churches. It is not for nothing that Miller's Rachel is not only 'lay' but female. Miller's book was first published in 1959, and part of it appeared several years earlier. That was not a world in which laywomen distributed holy Communion in a Catholic monastery, even after it had fallen down, and the significance of Rachel's action is that of a radical departure from expectation and even propriety. In the little Churches now finding themselves in Church roles, boundaries have melted, but not into vagueness. The old boundaries which have melted were needed in their time (and still are in many places) to facilitate and protect essential exchange. The old roles did the same; they articulated the body of Christ in ways both socially appropriate and symbolically beautiful and meaningful. But they are not, and never were, the only way in which the body of Christ could know itself and give itself.

As Vincent Donovan realized when he baptized his Masai converts, new Churches must discover their reality as body of Christ out of their own cultural identity, transformed but not obliterated:

The baptisms, as they took place in the six communities, were simple affairs . . . it would be up to them, not me, to enhance those essentials in any way they wanted in later ceremonies, and enhance them they did, as the months progressed, into very elaborate baptismal liturgies. They were makers of liturgy, in their own right, as pagan. Liturgy is part of a culture. So is a

257

way of praying. Now that the gospel had come to them, they would have to have their own liturgy, their own way of praying. That was their affair. Mine was the gospel. (*Christianity Rediscovered*)

It is a little like what one might see if one dropped some brightly dyed and oily liquid into a glass vessel of clear water which was swirling quite quickly through and round and among lumps and arches and spikes of stone placed in it. As long as the water was clear (before the dye was put in) the solid objects in it would give the obvious 'shape' to the colourless water, indeed they would appear to be the essential things without which the water would have no 'shape'. But once the dye was dropped in it would follow the currents of the moving water, and the pattern of the actual flow of the water would become apparent. It would become clear that this flow of water was itself the essential; the stones could even be removed altogether, after which the pattern, though different, would still be beautiful as long as the water moved. This is a clumsy comparison, but it may serve to illuminate a shift in the mode of awareness which is hard to describe. It suggests the reason why traditional hierarchical and ministerial roles, in the context of the Eucharist and elsewhere, seem only marginally important in many of the new little Churches, and why there is a stretching of older theological concepts which will not serve because they were developed to fit an experience of life which is now irrelevant. But it is all very confusing because an adequate poetry has not yet been developed for it. It awaits its Taliessin, the king's poet who can accurately trace the diagram of glory in this new fellowship of the Round Table. (Perhaps she will be African.) So, around this table, priest and philosopher, buffoon and princess, child and wizard, poet and king, exchange life and meaning. Equal and unequal roles are not fixed solids but points of identity apparent only in the flow of exchange.

There is one other sign of the End which we can discern in the symbolic scenario of Miller's novel and in the life out of death in the Church which we are actually seeing, but it comes at us also, as it were, from the End itself. It has to do with Rachel, who is 'lay', female, 'marginal' and very odd indeed, and it has to do with Wisdom, the feminine experience of divine activity, and so with Christ, who is incarnate Wisdom. It has to do with the new com-

258

munities, and with the End and the signs of the End, for among these is 'a woman clothed with the sun, and on her head a crown of twelve stars'. The detailed study of this must be pursued in the next chapter, for we can see now how the theology of the Church is intimately linked to the theology of the last things. The Christ who is to come is Jesus who was born at Bethlehem and died on Calvary and rose from the dead. His body is the gathered people who have died with him and live by his new life, but just as that life on earth passed through sphere after sphere by the force of passionate love, so his glorified body comes to its fulfilment because the same love thrusts against the barriers of refusal, wherever there are those who are willing to become the God-bearers, bearing into the dying world and dying Church the body of its new eternal life. So the experience of the uprush of passionate awareness brings men and women together in painful and joyful community of recognition of the life they share, and this is indeed the End, anticipating its proper time, just as in the earthly life of Jesus the power of resurrection broke through before due time, because love required it.

Whenever the thing happens which must happen, it will come as it did at first. It will come when obscure longing and need have prepared the way, when bewilderment and the failure of all that seemed secure have shaken minds and hearts. It will come where and as it is not expected, and it will come on the other side of a gap so unimaginable that it annihilates all expectation.

It will come quietly, for the uproar and the destruction will be the uproar and destruction of its enemies, and they will make much noise and will persecute the tender body of Christ as they did before. And his enemies will be those of his own household, inevitably, for the lover is the fool of the family, contemptible and irrelevant. Brother will denounce sister, and the Round Table will be split and the Grail withdrawn, but those who have seen will be drawn after it, yet always quietly.

Perhaps the day of judgement, of the final choosing and refusing of Exchange, will be very quiet. What is there to shout about? The trumpets are in the ears of those who turn away. What comes then must be strange and terrible to human imagination, but we do not need imagination for this encounter. After all, we have known him a long time.

7 Clothed With the Sun

It is clear by now that there is an intimate connection between the 'last things' and the contemporary being of the Church. The naming of Jesus as incarnate Wisdom provides the bridge between the two since it is his body which has been growing towards its maturity through the centuries and has come to a particularly important crisis of growth at this point in history. It is in the light of this realization that we are now able to understand the way in which the Church has to live its inbetween state, actively exchanging the life of resurrection so as to hasten the coming of the End. From one point of view, the work of the Church is simply to bring about the 'second coming', since all depends on the free response of human beings to the courtship of God's love.

One of the most complex and mysterious figures of the Apocalypse is the woman 'clothed with the Sun' (Rev. 12:1–5) who was in labour with the child who is to 'rule all the nations' and had to be rescued from the vengeful dragon. This is clearly, in some sense, Israel, 'mother' of the Messiah, but she has also been seen as a figure of the Church who is to be saved from the dragon of persecution. She has also been identified with Mary, who bore the saviour, and indeed at one point the woman's child is distinguished from 'the rest of her offspring' on which the dragon went to 'make war' when he could not catch her. But there are two things about her which are clear, in any case: she is a figure who belongs to the End, and she is female. This is a woman who is a mother, in some sense the mother of Christ but also of the Church. And she appears at first 'in heaven', 'clothed with the sun, with the moon under her feet, and on her head a crown of twelve stars'. But she is also on earth, where the dragon attacks her and she has to flee 'into the wilderness' where God will keep her safe and 'nourish' her. The enmity of the dragon is directed at the woman herself, not just at her child, for he pursues her even when the child has already been born and 'caught up to God and to his throne'.

260

It does not seem particularly fanciful to connect this image with that of the feminine Being who 'is more beautiful than the sun, and excels every constellation of the stars'. I am not trying to pull any tricks of interpretation out of the apocalyptic hat but only to suggest that the femaleness of Wisdom, of Israel, of the Church and of Mary are symbolically linked, not because anyone plans it that way or necessarily notices the links, but simply because symbols work like that. This female figure, then, will also be linked to pagan goddesses, to the feminine images of the Magna Mater, of fertility, of night, and so on, all of them (including the scriptural personifications) appearing in dreams and myths at all times. But the Book of Revelation, which is a Christian work, firmly places this archetypal female in the context of the End. Even if the author's symbolism was intended to apply to a particular set of historical circumstances, which are not ours, it remains true that this 'dream' is a powerful poetic account of what the writer considered to be in some sense the ultimate events of history. So his description of the woman is not simply an evocation of the *Ewig-Weibliche* in a Christian context, it is the result of a definite sense that, whatever her other symbolic associations, she is an inextricable part of these final events.

Curious parallels do emerge between the account of the adventures of the woman who was 'a great portent in heaven' and the other events I am about to assemble very briefly, but they may well be quite coincidental and I do not want to stress them, unless perhaps they seem to come under the heading of 'oddness' in the category which Jung called 'synchronicity'—that is, things which have a real connection which is not a causal one. All I want to do here is to set the strange figure of the Woman in heaven at the head of this part of my study of a Church which is struggling to discover and live a new kind of being in the image of Wisdom.

In the last chapter I noticed that two characteristics of the 'new' Church are the fluidity of roles and the 'overturning' of the structures. It is clear that the increasing prominence of women in ministerial roles in the Church is not due to women being 'promoted' to male clerical roles but more to the fact that older ministerial roles are dissolving and new ones have not replaced them, but a whole new experience of ministry is emerging instead, in which it seems no odder for women than for men to be doing all kinds of things in and for the church, not all of which have been thought of as 'ministerial'. They include going to prison, healing people, preaching and political agitation, for instance. By these means, among others, the older structures are effectively overturned, and that means that the 'bottom' people come out on 'top', as indeed Jesus said they would, but 'on top' does not mean that the situations have been reversed and the oppressed are now the oppressors, as in the usual revolutionary model. It means that the vitality of the 'grass roots', the place where things have always grown, is now recognized as having primary significance and is therefore to be served by those who formerly merely organized. It is in this situation of radical change that the meaning of the feminine in the Church has to be understood. The radicality of the change can actually be measured by the fact that it makes not only possible but easy and obvious a change in the 'feel' of sexual roles in the Church which at one time would have seemed unthinkable.

Whatever other divisions there may be, of race or function, sex roles are the most obvious and ultimate, and their symbolism is at the basis of myth in every culture. Through most cultures the symbolism of the feminine has been connected with all that is earthy, dark and unconscious. It is the realm of night and of hidden, mysterious things which are often dangerous and even deathly. It is also the place from which new life comes, for all growing things and for people, born from the earth's womb, and therefore it is also the source of inspiration and of mysterious knowledge. (The Muses, as well as the Fates and Furies, are feminine.) The realm of the feminine is initially a hidden region; its wisdom is conveyed in ambiguous signs and imparted in secret rituals, in caves and grottoes and wooded places. It is contrasted with the realm of sky and consciousness, the masculine which is the place of daylight and clarity and reason and conscious decision.

Real men and women have always reflected, or rather embodied, these symbols, though the relationship is not simple. Therefore (to simplify in a way which is inevitably misleading) when people feared the dark and secret things, or when urbanized cultures grew to despise and dislike the earth and its fertility, women suffered accordingly—and women themselves often enough felt it to be right that they should do so, because they too knew themselves in that way, since their conscious minds moved in the only available con-

262

scious patterns, which were masculine ones. But some knew in themselves a power to rule and guide or to enslave and possess; they were priestesses or queens, or witches. They claimed and got worship and service from the men they guided or captured. Adored or suppressed, the feminine was the hugely powerful, fertile thing from which all life came; but it could not know itself as itself in human terms. It could be Divine Proserpina or Holy Wisdom, but it could not be human; it was just the *un*-human quality of the feminine in women that made them so suspect and so mysterious and so powerful. They, or rather their femininity, emerged from some strange region which could not be made everyday or tamed.

But at a certain point Wisdom took flesh, became conscious, made decisions and shone with a light that enlightened the nations. As we have seen, this did not alter everything all at once; in fact it altered some things only very slowly and some (it seems) scarcely at all, because the blockages to resurrection were so great. The awareness of the drastic change in the meaning of the feminine did change things at first. Women in the early Church had a new sense of themselves, and the men had this sense about the women, so they took on new status and roles very quickly, but this did not last. It was one of those breakthroughs which come too soon and cannot be assimilated into the rest of life. But something emerged into the awareness of the church in the gap left by the lost sense of Christian women as mediators of Wisdom. This was the cult of Mary.

It was not, as some have supposed, a thing devised in order to suppress women. The desire to suppress the woman altogether was certainly very strong, and the 'dragon' tried very hard indeed to destroy her. The viciously anti-feminine language of some of the Fathers of the Church (otherwise, it seems, kindly, pious and reasonable men) is a sign of how unnatural it was for Christians, sharers in the body of him who is incarnate Wisdom, to suppress the feminine in the Church. The fear of the feminine was so strong that they had to do so, but unlike their pagan contemporaries, who found it quite easy to despise women without getting angry about it, these Christian men worked themselves into a fever of neurotic repulsion at the physical femininity of women. This is one more example, indeed, of the way in which the spread of the power of resurrection in human lives often actually *increases* sin at the point of contact.

263

The emergence of the cult of Mary in the following centuries is an example of the way in which the power of love pushes its way through whatever channels are open. If one is closed it will find another, and when the way to the freeing of the feminine as incarnate was blocked in the conscious minds of Christian men and women it found a way to penetrate Christian minds symbolically. But the symbol was no goddess but a living woman, and although there have been times when Mary of Nazareth seemed almost to disappear into the 'Woman clothed with the Sun', she never entirely did so. The crowned and adored Madonna was still the girl from Galilee, and she kept Christian feet on the ground. She worked in many ways, but all of them were more or less earthed. She was the lady of the Romance cults and made a real though minor breakthrough into consciousness in the women who were the poets and arbiters of Romantic love. She was clearly Beatrice, and she was even (rather weirdly) Good Queen Bess, the Virgin Queen.

Hers also was the strange and misleading aura which gathered around 'religious' women in the nineteenth century, though it never touched the *men*, however holy, unless they were young enough to be capable of carrying a feminine projection. This 'aura' made it hard for them to think of themselves as Christian women, since they were invested with a symbolic role as Brides of Christ which was as heady as it was paralysing to them as ordinary sinners in search of love and death. (When they finally succeeded in shaking off this symbol it left them feeling so naked that they were not sure who they were any more, and many of them left their convents to try to find an identity.)

Another emergence of Wisdom-consciousness took place in that off-shoot of English Quakerism which flourished in the United States for over a century but has now dwindled to a handful surviving in Maine. The 'Shakers', so nicknamed because of the ecstatic dancing which was a feature of their early worship-meetings, began with revelations received by their Foundress, Mother Ann, the wife of a blacksmith. She and a few followers emigrated, and from that group grew a new and unique lived theology. Throughout the history of the Shakers both sexes lived and worked side by side in a state of absolute equality at every level, but with differences of function which divided along fairly traditional lines. They were always celibate, though men and women lived in the same houses

264

and at one time they adopted children as part of their work. Their theology reflected this sexual balance (or the other way around, whichever you prefer). To them, the Holy Spirit was 'Our Mother the Spirit', and the male incarnation in Jesus was balanced by Mother Ann, who was regarded as the female incarnation. The result of having an explicitly feminine source of divine inspiration can be discerned not only in the equal status of the sexes but in their attitude to material reality though they shared the suspicion of sexuality and the body with the rising evangelical movement of the time, and it was reinforced by Mother Ann's early experience of sex, as forced on her in an unwanted marriage, and her loss of several babies before birth.

This fear of sex was common to most of the many sects which flourished and soon died in the New World at that time and was usually combined with a rejection of all natural and man-made beauty and a cult of primitiveness for its own sake, even among purely secular Utopian sects. But the Shakers, on the contrary, had a very positive attitude to beauty and craftsmanship. To them it was deeply and religiously important that what they made should be beautiful. Simplicity was emphasized, but each thing must be as perfect of its kind as they could make it. They saw no special value in being primitive; their farm and domestic equipment was efficient, and they planned some advances in farm machinery. They felt that in making things well they were co-operating with God—a very 'Wisdom' concept. The result was that the buildings, clothes and furniture they made reached a level of functional grace whose simple decoration is inextricably linked to structural necessity and which has never been surpassed and seldom equalled. Genuine Shaker furniture is now prized very nearly 'above rubies', and even copies of it are more and more popular, and rightly so. To visit one of the Shaker villages, now repaired and furnished as museums, gives an insight into a way of life of astonishing harmony and integrity. Shaker worship used unaccompanied singing and above all dance, and this also is evidence of the strongly incarnational feeling for life expressing itself in a 'Wisdom' way, for music and dance articulate better than anything else the mobile and penetrating characteristics of divine Wisdom, present through all material reality not as 'static' but as giving and receiving life in the dance of continuing creation.

The Shaker phenomenon was isolated, and its accidental oddities

265

no doubt helped to reduce its influence. In any case it had no links at all with the feminist consciousness which had been developing for decades alongside it in America. The full theological significance of that movement, not only in America and Europe but eventually everywhere else as well, can best be seen in the light of a theological event which appears, at first sight, to have nothing whatever to do with feminism.

In the twentieth century something happened which showed that the symbol had been working, spreading and changing things by the ways of exchange in the characteristic manner of Wisdom as Scripture describes her, until it reached a point at which it had to break though, and then to find a language, a definition of itself. The breakthrough was in practice multiple and scattered in time and space, as it must be when it is working in real, earthly circumstances and having to wait for appropriate weak spots. First there emerged a few isolated eighteenth- and early nineteenth-century feminists, upper-class and highly educated, thus able to be freer of the usual conditioning of women. Then more and louder and more strident voices were heard, and eventually the whole wave of the Women's Suffrage movement gathered, and there followed in time changes in the political, social and economic status of women. With these changes and in them, preceding them and yet dependent on them for 'incarnation', the self-awareness of women changed, rapidly and forever, first in northern Europe and North America and gradually in other countries as the awareness spread.

That was the breakthrough, but its language was, inevitably, inadequate, for it spoke much in terms of political and professional and sexual freedom but little in terms of spiritual development, and still less in terms of the body of Christ. Since then a search for appropriately inclusive language has gone on, with some success, and that search has strengthened and extended the awareness itself and so also its practical results in the Women's Movement. But Christians, if they were not trying to oppose it as irreligious and immoral, accepted the change in secular terms and saw no special religious significance in it at all. Yet the thing was at work in that place above all where it had to be at work, the body of Christ, and if it was allowed no conscious language it could continue to work underground, powerfully and increasingly, until at last it broke through in a new way, yet in the same 'place' as it had done

266

originally—that is, in the context of the God-bearer: not just any woman, but the woman clothed with the Sun which is the symbol of day and intellect and consciousness; not just any Lady (however Romantic) but *our* Lady, the one for us all.

In the history of the Catholic Church there are far more instances of people having, or claiming to have, visions of Mary than of Jesus. They vary a great deal in imaginative value, from those whose inner logic carries conviction to the merely silly, but all of them are, as it were, the 'dreams' of the Church, bringing into its daytime consciousness the symbols it needed. And in the nineteenth and early twentieth centuries the visions became more urgent. At Lourdes above all, and at Fatima and other places, visionaries (all women or children) saw Mary and heard her speak, and her words were always connected with two basic Christian ideas: the need for repentance and the promise of healing. The effect of these visions was more widespread than that of any previous ones, and the double message and its bearers, viewed as communication of the Church's 'unconscious', are very significant. There was indeed much to repent, as the second Vatican Council finally acknowledged, and only when the suffering implied had prepared minds and hearts could the real healing take place.

Healing was needed for the wounds of a culture which could not see its own limitations. It was a culture in which the feminine had been as violently suppressed as the breasts of women who wore bandages in order to look like boys, a 'scientific', 'rational', 'efficient' world which prided itself on having relegated the unspeakable to the realm of non-existence.

The breakthrough in a culture which would not acknowledge the hidden power of the feminine took a negatively feminine form, a manipulative, cruel and possessive one. The evil which broke through in Nazi Germany had all the virulence of the Furies whose work was to revenge crimes against the proper order of the community. We think of Nazi crimes, but the whole Nazi phenomenon appears as a vengeance, inexorable, impersonal and unmerciful as the Furies themselves, for the crime of the rich nations in steadily and smugly dehumanizing the lives of millions, in Europe and in all the peoples whose self-respect, cultural identity and future had been sacrificed to the masculine gods called Progress and Profit, with all their attendant godlings and their cults and their ethical codes.

267

But if the dark goddesses thus revenged themselves, the promise of healing came from the same place, the deep place of Wisdom. In 1927 a French priest named Doncoeur is reported to have said: 'There yet remains the achievement of the discovery of the Madonna.' He did not know—perhaps he found out—what horrors had to shake up minds and hearts before the Madonna could indeed be discovered in a sense none could have conceived at that time. In 1950 Pope Pius xii defined as of faith that Mary, when her earthly life ended, was taken up body and soul into glory and suffered no corruption. Protestants were angry at this unnecessary complication to ecumenical relations; humanists smiled and shrugged at this evidence of the incurably medieval imagination of a senile church; 'progressive' Catholics were embarrassed and militant ones were delighted to have yet another banner to wave provocatively at the world, the flesh and the Communists. But few people recognized the nature of what had been done in terms of the growth of the body of Christ towards its final glory. It was Carl Jung, Protestant psychologist and sage, who made the statement that the definition of the dogma of Mary's assumption was the most important religious event for four hundred years.

What Pope Pius was doing, whether he knew it or not, was to provide the poetic language which could say what had been happening to human consciousness *as Christ*. Here, it said, is the archetypal woman, once queen of the unconscious earth, of the dark of night and death and mystery, from which life springs. But her great power, once feared, adored or shunned in symbol, has been shown to us as the light, from which light is born, and its proper home is in that light. Eve, mother of all living, becomes mother of the One who lives, and so we know in ourselves, who are his body, that which is She. We know her not as a secret but as daylight fact. And we know that fact not only on earth, in Galilee and Jerusalem, and maybe finally Ephesus, but in Heaven, which is the place of perfect Exchange. There, she is at home, she is exchanged in and by Them. She is their Fourth who is Us. She is creation, and she is Mother of God, and so God is in her and we in her and we in God, and all is in the exchange which is glory and this is true *now*.

This is present fact but also a fact of the End, in the body of every woman—and every man. Pictures of the assumption of Mary often show her 'clothed with the sun' and crowned with stars. The

268

symbolic identification is a natural one, but it clearly 'says' that Mary is a fact of the End. Human nature, one with hers in the way of exchange, can 'already' be seen in its proper relationship to the Three-in-One of whom it is the image, yet the relationship is 'not yet'. Its fullness belongs to the End, but we need the symbol of it consciously understood to show us how to 'hasten the end' by the way we live here and now.

Nothing will ever be the same again, because once a fact has been stated it cannot be un-stated, and we have to deal with it, either by responding to its implicit demand or by refusing to do so. It has its effect anyway, so that from that time on, explain it how we will, the build-up of longing and need in the Church became increasingly impossible to contain. It found its weak spot in a man called John who summoned a General Council when everyone had been saying there never could be such a thing again. As it was through John that Jesus came to his baptism and knew his being as beloved of the Father, and the end and purpose of that in death towards life, so, through this John, the body of Christ came half-knowing to baptism and learned in great agony its own name and its own nature as dedicated to death. Old ways fell apart; the will of the Father was spoken.

The dam, solid for centuries, broke, and through the breach flowed the fury of long-restrained waters. In its destructive onrush it met the inflow of other waters, and they carried away in that combined flood not only much of what had been thought to be essential in Roman Catholicism but large and structurally crucial chunks of other Churches as well. As it went it overran the banks assigned to it and flowed far and wide into secular regions and into other religious traditions. The half-demolished structures showing above water could still be used after a fashion, but the life-giving water of regeneration lapped along new shores once thought infertile. In the moistened soil seeds long dormant woke and put down roots and thrust up shoots, and strange new plants grew along these 'wilder shores of love'.

Among the things done by that superbly destructive Council was the re-presentation of the figure of Mary as essentially to be seen in the context of the Church, for it had become impossible to isolate her in impotent splendour. There is about this both an historical justice and good psychological sense in terms of Mary's role in the

269

Church. In the record of the early Church Mary does not appear at all after the day of Pentecost, nor are we told if the risen Lord appeared to her, and most of Jesus's earthly family are similarly absent. They were, however, a closely-knit and 'highly motivated' group, as we can tell from the Gospel accounts of earlier days, and it is easy to believe that they might claim a share in the direction of the new Church which posed a threat to its deeper sense of what Jesus meant by 'brotherhood' and 'family'. If so, there was probably considerable conflict, and the non-mention of Mary and her relatives makes sense. In a sense, she was too important. The leadership of a woman with her gifts and her unique relationship to the Lord would have been bound to distort the attempts of the young Church to make its own misakes and find its own way to be the body of Christ. She who had borne that body in Bethlehem must have known this as any intelligent and sensible mother knows it.

After this necessary separation the relationship of children to their mother often involves 'using' her symbolically, either positively or negatively, but eventually, if all goes well it becomes possible to discover a new, deeper and much more 'real' relationship, in which the mother can be, indeed, at the heart of things, though not necessarily with any great need for outward show. It is just 'natural' for her to be there. This is, in a sense, what the Catholic Church has been doing with the figure of Mary since the Council. She is 'there' in the persons of ordinary people, but especially of course of women. One of them drove a modest but effective end of the wedge into the vast structure of male ecclesiasticism, by being physically present at the Council, even if only as observer.

That was long ago, and what is happening now is something nobody foresaw. Even those who press for the ordination of women can only see that as introducing women into the older structure. But what is actually happening is that the feminine in women and men is becoming the body's genuine life, not displacing the masculine but, at last, married to it.

The obviously changed and clear influence of the feminine in this new sphere into which the Church has broken is a sign of a new degree of integration of the body of Christ in all its members. When this kind of Wisdom has appeared symbolically in myths it has always signalled the destruction of a religious system which had included God in itself. In the Northern myth (in Wagner's powerful re-working of it) Brünnhilde was the favourite daughter of Wotan, Father of the Gods; she was his faithful reflection, doing his will on earth. But Wotan became spokesman of a system designed to protect human beings from the challenge of love; law allowed no exchange of love outside its own structure. Out of compassion Brunnhilde opposed her Father's decree that Sigmund should die, and when he had died nevertheless she saved his sister-wife Sieglinde, hiding her in the forest so that she might bear the expected hero-son. For her disobedience to the system of the gods Brünnhilde, the immortal Virgin-warrior, was banished to mortality. As a mortal woman she was woken from her fire-protected sleep by Siegried, whose birth she had made possible, and as mortal woman she loved and was loved. But the Law, in its Teutonic avatar, had its revenge. Deception and hate and treachery (the world of sin, which the law cannot change but can only organize) brought humiliation to Brünnhilde and death to Siegried, and at last she mounted her great horse and rode into the fire of his funeral pyre and died with him. But her action, her *kenosis* and death for love's sake, brought the whole structure of the old gods crashing down in the flames of the final *Götterdämmerung* and made way for a different kind of God.

In another idiom, Sophocles told the tale of Antigone, who also disobeyed. When her brother Polynices led an army against Thebes to recapture it from the new king, Creon, his brother Eteocles fought on the side of the defenders and won. Creon upheld a morality of Law, saw the welfare of the City as dependent on order and interpreted order as loyalty to the City embodied in himself. He gave orders which symbolize his priorities: Eteocles was to be given the burial honours due to a dead hero, but the body of Polynices was to be left unburied for crowns and dogs to feed on, and anyone who tried to give him burial must die. To deprive the dead of the rites was sacrilege and injury almost unthinkable, it was to de-personalize the dead by excluding him from even the shadowy human company of the underworld; it was this belief which gave symbolic force to the decree, and it is a measure of the lengths to which the embodiment of Law will go to suppress any challenge to its authority.

Antigone, the sister of both the dead warriors, defied the edict and ritually buried her rebel brother by pouring earth over his body, and when she was brought before the infuriated Creon she

271

answered him in words which sum up the whole issue. Here is the dialogue of the moment when the point becomes clear; it shows with jolting clarity how it is the feminine presence in the revivified Church which reconciles the apparently irreconcilable, and by doing so rouses such fear and anger in those who embody a religion become Law (this is the Penguin translation of *Antigone*):

Creon:	. . . none of my subjects think as you do.
Antigone:	Yes, sir, they do, but dare not tell you so.
Creon:	And you are not only alone but unashamed.
Antigone:	There is no shame in honouring my brother.
Creon:	Was not his enemy, who died with him, your brother?
Antigone:	Yes, both were brothers, both of the same parents.
Creon:	You honour one and so insult the other.
Antigone:	He that is dead will not accuse me of that.
Creon:	He will, if you honour him no more than a traitor.
Antigone:	It was not a slave, but his brother, who died with him.
Creon:	Attacking his country, while the other defended it.
Antigone:	Even so, we have a duty to the dead.
Creon:	Not to give equal honour to good and bad.
Antigone:	Who knows? In the country of the dead that may be the law.
Creon:	An enemy can't be a friend, even when dead.
Antigone:	My way is to share my love, not share my hate.
Creon:	Go then, and share your love among the dead. We'll have no woman's law here, while I live.

Antigone expresses the passion of Exchange which recognizes the underlying falsity in what seems a good and noble system when, misunderstanding its own commission, it becomes blind to love and so is involved in Refusal. But 'in the country of the dead', the kingdom of the baptized, the judgement between 'good' and 'bad' looks different and one may indeed give them equal honour, for all have died and so former living is irrelevant. But this is, as Creon so rightly says, 'woman's law', and he will have none of it, nor will any who think like him 'while he lives', but that is not for long. Antigone is condemned to a living death walled up in a cave, as so many seek to *contain* the 'woman's law'. She hangs herself, and her betrothed, Creon's own son, kills himself also and dies in her arms. His mother, hearing of this, kills herself at the altar of her own home, and Creon, realizing at last what he has done (as the prophet Teiresias warned him) goes also to death. In this way the reign of Law is destroyed by the passionate disobedience of the feminine which follows a deeper obedience, the 'woman's law'. Her fate was to share love 'among the dead' who have died with Christ, even though they do not at first fully understand the significance of what has happened to them.

Another example of the way in which the feminine overturns masculine structures comes very fittingly from the Gospel account of the resurrection of Jesus. Here, too, we find the 'woman's law', the law of those who are driven by their feminine view of reality to 'share love among the dead'. It has often been noticed that Jesus appeared first of all to the women, who indeed had been the only people, apart from John, who did not abandon him in his last hours. This privilege of being the first witnesses has usually been regarded as a fitting reward for courage and devotion. But I think there is more to it than that.

One woman at least had, unlike the Twelve, heard and believed the words of Jesus about his own imminent death and burial. As I suggested in an earlier chapter there were no words in which she could communicate to him the knowledge they now shared, but she did communicate it in the gesture of anointing him, and Jesus knew what she meant and said so. He gave to the incident an extraordinary prominence in his prophecy that it would be spoken of 'wherever the gospel is preached'. It would be very surprising if the other women had not shared her awareness. They were a small, close-knit group, as isolated from other women by their discipleship as they were isolated from the male disciples by custom and prejudice. They habitually did things together, and they must have recognized fully the significance of Mary's action, even if they had not known her intention beforehand, though it seems most probable that they did. So this little group of disciples knew, at least partly, the pattern of things as Jesus knew it, and with him they pondered and prayed, and with him, when the time came, they went to the cross and to the grave.

As women they were more likely to have a sense of the essential

273

physicalness of the work of Jesus. As Mary showed when she anointed him, they knew, however obscurely, that it was important to
'be with' his actual physical body. At the earliest possible moment
after his burial they needed to be back there with him, and the
words of Mary to the 'gardener' show that they thought of the body
as 'him', not 'it'. They were, therefore, much better prepared to
accept the evidence of their own eyes. The contrast is striking. The
Eleven, when they did finally see Jesus, were inclined to think him
a ghost, and Thomas took a deal of convincing that what his friends
had seen could be anything more than that, but Mary actually had
to be warned not to 'cling' to the body whose solidity it never
occurred to her to doubt.

The attitude of the women shows a directness and simplicity
which is, in masculine terms, quite 'unreasonable'. They display a
typically feminine attitude to truth. The women perceived the situation from within as a whole. In theological terms this is important,
for the focus of their vision is the body of Jesus. They clung to the
body because it was not just a body but himself. The masculine
logic, applied to the appearance of the risen Lord as in other cases,
is: 'it can't be so, therefore it is not true'. The women, turning the
logic upside-down, say, 'It is so, therefore it must be true'. The men
had been unable to make sense of his assertion that he must, in his
body, suffer and die, so when he was arrested they abandoned him
physically and witnessed neither his death nor his burial. To them
his body, once dead, was a corpse, a thing. In a way, they were
viewing it just like the chief priests, and like Pilate, to whom it was
an object which might be manipulated for political purposes. As
Creon saw the body of Poliynices, so Pilate and the Sanhedrin saw
the body of Jesus, and so, reluctantly, did even his closest friends.
But to Antigone the body was her brother, and to the women the
body of Jesus was 'my Lord'.

That was how the women did, by identification, go into the grave
with him and were baptized with him into death. It is significant
that the practical difficulty of moving the huge stone only struck
them when they were almost at the tomb. Their thoughts, their
being, were *with* the Lord, beyond the stone. That is why they had
no difficulty at all in believing that it was himself whom they saw,
once they had got it clear that he was 'not there' in the grave. 'Why
do you seek the living among the dead?' asked the angelic messen-

gers. They might have answered, very simply, 'Because that is where we last saw him.' It was merely a factual mistake, not a refusal of belief. And so he had no difficulty in communicating with them and could rely on them to convey his message accurately no matter what the result. The particular kind of truth which is Wisdom incarnate evidently 'gets through' to the feminine type of thinking, but is easily blocked by the masculine kind. It is the fate of Brünnhilde, and Antigone, and the women at the tomb, to be (like poor Cassandra) disregarded and despised for their ability to cut through all intervening considerations to the heart of the matter and act on it. But Brünnhilde brought Valhalla crashing down in flames; Antigone's action destroyed the house of Creon and with it the logic of Fate as ruler of mankind, and the witness of the women at the tomb finally destroyed the credibility of Law and Prophet *except* as summed up in the body of the risen Lord; at the same time, and equally, they descredited the old pagan myths as real ways to God. Παν ὁ μεγαζ τεθνηκε, 'Great Pan is dead', and women (who had once been his devotees in his Dionysian personality) killed Pan, first in the cave at Bethlehem, and then at the Cave by Calvary.

Now, in the latest emergence of the disruptive feminine in our own time, we find the same thing. One English priest, when he discovered what was going on in Latin America, was moved to almost incredulous awe by the realization of the existence of thousands of little, informal *communidades de base* which have grown up all over the sub-continent. These small 'basic communities' of mostly lay Christians are, as I suggested in the last chapter, visibly the place where the reborn Church is growing. 'The structure of the Church has been turned on its head', he said, summing it up. With the approval and support of many bishops and clergy, this is the new body of Christ, growing from within the old situation, reaching out and recreating in Wisdom's way. Men and women work together as equals in a way characteristic of the new Church everywhere.

In the last chapter I looked at baptism as the way towards an understanding of the ultimate being of the Church and saw how the End is the event which, as it were, retroactively works in the lives of men and women now, but it does so as the Church, and in particular in the sudden and wholly unexpected emergence of the reborn form of the Church. Now, seeing how closely this phenomenon is linked to the emergence into consciousness of the feminine, we can also begin to see (symbolized in the 'great portent' of the Woman in heaven) why this emergence is itself the most powerful of all the signs of the End, working retroactively to form a Church which shall indeed and visibly be Christ's bride, mother and daughter, and finally himself, the eternal feminine who is Wisdom. In himself, in his human and earthly life, masculine and feminine were wedded. In his body, the Church, that union is at last able to be lived consciously and more and more fully. This is indeed a sign of the End. The long differentiation is giving way to a new and conscious and passionate union, in the minds and hearts of those who are the work of the Spirit as he revivifies the body. They not only are, but know they are, both bearing and borne, Wisdom and incarnation, bride and bridegroom. 'Flesh knows what spirit knows, but spirit knows it knows.'

At the Table where this body is broken, the masculine symbolism of the victorious hero who overcomes in the struggle (the *agon*) engages in joyful exchange with the feminine symbolism of the giver of the food which is life. This is evident in the consciously symbolical elements in ritual of the Lord's Supper in many different kinds of gatherings. One such is the exchange of 'peace' which becomes bodily encounter uniting many levels of awareness. Another is the variety of ways in which the body and blood are actually shared out in the gathering—by neighbour to neighbour, by people who offer to do so, by people asked to do so, as well as by those who have explicit symbolic ministry. This shows the fluid quality of the signification that goes on, and people learn, without realizing they are learning, to live their being as body of Christ in their bodies, as bodies becoming spiritual, as spirit articulated in body. Wisdom is incarnate in this newly-born Church which knows itself, more clearly than it has ever done, as the Grail, the feminine physical vessel of vision, which is no merely passive container but the vital, particular human body which is full of Christ.

This is where the beginning of the End has to be, as it was at the beginning of incarnation, and as it was at the beginning of creation itself, when Wisdom 'covered the earth like a mist'. From the feminine principle comes all life, but now the feminine is not goddess but both human and divine, the son from the mother and the mother in the son, clearly, consciously, particularly, men and women who are in their particularity the body of Christ. As she comes to consciousness and to clearer and clearer articulation, so he grows towards his full stature. As he reaches 'from glory into glory' becoming more and more clearly himself in his earthly body, so the passionate desire of the bride for her lover reaches out to his passion for her, and they will no longer be denied.

We cannot tell how close that moment may be, for its coming depends on many things. It depends on the way in which exchange may be speeded or impeded by circumstance. It depends on the blinded but ruthlessly intelligent movement of desperate Refusal, feeling that its time is short and anguished with the fathomless hunger of ultimate negation. But, finally and above all and beyond all, the time of the end depends on the response of human beings to the love they perceive. It is only in those who recognize the coming of love, and give themselves to it, that the End is able to come. Here, again, the Lover must wait, in his need, for the response he cannot compel. It is in those lovers that the final baptism must be accomplished. As John's vision sees it, even the forces of destruction must wait 'until we have put the seal on the foreheads of the servants of our God', for they are those in whom the End comes, as it was coming in the dying Irish barmaid.

In the second letter of Peter, we also found this idea that the members of the body of Christ are somehow in charge of the coming of the End. It is up to them to 'hasten' the coming of the day of God by living 'lives of holiness and godliness', and there, as in Paul's reference to the custom of baptism 'for the dead', the truth underlying the statement is made more telling for us by the fact that the writer feels no need to explain it, but takes it for granted that his readers will know what he means and recognize in it a reality of Christian experience so basic that structure of custom and conduct can be built on it without hesitation.

It is against this background that we must, then, consider what comes under the heading of 'moral theology'. In the curious, suspended, 'inbetween' existence which is human history until the End, we have to find ways to live in relation to that End, but ways which take account of the fact of sin, since resurrection has not yet transformed all reality. And at this point in the history of that transformation we have a great deal of re-thinking to do in the light of all that has been said here to show the almost incredibly great signifi-

277

cance of the changes taking place in the life of the Church, as she becomes more and more the body of incarnate Wisdom. Therefore the work of the next chapter has something to do with what is usually classed as 'moral theology', but the associations of the phrase are misleading. It must be apparent from the study of the symbolism of the feminine and its relation to the End time that the demands made on Christians who respond to the contemporary challenge extend into regions unclassifiable in terms of traditional theological categories. The breakthrough in which the whole body of Christ (conscious and unconscious) is involved demands the service of *amour voulu* in areas of, for instance, politics, aesthetics, medicine, agriculture, sexuality, food production, industrial economics and mysticism. All of these belong together and cannot be separated because all of them are expressions of incarnate exchange.

8   Dying Each Other's Life

On the day of Pentecost, having heard and been convinced, the first converts asked, 'What must we *do*?' The question is the one which Romantic passion must ask if it is to be genuine *amour voulu* and not merely a transient and self-indulgent *amour fol*.

The response to God, in relation to the End and in the exchange of resurrection, must be about morality and politics, about sexuality, about ritual, about prayer and finally about martyrdom. Here again, we need proper conceptual tools which can help us to answer the question in each person, in each situation, since each is particular; and such tools must be not purely intellectual but rather means whereby the whole person may discover his or her reality-in-exchange.

The right kind of language must have two characteristics. It must image the real nature of the Exchanges which are the life of God, and of God in humankind. But it must do so in a poetry which reflects for those who hear it the known truth of their particular cultural and personal experience. In other words, the poetry of good theology must grow from deep within the actual and concrete experience of people, so deep that when they hear that poetry they recognize in it *both* the accurate expression of their problems and hopes and loves *and* the evocation of deeper layers which they cannot touch but of which they are mutely aware, afraid and desirous.

The need for such a language has been a problem weighing on the minds of many Christians. In particular, the 'theologians of liberation' were forced to recognize that there was just no way they could articulate the connections they perceived between the suffering of oppressed people and the freedom of cross and resurrection, in the categories made available to them by a theology emerging from a culture with a totally different kind of experience. The culture which shaped 'traditional' theology was one in which, for instance, the thing called 'capitalism' did not exist as the basically constitutive element in human society which it has become, shaping

279

not only the forms of government but the thinking and feeling of both oppressor and oppressed. Therefore different categories had to be found, not only for intellectual clarification (though that is part of it) but so that the lover might discover means to be and do what his Lady required.

To ask the question 'What shall we do?' is to reach out into the whole of human life, and in order to make some sense of such multiplicity of concern and create the possibility of continuing the lived analysis in any one direction there has to be a reference point. We have that reference point, essentially, in the cross, as we have seen, but in order to articulate that central fact in poetry which images reality as people experience it *now* we need a statement of it which shows us the cross as it is lived in an acutely and inescapably contemporary idiom. We need to see how, here and now, those who die with Christ are indeeed making up what is wanting in the suffering of Christ for his body which is the Church *now*.

In earlier chapters I looked to the lived experience of Jesus himself, with his lovers, to discover the ways of Exchange which are saving. This culminated in the search for the central point of Exchange, the cross itself. In this one I have chosen to take as my central poetic statement of the cross the experience and words of one of the lovers of Christ, a man who died in a factory accident fourteen years ago, aged thirty-four.

I have chosen this particular man for various reasons. He was a worker-priest, a young Jesuit who chose to go and work in a factory, and live with and as others who worked there, out of love for them and for no other reason. 'They are fooling themselves', he wrote scathingly, 'if they think I am going to live with the de-Christianized outcasts to do pioneering work, to bring honour to the Society of Jesus, or to write books. I am going to do this as the Father's work, in order to love them, to gather them to the Father in the Son by the power of the Spirit. This is the only reason, and it is quite enough.' Therefore he lived intimately the deepest and most acute theological issue of our time, the issue of poverty and oppression in a world of unprecedented possibility for prosperity; also a world which, in its nastiest manifestations, is often anxious to call itself 'Christian'. I chose him because he was a passionate man and knew it and knew what it meant. I chose him, perhaps most of all, because the kind of theology he discovered and lived was the expression of

280

the Wisdom way. He lived 'from inside outwards', being the *source* of the Church, quietly and patiently, within the given human situation. He was Wisdom incarnate in his place and time.

Finally, I chose this man as my reference point here because the book of extracts from the spiritual journal he kept came into my hands exactly at the point in writing this book when I needed it, as a writer but also as a Christian, and therefore it constitutes a significant breakthrough for the book and for myself, or rather for myself in the book. (This is not an unusual kind of occurrence, I think. Other writers, together with poets, artists and musicians, as well as people whose poetry does not have to take such specific forms, will recognize how it works.) The diary is that of a man who was not a writer except from necessity and often wrote in snatches at the end of an exhausting day. It is also couched in the frequently inadequate categories and images which were available to him. Constantly his lived experience pushed against the barriers of language, and the sheer force of his need and his love makes one see the reality beyond his words, but the language remains insufficient. So in practice I have made use of a kind of counterpoint between the lived passion of this cross-bearer and the other kind of intensity which is that of the poet, calling once more on the dense and vivid images of Charles Williams to illuminate the brief sentences of the worker-priest.

Egide van Broeckhoven died in a factory accident on 28 December 1967. He had been trying to detach a stack of twenty-foot steel plates weighing several tons, which had become stuck while being moved. While he was doing this the supports broke, and the whole stack fell over on him, throwing him back on to another plate, and breaking his back. He died instantly, his arms thrown wide under the plates which had killed him.

He was a man whose most obvious characteristic seems to have been his great likeableness. He was lively, funny and sociable. There was about him a quality of joyful and undeceived and even blatant courage which annoyed people in authority, and he had an outspokenness and lack of polish, together with great warmth and openness of manner, which drew some and alienated others. He was also a mystic, but of a kind which many would find hard to associate with that word. Even in this brief description we can perceive an obvious resemblance to another young man who died at about the same age and for the same reason, for the most important, as opposed to the most obvious, thing about Egide was that he was a man passionately in love with God. Because of that, and in that, he was deeply in love with a great many people. He knew where he would find God and where other people must find him, and he died at that point of exchange of love which is the cross of Christ. Something he wrote during the year before he began working in the factory indicates the place at which it is necessary to begin asking and answering the question, 'What shall we do?'

> The preaching of the historical Christ, of the salvation brought by His death and His life, is the final, concrete form, proper to every expression of love, of the divine life which is in us and which we know by faith; this concrete expression of love is thus the promise that the deep desire which is in us will be fulfilled, that desire which is the form assumed today by the expectation of the Old Testament . . . .
>
> If Christ today still has something to say to men, it will be an answer to their deepest desires, not a message that goes over their heads and doesn't reach their hearts.
>
> . . . Thus we have got to find out how men of today desire God with their whole heart, with their whole being, in their whole life; or better yet, how God is making them desire Him. How can we do this if we have not come to know the men of our time deeply, with a knowledge that only love can give? How can we love them if we do not go to them; if we do not imitate at least partially that total self-giving which moved God to make Himself man, so that men will let us approach them?
>
> (E. van Broeckhaven, *A Friend to All Men*)

This is what he did, and he discovered a mystical depth of identification with his friends in suffering love which was finally summed up by the manner of his death. He knew what incarnation was about, and he went to meet people where they were at home, in themselves, because there he found Christ, and so they too were enabled to recognize that Christ who had previously been no more than a meaningless name. He went to live, work, eat, drink, play cards, talk and listen. He went to them where they were 'at home' because that is where God always is.

He went to them, touched them, ate with them, sweated with them; he shared their bodily lives, because it is as bodies (not *in* bodies) that people live, and live in Christ. Bodies are the places where Christ is at home in his people, and the vision of human life which is explicit in the doctrine of incarnation and articulated in the language of Wisdom's 'feminine' consciousness shows us human bodies as symbolic systems. But the symbolism of our physical being is not something which became arbitrarily attached to it. We do not apprehend parts of ourselves as symbols because they happen to have functions which make that kind of association of ideas a natural one; rather, the physical and the psychic functions are expressions of each other, though the level of meaning may vary. Charles Williams loved the symbolism of the seated body, the straight but flexible spine, finding poise and equilibrium and rest because of the wide, firm base of the buttocks, 'the frame of justice and balance set in the body, the balance and poise needful to all joys and all peace'. They are, in the poem called 'The Vision of Empire' (*Taliessin Through Logres*) the 'rounded bottom of the Emperor's glory', but this Emperor is God, and the bottom of his glory is, in Williams' imagery, the area of the Caucasus, on a map which becomes (drawn on the end-paper of the book's first edition) a girl's naked body, and her body the 'Empire'. This is Byzantium's Empire, but it is also the extent of the reign of God acknowledged in the flesh-taking, and so if that flesh-taking is denied, by doctrine or deed, it fails. In the 'Empire' Caucasia is the region of the joyful, natural, unspoiled flesh, the region of the proper delight of the senses, and of the fertility which is theirs. This becomes something more in the light of the Emperor:

The Empire's sun shone on each round mound, double
fortalices defending dales of fertility.
The bright blades shone in the craft of the dancing war;
the stripped maids laughed for joy of the province,
bearing in themselves the shape of the province
founded in the base of space,
in the rounded bottom of the Emperor's glory.
Spines were strengthened, loves settled;
tossed through aerial gulfs of empire
the lost name, the fool's shame,

fame and frame of lovers in lowlands of Caucasia,
rang round snowy Elburz.
The organic body sang together.

The sexual imagery is emphatic and joyful. Natural sexual love
is 'shame' only to a 'fool', it is the '*fame* and frame of lovers', and
in its proper use and celebration it provides the firm base for the
whole body of Christ. The idea of the life of the senses as the
stability of the spiritual body is one that may seem odd at first, but
it is a conclusion from seeing creation in terms of incarnation. A
proper sensuality must be the basis from which all upreaching of
the spirit is possible. If it ceases to be part of the Empire, it becomes
a place of sin, but the denial of the glory of the sensual flesh is
finally a denial of the flesh-taking, a return to the gnostic doctrine
that 'I have a body, but I *am* a spirit':

> . . . none
> cared how men were shaped in body or mind,
> nor pined for the perfect Parousia; all gave
> their choice to the primal curse and the grave; their loves
> escaped back to the old necromantic gnosis
> of separation, were it but from one soul.
> Frantic with fear of losing themselves in others
> they denounced and delivered one another to reprobation.

Williams makes a direct connection between the loss of a proper
awareness of the body and the loss of love in the body of Christ, by
which people 'denounce' each other and consign to 'reprobation'
those whose opinions they disapprove. This is what happens. First
we fear the senses because they are involved in sin, then we react
against that fear, making the senses an idol. The *inherent* symbolism
of the body must be studied, and that means it must be loved, but
wisely loved, for Wisdom is never of the intellect alone, but neither
is it mindless or self-indulgent.

We easily lose any sense of the meaning of the human shape. One
result of this is to lose the sense of human scale in the environment.
It has taken about a century of bigger and increasingly less
human-scale planning (in apartment blocks, industrial complexes,
hospitals, schools and farms) and the conscious and unconscious

reaction to them in urban vandalism, industrial unrest and agrarian cynicism and despair before people began to realize that health and happiness had a close connection with scale. Human beings need human-scale contexts as much as they need clothes that fit them and food their bodies are designed to digest. Inhuman urban planning in practice goes hand in hand with adulteration and denaturing of food. Body-symbolism is at the root of 'moral theology' of any kind.

Yet it seems possible that the very abuses have made us aware of the underlying principles in a way which was not possible when people just 'naturally' lived out their body-symbolism, more or less. For although people are at home now in bodies whose sexuality is a problem in new and different ways, the very problems create a possibility of seeing the 'organic body' as a whole that can sing. The collapse, or near-collapse, of traditional systems of sexual behaviour in the West (and gradually elsewhere) has been tragic for many. Not all these systems were morally equivalent by any means, but they can be taken together up to a point, and they did (and still do where they can still work) provide people with a sense of sexual identity, a strong and reliable framework of custom and taboo and expectation within which the vulnerable individual feelings could discover themselves. The limits might be painful, but they were safe, and they were supportive. There were those who found them intolerable and broke free, but for most they were 'where they were at home', they were the demarcation of their sexual selves. Even in being disobeyed, the norms provided categories for self-understanding.

This was what made it possible for people to say, at one and the same time, that adultery was a sin, but that (for them) it was right. 'Adultery', in context, was a word for a certain kind of sexual behaviour which was in the category of 'sin'. But love for a person to whom one was not married could lead to a strong conviction that to make love to that person was really good, and indeed the cult of Romantic love spelt this out and even codified it. But everyone went on saying that it was a sin as well. In time, the moral contradiction became intolerable, and when the Romantic revival came six centuries later it blew this kind of thinking apart. The point is that such unexamined categories do help people to know specifically on which side of a boundary they are, and therefore how they may

285

think of themselves and others of them. This is an important function of social morality; it is part of what Paul called Law, which he said came in to cope with sin, but actually increased it—because it makes people aware of some actions as guilty and sets up conflicts. But also it was suitable during the stage of 'tutelage' when children of God could not yet cope with the real freedom of Christ. It is 'holy and just and good' in its own way, but its goodness lies in the way in which it protects immature people and societies from having to cope with the deeper challenges of love, at least until such a time as they are able to recognize such challenges without either panic or bravado.

The danger is, as Paul pointed out, that the protection becomes a prison, even if a self-chosen one, but where there is no protection at all (as there is not for so many now) the anxiety, the vertigo of too many choices and no foothold, is intense. New languages of sexual behaviour are invented to try to give people a way to make sense of their emotions, some kind of basis for decisions which are decisions and not just rationalizations. But often these languages are themselves rationalizations of lust for domination, or of fear of responsibility, or of desire for revenge for the basic horribleness of life.

The root of the matter is indeed language. There is no available language of body-symbolism which could provide a really truthful awareness of the meaning of being bodily, and therefore a criterion for moral decision in the absence of older socio-sexual language. The older languages of sexual behaviour will not do because they were not essentially languages about sexuality at all and so were never truly moral. They were offshoots of quite different language systems which had to do with property, or the need for racial continuity, or social stability, or the pursuit of pleasure, or the suspicion of pleasure. Such phrases as 'the *bonds* of matrimony' or 'to *lose* one's virginity' or '*fille de joie*' or 'the marriage *debt*' or 'a *kept* woman' or '*play*boy' show very obviously the attitudes and categories from which they derive. If we are to answer the near-despairing question 'What shall we do?' in the area of sexuality, this is where it has to begin. We have to take bodies seriously precisely as bodies, whose detailed form in action, and functional form, are the one proper source of a language which may clearly express the *amour voulu* of loving response to God in Christ.

286

This is a fundamentally different moral approach. In a situation in which all kinds of non-physical criteria are used for making judgements about how people should behave physically, including sexually, love melts away or gets knocked down. There is great distress, and the destruction of lives and minds has been terrible. Yet this language vacuum has created a possibility (perhaps not very great, but real) that at least people who know about incarnation may begin to discover that the proper language in which to articulate the moral significance of the body's action must be based on awareness of the body as a human person, but not a person in isolation. I referred earlier to the way in which the 'feminine' awareness of body as person had a revolutionary effect both mystical and political, and now we can see how this kind of awareness is the only possible source of a genuinely incarnational moral theology. 'The organic body sang together', as the whole person lives *as* (not *in*) his or her body. As the body is discovered as risen with Christ, so must the reflection on this discovery move towards a greater and greater awareness of its own bodily meaning. At the same time, as the spiritual awareness of inherent body symbolism grows, so must the awareness of the communal dimension, the essentially exchanged natures of bodily being, grow also. The 'organic' body is both the individual and the whole, at one and the same time.

The whole area of sexuality is so fogged by anxiety, prejudice, guilt and sheer ignorance that it may be easier to look for a moment at the inherent symbolism of a part of the body, the hand, which is not felt to be obviously sexual but which is important in itself and sexually meaningful also, as all lovers know.

'Hand' is a word used to signify the whole person when he or she is being considered as a unit of labour. 'Factory hands' are people but scarcely considered as such, and this use of body-symbolism to degrade, implicitly and routinely, is a good example of how powerful the inherent symbolism can be, in this case for harm. It was precisely this sense of the blasphemous nature of the assumption about human beings underlying the organization and practice of factory work which drove Egide von Broeckhoven to insert himself in that appalling gap which had been created between 'hands' and 'people' and to try to establish a renewed exchange at that point which was himself. Inevitably the only possible point of exchange was the cross.

But hands make things, they mean the human being as creator of the human environment, and so a hand can fittingly symbolize God the Creator, linking God and creature by recognition of a shared character, that of maker. In Michelangelo's fresco on the Sistine ceiling, the vibrant hand of the Creator has just brought into being the human thing, Adam, whose responding hand is still limp with a life not yet fully aware. In that painting, the hands are what one remembers.

Hands have this meaning in themselves but not by themselves. What is made is not for the maker alone. To make is to share onself; hands therefore mean giving, offering of self as one offers something good to another. The lifting or joining of hands in prayer is a gesture which expresses this sharing of self in such a basic way that there is no altering it. It is unimaginable, for instance, that a gesture of clasping the hands behind the back could be the symbol of prayer. The hands stretched out, to other human beings or to God (and both are meant, and must be, in the same gesture) do not just *mean*, but *are* a giving of the whole person. The symbolism is inherent in the action, the action 'takes' the person into the meaning; the act *is* the given person.

Not only the gesture but the actual shape of the hands, which makes the gesture possible, has inherent meaning. Williams was fascinated by thumbs, which make hands human and able to do human things. In 'Bors to Elayne: on the King's Coins', *Taliessin Through Logres*, it is Bors, the father of a household, who comes home to his wife Elayne and greets her as the one who gives shape and life to the household:

... I am come again
to live from the founts and fields of your hands ...
On the forms of ancient saints, my heroes, your thumbs,
as on a winch the power of man is wound
to the last inch; there ground is prepared
for the eared and seeded harvest of propinquent goodwill,
drained the reeded marshes, cleared the branched jungles
where the unthumbed shapes of apes swung and hung.
Now, when the thumbs are muscled with the power of goodwill
corn comes to the mill and flour to the house,
bread of love for your women and my men;

288

at the turn of the day, and none only to earn,
in the day of the turn, and none only to pay,
for the hall is raised to the power of exchange of all
by the small spread organisms of your hands; O Fair
there are the altars of Christ the City extended.

Hands—and especially thumbs which give them their special power and skill—bring the human person to a point of distinctively human activity, and that activity is one of making, giving, receiving, typically the exchanges of the household, the work of the kitchen. But the meaning of the thumbed hand reaches out to the earth from which food comes, to give to it and receive from it. Thumbed hands build the house and make it home, and all in it both 'earn' and 'pay' not as an arbitrary allocation of wealth but by the nature of hands, which give and receive in every act of making, for the making can only be done in virtue of what is received, the corn to the mill and the flour to the house. So thumbed hands mean the human community and the whole human beings in it and all of that as the body of Christ—so Christ as sacrifice, but also Christ as social organism, in 'the altars of Christ the City' which lie in the inherent function and shape of a particular woman's strong little hands.

But hands can also destroy, with that efficiency which must be theirs if they are to make and share efficiently. They can pull apart, smash, seize, crush, kill. The closed fist is a symbol of implacable hatred because that is what a closed fist *is*—it is closed against all possibility of exchange, it is the negation of making.

For good or ill, then, moral decisions are inherent in the movements of hands. That is why we feel a kind of basic outrage when the hands' movements contradict the heart's intention. We are aware of a horrible and improper separation, whether it be in the hand of friendship which conceals plans for revenge, or the heart full of love which is obliged to hide itself behind folded and unyielding hands. We do not have to *invent* the significance of moral directions articulated in the movement of hands; they are there 'in our hands'. But if we wish to discover the truth of our hands' meanings, and make decisions as the truth of our hands reveals choices, we need consciously and laboriously to become increasingly sensitive to the meanings of our hands. We can easily silence them, and indeed we are trained to do so, because that is one of the deathly functions of Law. The diplomat's handshake; the seducer's caress; the child's hand held—to keep him tied rather than to guide; the delicate surgery of Hitler's concentration-camp experiments; the folded hands of un-adoring worship rendered under threat of punishment; all these are things people are trained to do, which contradict the meaning of hands. They are fundamentally untruthful, and we can recognize such a blasphemous insult to the inherent meaning of bodily being without any trouble at all.

But the same thing applies to specifically sexual parts and actions. It is more difficult to understand wisely in this area because the emotions involved are so profound and so violent, but the same kind of insight is needed. The symbolism of the actions of human sexual intercourse is inherent, and this applies to those parts which are not seen, the places where seed grows in the man and is implanted in the woman. But the fact that the bodies of men and women have different functions and forms adds a dimension which was absent in considering hands. The need of one for the other in order that the act of generation may be completed is an essential element in the meaning of the body as sexual. On the very precise interaction of two bodies depends the degree of pleasure which they are able to share, and this giving and taking is of whole persons, a giving and taking which draws to a point of exchange all the levels of sharedness which make up human life, from the most earthy to the most heavenly. And it becomes heavenly not by distancing itself from the physical and 'offering' all this to God, but precisely by paying detailed and loving attention to what is being done, and precisely how.

Because of the complexity of the exchanges which are summed up in the idea of sexuality, it is not possible for any couple at any one time to experience the full range of possible meaning in sexual exchanges. The emphasis will differ from one couple to another and from one time to another. The discoveries they make may be predominantly of sheer delight, or of a kind of quiet tenderness, or perhaps of the need and beauty of restraint and sacrifice for the other's sake. They may come upon fear, or ecstasy, or tremendous laughter. They will also discover the evil in themselves, even without intending any. Some men and women will be joyfully aware of the life-bringing outcome of their intercourse, and desire it, while others may not advert to it at all. Because of this variety of levels and of categories of feeling and intention in specifically sexual exchanges, and especially because of the ambiguity of the procreative possibility, it is harder to become sensitive to the moral directions inherent in sexual form and action. But, just as with the hands, the body-symbolism of sexual behaviour is that of the whole person, inescapably, and not only of the whole person but of the person as part of the organic body, whose actions are therefore without exception the actions of that communal body and have no human meaning apart from it. This is why the claim to moral autonomy in the area of sexuality is mistaken, if understandable. There is no such thing as private sex, not because people (in State or Church) have made rules about it but because the shape and function of the body, as it discovers itself sexually, says things about sharedness in every aspect. Sexuality threads people into the network of human community historically and socially. That is its nature.

It follows from this that we have to say something which sounds impossibly hard: to be truthful, sexual behaviour must be directed to a greater and greater conformity to the actual bodily facts, experienced as the facts of whole human persons-in-exchange. As the hands discover and articulate moral direction and spiritual insight and aspiration, so also, and even more deeply, do the specifically sexual parts and functions. Even more, here, does an untruthful gesture betray the human integrity. All this, when we try to apply it, creates a necessity to make what look like appallingly rigid judgements about such things as the use of contraceptives, about homosexuality, about the indissolubility of marriage. This criterion makes us perceive as untruthful any use of bodies (that is, of people) as sexual which fail to express at every level of the human person the full symbolism of bodily sexual being, which is to be exchanged physically and emotionally and in relation to history and to the community, and as particular and passionate incarnation of divine love, totally given and received, creatively poured out without reserve and in eternal fidelity. That is the kind of thing sexuality is and says, in itself. That is why the conscious commitment to such an exchange has to have the character of 'sacrament', for it makes actual and bodily in a special and particular way the passionate love of Christ, which gives life. And that is why it can only be fully seen 'in Christ and in the Church', as Paul says. That *is* its meaning,

291

in the context of the whole Body, yet it is a meaning hard to discern and quite impossible to live.

It is impossible to live it—literally impossible. It is impossible to put into practice fully what I have just been saying has to be done, because of one huge fact which, literally, 'gets in the way'. That fact is sin. We live, bodily, not only in exchange of the body of the risen Christ but in the exchange of sin. The whole bodily situation is a sinful one, whether or not anyone wills evil. The greatest saints, the most ardent and selfless lovers, are in it. It is how we relate to each other. Sin is refusal, it blocks and distorts, and it does this 'in the nature of things'. Because it is in the network of exchange, that is how life, bodily life, *is*. And so the very sensitivity which shows us the truthful direction of bodily action and function also shows us, over and over again, that it is impossible. This is, of course, the situation which necessitates the phenomenon of Romantic passion, as we have seen.

What does this mean for our bodily being in the ways of love? It means that, over and over again, the ways to the proper and fully significant exchanges are blocked. They are blocked by heredity, or by conditioning, or by circumstance. People are made incapable of the 'proper' exchange of love by false ideas about sex which make free and joyful self-giving impossible; they are blocked by economic pressures, creating fear of more children; they are blocked by the kind of systematic destruction of male sexual sensibility which makes tenderness to a lover impossible; they are blocked by deep-seated fears of the feminine (in men *and* women); they are blocked by physical and nervous illness; they are blocked by political propaganda or the huge pressure of public opinion; they are blocked by sheer unhappiness; they are blocked by the little-understood psycho-physical factors which can make the opposite sex repellent as a sexual partner. There are as many kinds of blockages as there are people.

But we have learned all through this book that when love comes up against an obstacle the thrust of passion will try to find a weak spot. If the obvious way ahead is blocked it will find another way, unexpected, unwanted perhaps. In the application of this to matters of sexual morality, sensitivity to the passionate nature of love in all human bodily relationships makes it clear that we must be able to say two things about them which are only apparently contradictory.

The first is that there is, indeed, an absolute rightness in this as in other matters. The discernment of it depends on a sensitive love for the actual bodiliness of God's beloved. There is 'absolutely' no room for compromise, the demand is total, in so far as it is discerned.

The second is that love must find a way to exchange, even when the way discerned as fully truthful is blocked. It will go round, under, over; it will smash and destroy; but it will get through by some means. And the very distortion, the weakness and sense of wrong, the unfulfilment and loneliness, are the ways in which love creates an even greater channel for itself. The prostitute with the heart of gold is not merely a sentimental cliché. The woman who sticks stubbornly to a brutal man, or the man who nurses an invalid wife for years, are living proofs of how love finds a weak spot and grows to heroic proportions in relationships which are basically 'wrong'. More problematically, the broken marriage may have been broken by love; many homosexual relationships exhibit a fidelity and tenderness whose holiness is evident; even the promiscuous may be in pursuit of elusive truth, though in paths narrowed to the point of asphyxiation by fears and false doctrines.

That is not to say that sexuality cannot be used as a way of refusal. It is one of the most effective ways of refusing exchange. As the hand made to give and comfort and build can also tear apart and smash, so sexuality, which means sharing and life-giving and passionate truthfulness, can deceive and corrupt and utterly destroy a human personality. This scarcely needs to be said. What I want to outline here, for others to fill in, is simply the way in which an understanding of body symbolism as discovered in the way of Exchange shows as simultaneously the possibility of true and precise moral judgement and decision and also (at the same time and by the same criteria) the glorious ruthlessness of divine love in finding a way to give itself in a bodily situation distorted by sin. Truthfulness and compassion, clarity of judgement and tenderness of action, are not opposites but two results of the same vision. This was how Jesus saw things. His demands were as absolute as heaven and hell, but that very fact made him furiously tender to the damaged and the weak and the muddle-headed. It is only by striving in all humility to see things as he did that his Church can be faithful to the stringency of his demands and the delicate sensitivity of his discernment of love's way in a sinful situation.

We cannot admit compromise, but we must admit compassion and indeed be filled with awe and gratitude because love does break through. And in all this we have to assert, especially, the truly heroic kinds of breakthrough which happen when a man or woman whose need for sexual self-giving in love is blocked (by a hideous marriage, by homosexual tendencies, by severe risk of damage in case of another pregnancy) strives even in this situation to live his or her body symbolism as far as it is possible according to its inherent meaning, and is therefore inevitably obliged to refuse to take the available paths of physical love which do not reflect that meaning. Such a choice is beyond question heroic, and if it is taken out of love it breaks through to that which fulfilled sexual love is also seeking. It breaks through because only in that further sphere of lived but transformed bodiliness can sexuality be recovered as human and holy. This is a real choice, and it has about it a deep and passionate rightness which does extraordinary things to such a person. But not all have, at the time when such choices must be made, reached a point of development at which such a decision can be made or even perceived as valid. For them, the *proper* way may involve a use of sexuality which is 'wrong', yet necessary as the only way through. We have to be very careful in moral judgement in this area, just because the body symbolism of sexuality makes clear an absoluteness of demand which must be known and adored but not idolized.

We tend to treat sexual life as a department, to be dealt with according to criteria we do not apply elsewhere. Exploitation, bullying, manipulation, deceit and petty meanness are practised in their sexual lives by people who would be astounded to find their behaviour described in those terms; for in other areas it may be quite different. But there are no other areas. Sexuality is oneself and is exchange with others in all kinds of ways, as it exchanges with God in them, because the specifically sexual is simply a point of most vivid awareness of the way in which we are our bodies. Therefore, in its less specific but equally vital ways, we know each person sexually, by sight and smell and touch, by concrete service and emotional response, and at the deepest level to which, perhaps, we can reach if we love enough. 'What they ask is not an encounter with impersonal goodness (someone who is charitable) but with one who loves their concrete being', wrote the young worker-priest in his diary. 'Such an encounter will then become for them a profound experience that will sustain them throughout their lives, that will give them back trust in life, in love, in God.' He wrote this when he was about to begin his encounter with real poverty and dispossession. He was already aware that 'all friendship has its beginning in the senses', because that is where it is indeed 'concrete', in the immediacy of a smile, a proferred cigarette, an offer of help, an embrace, the loyalty which will stand by a friend in trouble with the foreman even if it means trouble for oneself. But it is dangerous, because this is the area, at the heart of the network of exchange which is the human body, where violent and unexpected and crucial things happen. Egide wrote of 'the desire for love which is already an experience of God' and then noticed that 'it often happens that when someone reaches deep into a person and touches this basic desire, he himself is shaken to his foundations. He then touches the fine line between trust in life or despair, faith in the living, existential God or unbelief, the desire for love or disillusionment.' This is a turning-point, it is the breakthrough of passion, with all its possibilities for good or ill. He himself broke through to so deep a level of mystical awareness of the meaning of such an encounter that he lived from then on in the sphere in which such things are fully lived instead of, as they are for most of us, fleetingly known and wistfully regretted. But to do that requires a special gift, which has to do with sexuality. This is the level of encounter with which the Romantic doctrine was concerned. When several times Egide wrote notes in his diary about sexuality as the place where love has to begin, it was Romantic love he was talking about. 'He who loves exposes himself to be wounded in order to be all the more completely dependent on the Beloved. This is true of sexual love, but it is also true of the love of God.' That seems an odd thing for a man to say who had taken a vow of chastity. It is important to see why his statement could be true and yet not invalidate his own choice but make it a necessary one.

Egide van Broeckhaven spent much time with people in their kitchens or in the one room which was also their kitchen. Kitchens are places where people are, willy-nilly, un-secret and exposed to each other and so have to work with the fact that they are not perfect. In this concrete, messy, intimate situation it is impossible not to be aware that not only are people morally imperfect, but they are obviously physically and psychologically imperfect. In this place which is 'home' in the most vivid and realistic sense, they experience inescapably each other's blemishes or sicknesses. They may have weak eyesight or suffer from dandruff or lung cancer. They may talk too much or not enough, avoid trouble out of cowardice or court it out of natural pugnacity. And all of such things are a combination of heredity, circumstance and choice, in what proportions it is impossible to tell. Therefore all the people who, in a 'kitchen situation', share food, talk, warmth and space (experiencing, often, the insufficiency of these things) are exchanging a great deal of negative influence and reacting off each other in destructive ways. But also they are sharing life in the proper flow of exchange which is love. And both of these ways of exchange are essentially bodily, and therefore sexual in the broad sense. People exchange life sexually where they are at home, in themselves as flawed and imprisoned and warped as well as having 'the desire for love which is already an experience of God'. They communicate, therefore, as wounded people, incomplete, desirous and bewildered. And the point at which this deathly experience crosses over and becomes the possibility of a real encounter with the concrete being of another is the cross, yet scarcely apprehended in that way.

The most obviously fitting way this can happen is that of fully committed sexual love, in which the initial breakthrough is worked out in the *amour voulu* of detailed, everyday, practical service and of self-giving at the erotic level and all that flows from it in the growing intimacy of bodies and minds. A man and woman discover each other as two halves of one person created by God to be his image *as a couple*, and they learn by their bodies. Out of this unfolding story of heroic fidelity other stories grow. The exchange of sexual love flows outwards to more and more others, who, by their involvement in that 'kitchen situation' of loving struggle, are warmed and challenged and comforted to discover a deeper and deeper encounter.

It was out of his concrete experience of people in their overcrowded, inadequate homes that Egide wrote that 'the most far-reaching apostolate has to be that of married people'. Christian marriage is an explicit commitment to the deepest exchange of many-levelled love in Christ, and since it is in him it is never private but is given, through and with the sexual practice, to all who so deeply need that

296

love, in concrete, practical terms. It is through the erotic encounter in this context of the body of Christ that each one is released from the prison of the deathly flesh and becomes capable of resurrection—begins, indeed, to live that life more consciously and fully, and therefore of course more painfully yet hopefully, than in any other way. But still it is a wounded sexuality, one enmeshed in sin as well as living in exchange of resurrection. Therefore, also, it is often in the experience of a difficult, broken, 'failed' marriage that the full glory of what has been exchanged in that willed self-giving is revealed, and this is to be remembered when we are thinking about divorce. There is always the need to keep in tension the two truths that the shared experience of sexual intercourse does something between two people which (in some measure) is part of them forever, because that is what their bodies 'say' and it is true whether they intend it or not; and also that the damaged nature of the exchanges may make it literally impossible to reach the deeper levels together in this way. The recognition of this has to be lived, and it can be as redemptive as the proper and sacrificial joy of a faithful marriage. Indeed a broken marriage can be simply the painful following out of that same fidelity, which is ultimately fidelity to God.

But there is another consequence of the inevitably flawed nature of sexuality. There is a certain kind of flaw in the sexual being of some people which does more than present obstacles to their deepening encounter with God in each other. It actually prevents them from encountering God in genital sexuality. They are people who, whether or not they marry or share explicitly sexual encounters of any kind, are not capable of responding to God in that way. They are spiritually eunuchs in a fundamental way. This is not the same thing as the tragic case of people who are indeed capable of full erotic encounters as a way to meet God but are prevented by circumstance, or the wrong kind of partner, from ever experiencing the fulfilment of their own capacity for love in this way. I am talking of those who *cannot* find God in genital encounter, no matter how fully they may believe in the possibility of this, and no matter how unselfishly they may try to do so. But the passion of divine love seeks the weak spot for a breakthrough. As in a loving marriage it breaks through in the erotic encounter; as in the failed marriage it breaks through in the agony of humiliation and grief; as in enforced

297

singleness it breaks through even in the acceptance of frustration and incompleteness; so in the case of those who have this fundamental incapacity for erotic breakthrough it uses that very flaw as the place of encounter with ultimate love. Egide himself put it very well, in the last years of his life: 'As a man has a need for a woman (for his wife) I have a need for God. As a man needs his wife, I need my God.' The acceptance of a 'call' to be celibate, then, may be not entirely a human choice between different possibilities of loving, but the recognition of a fact—a fact of the sinful human condition operating in this particular way in this person and therefore providing that weak spot by which the floods of divine love may enter. But the obscure awareness of this and the possibility—even certainty—of suffering and failure and misunderstanding which acceptance must bring makes it very frightening, and so it is essential that the choice made in response to such a call should be made out of the deepest humility; there has to be a trust in the strength of that love, and in nothing else, which only a rather crazily literal belief in God's promises can make possible. It is a choice which has to be made and maintained in a close and conscious awareness of it as being the result of sin, in the sense of 'what is wrong' with human life, and *therefore* as potentially redemptive. The incarnation of Christ was an acceptance—as a personal, intimate, concrete situation—of sin in that sense. It was by being made sin that Jesus was able to open the way for the full flood of the Father's love to enter that sinful situation. As the full acceptance of another in erotic discovery of God is a bearing of all the pain of the sin that the encounter discloses, and so lets God into the world of sin, so also the acceptance of being the one who cannot do that becomes the 'place' where a passionate response to God is made possible.

It is, it must be, a fully 'sexed' response, although it is not sexual in the sense that genital encounter is sexual. And as 'sexed' it is a response to God encountered in others, and it is a response *to each one* which is potentially passionate and single-minded and total in a way which is not possible for those whose primary means of exchange of divine love is through genital sex. But the body symbolism has to be fully lived; as it seeks for what it desires, as all bodies must do, its incapacity drives it with such force that it breaks the barrier to another sphere, the sphere of glory. As Rilke expressed it in the first Duino Elegy:

... Is it not time that, in loving,
we freed ourselves from the loved one, and, quivering, endured:
as the arrow endures the string, to become, in the gathering
   out-leap
something more than itself? For staying is nowhere.

In Egide's own phrase, that kind of celibacy is 'a dive into the River at its source'. That is where it must be lived, but not because this state is chosen as a better way. Nobody can choose it, it only happens in the passionate exchange of love between God and a human person; it is lived there because that is the only way such a person can live it at all.

If we can get it clear that God comes to meet us in our weakness, not in our strength, then we can understand both why marriage is *the* crossroads of exchanged love, in the Church which is God's rather chaotic kitchen, and why celibacy 'for the kingdom' is both humiliating and glorious, and absolutely essential if the full power of the passion of Christ is to be released in his world. And (as it were spelling this out) we realize that marriage vows are not so much the statement of a choice made by two people as an echo by them, to each other and in the Church, of the Word of God which they hear in their bodies about themselves as a couple; similarly the vow of chastity is not a choice made and a promise given to God but primarily the acknowledgement of a fact about one's own bodily being, and the surrender made in that knowledge to whatever use God may wish to make of this weak spot, as Mary 'echoed' God's Word in her. In both cases the possibilities of misapprehension and mixed motives are enormous. But the basic realities are there and need to be very sensitively discerned.

No doubt in reaction to excesses of 'permissiveness' there has been a curious 'romantic' exploration of the possibilities of a quasi-mystical, non-consummated erotic love. Little pamphlets and books have appeared, explaining that spiritual energy should only be used in full genital intercourse when conception is desired, and that to use it at other times is an aberration resulting from 'distorted emotions'. This has nothing to do with puritanism, and it is a doctrine for married couples and for all lovers. They are encouraged to learn how to use their sexual energy in a non-genital experience

299

of passionate love. It is as if Donne's 'ecstatic' lovers were held up as a sexual norm, rather than seen as a prelude to fuller physical intimacy. This has been proposed in the context of 'natural birth-control' also, but it is primarily a doctrine about an experience of love which is very explicitly Romantic, a deliberate by-passing of 'natural' fulfilment in order to arrive at the further meaning of the love between the couple. It is in keeping with the body symbolism, as celibacy is, though in a different way. It seems unlikely, at this stage of our culture, that it could be more than a very small minority movement, but even parenthetically it is significant.

This is a far cry from the warmth and chaos of the normal human 'togetherness', but in any case we have to move out of the unpredictable intimacy of people 'being themselves' in a kitchen and think about the kind of thing most people have to do to keep any kind of food coming into that kitchen. My reference-point in this connection is still a man who in his living with Wisdom chose to share the heaviest and most unpleasant kind of work with those whose inevitable lot it was, and who were glad to have the chance to do it. The things that happen to the bodies and minds and hearts of people who work in factories have rightly become one of the central moral issues of our time. But I want to include, under this heading, others who work in bad conditions and under systems which dehumanize them, though the circumstances may look different. Landless rural labourers in many countries must be considered along with those who work in factories, but in another sense equally oppressed are those whose standard of living is much higher, even luxurious compared with that of an Arab foundry-worker in Brussels, but whose work is inherently meaningless and degrading, whether it be endlessly packing cheap cosmetics in unnecessary plastic display wrapping, or serving drinks or typing letters for men whose business is to make money at the expense of people who lack it. The difference is that the underpaid and underprivileged factory worker or labourer knows he or she is oppressed; the others often do not, and even happily connive at or promote their own oppression.

Once again, we have to keep two things in tension. One is that this kind of thing is evil, and nothing can alter that, though the effects may be alleviated; the other is that it is right to get into the middle of all this. Both these things are true, but to accept either of them without the other is spiritually lethal. If we say that oppression is evil, in its effect on the oppressed but also on the oppressor, we have to remember what kind of thing evil is—not a thing-in-itself but basically a distortion of things inherently good. Evil is a lying use of good. Injustice is not an alternative to justice, it is a refusal to recognize the nature of justice. The *facts* about human beings are those of exchange; people are people in the network of exchange, which is love. 'Justice' is the clear recognition of this and is therefore concerned with the kinds of actions which result from seeing human society in those terms. Injustice is simply a view of, and resulting decisions about, human society which are false, and this is so even when those who hold and practice injustice are sincere and highly motivated. It is important to hold on to the fact that injustice in the political sphere means basically an *unreal* vision of things, resulting from a failure to perceive the proper relationships in the organic body, in just the same way that sexual sin is the result of failure (culpable or not) to perceive the inherent meaning of being bodily. In fact, we can reverse those statements and say that sexual sin is due to failure to recognize the proper relationships ('proper' in the sense of appropriate, fitting, *necessary*) in the organic body, and injustice is due to failure to perceive the inherent meaning of bodiliness. Social and sexual sin are both, at bottom, the result of false statements about the nature of reality.

Egide van Broeckhoven was not politically minded in the usual sense, partly because his available language for making political judgements was very inadequate. At that time, a few people were already beginning to try to find ways to articulate as Christians the inherent contradictions in the languages of modern economics and politics which made such systematic dehumanization as Egide experienced in the factory more or less inevitable, but he himself had not heard of them. Although there are signs that he was groping for them it did not occur to him to find his point of insertion into an unjust situation by seeking an adeqaute analysis of it. His way was the 'inner' way of Wisdom, living the reality from within until its nature became so evident that others, perhaps, could be challenged to the point of a linguistic/philosophical breakthrough. The analysis has to be done, it is a vital work of Christ's body now, but it has to be done truthfully. I mean by this that it is not enough to find a language which adequately articulates human life at the levels of social organization or of economics and politics strictly so called—necessary as it is to speak of these fully and accurately. A language which does this, but leaves out the dimension of ultimate meaning in the movement towards the whole Christ, is not accurate. An accurage language must articulate the whole of the 'organic body', including the fact that it is diseased, and that the disease is not simply an external growth which can be cut away, leaving a basically healthy body. The truth is that the body carries disease in its bloodstream, and the growths on it are the result of this. If they are removed, by revolution or war, they will only grow again somewhere else, unless the illness itself is 'reversed' and the flow of life reestablished. And this cannot be done unless the condition is correctly diagnosed.

This does not, of course, mean that the growths are irrelevant or inevitable. Quite the contrary. In the more enlightened kind of medicine which is beginning to get a hearing (a fact which is in itself part of the process of 'reversing' the sickness of society) the first aim is to foster in the body those forces which will resist disease and drive it out by giving it nothing to feed on. Symptoms may then gradually disappear, without need for surgery or suppressive drugs, but for this to happen it is not enough simply to stop doing or eating what is known to be harmful—the disease is too well established for that to be adequate. It is necessary to take conscious and positive and often painful steps to establish different patterns of exchange in the body. And that requires an accurate knowledge of the workings of the whole system.

One can apply all that equally well to the organic body of the individual and to the social organism, and it must be clear from all that we have considered so far that the former is much more than a metaphor for the other. It is literally the case that the possibility of recovery for the social organism depends on what it· eats and what it breathes, and on where it lives and where it works and how it travels between the two, and also on how it 'plays' and how its relationships are managed, both the domestic or personal and the economic and political. A society is sick if it lives off food that is kept artificially expensive and is also basically unbalanced, debilitating and disease-promoting, as most food in the 'civilized' world actually is. This is true not only because the members of such a society are, due to such eating habits, less prosperous, less healthy and less intelligent than they could be (and that is a very mild statement of the case) but because the processes by which such food is produced and marketed are destructive to the soil on which the health and even survival of the cities depends and are also destructive of the sense of values of those engaged in processing and marketing. Such people either know, or try not to know, or are conditioned to think in such a way as not to recognize, that what they are producing for people to eat is bad. It is as bad for them to know or not know this as the stuff they produce is bad.

It is bad at all stages. It is bad for the farmers, who are forced by untruthful economic structure to use methods which lower soil fertility, adulterate the produce, abuse animals, and in the process dehumanize those who 'farm' like this. It is bad at the stage of the cynically exploitative processing systems which take out nutrients expensively, and expensively sell back to people the nutrients they then lack. It is bad at the level of the marketing business which spends huge sums on 'convenient' and showy packaging, wasting resources and raising prices. Food, then, is one of the big things which makes society sick. People who are involved in producing and consuming bad food are sick in body and mind. As bodies, they are heavily handicapped in their exchanges and their political judgement is corrupted and untrue because of their conditioning, which requires them to *need* food which is inherently untruthful about its meanings, or which indeed has distanced itself from meaning anything at all except sensation divorced from function. It is not food for proper nourishment and enjoyment but food for obsessive and un-delightful cravings. If this connection between food and political structure and decision seems far-fetched, we can verify it easily if we consider the violent reaction when what is thought of as our 'standard of living' is threatened, for this 'standard' is closely tied to certain kinds of eating expectations which are in fact based on no actual needs of body and mind but are the result of conditioning.

The same can be said of housing, city planning, transport, medical care, education, and above all of the patterns of industry and commerce which support all those things. The whole lot is corrupted, and each area individually is corrupted, by false expectations deliberately or semi-deliberately fostered. All these expectations are shaped not by real human needs but by the demands of a system whose values have no reference-point in the sense of exchange as that of the organic body. Therefore, when we are thinking about political relationships which are the wider reach of the human organism we are dealing with a situation which is not curable simply by reforming the pattern of industrial and economic relationship from the outside. This is true even when the illness in these areas has been accurately and sensitively diagnosed using a language, such as the Marxist one, which can deal with real and concrete experiences as they are now known.

How basically inadequate the approach solely from 'without' can be we can now see very well in China. This is the place where the most complete and comprehensive re-shaping of a society ever known was undertaken. It was far more searching and more aware of the sheer complexity and 'organicness' of human society than the Russian revolution. It aimed to re-train people's minds along lines which accorded better with the truth about basic human relationship in society. It promoted real exchange and articulated properly human values. It succeeded to a great extent precisely because it was truthful over such a wide field. In the end it did not succeed; minds were changed but not transformed. We can see how superficial was the change now that the whole organism is deliberately subjecting itself to the values of cultures it rejected, because it cannot face being outdistanced in prosperity by other nations, and because it cannot abide the threat of Russian power on its border. So the technology of the West comes in, and with it Western values, and the great cultural experiment has failed, though not entirely.

It failed because it had, as a doctrine about reality, one huge lack; it had no doctrine of sin. Evil had still, as in 'classical' Marxism, to be attributed to particular people in particular systems, thus assuming that to eliminate these would be to eliminate evil tendencies in society. This proved to be untrue. Sin cannot be dealt with in such a way, not so much because the process of 'purging' is cruel but because it is based on a false premise. It does not work because the 'organic body' is not like that, and no amount of sincerity or determination will make it so.

This is the reason why the remedy has to be sought in a different approach altogether. I use the word 'approach' deliberately, because in practice most of the things which are being done (or attempted, or hopefully planned) by reformers and revolutionaries and resistance movements and human-rights campaigners and

304

peace organizations and all those who articulate, in theory and practice, the proper needs of human beings are indeed things that need to be done. When they fail it is not because their ideals are false or their movement unnecessary, but (apart from the high risk of being imprisoned, disgraced, sacked, tortured, publically vilified or killed) because they are insufficiently radical in their approach.

This radicality, really 'getting to the roots', means seeking to approach the service of human beings as what they are: the body of Christ, people in some degree and way engaged in exchanging resurrection, whether they know it or not, but all prevented from full awareness and response by that other kind of exchange which is deathly. If these are the basic facts about human beings as they relate to each other, then obviously only an approach which takes these facts as its point of departure has a chance of accomplishing anything of permanent value. The older methods employed by Christians to bring Christ's Kingdom closer failed because they were not sufficiently radically Christian. They were only, in many cases, adaptations of 'worldly' structures, ideals and methods to would-be Christian purposes. 'The world' is where we are, and such adaptations are necessary and effective. To build hospitals, teach, relieve poverty, do research, work in politics—these and other things have been important in exchanging resurrection, and they still are to some extent, though it is harder and harder to justify a Christian presence which, in effect, underwrites the values of institutions whose whole existence is based on untruths about the nature of the organic body. But more and more Christians are discovering that they cannot discern in this approach the genuine passionate thrust of God's love towards humankind. The only kind of involvement that seems to have that meaning is involvement with the ones who suffer—the oppressed, the misled, the under-privileged in mind, body or political status. Egide van Broeckhoven was speaking for many then, and more since, who began to feel that 'it seems there is not a single person any more who is sure of the right choice', in discovering a means of 'Christianizing' society. 'The structures which once inspired blind trust (School, Church) are placed in doubt; we have been driven into a corner where we are face to face with what is essential to the apostolate: "He who receives you receives Me and Him who sent Me"; to the apostolate of love: "as my Father loves me, so I love you, love one another".'

305

To the anguished social worker or the member of a resistance organization, this may sound like a kind of cop-out, a religious evasion of political responsibility. But it is not. It is where responsibility begins, because the real responsibility is not something one takes on or leaves, as if there were a choice. It is simply a fact. We *are* responsible for each other, whether we like it or not, and if we refuse to recognize it that does not alter the fact. So the first step in realistic political and social action for the Christian is the step into Christ, the step which identifies with him and goes to meet people as Christ, finding him in them and simply loving them for what they are, where they are. For Egide 'the apostolate', the exchanging of the good news of resurrection, was first and last a matter of friendship, or simply loving. 'It is not organisation. Not in the first place doing something. It is increasing the presence of God, the presence of Salvation.' By being there, by working in the foundry, eating and joking with the other men; by being injured at work and suffering from clumsy treatment at the accident clinic; by being insulted and despised by petty officials; by losing his job; finally, by dying, this man lived Christ in the world of industrial Brussels. 'The world of today is the Burning Bush of God's presence', and that is where 'salvation' happens, where resurrection is exchanged.

Egide lived before the new kind of 'Church' began to be apparent. The Wisdom kind of Church was not present in the ecclesial language he used, but it was very much present in the way he lived his calling as minister to the body of Christ. His experience of being the Church in that way was where his political action began, where all our political action has to begin, though he himself did not think of it like that. He said we had to do our best to find out what were the human structures 'that God will save at the end', that is, the ways of living which can truly carry the flow of exchange in God's love. In that situation 'I must become myself God's message of love' to 'let God's life flow through me to others and through others to me'. That is the exchange of resurrection, and it is not a means to another and practical end, it is itself the beginning and the end, and all else flows from it, whether it be comradeship over a difficult job shared, the occupation of a plot of land to prevent the building of a nuclear power station or a military installation, or the gift of life itself. Achievements of change which do not grow from this

306

awareness of what love requires eventually turn to the same hatreds, the same oppressions, which first drove people to oppose such things.

Jesus meant what he said and so did Paul. The warning that the one who takes the sword will die by the sword is simply a statement of fact. So is the statement that it is difficult for a rich man to enter the kingdom of God. These are not condemnations, just facts. To say that prophecy and extreme generosity and great faith and even martyrdom itself are all useless without love is, again, simply a statement of fact. That is the nature of reality. Unless such things are themselves articulation of the flow of exchanged love they are a denial of the statements they appear to make; they are false and illusory and therefore unstable.

'Like a dream one wakes from, O Lord, when you wake you dismiss them as phantoms.' This sentence of the psalmist (Ps. 72 [73]) refers to the structures of oppression and injustice, but it applies also to all inauthentic action and achievement. That psalm is the agonized prayer of a man driven almost to unbelief by the apparent triumph and sheer contented prosperity of oppressive groups. In the end, he recognizes the flaw in the apparently impregnable thought-control by which oppression of any kind (conscious or unconscious) perpetuates itself. However convinced and convincing it sounds, it is based on a lie, it is not real, it is 'phantom' and will dissolve in the face of reality. Where, then, is reality to be discerned, if all the available language is the language devised by injustice to preserve itself from knowledge and to keep others equally ignorant? What we are trying to discover is how the necessary and proper exchanges of earthly political and social life can be, in their own distinct way, also exchanges of love. How can they be what Egide (fumbling for words) called 'definitive' structures—those which, though purely earthly, yet carry an eternal traffic? Is it possible, or are we obliged to reject the one in order to engage in the other? It often looks like that, and indeed it often is so; the way in which, in our time, so many Christians feel obliged to disengage themselves from the structures of 'the world' is proof enough that it is all too easy for earthly exchanges to become systems of the refusal of true Exchange.

Charles Williams saw both choices and the possible coincidence of them in an essential ambiguity which has to be lived. It is worked out in the dense and singing images of 'Bors to Elayne: on the King's Coins' in which Bors comes to Elayne his wife for reassurance of the existence of the truthful exchange of food and service in the household of God's people. The reason for his dismay, and his intense need of the comfort her hands can give him, is that he has just returned from a conference about money, for the King is about to mint the first coinage. Each in his own way, Bors and three other people realize the different kinds of exchanges made possible by a currency which is symbolic and is not merely the exchange of actual goods and services. In the reaction to this new thing we see in miniature some of the answers which may be given to the question 'What must we do?' in the area of economics and politics.

In the poem, Bors feels himself bewildered. He is a practical man who can see the convenience of coinage, yet something in him revolts, and it is only in the presence of Elayne, who means to him the basically sane and human exchanges, that he even dares think about the implications of this new thing. He speaks, then, to her of the new-minted coins, each with the dragon on it which is Arthur's device, and having Arthur's head on the other side.

> They carry on their backs little packs of value . . .
> the King can tame dragons to carriers,
> but I came through the night, and saw the dragonlets' eyes
> leer and peer, and the house-roofs under their weight
> creak and break; shadows of great forms
> halloe'ed them on, and followed over falling towns.
> I saw that this was the true end of our making;
> mother of children, redeem the new law.

He begs Elayne, mother and house*keeper*, to keep the houses and cherish the children, all threatened horribly by the power of the released 'dragonlets'. His fears echo the vision of the psalmist, who saw that those who hold political power dictate not only law but thoughts, because they hold, or seem to hold, all ways of exchange. 'They scoff, they speak with malice', says the psalmist.

> From on high they plan oppression.
> They have set their mouths in the heavens
> and their tongues dictate to the earth.

308

So the people turn to follow them
　and drink in all their words.
　(Ps. 72: 8–10, Grail translation)

The poor can use only the language offered them, and so they think as their oppressors think, they accept 'market value' as absolute, even though their houses and towns are destroyed by the weight of an economic system based on a lie. The first and radical lie is to be discerned in the impersonality of a system, symbolized by the use of coinage, which shifts the criteria for the propriety of an exchange from need and service between real human beings to the demands of a self-validating system in which men and women become means to keep the mechanism of this idol-robot in working order.

But Bors' reaction is inarticulate. He feels a huge dread but cannot really say why, and he knows that others, cleverer or wiser than he, see things more clearly, though they do not agree in their interpretation of what they see. He describes the debate in which he took part, presenting each argument with the fair-mindedness of the truly good man, whose basic rightness is so integral to his being that he can seldom consciously justify his intuitive judgements. He remembers, then, the very convincing arguments of 'Kay the King's Steward, wise in economics', who sees all the practical advantages of precisely that impersonal and impartial economic standard which frightens the instinctive sympathies of Bors.

> . . . gold dances deftly across frontiers.
> The poor have choice of purchase, the rich of rents,
> and events move now in smoother control
> than the swords of lords or the orisons of nuns.
> Money is the medium of exchange.

Certainly, the impersonal economic control is smoother than the violent exchanges of war or the hidden exchanges of substitution, sacrifice and love. But who controls? Kay sees himself as controlling, for his job is to control supply and demand for the king's household. But is he really in control? Will not the power he has helped to loose end by controlling him? 'How slippery the paths on which you set them', says the psalmist, for the apparently secure and prosperous who 'dictate to the earth' are living according to doctrines radically untrue and are therefore unable to stand up when truth breaks out. 'You make them slide to destruction.'

They will be destroyed, and discovered to be 'as phantoms' because the whole thing is based on what Taliessin, the king's poet, calls a 'convenient heresy'. The poet knows the huge power of symbols. In a few lines Taliessin/Williams provides an analysis of the whole meaning and danger of any political ideology whose reference-point is not people but the maintenance of an economic system, however rational and efficient.

> Taliessin's look darkened; his hand shook
> while he touched the dragons; he said 'We had a good thought.
> Sir, if you made verse you would doubt symbols.
> I am afraid of the little loosed dragons.
> When the means are autonomous, they are deadly; when words
> escape from verse they hurry to rape souls;
> when sensation slips from intellect, expect the tyrant;
> the brood of carriers levels the goods they carry.
> We have taught our images to be free; are we glad?
> are we glad to have brought convenient heresy to Logres?

In this passage we see precisely why Christians, finding their own being as they echo the Word of God spoken in them, are driven to put themselves among those in great danger of this rape, those who are undefended because their intellect has been carefully separated from sensation by a type of education designed for that purpose. The tyrant knows all about that – 're-education' is the first thing a dictator attends to. Once 'the means are autonomous', there is no way they can be judged, because there are no criteria except their own internal ones. The worker-priest in Brussels knew this and fought it in the only way it could be fought, by simply being, himself, the only possible argument against the false autonomy of human symbols. By working and living among the oppressed, God's little ones, he recreated the links with human reality which the autonomy of the economic system under which he and they together suffered was shown up as the 'phantom' it is. By being there he spoke more profoundly than Kay, the Steward, or even than Taliessin, the poet, for he lived the inescapable ambiguity: this system

310

is evil, yet it is where God dwells and is to be encountered in the exchange of everyday hardship, friendship and precarious hope. In the poem, it is finally the voice of Christian insight, in the person of the Archbishop, Dubric, which expresses that ambiguity, the lived tension which reconciles the irreconcilable, the ambiguity we call incarnation. He sums up the whole thing—the inescapable folly and sinfulness, yet *in* that the genuine exchange, which makes present in this world the coming kingdom, even money is one medium of exchange in the traffic of the spheres:

The Archbishop answered the Lords;
his words went up through a slope of calm air.
'Might may take symbols and folly make treasure,
and greed bid God, who hides himself for man's pleasure
by occasion, hide himself essentially: this abides—
that the everlasting house the soul discovers
is always another's; we must lose our own ends;
we must always live in the habitation of our lovers,
my friend's shelter for me, mine for him.
This is the way of this world in the day of that other's;
make yourselves friends by means of the riches of iniquity,
for the wealth of the self is the health of the self exchanged.
What saith Heraclitus?—and what is the City's breath?—
dying each other's life, living each other's death,
Money is a medium of exchange.'

There is no escapting the dilemma, but in living it as Christ there is salvation. That is why we have to say not only that every kind of practical involvement in the world from housework to medical research is valid, but also that even strictly political activity can indeed be a medium of exchange, but only if all these are lived *as* exchange, 'dying each other's life, living each other's death'. And that is why we have to say also that apparent non-involvement in important causes and issues can be and often is a deeper and even more effective involvement; the one who simply lives, and loves, and prays and suffers, visibly with the poor or invisibly and 'uselessly' united with them in the poor Christ who died a 'useless' death, is engaged equally and powerfully in exchanging resurrection and so struggling to reverse the tide of Refusal.

311

But in this life and death struggle, how can we see clearly enough to know what and whom to oppose, what and whom to embrace? How can we be un-deceived by the phantoms whose voices speak with such assurance? When we ask 'What must we do?' we must ask it out of the place of ultimate exchange, or the answers will be false, or partial and misleading.

The word 'prayer' is, to many, a narrow and specialized word. To pray is to do something extra. It is good, perhaps the highest good, but quite apart from actual *doing*. Indeed we can manage very well without prayer, and most people do. But without prayer what is it that we do? Prayer is not a separate activity, but simply a living from the centre, from the place of Exchange, in an awareness of its nature which is sometimes fully conscious and sometimes implicit, but always present. It is the place to which the psalmist turns, finally, driven by his desperate need to understand the congruence of misery and prosperity, of the guilt of the oppressed and the 'untroubled' minds of the oppressors, the 'punishment' of the innocent and the 'sound and sleek' bodies of the proud. When he was 'stupid and did not understand' it was because he was still under the sway of the phantom world of false autonomy, but *all the time* the reality was there, it needed only the courage of love to discover it:

> Yet I was always in your presence,
> You were holding me by my right hand.
> You will guide me by your counsel
> and so you will lead me to glory.
> What else have I in heaven but you?
> Apart from you I want nothing on earth.
> My body and my heart faint for joy;
> God is my possession for ever.

In this place, and here alone, Wisdom is at home. And the special importance of the life and death of Egide van Broeckhoven lies in the fact that he knew, lived and articulated the oneness of the political, the sexual and the mystical. In that place where he was one with God he found those who were his friends, and in his friends he encountered his God. And by that discovery he liberated, in them, the Wisdom who before had been imprisoned and dumb. He is, before the time when it was recognizable, the prophet of the new Church which 'turns the structure of the Church on its head', in the words of another worker-priest. Around Egide such a Church formed itself, for Wisdom found a home among those who loved her in him. She lived in and between them, she was their exchanges, of fumbling words, of sudden smiles, of awkward acts of kindness or gestures of solidarity. She it was who put on the coffee-pot late at night; she it was who exhausted herself in over-driven and unjustly rewarded labour; it was she into whose arms came the small son of an Arab labourer, rushing to be kissed by his friend; Wisdom in him suffered when unsafe machinery caused an injury, made worse by careless treatment, and she made that pain redemptive. Egide knew this and lived it more and more consciously and fully as his short life moved to its fulfilment.

His prayer in *A Friend to All Men* was very like that of the psalmist, feeling the weight of a guilt which is his and yet not his: 'Lord, behold my sin and the responsibility that weighs on me. But you will give me your Spirit. I want to cling to this hope, this love, this grace, without ever letting go', he wrote, and we can hear in his words the echo of the psalmist's cry: ' . . . I was stricken all day long, suffered punishment day after day . . . you were holding me by my right hand, you will guide me by your counsel . . . God is my possession for ever.'

So his movement was always outwards from that deep place and inwards to it from that same 'place' discovered in his friend. As André Louf makes clear in his book *Teach Us to Pray*, prayer is essentially exchange:

> So long as we ourselves were still intent on the Word of God in our heart, we had come no further than the prelude. There comes a moment when we yield up God's Word to the Spirit within us. Then it is that our heart gives birth to prayer. And then at last the Word of God has become truly ours. We have then discovered and realized our most profound, our true identity. And then the Name of Jesus has become our name also. And together with Jesus we may with one voice call God: Abba, Father!

In order to be able to yield up God's Word in that way, as Egide knew, all else had to go; we must not keep anything 'except our

313

vital centre in all its purity' because that is the place of exchange. And so his life, his prayer, his mystical experience and awareness, were known in that exchange. We must 'live the gift of your whole self to God and the gift of your friend to God'. He knew that it was not enough to give oneself to others, for that outpouring might spring from an ignorant pride that felt itself able to bring love and peace and hope on the sole impulse of natural generosity and proper indignation; many, indeed, try to do it like this, and fail, and become cynical or despairing. 'Giving yourself over to men to the point of losing yourself leads to empty nothingness if you stop giving yourself over to God to the point of losing yourself in him.' Yet this apparent loss, this 'impractical' mystical way of 'dying each other's life' is the place where genuine personal, social and political changes can begin. 'The nakedness of love is a path surer than all the paths which human wisdom builds in its own certitudes.'

The mysticism of political commitment? The politics of mystical awareness? One of Jesus' most obviously political acts, the choosing of the Twelve who were to be his Church, was preceded by a night-long vigil of prayer. We cannot draw a line, the one can only come to its proper reality in and through the other, whether the two be incarnate in the hermit who never even goes into town to vote, or in the activist making speeches and organizing protests, or in the dumb agony of the tortured political prisoner whose name is not mentioned in the press.

It is true that there are mystical gifts which are uncommon, and deeply important to the work of the whole body; it is true that prayer, if it is to be the point of intersection of vital exchange, must have its special times and places and methods so that it may be known, articulated and entered into, as fully as possible. This is necessary because the organic body, individual or social, is full of sin. It resists the exchanges of mystical love, so there is an absolute need to clear out, violently if necessary, the channels for exchange which have become silted by apathy and selfishness. But all this is necessary only because of sin; essentially, mystical awareness is simply knowing who and what one is, with one's friend, in God. Prayer is the movement of exchange in that awareness. And so prayer is our life, the ultimate and deepest life, and it is lived in and by the whole body—the individual limited body and the myst-

314

ical body which is Christ's, still limited at present but transcending many limitations even now.

The kind of mystical awareness which Egide articulated in his diary is not new, but he was able to bring a needed lucidity of personal and vivid experience to those facts about being-with-God which make it especially clear that it can and does and must happen between people, in those exchanges which are the bloodstream of Christ's body. It is ecclesial or it is nothing: it happens in and as Christ's body, and once more we experience the concept 'Church' not as organization but simply as the being of the risen Jesus. 'The Church should become in us the tangible reality of God's love for the concrete world of today.' 'This is not an individual venture; it is the Church itself which, in our person, penetrates even further into the desert, filled with the joy of the Lord.' Prayer which focuses this is prayer known as lived from and to the other, at the same time that it is lived from and to God. It is a prayer which can break through, thrusting with divine passion at the obstacles to love in the un-lovingness of an alienated and self-destructive society. Egide knew he must 'strive to find where, in the narrowness of so many human lives, there is a tunnel that leads down into the depths'. To do this means to do as Christ did; 'the prototype of this reality is the concrete existence of the historical Christ' and so to become incarnate with him in that situation.

A few days after he had had a thumb badly crushed by a faulty machine and (still in great pain) was on the way to the clinic for treatment, Egide experienced this mystically. Afterwards he recorded it in dense, highly theological language which is the only way to express a personal reality so intimate and universal that everything else falls to triviality beside it:

> ... how, from the ocean of God, the Son came to me; how, in a personal encounter, I was placed in this world, in the Son and by the Son in His divinity and His humanity; and how I am going towards the world in order to go to the Father with the world in the Son. How the suffering that passes through me is redemptive, as was the suffering of Christ, for it means accepting my own sin and that of the world and submitting myself to suffering in a redemptive way. . . . How I myself lived all the encounters with my friends in this encounter with Christ, who,

315

from the divine majesty, came to me, was with me, who was placed at my side by the Father and who returns to the Father; how, by this encounter, *I have saved them*, and how I saw that they were thus on the way to their fulfilment. I felt the Fullness of life flow through me, and I felt thereby a great power come to life in me, in a great peace, knowing that I am in the situation where love wants me to be.

This was a major breakthrough, a passage through the spheres, and the language he uses makes clear the Romantic nature of the experience whose result and 'being' he describes in the first paragraph. The whole thing is known in terms of exchange, of that tremendous outpouring of love from the Creator to the created, in and by incarnate Wisdom. The whole of Christian theology is here, but it comes to us—as it always should do—as the stumbling words of the lover, unable to find language adequate to the thing Wisdom is showing him, yet in its very inadequacy expressing a glory of humility and adoration. There is a stark theological simplicity about Egide's record of his experience which to some will seem abstract, because the symbols he uses, which for him were vehicles of intensely experienced reality, are so familiar in an alienated type of theology that they read like little more than a kind of religious puzzle. This is Pauline theology, but with less concession to human imagination than even Paul was accustomed to make.

One way in which we can experience this imaginatively so as to illuminate but in no way weaken Egide's description is by thinking of a completely different way in which the intense search for a special kind of personal perfection is at the same time a search for the deepest communication. Not long ago a television documentary was made about the Russian dancer Natalia Makarova (now working mainly in the United States). The interviews with the dancer, with her teacher, her partners and one of the best of her choreographers demonstrated vividly the nature of the relentless, life-long quest for a perfection 'which one can never reach but must always strive for', as she said. The discipline that never slackens, the hours of practice, the constant self-criticism, the correction (by what one is tempted to call a spiritual director) which is needed even by the greatest are the marks of a classic conception of ascetical and spiritual development. The results in such an artist contradict flatly the

316

popular image of the dour ascetic. One of the things which came through most clearly in this programme was the delight in life, the humour, the deep satisfaction which lives alongside the 'humility' (her own word) which knows it must ever fall short of the vision it sees. 'Her body is a finely tuned instrument', said Glen Tetley, who finds that her ability to *be* the roles he creates releases new levels of creativity in him. To be this kind of instrument she is always 'fighting with my body', as she put it, and we are reminded of Paul of Tarsus, fighting with himself to make of himself the Lord's 'finely tuned instrument'.

All this single-minded, dedicated discipline is directed to transforming the 'gift' of natural grace, musicality and good physical proportion into a perfect means of communication, and like all genuine asceticism its result is a freedom and spontaneity in performance in which all conscious awareness of effort is absent. This is a description of a *spiritual* development, one which makes possible a constantly greater and deeper level of exchange between dancer and choreographer, dancer and dance, and most of all between dancer and audience. The audience is 'converted' as the full force of a passionate givenness is released upon it, and what is given is not the personality of the dancer, but rather her person is the 'medium of exchange' by which 'something else' is given and received. The dance catches up hearts and minds in an experience of intense communication, and this must be prepared for not only by all the long years of early training but by constantly renewed study and work between performances. The result of all this is that each performance is a genuine Romantic experience, for dancer and audience, as many can testify. How truly romantic such an experience can be is easy to verify by looking at the faces of people coming out of the theatre after a performance or by reading any of the many novels which have been written for the dance-struck young.

It is not hard to see in Egide van Broeckhaven's mystical experience of the meaning of friendship the results of a parallel process of single-minded and total commitment to the calling discerned in personal gifts and opportunities.

Finally, in rich exchange of images with these two, we have the language of the one who has the poet's special charism. He must help us to hurl our cowardly imagination into the heart of this mystery, and to encounter at least in that way what it is our greater business to encounter in the darkness of utter presence, which annihilates imagination only to bring it to rebirth as Wisdom. For the poet can evoke with piercing accuracy the things which are beyond speech but not beyond imagination. What he here evokes is the living of exchange of resurrection at its most consciously and deeply lived point, beyond what is required or even proper in most times, places and peoples. It is not a matter for an élite; it is the being of the body, but a few are chosen to know explicitly 'the whole charge' of what others live unconsciously yet fully, or with only occasional knowledge. So, this degree of lived knowledge is only separated from other ways of fully living exchange for convenience of naming, for all is in and for 'the common union'. Nevertheless, this degree is necessary, and in Williams' images we see the worker-priest in the sweat and danger of the foundry and the dancer, grotesque in woolly leg-warmers at unglamorous barre-practice, and both shining with their proper glory. The poem called 'The Founding of the Company' (*The Region of the Summer Stars*) tells how, in the household of the king's poet, a certain conscious and courteous awareness of Exchange became a way of life, to the point of being articulated in 'a gay science devised before the world', and therefore not a thing invented but a living out in joyful obedience that which is the very nature of human being. It was known in three degrees ('no Wisdom separate but for convenience of naming') and at the first were 'those who lived by a frankness of honourable exchange' which all humankind must know, if it is not wholly surrendered to Refusal. So 'servitude itself'

> . . . was sweetly fee'd and freed by the willing proffer
> of itself to another, the taking of another to itself
> in degree, the making of a mutual beauty in exchange,
> be the exchange dutiful or freely debonair.

This is the loveliness of everyday exchange, of the kind which Bors saw in Elayne as she stood to greet him in the hall of their home; of the kind which happens in kitchens; of the kind Egide had with his friends in the factory canteen or in their overcrowded homes; of the kind which Makarova had between performances, nervously chain-smoking and smiling, enjoying her baby. Yet it opens immediately and simultaneously into the 'second mode' which 'bore

318

farther the labour and fruition', for it took on consciously the work of atonement by the 'one adored Substitution', and each one, in this, worked that work in the organic body by voluntary substitution, one for one, 'dying each other's life, living each other's death', not more than the others but more explicitly and in greater detail. The poem continues:

Terrible and lovely is the general substitution of souls
the Flesh-taking ordained for its mortal images
in its first creation, and now in its sublime self
shows, since It deigned to be dead in the stead of each man.

But there is a further degree, again not a degree of separation but, on the contrary, a degree of even deeper identification and total surrender in and for the sake of the other, the friend. It is the degree described by Egide in the passage quoted, the place where all exchange, all substitution is known in its origin, yet by that very originality all the more concretely and particularly effective. Williams again:

Few—and that hardly—entered on the third
station, where the full salvation of all souls
is seen, and their co-inhering, as when the Trinity
first made man in Their image, and now restored
by the one adored substitution; there men
were known, each alone and none alone,
bearing and borne, as the Flesh-taking sufficed
the God-bearer to make her a sharer in Itself.
Of the lords—Percivale, Dindrane, Dinadan, the Archbishop;
of the people—a mechanic here, a maid there,
knew the whole charge, as vocation devised.

'Few—and that hardly' come to this because it is not necessary that all should; others live the exchange deeply, perhaps beyond the degree of fullness of some whom 'vocation devised' for the more deliberate degree. It is not a matter of 'better' but of divine love searching out in the nature of each one the especial and unique possibility of transformation. But it is in this third degree that we can see most clearly what prayer and mystical awareness are all

319

about. 'Each alone and none alone, bearing and borne', men and women, and children too, encounter God in each other, and each other in God, and all in the Body of Christ which is theirs: their meaning, their medium of exchange, their hope and their bliss, and also their death, for this is the 'last enemy' and the greatest glory.

Christians have always given the highest honour to those who voluntarily gave their lives out of love for Christ, because their witness ('martyr' means witness) is so clear a statement of the essential nature of Christian death, no matter what the manner of it. Here, also and finally, an answer must be sought to the question 'What must we do?', and the answer this time is clear and yet not as clear as it seems. The answer is 'you must die', but not any kind of death will do. It must be a martyr's death, a death for love's sake, the finally Romantic action. It must be the passionate break-through which, above all other actions, allows the flood of divine love to flow through the channels of exchange and carry resurrection strongly through the organic body, 'hastening that coming of the Lord' which must await the completion of the number of those who witnessed by their lives.

In Williams' poem called 'The Last Voyage' (*Taliessin Through Logres*) the great enterprise of Arthur's kingdom has failed, as even the most idealistic human enterprises do fail, through cowardice, treachery, vanity and sheer foolishness. But the thing the enterprise tried to incarnate goes on. Three people symbolize the 'three ways of exchange' in that enterprise; Bors is the symbol of earthly concern, he whose very earthy exchanges have been loved to an eternal veracity; Percivale is the symbol of the philosopher, of Wisdom herself, as a human and intellectual gift; and Galahad is symbol of mystical transformation, the 'alchemical Infant'. These three take ship for Sarras, the 'land of the Trinity'. There, that which transforms humankind awaits always the need and call of some new enterprise. But there is something else on the ship which finally delineates the meaning of the voyage. It is the dead body of the one who, all through the poems and Arthur's kingdom, was the deepest symbol of exchange. This one is Blanchefleur, sister of the wise Percivale, Elayne's friend, and 'farther from and closer to the King's poet than any', for both were withdrawn from the exchange of married love, yet totally given to exchange through and beyond each other. In the convent where she went, she was portress, 'the

320

contact of exchange', and the one who received from the wise Merlin the infant Galahad, so that he might be nurtured in safety. In a blessed tangle of sinful and holy exchanges she who bears no child mothers this child, whose own mother bore him out of an enchanted conception, from a man who thought her another woman: Lancelot's lover, the Queen Guinevere. In this last scene Blanchefleur has died because, travelling with her brother, she came to a castle where a lady lay sick who could only be saved by the blood-shedding of one who was both Princess and Virgin, as Wisdom herself is. Against the protests of her companions, Blanchefleur cut a vein and bled into a dish, losing so much blood that she died. But the other woman lived, receiving her life from that death. And in her death Blanchefleur is one, also, with the symbol of the thigh-wounded Grail-King Pelles whose sickness made all his land barren. Pelles might only be healed by the coming of Galahad, himself the child of such strange exchange, since his mother was the daughter of that wounded King and herself the guardian and bearer of the Grail. The dead Blanchefleur, then, is the symbol of all martyrdom and all substitution, the culminating point of many passionate exchanges which find here their visible, concrete expression. On the magical ship which speeds towards the Trinity, between those three who are the three-in-one of the earthly City on its way to become the heavenly City, lies

. . . a saffron pall
over the bier and the pale body of Blanchefleur,
mother of the nature of lovers, creature of exchange;
drained there of blood by the thighed wound,
she died another's death, another lived her life.
Where it was still tonight, in the last candles of Logres,
a lady danced, to please the sight of her friends,
her cheeks stained from the arteries of Percivale's sister.
Between them they trod the measure of heaven and earth.

This is the feminine symbol of what passion is all about. It is a ruthless but accurate exposition of the answer love gives when it is asked 'What must we do?' We have to do what Blanchefleur symbolizes, because that is what wisdom in Jesus did, and there is no other way in which salvation can come. The poem makes clear the immediacy and practicality of martyrdom; a real woman is alive and dancing because of this death. But this happens at the heart of a web of ambiguous exchanges, many of which look accidental, yet all are essential. Blanchefleur does not elect herself 'mother of the nature of lovers', she just is, because of the way divine love comes to her. In her death she is once more portress, she is the weak spot at which the power of love breaks through the spheres. She is the God-bearer, the Grail itself, vessel of incarnation, but she is also Christ, from whose body all of dying creation is given new life, its 'arteries stained' with his blood. And so creation dances in the candlelight, the 'last candles' before the end. But this is a proper time for dancing, and the dead dance with the living 'the measure of heaven and earth'.

There are many deaths that lead to death. Baptism leads to baptism. Martyrdom is not a sudden end but the fulfilment of a long process, and that process is practical and concrete, incarnate in the everyday. On Christmas Day 1967, three days before he died, Egide van Broeckhoven was renewing that dedication to death which was the meaning of his life. He had, earlier that month, repeated to himself the command 'Abandon everything, risk everything, sell everything—for God.' And on the feast day he was, once more, recognizing what this meant. To him, death was not a leaving of those friends to whose love he had given himself so totally. It was the way of redemptive love, seeking the only finally effective means of being their friend. So he wrote four brief phrases which sum up what he knew to be involved in his obedience:

1) Abandoning everything for love.
2) Friendship; losing and finding it in God.
3) Giving my life totally and *losing it for this world in its most concrete reality.*
4) The unity of these three things.

To him, friendship was 'giving my life totally' because at its deepest point, in God, it might and did mean losing its satisfaction, even the visible presence. Friendship involved 'abandoning everything for love'. And life was to be given—totally—for *this world*, for particular people, and the salvation of the real human situation, as

322

Blanchefleur's death revivified the dying woman and restored her to her friends.

The day before he died, Egide was reminding himself of that routine means of dying which is 'practical discipline and mortification', because, he said, these were ways to experience 'new spaces' in which God could enter. But the channels of divine exchange were now fully open in him and divine love could flow unchecked to give life to those whom he loved so much. The last thing he wrote in his diary was a renewed sense of 'my desire to encounter and reach men in depth'. He reached them in the deepest depth of all, next day. He died under the weight of the steel which symbolizes the impersonal, efficient sin of the society whose victims he lived and died to redeem.

This man brings to a point the meaning of passion. He is not alone. Like Blanchefleur he died the life of others, others live his death, and his life and death are the life and death of the man Jesus. In the whole body of Christ this exchange goes on, day after day, until the End.

9   Envoi

Any book about Christianity must properly be a call to mission, for Christianity is a 'sending out' of people to share the good news that life is possible. In its measure, this book is a call to the particular kind of mission which God requires of his people at this point in history. This final section, therefore, is literally an *envoi*, my bit of the exchange which is the giving and receiving of the Word. As *envoi* it is also a 'tradition'. It is the handing on to others of a message. It is now their turn to discard what is unhelpful or unnecessary and to make what is true a part of the message they themselves must carry.

This is a long book, yet there are huge gaps and huge questions raised which I have not even attempted to answer. For instance we are able to see perhaps more clearly than ever before the human and divine centrality of the Eucharist, but it is now impossible to categorize this—this what? Event, ritual, symbol, person, food, community? At some point it has quietly become impossible to think of Eucharist in terms of 'validity'. The sheer physical reality of the thing makes us aware of Eucharist in a hundred ways in which it happens more or less intensely and faithfully, with more or less truthfulness to its inner exchanges whose fullness lies only in eternal celebration which we call heaven. There is no line around it, but a continuum from the simplest sharing of honest food in honest love to the kind of celebration which takes place among a group of Christians who are facing death for the sake of the Christ to whom they have given themselves—obeying as fully as they can the command: 'Do this in memory of me'. In between are all kinds of ritual and non-ritual gatherings to share bread and life, in some of which Christ is known, in others unknown. And those who 'know' may sometimes welcome him less warmly than those who do not know. To understand this is vital to the future Church. There are those who will seek such understanding, and to them the tradition passes. I am reminded once more of a passage in Vincent Donovan's book in which he says that 'the immediate and infallible result of baptism is a eucharistic community with a mission'.

Linked to this are questions about the nature of ministry and ministries. Using the model of Exchange in thinking about the nature of the Christian gathering which is the Church makes it impossible to live with a stratification based on a medieval (and then necessary) division of the educated and literate—the clerics or 'clerks'—and the illiterate 'people'. Awareness of the beautiful and complex exchanges by which one person discovers gift as call, from and to the community, and comes to recognize and be recognized in specific ministerial roles, far surpasses in theological truth and human richness anything possible in structures conditioned by thinking of people as essentially separate islands, linked only by a certain amount of boat traffic.

Arising from this same awareness of Church as exchange in and with Christ, in and with each member, we have to deal with the question of how the body of Christ should reach crucial decisions, both doctrinal and practical (here the great tradition of the Society of Friends is relevant). It throws new light on mission (who goes and who stays and how are they related?) and on marriage as sacrament (when does it become consciously the thing it symbolizes? Can it be sacrament before that?). We need to think about children and their responsibility and their Christian status, and what kind of education truly leads them into personal exchange in Christ. There are, too, far-reaching questions about the inner reality of 'religious life'—to use a phrase itself divisive and misleading. Is it perhaps the case that the special insights and gifts nurtured in necessary (though often exaggerated) separateness by various religious orders and groups should now be given back to the new Church as generously as they have been received and shared in isolation, which was itself for the sake of the Church? Must the 'death' of religious life be to let go the older conditions of particular 'spiritualities' in order that these may come to new birth in and for the reborn Church? From one point of view, a book like this only exists to stimulate others to answer the questions it raises, including those I have not even noticed, or those provoked by the inadequacy of my presentation.

So at the end of this book I am not even trying to tie up loose ends. Apart from the fact that any work of theology is necessarily incomplete because it is in a tradition, there is another reason why it cannot be done here, and that is that the kinds of 'ends' are as impossible to classify in familiar compartments as the parts of the book itself, because the way I have chosen to explore the realities of Christian experience dissolves all the categories which have usually served to make things more manageable. It seems to be impossible to divide up theology into 'dogmatic', 'biblical', 'moral', 'ascetical', 'mystical' or even 'liberation' compartments. Theology just is not that kind of thing. But once these divisions are abandoned (or rather, once they are discovered to have somehow disappeared) there is no way to divide up theology at all. It has to be grasped as one whole, even if, naturally, our small human hands only feel one bit of it at a time.

Therefore, rather than try to sum up and draw together the themes studied in this book, I want to take the whole thing and focus it in a very practical way on the present and future challenge to the Church, as that becomes clear to us from what has been explored so far. This does not mean that the 'point' of the book is to help us to make realistic Christian choices now. The 'point' of the book is the 'point' of Christianity, which is Christ, incarnate Wisdom, the man called Jesus. But it does mean that we need to discover him newly, so the practical focus must be simply the word of Christian awareness at a particular point in time.

There is one word which brings to a point the particularity of the Word in our world, now, and it is the word 'poverty'. What is being said is that the Church must be the Church of the poor; and there are many ways in which that is true.

First of all it means what it most obviously meant in the life of Jesus himself and has meant through the centuries: that the gospel message gets through very easily and directly to people who have little to lose. Poverty means that people cannot find security in the circumstances of their lives. The certainties are the regularity of the landlord's demands for rent, the contempt of officials of whatever kind, and death. Virtually everything else can and does fail—jobs, crops, health, justice, the Church. Family members may support each other but they cannot create jobs; they may reject, they may be split up, they may die. So the poor have always been the beloved of God in the very simple sense that being poor means being vulnerable, and therefore divine love finds it easier to break through.

326

There can be a 'pie in the sky' element in the search for comfort in religion, and in places where the religious establishment is identified with the oppressor the 'cry of the poor' which the Lord hears may take a secular form. But it is still a cry for God. The psalms ring with the universal language of human longing for God, the only hope of the oppressed, in the fierce confidence that somehow the poor will find redress:

> Lord, why do you stand afar off
>> and hide yourself in times of distress?
> The poor man is devoured by the pride of the wicked
>> he is caught in the schemes that others have made.
> . . . In his pride the wicked says, 'He will not punish.
>> There is no God.' Such are his thoughts.
> . . . He thinks: 'Never shall I falter:
>> misfortune shall never be my lot.'
> . . . He lurks in hiding to seize the poor;
>> he seizes the poor man and drags him away. . .
> Arise then, Lord, lift up your hand!
> O God, do not forget the poor!
> But you have seen trouble and sorrow,
> you note it, you take it in hand.
> The helpless trusts himself to you;
>> for you are the helper of the orphan. . . .
> Lord, you hear the prayer of the poor;
>> you strengthen their hearts; you turn your ear
>> to protect the rights of the orphans and the oppressed
>> so that mortal man may strike terror no more.
> (Grail Ps.9, Part 2: 1–2, 4, 6, 9, 12, 14, 17–18)

It is the cry of the oppressed through the ages, and it is the cry which Jesus heard and to which he responded with such passion. It is a cry which echoes now more insistently than ever, from the slums of Lima, from the semi-deserts where flocks die for lack of pasture, from the prisons of Brazil or Belfast, from tenements where rats bite the children, from the huts of landless labourers, from the mines of South Africa or Bolivia, from the streets of Calcutta or London or Chicago, where people who sleep under roofs can, if they

327

go out early enough or late enough, step over the bodies of those who do not.

But it rises also from people who are hungry, with a hunger near to madness, for some sense in life, for something to tell their children which will make their world seem worth living in. They also are the poor, and they turn to the Lord, calling him by some name or other, and swear at him and denounce him and plead with him and bribe him and expect him with an obstinate hope concealed, often enough, by angry cynicism. Once, the hands of the Lord were there to heal, the word of the Lord brought hope and courage, and ever since then there have always been those who knew that to be body of Christ means, before anything else, to be drawn to these poor by the pull of irresistible love.

But real love can only be offered from a position of equal neediness. The proud lover is rightly repulsed. The Christ who went to the poor like steel to a magnet was poor himself. He was poor in his origins and in his birth, but even more so when he left behind the uncertain but more or less stable life of a village tradesman and took to wandering about the country without job, home or income. Yet finally even that was not enough, for economic and cultural poverty only symbolize the deeper poverty of human beings. The deepest poverty is the lack of God, and only a poor God could be vulnerable enough to share that, a God who had 'emptied himself' and become 'obedient even to death', as the poor have to be, who die young at the will of others. The poor Christ is not just the wandering preacher who had nowhere to sleep unless somebody took him in, he is above all the one who died.

It seems, at this time, that this is what the Church has to do. Individual Christians know that they have to die with Christ, but if the Church is truly his body then the Church, as a body, is called on to die, in order to be available to those who cry, 'O God, do not forget the poor!' In a sense this is always required, but there are times in the history of the Church when the shape of the demand at the corporate level becomes much clearer. We have seen it at a local level in many places where churches established as missions in 'undeveloped' countries, and living (even unintentionally) a privileged existence under the protection of a colonial power, faced their moment of truth when the country achieved independence. Many, at that point, recognized the call to die with Christ, to be really

328

poor, helpless, vulnerable. Missionaries stayed with their people, and some were imprisoned and some were killed, but some, then or later, were recognized as being truly poor with the poor, oppressed with the oppressed. They were recognizably the body of the man who lived and died with the poor.

Now, in Latin America, a Church which for centuries identified itself with the possessors has in many places and many people undergone a conversion more complete and rapid than anyone would have believed possible ten years ago, before the famous Medellin conference of bishops aligned the Church firmly on the side of the poor. A Church identified with the poor and oppressed is extremely inconvenient to dictatorships, and many Christians have suffered imprisonment, torture and secret death. As an article in the *Catholic Worker* pointed out, 'If this life of solidarity with the poor is taken seriously by the Church in Latin America a more intense persecution may be inevitable; but its courage in doing so may prevent the ultimate despair of a continent awaiting its liberation.'

At all times in its past history, when the wealth and smugness of the Church led to revolt and schism, a few people have known what it was all about and have come together in their response to the poor Christ. These lovers of God saved the Church; in a sense they *were* the Church. The mendicant orders, the Jesuits, the Quakers, the Salvation Army—there have never been very many, but in their poverty Christ died and the Church, his body, rose again.

It seems most likely that this will be the pattern once more, that a 'little flock' will save the blind and indifferent mass. It seems all too possible that the Church, or at least large parts of it, will indeed 'die', but through gradual stiffening of terrified structures, through creeping demoralization and apathy. Yet the Church cannot really die, it merely sheds its dead limbs, as the head of Mrs Grales hung dying on the shoulder of the newly alive Rachel and would eventually dry up and fall away. But there is at least a chance that at this time of unprecedented challenge there might be a clearer vision of what is needed.

There are two reasons for hope. One is the truly unique nature of the changes which are taking place in the life of the Church. As Walbert Buhlmann has said in his remarkable book on *The Coming of the Third Church*:

329

The Western Church, in particular the Roman Church, finds herself today in something like the situation of the primitive Church among the Jews, for we too must beware of handicapping with the trappings of history the arrival of the new 'Church of the Gentiles', the Third Church. We have the opportunity of becoming the Church for the whole world but we must pay the price, that is, strip ourselves of Western bias.

As he did with Peter and the little group which went to the house of Cornelius, God has taken a great deal of trouble to show us that we have to overcome not only 'bias' but assumptions about what is and is not proper for Christians to do, so deep-rooted as to have the nature of taboos. Peter's change of heart involved a struggle with religious repulsions which he, and no doubt many others, did not overcome easily, and we know that Peter himself was still struggling and failing years later, when Paul (whose conversion experience had cleared all that away and made it easy for him) felt obliged to take his erring confrere to task publicly. This is the kind of dying which is asked of the Church now, but the demand is now not only on a larger scale than at any time since God made clear what he had been doing in the house of Cornelius, it is also qualitatively unprecedented since then. If the evidence is examined with a mind open to the Spirit, that conclusion appears unavoidable, though there is no way of telling how the 'new' Church will develop. There are no guarantees; the demand is for a leap of faith, for a dying, a baptism. Walter Buhlmann has put the issue clearly:

> The crisis facing the Church is such that only our instinctive attitude of self-defence prevents us seeing it in its true proportions. Those who wish at all costs to preserve the structures developed through the centuries are full of anguish. Others, who see that the structures are threatened but think it worth while sacrificing them for the greater spread of the gospel, are full of confidence. It is not possible to put the brake on the rapid changes; they will accelerate still more. But amid all the turmoil there will remain the community of Christ's disciples who have renewed the faith in the Father and his Son and who bear it through the world as a sign of hope for all. This is what is contained in the promise of the indefectibility of the Church.

330

Thus, this crisis becomes a challenge and an altogether special call to us.

The uniqueness of the demand, the unmistakable oddness of what is going on, is one reason for hope that this 'altogether special call' will be heard. One should never underestimate the human capacity for not seeing what one does not want to see, but if the situation is recognized at all it must be obvious that no rummaging in the filing-cabinets of precedent will provide blueprints for the future. If a response is made at all it has to be radical.

The other reason for hope lies in the character of the emerging pre-Church gatherings, and the Churches which crystallize in them. I have called this the 'Wisdom' character, and I have spelled out the fact that it is not only closely but causally linked to the emergence of a feminine type of consciousness. The way in which writers such as Robert Graves, Geoffrey Ashe and Theodore Roszak have expressed this in terms of the return of the 'Goddess' is significant, but they have all failed to see that this is not a 'return' but an ecclesial incarnation. A Goddess, or a God, is a symbolic evocation of an *un*conscious experience of the divine, but Wisdom is not a Goddess or a God but the nameless 'I am' who is incarnate, subsisting in its Church, and has now managed to get that erratic body to become consciously aware of the element in itself which has been hitherto unconscious and available only symbolically.

In an individual, the 'withdrawal of projection' means not only an immense enrichment of self-awareness but also the immediate release of energies previously occupied in policing the unconscious. The two things, which are really one, mean that the person can become not only wise but wisely powerful. If I am right in my description of what has been going on in the 'psyche' of the Church, then the equivalent thing must happen. In so far as the Church allows herself to be consciously aware of the Wisdom becoming so visible in and around her, she will acquire both a new vision and a new spiritual energy. Nothing like it has ever been possible before.

There are, therefore, grounds for hope that this time the Church may be rescued from the gates of hell not by one tiny heroic remnant but by a vast number of such 'remnant' communities of the 'poor of Yahweh', who use their heads and their hearts, who read the signs of the times as Jesus told them to and respond accordingly.

331

But even to begin to think along these lines easily makes people confused and anxious. Shut in by the unquestioned and constant demands of daily life, they feel helpless: 'Yes—but what can we *do* about it?' I have stressed all through this book the very bodily and practical nature of a religion rooted in incarnation; therefore it cannot end on a merely rhetorical note. Wisdom may 'cover the earth like a mist', but at a certain point she has to take root and give herself a chance to grow in good soil—or rather, *we* have to give her a chance to grow, for divine love waits for the *fiat* of human love, now as it did in Nazareth, while all creation holds its breath in tremulous hope.

What kind of soil can we prepare for Wisdom's growth? The answer is the one with which I begin this chapter; the answer is poverty. It was in the poverty of a human life that Wisdom took root, it is in the hearts of the poor that then and ever since the shoots have flourished. It is to the neediness of the lover, as he waits in the streets, that the beloved responds.

The poor Christ, the oppressed, denounced, shunned, tortured and dying Christ, is the place where Wisdom finds a home, now as then. Sometimes those with whom she has moved in do not recognize her until someone points her out. The 'missionary' character of the new Church has to be, like Peter's, the discovery and celebration of divine Wisdom very much at home in a place where no one had expected her, and wearing an apron rather than a crown. And surely it is important that it was Peter who was first sent to find this out, Peter who was 'the rock', the leader, in spite of all faults. He has to make that discovery all over again, in our time, and he will find it as hard as he did then to set aside ancient preconceptions and abandon direction and be content to sit down with Wisdom in her new home and learn her language and take a broom in hand.

To make such a discovery, poverty is needed. To 'lay aside bias', to strip oneself of the protection not only of colonialism and a cassock but of the cultural self-confidence of those with a rich and deservedly loved tradition is the kind of *kenosis* demanded: to go to the poor, and be poor, means to give up all the props of social and emotional security. It is not just a 'spiritual' poverty, if by that we mean a kind of poverty which allows us to go on having all things we think we 'absolutely have to have'. It means just plain poverty.

332

Here, also, we cannot separate body from spirit. To be poor means to be poor, to do without, to need things and not have them, to be uncertain of the future and dependent on other people. That is what is required of the Church, and that is what is required of each Christian. It is required in the measure in which such a demand can truly be personally and communally recognized. Anything else would be a form of oppression, but that means that those who do recognize it have the inescapable work of helping the rest towards realization as fast as realistic love allows.

This is the key. The effort—in however inadequate, clumsy or ludicrously naive a form—unlocks the door to Wisdom. Until it is unlocked, nothing much happens. It is true, she can whistle shrilly through the keyhole and create discords in the ecclesial harmonies, but until the door is opened she cannot come in and teach people to sing a new song altogether.

But when people begin really to practice poverty in the most basic and simple-minded and practically 'useless' way, then things begin to change. 'The one who lives with Wisdom' sees things differently. Material poverty (even the very comparative kind) sets people free. When the clutter has been removed they can see each other.

In that new clarity other kinds of Christians look different, and their differences are suddenly a source of richness and delight. Other faiths reveal themselves as the places where Wisdom has been home-making for a long time, preparing through centuries 'a people for herself' towards a moment when she may be discerned as in-carnate. The gatherings of a-religious seekers, the mute assemblies of the suffering, as well as the more vocal kind, are discovered to be places where 'Wisdom is known in her children'.

So that is where we end, and begin. It began with the awe-ful vulnerability of an adolescent girl, called to an exchange of love which required of her the sacrifice of most things that make rich a young woman's life. 'Seven sorrows' seems a conservative estimate of the wounds which made her life one of radical poverty. Her poverty was necessary so that divine Wisdom might take root among the poor who waited, so that she might grow among them unnoticed, so that she might shine among them with a brief and equivocal glory, and might die for them, as the poor do die, for whom justice is a rare luxury. In the deep water of his baptism 'death and life

333

contended', and the victory was one which left behind everything which could impede his 'purely proceeding spirit', to use Rilke's phrase.

So in the literal denudation of baptism those called to be his body enter into a poverty of his death, symbolically leaving in the water all that separates them from the love of God, and therefore from each other. They must learn how to be 'dying each other's life, living each other's death', and for them poverty is an absolute requirement, for each thing we cling to, however innocently, is refused to that exchange of love.

Through the centuries those who knew this have been the ones in whom the Church lived. Every time, the one absolute requirement for genuine renewal in the Church has been poverty. It is not enough by itself, but it is a precondition. To be poor without love is 'to do the right thing for the wrong reason' and that, as Eliot's Becket knew, is 'the greatest treason', yet there can be no love without poverty, at least in desire, and if love is real then it desires poverty and gets it.

Poverty makes way for the Spirit, it lets God work. It is very simple and obvious. Every possession or personal preoccupation requires energy for its upkeep. Some there must be, but the more there are the more of a person's spiritual energy is unavailable for anything else. It is a kind of refusal of exchange, however inculpable. Conversely, each single thing which is let go means that much more love released into the exchange of life with the Three-in-One.

At this point in the history of the world and of the Church, which is the point where 'Spirit knows it knows' and is aware of Wisdom at work in all creation, there is a great deal to do in very particular ways, but if the practical choices are to be rightly made they must be of the kind that Wisdom inspires. They will not be discovered by 'think-tanks' and teams of experts (though these may come in at some stage) but only discerned by minds and hearts open to the exchange of love. There is a need to be 'wise as serpents and simple as doves', to try to think with the ruthlessly honest intelligence of Jesus and love with the terrible folly of Jesus. We are always glad to be thought wise, but an older meaning of the word 'simple' was less complimentary than our modern one, which implies a certain admirable and elegent spareness. 'Simple' meant foolish, even half-witted, and certainly poor. In the end, that is the kind of

334

poverty which is required of the companion of Jesus; for Wisdom herself puts on the fool's gear and in that guise can only be recognized by those who are themselves fools. 'For since, in the Wisdom of God, the world did not know God through Wisdom, it pleased God through the folly of what we preach to save those who believe. For Jews demand signs and Greeks seek wisdom, but we preach Christ crucified, a stumbling block to Jews and folly to Gentiles, but to those who are called, both Jews and Greeks, Christ the power of God and the Wisdom of God' (I Cor. 1: 41–4).

Select Bibliography

Ashe, G., *The Virgin*. Routledge and Kegan Paul 1976.

Blake, W., *Complete Poems*. Penguin 1977.

Broeckhoven, E. van, *A Friend to All Men*. New Jersey, Dimension Books, 1977.

Buhlmann, W., *The Coming of The Third Church*. St Paul Publications 1976.

Dante Alighieri, *The Divine Comedy of Dante Alighieri*, tr. Dorothy Sayers and Barbara Reynolds. Penguin 1975.

Donovan, V., *Christianity Rediscovered*. Indiana, Fides Claretian, 1978.

Divine Office. Collins 1974.

Eliot, T. S., *Four Quartets*. Faber and Faber 1959.

Green-Armytage, A. H. N., *John Who Saw: A Layman's Essays on the Authority of the Fourth Gospel*. Faber and Faber 1952.

Guerric of Igny, *Liturgical Sermons*. Michigan, Cistercian Publications, 1970.

Hügel, F. von, *Selected Writings of Baron von Hügel*, ed. Chambers. Fontana 1965.

Writings of Julian of Norwich. Penguin 1966.

Jungk, R., *The Nuclear State*. John Calder 1969.

Jeremias, J., *The Eucharistic Words of Jesus*. S.C.M. Press 1970 and Philadelphia, Fortress Press, 1977.

Keats, J., *Poems of John Keats*, ed. J. Stillinger. Heinemann 1978.

Kipling, R., 'Wireless' in *Traffics and Discoveries*. Macmillan 1904.

Koestler, A., *The Act of Creation*. Hutchinson 1969.

Lewis, C. S., *The Allegory of Love*. Oxford University Press 1965.

— *Out of the Silent Planet*. Pan Books 1968.

— *The Last Battle*. Fontana 1980.

Louf, A., *Teach Us to Pray*. Darton, Longman and Todd 1974.

Luke, H., *Dark Wood and White Rose*. Benedictine Abbey, New Mexico, Dove Publications, 1975.

France, Marie de, *'Lays' of Marie de France*, tr. E. Mason. Everyman, J. M. Dent, 1911.
Macdonald, G., *The Princess and the Goblin*. Puffin 1979.
Miller, W., *A Canticle for Liebowitz*. Corgi Books 1970.
Rilke, R. M., *Duino Elegies*, tr. J. B. Leishman and S. Spender. Hogarth Press 1959.
— *Selected Poems*, tr. J. B Leishman. Penguin 1969.
Robinson, J. A. T., *The Body*. S.C.M. Press 1952.
— Re-dating the New Testament. S.C.M. Press 1976.
St Ambrose, *On the Mysteries*, tr. T. Thompson. S.P.C.K. 1919.
St Teresa of Avila, *Complete Works*. Sheed and Ward 1972.
Sophocles, *Antigone*, tr. E. S. Watling. Penguin 1953.
Tolkien, J. R. R., *The Lord of the Rings*. George Allen and Unwin 1979.
Turner, W., *Essays on the Ritual of Social Relations*, ed. Gluckmann. Manchester University Press 1962.
Williams, C., *Taliessin Through Logres*. Oxford University Press 1938.
— *The Descent of the Dove*. Longmans Green 1939.
— *All Hallows Eve*. Faber and Faber 1945.
— *The Figure of Beatrice*. Faber and Faber 1950.
— *The Region of the Summer Stars*. Oxford University Press 1950.
— *The Place of the Lion*. Faber and Faber 1964.
— *Shadows of Ecstasy*. Faber and Faber 1965.
— *War in Heaven*. Michigan, Eerdmans, 1965.

Index of Names

Taliessin Through Logres (Williams) 234–7, 256, 283–4, 288–9, 308–11, 319, 320–2
Teach Us to Pray (Louf) 313
Teresa of Avila, St 211
Tetley, Glen 317
Thomas, St 206, 208–11, 274
Tolkien, J. R. R. 2, 40, 66
Trinity, doctrine of the 90, 154, 172, 208, 231, 269
Turner, Victor 216
Tyre and Sidon, district of 75

van Broeckhoven, Egide 281ff, 295–6, 299,

301, 305–6, 312–16, 317–18, 322–3
Vita nuova (Dante) 49
Virgin, The (Ashe) 133
von Hügel 227

Wagner, Richard 143, 270–1
War in Heaven (Williams) 123
Weinberg, Alvin W. 110
Wheeler, Archibald 33–4
Williams, Charles 2, 16, 20, 46, 51, 52, 54, 91, 102, 104, 109, 123, 134, 161, 234–7, 256, 283–4, 288, 307–11, 318–22
Women's Suffrage Movement 266

Index of Subjects

340

341

342

344